In Defence of Fundamental Rights

William E. Conklin,
Faculty of Law, University of Windsor, Canada

SIJTHOFF & NOORDHOFF   1979
Alphen aan den Rijn   The Netherlands
Germantown, Maryland   USA

© 1979 Sijthoff & Noordhoff International Publishers B.V.
Alphen aan den Rijn, The Netherlands

ISBN 90 286 0389 1

Library of Congress Catalog Card Number: 89777

Printed in The Netherlands

In Defence of Fundamental Rights

For the memory of my Dad

Table of Contents

Part three:
Implications for Constitutional Analysis

Preface

The lawyer trained in the common law generally relies upon judicial decisions, statutes, regulations and constitutional documents as the primary resource material for the law. He seeks out the *ratio decidendi* of earlier judicial decisions, he distinguishes the material facts of one judgment from the material facts of another, and he analogises in hard cases where precedents cannot be found with respect to an issue or where two or more lines of precedents collide with each other. The lawyer construes statutory, regulatory and constitutional provisions in the context of the statute, regulation or constitution as a whole in an effort to ascertain the true purpose of the provision as intended by the legislature, regulation-making authority or the constitution framers. He then chooses that construction of the provision which gives the closest fit with the overall purpose of the instrument. This process of legal analysis, the common law lawyer is taught to believe, will tell him what constitutes the law.

Insights as to the content of the law no doubt do flow from such analysis. The possibility always remains, however, that the lawyer's inquiry has merely skimmed the surface; that the law is much more than the *ratio* of cases and the words of legislative enactments; that the very process of analysis which the common law lawyer has been trained to follow for over a century has directed him to ask the wrong questions.

The study of the law in a common law country such as Canada can be compared with life in one of those grand medieval castles overlooking the Rhine. At one period in history the castle served as the framework for a vibrant life. It offered physical, social and economic security to its inhabitants. It often replaced the fears, hopes and tribulations of its friends and foes with certainty and stability. But, over the centuries, the socio-economic environment within which life was secured as well as the political, religious and moral preconceptions of its friends and foes gradually altered. Ivy and wild grapevines grew over formerly majestic portals. Winds sealed the shutters. Light dimmed. Chambers and court yards grew dark, cold and forgotten. As with life in the medieval castle, the sights of the lawyer trained in the common law tradition have increasingly become focused to little, specialised closets. Isolated in his comfortable cloisters of the court room or the law faculty, the lawyer has defended his claims in a world barrenly insulated from the insights of other disciplines. Windows which formerly ushered in fresh air have been long closed.

I wish to try to push open those windows with respect to one area of the common law. I have chosen the subject of liberty and I have studied that subject with reference to the constitutional experiences of Canada and the United States and, to a lesser extent, Great Britain. My aim has been to elucidate the character of arguments which common law lawyers have implicitly as well as explicitly employed in the three countries in defence of fundamental rights and to question whether, if those arguments possess shortcomings, an argument can be made which can consistently support the existence of fundamental rights. I want to show that fruitful insights to hitherto unresolved constitutional problems do flow from another discipline and that the insights are not mere "pie in the sky". Rather, they evolve from and can be connected to concrete legal problems.

During the span of tine when I was carrying out the research for this book I was most fortunate to have been a student under several great teachers and scholars who have helped shape my theses and arguments. In particular, I cannot let the opportunity pass without acknowledging my gratitude to Professors C. B. Macpherson and Peter Russell of the University of Toronto, Frederick Northedge of the London School of Economics and Kent Greenawalt of the Columbia Law School. The early drafts of several parts of the manuscript were submitted in the form of essays in the partial fulfilment of the LL.M. degree at the Columbia Law School during 1976-1977. The invaluable criticisms of Kent Greenawalt, Ernest Nagel, William F. Young, James Nickel and Charles Frankel helped me to clarify and substantiate my arguments. Joseph H. Smith renewed my interest in the judgments of Chief Justice Coke. William Christian of the Political Science Department, University of Guelph read the whole of my manuscript and for his perceptive criticisms I am indebted.

I have found that the writing of a book requires an environment where students and colleagues are continually prepared to challenge one's arguments with goodwill and encouragement. I have found such an environment at the Windsor Law Faculty. Leon Lysaght continually questioned the clarity of my theses. Julio Menezes helped me to apply my arguments in chapter II to a concrete problem in "Capital Punishment and a Democratic Society," to be published in Julio Menezes, ed., *Decade of Adjustment: Legal Perspectives on Contemporary Canadian Issues* (Toronto: Macmillan & Co., 1979). And I am especially grateful for having had the opportunity to teach under a Dean, Dr. Ronald Ianni, whose encouragement and administrative support have meant a great deal to me while writing the final drafts of my manuscript. I am also grateful to Patricia Thornton and Deanna Gadoury for typing the later versions of the manuscript as well as to Tim Mathany for checking citations and preparing a table of cases and statutes.

There are, however, two persons whose ideas and whose respect for my efforts have been indispensable to my study of the subject of liberty. The one, Marjolijn Doedijns, carried on a dialogue so necessary to crystallize my criticisms of the liberal tradition in chapter IV as well as to elaborate my own defence of fundamental rights in chapter VI. The other, in whose memory I am dedicating this book, read and commented upon all but the later drafts of my manuscript. That he encouraged me to pursue the line of inquiry in this book there can be little doubt, and for that experience I am deeply grateful.

I alone remain responsible for any errors and omissions which remain.

Kingsville, Ontario,   *William E. Conklin*
January 26th, 1979

XI

Table of Cases

Buckley v. *Valeo*, 424 U.S. 1, 96 S. Ct. 612, 46 L. Ed. 2d. 659 (1976).

Calvin's Case (1608), 7 Co. Rep. 1a, 77 E.R. 377, 2 Brownl. 198, 265 Hard. 140 (K.B.).

Campbell v. *Hall* (1774), 1 Cowp. 204, 98 E.R. 1048 (K.B.).

Case of Adam de Ravensworth (1336), Coram Rege Roll, No. 306, mem. 27.

Case of the Lords President of Wales and York (1609), 12 Co. Rep. 50, 77 E.R. 1331 (K.B.).

Case of Proclamations (1610), 12 Co. Rep. 74, 77 E.R. 1352 (K.B.).

Chemicals Regs, Ref Re, [1943] S.C.R. 1, [1943] 1 D.L.R. 248.

City of London v. *Wood* (1701), 12 Mod. 669, 88 E.R. 1592.

Co-operative Committee on Japanese Canadians v. *A.-G. Canada.* [1947] A.C. 87, [1947] 1 D.L.R. 577 (P.C.).

Curr v. *The Queen*, [1972] S.C.R. 889, 26 D.L.R. (3d) 603, 18 C.R.N.S. 281, 7 C.C.C. (2d) 181.

Dandridge v. *Williams*, 397 U.S. 471, 90 S. Ct. 1153, 25 L. Ed. 2d 491 (1920).

Daniel v. *Family Security Life Ins. Co.*, 336 U.S. 220, 69 S. Ct. 550, 93 L. Ed. 632 (1949).

Debs v. *United States*, 249 U.S. 211, 39 S. Ct. 252, 63 L. Ed. 566 (1919).

De Libellis Famosis (1606), 3 Co. Rep. 254 (1826 edn.), 77 E.R. 250 (Star Ch.).

Dennis v. *United States*, 341 U.S. 494, 71 S. Ct. 857, 95 L. Ed. 1137 (1951).

Dominion News and Gifts Ltd v. *The Queen*, [1964] S.C.R. 251, 3 C.C.C. 1,42 C.R. 209.

Douglas v. *California*, 372 U.S. 353, 83 S. Ct. 814, 9 L. Ed. 2d 811 (1963).

Drewary et al. v. *Century City Developments Ltd. et. al. (no. 1)*, [1975] 6 O.R. (2d) 288, 52 D.L.R. (3d) 512 (Ont. H.C.).

Duke of Argyle v. *Commissioners of Inland Revenue*, [1914] L.T. 893 (K.B.).

Duncan v. *Louisiana*, 391 U.S. 145, 88 S. Ct. 1444, 20 L. Ed. 2d 491 (1968).

Dupond v. *City of Montreal* (1978), 19 N.R. 478, (1978) 84 D.L.R. (3d) 420 (S.C.C.).

Ellen Street Estates v. *Minister of Health*, [1934] 1 K.B. 590, [1934] All E.R. 385 (K.B.).

Essex County Roman Catholic School Board and Porter et. al., Re (1979) 21 O.R. (2d) 255 (Ont. C.A.)

Flemming v. *Nestor*, 363 U.S. 603, 80 S. Ct. 1367 (1960).

Frohwerk v. *United States*, 249 U.S. 204, 39 S. Ct. 249, 63 L. Ed. 561 (1919).

Frontiero v. *Richardson*, 411 U.S. 677, 93 S. Ct. 1764 (1973).

Ft. Francis Pulp and Paper Co. Ltd. v. *Manitoba Free Press Co. Ltd.*, [1923] A.C. 695, [1923] 3 D.L.R. 629 (P.C.).

Furman v. *Georgia*, 408 U.S. 238, 92 S. Ct. 2726, 33 L. Ed. 2d 346 (1972).

Cagnon and Vallieres v. *R.* (1974), 47 D.L.R. (3d) 378, 25 C.R.N.S. 217 (Que. C.A.).

Gallant v. *R.* (1949), 35 M.P.R. 214, [1949] 2 D.L.R. 425 (S.C.P.E.I.).

George Gray, Re (1919), 57 S.C.R. 153.

Gitlow v. *New York*,, 268 U.S. 652, 45 S. Ct. 625, 69 L. Ed. 1138 (1925).

Green v. *Mortimer* (1861), 3 L.T. 642, 35 (Repl.) 324 (H.L.).

Gregg v. *Georgia*, 428 U.S. 153, 96 S. Ct. 2909 (1976).

Griffin v. *Illinois*, 351 U.S. 12, 76 S. Ct. 585, 100 L. Ed. 891 (1956).

Harper v. *Virginia Bd. of Elections*, 383 U.S. 663, 86 S. Ct. 1079 (1966).

Harrison v. *Carswell*, [1976] 2 S.C.R. 200, 62 D.L.R. (3d) 68, [1975] 6 W.W.R. 673, 25 C.C.C. (2d) 186.

Hebert v. *Louisiana*, 272 U.S. 312, 47 S. Ct. 103 (1926).

Henry Birks and Sons (Montreal) Ltd. v. *Montreal and A.-G. of Quebec*, [1955] S.C.R. 799, [1955] 5 D.L.R. 321.

Hirabayashi v. *United States*, 320 U.S. 81, 63 S. Ct. 1375 (1943).

Hoani te Heuhen Tokino v. *Aotea District Maori Land Board*, [1941] A.C. 308, [1941] 2 All E.R. 93 (P.C.).

Hogan v. *The Queen*, [1975] 2 S.C.R. 574, 48 D.L.R. (3d) 427, 26 C.R.N.S. 206, 18 C.C.C. (2d) 65, 9 N.S.R. (2d) 145, 2 N.R. 343.

In Re Cape Breton (1846), 5 Moo 259, 13 E.R. 489 (P.C.).

In Re Initiative and Referendum Act, [1919] A.C. 935, 48 D.L.R. 18 (P.C.).

Irvine v. *California*, 347 U.S. 128, 74 S. Ct. 381, 98 L. Ed. 561 (1954).

John Lamb's Case (1611), 5 Coke 108 (1826 edn.), 77 E.R. 822 (Star Chambers).

Kielly v. *Carson* (1842), 4 Moo 63, 13 E.R. 225 (P.C.).

King v. *Earl of Banbury* (1694), Skinner 517 (K.B.).

Korematsu v. *United States*, 323 U.S. 214, 65 S. Ct. 193 (1944).

Kotch v. *Board of River Pilot Comm'rs.*, 330 U.S. 552, 67 S. Ct. 910, 91 L. Ed. 1093 (1947).

Kramer v. *Union Free School District No. 15*, 395 U.S. 621, 89 S.
  Ct. 1886, 23 L. Ed. 2d 583 (1969).
Labrador Company v. *The Queen*, [1893] A.C. 104 (P.C.).
Lee v. *Bude and Torrington Junction Ry. Co.* (1871), 6 L.R. 576
  (C.P.).
Levy v. *Louisiana*, 391 U.S. 68, 88 S. Ct. 1509, 20 L. Ed. 2d 436
  (1968).
Lindsley v. *Natural Carbonic Gas Co.*, 220 U.S. 61, 31 S. Ct. 337
  (1911).
Liyanage v. *The Queen*, [1967] 1 A.C. 259, [1966] 1 All E.R. 650
  (P.C. 1965).
McBratney v. *McBratney* (1919), 59 S.C.R. 550, 50 D.L.R. 132,
  [1919] 3 W.W.R. 1.
McCann et al. v. *The Queen* (1976), 68 D.L.R. (3d) 661, (1975),
  29 C.C.C. (2d) 337, 1 F.C. 570 (Fed. Ct., T.D.).
McDonald v. *Bd. of Election Comm'rs.*, 394 U.S. 802, 89 S. Ct.
  1404, 22 L. Ed. 2d 739 (1969).
McGowan v. *Maryland*, 366 U.S. 420, 81 S. Ct. 1101, 6 L. Ed. 2d
  393 (1961).
McKenzie v. *Stewart* (1754), 9 Mor. Dict. 7443 (H.L.).
Magor and St. Mellons Rural District Council v. *Newport Corp.*,
  [1952] A.C. 189, [1951] 2 All E.R. 839 (H.L.).
Martin v. *Law Society of British Columbia*, [1950] 3 D.L.R. 173,
  [1949] 1 W.W.R. 993 (B.C.C.A.).
Massachusetts Bd. of Retirement v. *Murgia*, 427 U.S. 307, 96 S.Ct.
  2562, 49 L. Ed. 520 (1976).
Masses Publishing Co. v. *Patten*, 244 Fed. 535 (1917), (Dist. Ct.
  S.D. New York).
Miranda v. *Arizona*, 384 U.S. 436, 86 S. Ct. 1602, 16 L. Ed. 2d
  694 (1966).
Morey v. *Doud* 354 U.S. 457, 77 S. Ct. 1344, 1 L. Ed. 2d 1485
  (1957).
Murray v. *West Vancouver* (1937), 52 B.C.R. 237, [1937] 3 W.W.R.
  269 (B.C.S.C.).
Murray's Lessee v. *Hoboken Land Improvement Co.*, 18 How 272
  (1856).
Nova Scotia Board of Censors and A.-G. for Nova Scotia v. *Mc-
  Neil*, [1978] 2 S.C.R. 662, (1978) 84 D.L.R. (3d) 1.
O'Connor v. *The Queen*, [1966] S.C.R. 619, 57 D.L.R. (2d) 123,
  48 C.R. 270, [1966] 4 C.C.C. 342.
Oregon v. *Mitchell*, 400 U.S. 112, 91 S. Ct. 260, 27 L. Ed. 272
  (1970).
Ouellet, Re (Nos 1 and 2) (1977), 72 D.L.R. (3d) 95 (Que. C.A.).

R. v. *Wray*, [1971] S.C.R. 272, 11 D.L.R. (3d) 673, 11 C.R.N.S. 235, [1970] 4 C.C.C.1.

San Antonio Independent School Dist. v. *Rodriquez*, 411 U.S. 1, 98 S. Ct. 1278 (1973).

Saumer v. *City of Quebec*, [1953] 2 S.C.R. 299, [1953] 4 D.L.R. 641.

Schenck v. *United States*, 249 U.S. 47, 39 S. Ct. 247, 63 L. Ed. 470 (1919).

Shapiro v. *Thompson*, 394 U.S. 618, 89 S. Ct. 1322, 22 L. Ed. 2d 600 (1969).

Skinner v. *Oklahoma*, 316 U.S. 535, 62 S. Ct. 1110 (1942).

Snyder v. *Mass.*, 291 U.S. 97, 54 S. Ct. 67 (1934)

Stockdale v. *Hansard* (1839), 9 Ad. & E.1, 8 L.J. Q.B. 294, 112 E.R. 1112 (Q.B.).

Switzman v. *Elbling*, [1957] S.C.R. 285, 7 D.L.R. (2d) 337.

Trop v. *Dulles*, 356 U.S. 86, 78 S. Ct. 590, 2 L. Ed. 2d 630 (1958).

U.S. v. *Caroline Prods. Co.*, 304 U.S. 144, 58 S. Ct. 778 (1938)

U.S. v. *Guest*, 383 U.S. 745, 86 S. Ct. 1170, 16 L. Ed. 2d 239 (1966).

Validity of the Wartime Leasehold Regs., Ref. Re, [1950] S.C.R. 124, [1950] 2 D.L.R. 1.

Vauxhall Estates Ltd. v. *Liverpool Corp.*, [1932] 1 K.B. 733.

West Coast Hotel Co. v. *Parrish*, 300 U.S. 379, 57 S. Ct. 578 (1937).

Whitney v. *California*, 274 U.S. 357, 47 S. Ct. 641, 71 L. Ed. 1095 (1927).

Williamson v. *Lee Optical Co.*, 348 U.S. 483, 75 S. Ct. 461, 99 L. Ed. 563 (1955).

Yates v. *U.S.*, 354 U.S. 298, 77 S. Ct. 1064, 1 L. Ed. 2d 1356 (1957).

Yick Wo v. *Hopkins*, 118 U.S. 356, 6 S. Ct. 1064, 30 L. Ed. 220 (1886).

Table of Statutes

Introduction

The words "human rights" and "fundamental freedoms" have been the great popular slogans of the twentieth century. Politicians throughout the world have repeatedly boasted that respect for liberty is a major policy of their governments. Constitution framers have "entrenched" articles of human rights in bold letters. Judges have confidently perceived themselves as the independent protectors of liberty. And yet, so much disrespect is demonstrated towards human rights from day to day.

The barbarism of the twentieth century has been so profound that the conscientious student has adequate cause to re-evaluate the foundation of liberty itself. That the Soviet Union, Uganda, Chile and India[1] — to mention but a few — inscribe such beautifully worded rights in their respective Constitutions leads one to suspect the claim that fundamental rights are fundamental simply because the rights are entrenched in a written constitution. For one to appreciate the extent to which rights are fundamental in any given society one must be prepared to pierce the veil presented by written constitutions and statutory enactments. One must penetrate deeper into the moral-political premises underlying the enactment, interpretation and enforcement of the constitutions and statutes themselves.

This inquiry attempts to do just that. It pries into the concepts underlying the decisions of judges, the statutes of legislators and the arguments of legal scholars in three countries. The countries which have been chosen are Canada, the United States and Great Britain.

These three countries, perhaps more than any others, have bragged to themselves and to the world of the fundamental rights protected in their law. Jurists, legislators and constitution framers in Canada and the United States in particular have often asserted that certain fundamental rights[2] underlie their societies. The various drafts of a new Canadian Constitution,[3] the Canadian Bill of Rights[4] and numerous provincial human rights codes[5] recognise the existence of fundamental rights. Some leading Canadian jurists[6] and scholars[7] have even believed that these same rights are implied in the present Constitution. With respect to the United States, the American Constitution expressly "entrenches" certain freedoms and rights. In more recent years the American courts have held particular rights to be fundamental even though the written Constitution was silent with respect to them. Judicial acknowledgment that these latter rights were fundamental has led to important legal consequences, not least of which is the principle that the American courts are obligated to exercise a high level of scrutiny over legislation which infringes the rights.

My inquiry begins with the above claim of jurists, legislators and constitution framers that fundamental rights are in fact and ought to be the foundation of their respective societies. My study is not directed to the question of why fundamental rights ought to be valued over other goods such as, say, virtue or happiness, although I shall argue at the end of chapter II and in chapter III that counsel and judge alike may ask normative questions as a legitimate inquiry into the content of the law. Rather than attempting to argue why one value ought to be preferred over another at this point in time, I begin with the claim of jurists, legislators and constitution framers that fundamental rights are in fact and ought to be the basis of the workings of civil institutions. The focus of this study is directed to the more modest question of what character of argument politicians, jurists and constitution framers ought to adopt if they are consistently to support their own claim that fundamental rights exist and ought to exist in their respective societies.

How should one go about identifying the premises of judges, legislators and legal scholars? The task is a formidable one. Should the student look to history with a view to isolating the predominant principles advocated by lawyers over a long period of time? Should one use sociology in an effort to abstract the socio-economic biases of the legal elite in each of the three countries? Or, alternatively, should the student interview and analyze the psychological boundaries of the judge's or lawyer's make-up?

No doubt each discipline could render fruitful insights. This student, being a lawyer trained in the common law tradition, will go to the common law lawyer's primary resource material: the decisions of judges, the statutes of legislators and the writings of legal scholars. I shall look at that material with only one critical question in mind: "Why are fundamental rights considered fundamental?" In particular, I shall examine the ideas and the arguments which esteemed judges, legislators and legal scholars have used to justify the existence of fundamental rights in the three countries.

In order to gain a better grasp of what I am looking for in the lawyer's primary resource material, we are aided by various dictionary definitions of the word "fundamental". The *Oxford* English Dictionary[8] gives two potentially applicable definitions. First, "of or pertaining to the foundation or groundwork, going to *the root* of the matter*." Secondly, "serving as the foundation or base on which something is built. Chiefly and now exclusively in immaterial applications. Hence, forming an *essential or indispensable* part of a system, institution, etc." "Fundamentalness" is defined as "a leading or primary principle, rule, law or article, which serves as *the groundwork of a system*; an *essential part*." Other dictionaries provide similar definitions. *Webster's Third New International Dictionary*, 1967,[9] for example, defines "fundamental" in this way:

> 1. producing, supporting, regulating or conditioning something (as a development or system): *basic, underlying...*
> a) serving as an original or generating source: being the one from which others are derived: *primary...: formative...*
> b) serving as a basis supporting existence or determining essential structure or function: forming the foundation on which something immaterial is built...
> c) constituting a necessary or elemental quality, part or condition: *indispensable...: irreducible.*

Ballentine's Law Dictionary[10] defines "fundamental" as "at the foundation; basic." And *Bouvier's Law Dictionary*[11] defines "fundamental" in this way:

> This word is applied to those laws which are the foundation of society. Those laws by which the exercise of power is restrained and regulated are fundamental. The constitution of the United States is the fundamental law of the land.

The thrust of these definitions makes it clear that something is fundamental if it is "at the root of the matter", "essential", "basic", "underlying", "primary", "formative" or "irreducible". These are very strong words. They require that we place a heavy burden upon those who would claim that the rights in any country are fundamental rights. The definitions also tell us that when reading judgments, statutes and legal writings, I should look for something which tells us why rights are "at the root" of the legal system, "essential", "basic", "underlying", "primary", "formative" or "irreducible" elements of the law in the three countries under consideration.

Let me be more precise about my intention. The first three

chapters of this book will show that jurists in Canada, the United States and Great Britain have offered various types of argument for the justification of fundamental rights. They have sometimes elaborated one type of justification, sometimes another. Their focus has varied from one historical period to another. Sometimes their argument has explicitly flowed from a conscious concern to justify fundamental rights; at other times their argument has implicitly hovered in a discussion about issues to which fundamental rights were less perceptively related. My purpose, however, is not to document which jurist advocated which type of justification and when. Nor is my inquiry limited to jurists who have consciously concentrated on fundamental rights issues. Rather, my objective is to move interchangeably from the jurists of one country to another and from one period to another in an effort to isolate the types of arguments which they have made in defence of the existence of fundamental rights. Having identified the arguments, I want to scrutinize them to assure myself that if judges and legislators consistently used the arguments in support of their decisions and conduct, the rights in their society would be "at the root of the matter", "essential", "basic", "underlying", "primary", "formative" or "irreducible".

The arguments which jurists have made for the existence of fundamental rights in Great Britain, Canada and the United States can be classified as "backward-looking", looking to "society's contemporary values" and looking to a written constitution. Sir Edward Coke appears to have been the first jurist in the common law tradition to elaborate the "backward-looking" approach in sophisticated depth. He held, briefly, that fundamental rights existed because and to the extent that they could be uncovered in legal tradition. The second "contemporary values" argument has followed three versions. Some jurists, such as Lord Devlin, have argued that fundamental rights exist because and to the extent that they are supported by the values of "the ordinary man on the street". Mr. Justice Marshall of the United States Supreme Court has in recent years relied heavily upon the conscience of "the informed citizen". Another version, elaborated in greatest depth by the early nineteenth century British philosopher, Jeremy Bentham, has fallen back upon the notion of "the will of the majority". A third, more common version of the "contemporary values" argument has been for jurists to rely upon the concept of "the intent of the legislature". The third general category of argument for the existence of fundamental rights has related to a written Constitution. Fundamental rights exist, so the argument goes, because they exist in a written Constitution.

Part one of this book will examine the general juridical arguments for the existence of fundamental rights in three respective chapters. I shall raise shortcomings with respect to each of them. I shall exemplify the difficulties by shifting back and forth between the Canadian and American constitutional experiences. The three arguments will be found wanting. Indeed, I shall suggest that the very nature of the British, Canadian and American constitutions directs us to leave the traditional legal materials in order to answer the critical issue of why fundamental rights are fundamental.

Part two of my inquiry will, therefore, examine the concept of liberty in Anglo-American political philosophy. Although some arguments and ideas of T. H. Green and Isaiah Berlin will be developed, I shall focus primarily upon the writings of John Stuart Mill, Jeremy Bentham and John Rawls.

But why have I chosen Mill, Bentham and Rawls over other political philosophers? For one thing, Mill and Bentham have influenced the thinking of common law lawyers over the past century in a very deep way. Mill's principle of "self-regarding conduct", for example, provides the basis of much reform-minded thinking in the field of criminal law to this day in Canada and Great Britain. Bentham's philosophy of the "greatest happiness of the greatest number", on the other hand, serves as the philosophic framework for the principle of legislative supremacy which is so important in the Canadian and British constitutions. His perspective also provides the justification for interest group politics as played in the United States Congress and as translated into legal analysis by Mr. Justice Holmes and Roscoe Pound. If objections can be made to the prevailing juridical arguments for fundamental rights in Part one, then it may be that the philosophic reasons for those objections can be found in the writings of Mill and Bentham.

Chapter IV, therefore, will examine Mill's important idea that "self-regarding conduct" ought to be protected. I shall set out what Mill meant by the term and why he considered it so essential to the concept of liberty. Mill's argument for the protection of "self-regarding conduct" was, for the most part, a utilitarian one. I shall raise some significant difficulties in Mill's argument. I shall try to show how these obstacles characterise what contemporary philosophers refer to as act and rule utilitarianism. Finally, I shall show how these same conceptual difficulties in utilitarian theory underlie Mill's own arguments for the protection of "self-regarding" conduct.

I have chosen Rawls over other contemporary philosophers because Rawls raises the important moral and constitutional issues which any argument for the existence of fundamental rights should face. Rawls does so, in addition, with remarkable comprehensiveness. Furthermore, he attempts to overcome the shortcomings of the utilitarian perspective of Mill and Bentham. Finally, he tries to come to terms with the relationship between liberty and equality, a relationship which liberal philosophers, politicians and judges have invariably assumed to be contradictory. Rawls is not alone in that regard.

Chapter V will briefly outline the major issues (as Rawls perceives them) for an argument for fundamental rights. We shall see, however, that Rawls leaves some issues unresolved. Rawls assumes, for example, that although basic liberties must be held equally, equality in the "worth" or effective use of the basic liberties is not required in a just society. I shall try to argue that liberty requires equality or, at least, a sufficient economic and social equality so as to permit each individual to *exercise* his of her *fundamental* rights and freedoms *effectively*. Furthermore, notwithstanding Rawls' disclaimers to the contrary, I shall attempt to establish why we are obliged to determine whether Rawls' principles of justice rest upon an *a priori* ontological hypothesis concerning what Rawls himself believes to be important to men and women.

We shall see that Rawls' ontological hypotheses do provide some indication as to why basic liberties are fundamental. His ontological hypotheses protrude from his two arguments showing why basic liberties must be distributed equally. The one argument begins with liberty of conscience and the second with self-respect. Whereas the former possesses serious weaknesses when it is extended to other freedoms, the latter is more far-reaching and more consistent with classical democratic theory.

Chapter VI will return to Mill's principle of "self-regarding conduct". I shall argue that the conceptual problems faced in Mill's utilitarian argument for "self-regarding conduct" can be overcome if one accepts the principle of respect for persons rather than "the greatest happiness of the greatest number" as the ultimate norm in a democratic society. I shall put forward a particular conception of the self. This conception will go a long way in chapter 6 towards resolving the apparent inconsistencies elaborated in chapter 4 in Mill's own application of his notion of the protection of "self-regarding conduct".

In Part three I shall return to constitutional law. In particular, my objective here will be to join the moral-political principle of "respect for persons" with constitutional analysis.

The first concern in Part three will be to ascertain which rights are fundamental ones. The issue is an important one for a country such as Canada which, for over a decade, has been considering various drafts of an entrenched Bill of Rights. Traditional rights of life, expression, due process, non-discrimination and the like, have been placed in the drafts without much discussion as to why those rights are fundamental. I wish to show why they are so. There has been concern in more recent years, in addition, that language rights and freedom of information ought to be added to the list of fundamental rights. Part one will have established that the traditional juridical justifications of fundamental rights do not, of necessity, leave room for the existence of these or any other fundamental rights. Chapter VII will show how language rights do have a role in the implementation of a "respect for persons" perspective in a country such as Canada. Finally, I want to show why equality and liberty are not so contradictory as liberal theorists, politicians and judges have so long assumed. Rather, an argument for fundamental rights should concern itself with the effective exercise or, to use Rawls' term, the "worth" of fundamental rights. As such, one should incorporate socio-economic considerations into any evaluation of the protection of fundamental rights in any one country. Several recent American Supreme Court judgments will be used to show how judicial analysis can take account of the interdependency of equality and liberty.

The second general issue in chapter VII will be the level of judicial scrutiny expected of legislation which allegedly burdens fundamental rights. As in the case of the enumeration of fundamental rights above, Part one will have demonstrated how juridical approaches toward fundamental rights have failed to explain why one standard of judicial scrutiny should be accepted over another. Because the level of scrutiny is critical to the ultimate outcome in any given civil liberties case, traditional analysis has correspondingly failed to bring certainty, consistency or principled reasons for judgment. The principle of "respect for persons" elaborated in Chapter VI will be shown to fill the vacuum.

A third issue which has confronted common law lawyers has been the scope of fundamental rights. Even if we have ascertained which rights are fundamental and what standard of judicial scrutiny should be exercised, the question remains: at what point should the protection of the right terminate? Bentham suggested that the protection should end when "the greatest happiness of the greatest number" so required. The constitutions of many Commonwealth countries require that the "national security", "public welfare" or "interest of the state" resolve the issue. The various drafts of an entrenched Bill of Rights in Canada have been no exception in this regard. By using Ronald Dworkin's distinction between a weak and a strong sense of rights, I want to show how

American and Canadian courts have, in subversive advocacy cases, adopted a very weak sense of rights. The weak sense will be seen to be alien to a "respect for persons" justification toward fundamental rights. I shall suggest how lawyers and judges ought to approach subversive advocacy cases if they are to live by the claim that fundamental rights do exist in their society.

Finally, chapter VII will suggest a method of judicial decision-making which is consistent with a "respect for persons" argument. After briefly examining Ronald Dworkin's theory of judicial decision-making, I shall show how my chapters I and II raise serious shortcomings to his theory. Indeed, I shall suggest that the principle of "respect for persons" requires lawyers to be forward-looking as well as backward-looking, contrary to what Lord Coke C.J. and Ronald Dworkin have advocated. That "respect for persons" lies at the foundation of fundamental rights raises serious new questions for the constitutional lawyer and, possibly, new answers to the challenges to liberty in our times.

Notes

1. The Constitution of Union of Soviet Republics (ed. John Hazard; Oceana Publications, Inc.: Dobbs Ferry, N.Y., issued September 1972) provides, for example, in Chapter X — Fundamental Rights and Duties of Citizens

Article 124

In order to ensure to citizens freedom of conscience, the church in the U.S.S.R. is separated from the state, and the school from the church. Freedom of religious worship and freedom of anti-religious propaganda is recognised for all citizens.

Article 125

In conformity with the interests of the working people, and in order to strengthen the socialist system, the citizens of the U.S.S.R. are guaranteed by law:
a) freedom of speech;
b) freedom of the press;
c) freedom of assembly, including the holding of mass meetings;
d) freedom of street processions and demonstrations.

These civil rights are ensured by placing at the disposal of the working people and their organisations printing presses, stocks of paper, public buildings, the streets, communications facilities and other material requisites for the exercise of these rights.

Article 127

Citizens of the U.S.S.R. are guaranteed inviolability of the person. No person shall be placed under arrest except by decision of a court of law or with the sanction of a procurator.

Article 128

The inviolability of the homes of citizens and privacy of correspondence are protected by law.

2. The terms "liberties" and "rights" are used interchangeably in this study since it is the fundamentalness of those liberties and rights with which it is most concerned. For careful enunciations of the differences of each term, see W. D. Lamont, "Rights," *Aristotelian Society Proceedings*, suppl., vol. 24 (1950); G. Williams, "The Concept of Legal Liberty," in R. S. Summers, ed., *Essays in Legal Philosophy* (Oxford: Basil Blackwell, 1968); H. N. Morse, *The Hohfeldian Place of Right in Constitutional Cases*, 6 Capital Univ. L. Rev. 1 (1976); C. J. Friedrich, *Rights, Liberties and Freedoms*, 91 U. of Penn. L. Rev. 312 (1942); J. Finnis, *Some Professorial Fallacies About Rights*, 4 Adelaide L. Rev. 377 (1972).

3. Known as the "Victoria Charter," approved by the federal and nine provincial governments at the Constitutional Conference in Victoria, June 1971. Also see discussion of Constitutional Amendment Bill, infra, Appendix.

4. S.C. 8-9 Eliz. II, c. 44 entitled "An Act for the Recognition and Protection of Human Rights and Fundamental Freedoms."

5. See, e.g., Ontario Human Rights Code, R.S.O. 1970, c. 318; New Brunswick Human Rights Code, R.S.N.B. 1973, c. H-11. Also see the Canadian Human Rights Act, S.C. 1976-77, c. 33.

6. See, e.g., *Ref. re Alberta Statutes* [1938] S.C.R. 100, [1938] 2 D.L.R. 81 per Cannon and Duff, JJ.; *Saumur* v. *City of Quebec* [1953] 2 S.C.R. 299, [1953] 4 D.L.R. 64, esp. Rand J.; *Switzman* v. *Elbling*, [1957] S.C.R. 285, 7 D.L.R. (2d) 337, esp. Abbott and Rand JJ.; *Liyanage* v. *The Queen* [1967] 1 A.C. 259, [1966] 1 All E.R. 650 per Lord Pearce (P.C. 1965) and *Rex* v. *Hess (No. 2)*, [1949] 4 D.L.R. 199, [1949] 1 W.W.R. 586 per O'Halloran J. A. See generally, text, infra, chapter I, sect. 4.

7. S. N. Lyon and R. G. Atkey, *Canadian Constitutional Law in a Modern Perspective* (Toronto: U. of T. Press, 1972), pp. 370-377; R. R. Price, *Mr. Justice Rand and the Privileges and Immunities of Canadian Citizens*, 16 U. Tor. Fac. L.R. 23 (1958); A. Brewin, *A Bill of Rights Implicit in the B.N.A. Act*, 35 Can. Bar. R. 554 (1957).

8. 1933, vol. 4, p. 604.

9. unabridged edn., 1967, p. 921.

10. 3rd ed., 1969, p. 508.

11. 3rd revised ed., 1914, p. 1323.

Part One

Traditional Juridical Arguments
for
Fundamental Rights

Chapter I

Chief Justice Coke's "Backward-looking" Theory of Fundamental Rights

The common law system is characterised by a heavy reliance upon precedent. In the formative years of the common law, precedent exhibited a persuasive role. Beginning in the 1830s precedent took on a binding character. Throughout the history of the common law system the doctrine of precedent has required that lawyers and judges look backward into history for their resource material. As early as 1250 Bracton had insisted that the lawyer must retreat to the past in order to find evidence of what constituted the law.[1] As recently as 1976 the Canadian Supreme Court has held that the judicial duty in the common law system is "to proceed in a reasoned way from principled decision and established concepts."[2] The common law lawyer seeks out the *"ratio decidendi"* of past judicial decisions, he distinguishes one decision from another in order to attain consistency, and he analogises in hard cases where past precedents seem silent with respect to an issue or where two lines of precedent collide with each other. This "backward-looking" process of analysis, it is generally assumed, will bring the lawyer closer to what constitutes "the law". The resolution of issues regarding liberty has been no exception to this assumption.

Sir Edward Coke (1552-1634) used the backward-looking nature of the common law system to refine a distinct theory of fundamental rights. Four principles underlay his theory. First, he constitutionalised the principle of the "rule of law". Secondly, he established specific fundamental rights during the course of private litigation. Thirdly, he believed that the lawyer alone monopolised the authority to ascertain and justify the existence of fundamental rights. Finally, he held that a violation of a fundamental right had the legal consequence of rendering a conflicting Act of Parliament, Royal proclamation or a customary rule null and void. The common element to his four principles was the backward-looking method by which he derived the principles themselves.

This chapter will show how Chief Justice Coke used the weight of tradition to support his theory of fundamental rights. Two modern cases, the one American and the other Canadian, will then be employed to exemplify how Coke C.J.'s backward-looking method can be applied in practice. In section 3, I shall raise significant problems with Coke C.J.'s method of argument. Finally, in section 4, I shall demonstrate these shortcomings by reference to the constitutional experience in Canada with respect to the rights of political participation and religious conscience.

Section 1. Chief Justice Coke's Theory of Fundamental Rights

One can appreciate Coke C.J.'s theory of fundamental rights only by bearing in mind the historical context in which Coke C.J. found himself. During the fifteenth century, England had been torn by an almost unbridled private war amongst the baronage. As one historian has noted, the baronage had been "far more interested in its own factious ambitions than in parliament or nation."[3] In addition, feudal overlords had abused the judicial process to their own favour in the words of a 1487 statute,

> by unlawful maintenances,[4] giving of liveries, signs and tokens; and retainers[5] by indentures, promises, oaths, writings or otherwise; embraceries of his subjects,[6] untrue demeanings of sheriffs in making of panels and other untrue returns by taking of money by juries, by great riots and unlawful assemblies.[7]

Against this background, the Tudors (1485-1603) thrived upon a new gospel of the "common weal" which played to the innate wish of the elite for comprehensive order.[8] Religious leaders attacked the inherent wickedness of resistance to constituted authority.[9] Lawyers, public officials, scholars as well as kings actively accepted that law was the command of a sovereign who, in turn, possessed the sanction of unlimited force at his disposal. James I's *Trew Law of Free Monarchies*,[10] which expressed the prevailing political thought in England at the turn of the century (1598), argued that the King's commands were "the commands of God's minister". As God's delegate, James claimed the authority to declare life and death over all his subjects.[11] The Tudor Kings and Queens had set the stage for Coke C.J.'s needed defence of fundamental rights.

The crucial factor leading to Coke C.J.'s theory of fundamental rights was that sixteenth century England had experienced the undermining of the judiciary's independence and, indeed, of the judicial function itself. The Tudor Council, for example, often advised, delayed and even ordered dismissal of cases before common law judges. Through the Star Chamber, Royal Council investigated, prosecuted and adjudicated offences violating the

King's peace.[12] In addition, the Star Chamber arrogated to itself jurisdiction over municipal and trade disputes, civil suits between private parties, miscellaneous criminal offences, offences against the administration of justice, and censorship over all written and verbal communications.[13] Common law judges were often expected to sit in the Star Chamber and its ecclesiastical counterpart, the High Commission. The purposes and procedures of the latter institutions, in turn, were deeply anathematic to common law principles. Furthermore, judges were required to draft legislation[14] and generally to advise the King as to legislative policy.[15] Since "the King could do no wrong," grievances against Crown servants were heard by the King's prerogative courts or the King's Council rather than by the more independent common law courts.

Coke C.J. reacted. As Chief Justice of the Common Pleas from 1606 to 1613 and as Chief Justice of the King's Bench from 1613 to 1616, Coke C.J. insisted upon the notion of the "rule of law". By this principle, the King, his officials and his prerogative courts lived *under* the law rather than above it. This inferred that the common law courts, not the King nor his advisers, were the ultimate arbiters of the subject's rights. In line with this perspective, Coke C.J. tried to contain and ultimately to undermine the jurisdiction of the King, the prerogative courts, the Court of Admiralty and the Court of Chancery.

The case of *Prohibitions del Roy* (1608)[16] illustrates how Coke C.J. looked backward into the legal tradition in order to establish the four elements in his theory of fundamental rights. Not least important was his assertion that the King was subject to the law.

Coke C.J.'s initial argument in support of the "rule of law" principle looked to past practice.[17] Because the common law courts had traditionally functioned independently of the King, they alone possessed the jurisdiction to arbitrate disputes involving the King's authority. Although the King was permitted to sit in the Star Chamber, Coke C.J. held, "it appears in our books" that the King even there could only consult with the Justices of the Star Chamber: the King could not sit *in judicio* (in a judicial capacity). Similarly, even though the King did sit in the King's Bench, the judgment had always been rendered by the court as a whole, (that is, *per curiam*). In addition, the King's Bench judges — as with all common law judges — were "sworn to execute justice according to law and the custom of England."

Coke C.J. proceeded to justify the "rule of law" principle by looking to more than past practice.[18] He went to two ancient Acts of Parliament dated 1328 (2 Edw. III, c.9 and 2 Edw. III, c.1). On the basis of these two old statutes Coke C.J. set out the proposition "that neither by the great seal, nor by the little seal, justice shall be delayed." From this Coke C.J. reasoned that "the King cannot take any cause out of any of his Courts, and give judgment upon it himself," although the King could stay a case if he himself were a party to it. The authority for the latter staying procedure was confirmed by a statute of 1410 (11 H. IV, c8). Coke C.J. confidently asserted in *Prohibitions del Roy* that

> no King after the Conquest assumed to himself to give any judgment in any cause whatsoever, which concerned the administration of justice within this realm, but these were solely determined in the Courts of Justice.[19]

He cited a statute of 1485 (1 H. VII, c.4) as holding that where the King's Council had reversed a common law judgment, the reversal was "utterly void for that it [that is, the King's Council] was not a place where judgment may be reversed." In the same light, reference was made to a 1403 statute (4 H. IV, c.22) which provided that

> judgments rendered in the King's Court are not destroyed, but a judgment stands in its own force until declared erroneous by a judgment of the King's Court.

That is, only the court, not the King, could declare a judgment erroneous.

By relying upon the past Coke C.J. did more than subject the King to the common law courts. He laid down principles of public law in the course of private litigation. These principles lay like loaded guns to be used in later centuries in other common law countries. Once again, he sustained his propositions by searching out legal precedents of centuries past.

It has already been noted, for example, how Coke C.J. used two 1328 statutes as evidence of the principle that neither the King nor the Chancellor could delay justice. A second public law principle flowing from *Prohibitions del Roy* involved an aspect of "equality before the law". In Coke C.J.'s words, "all persons, the lowliest as well as the highest, shall have and receive justice in the court of our Lord the King."[20] Evidence for this proposition could be found, according to Coke C.J., in Magna Charta as well as a 1352 statute (25 Edw. III, c.5). Thirdly, on the authority of a statute dated 1370 (43 Edw. III, c.3) as well as "the ancient law of the land", Coke C.J. held that no defendant could be tried without the Crown satisfying the proper procedure. The latter procedure included the presentment before the Justices, the matter of record, due process of law and the original writ.

Prohibitions del Roy reflects a third element of Chief Justice Coke's theory of fundamental rights; namely, one's rights were ascertained by looking, not to social, economic or political history, but to legal history. As a consequence, Coke C.J. insisted that the lawyer alone monopolised the authority to determine and to justify fundamental rights. When James I claimed in *Prohibitions del Roy* that he himself could resolve legal disputes because "the law was founded upon reason, and that he and others had reason, as well as Judges," Coke C.J. reported his own reply in these words:

> ... true it was, that God had endowed his Majesty with excellent science, and great endowments of nature; but His Majesty was not learned in the laws of his realm of England, and causes which concern the life, or inheritance, or goods, or fortunes of his subjects, are not to be decided by natural reason but by the artificial reason and judgment of law, which law is an act which requires long study and experience, before that a man can attain to the cognizance of it...[21]

To this James was "greatly offended" for if Chief Justice Coke were correct, the King replied, then the King would be under the law. This would be treasonous to affirm. Indeed, one account states that the King became so angry, shaking his fists at the Chief Justice, that "Coke fell flat on all fower" and begged James' pardon.[22]

The case of *Prohibitions del Roy* reflects a fourth and final element of Chief Justice Coke's theory of fundamental rights. On two occasions in his judgment Coke C.J. indicated that if the King followed a procedure which conflicted with fundamental rights, the latter were to prevail so as to render the former void in law. Coke C.J. cited one case during the reign of Henry VII (dated 1485) when it was held that a reversal of a common law court's judgment by Henry's council of state was void.[23] The reversal, Coke C.J. reported, "was held utterly void for that it was not a place where judgment may be reserved." On a second occasion in *Prohibitions del Roy*, we have noted how the Chief Justice relied upon "the ancient law of the land" to support the proposition that the Crown had to satisfy proper procedures during any trial. The consequence for not following the proper procedure was that the trial was void. For, in Coke C.J.'s words, "and if any thing be done against it [that is, "the ancient law of the land"], it [that is, the Crown's procedure] shall be void in law and held for error."[24] In his typical "backward-looking" method of justifying such a proposition Coke C.J. cited statutes dated 1370 (43 Edw. III, c.3), 1355 (28 Edw. III c.3), 1364 (37 Edw. III, c.18) and 1394 (17 R. II, *ex rotulis Parliamenti in turri*, Art. 10).

Prohibitions del Roy was not the only case which mirrored

Coke C.J.'s theory of fundamental rights. His theory pervaded his general attack upon the prerogative courts, the Court of Admiralty and the Court of Chancery. In the *Case of the Lords President of Wales and York* (1609),[25] for example, the King insisted that the King's Commissions to the Councils of Wales and York had granted authority to hear and determine riots and routs according to law "or their discretions." Coke C.J. held that the two prerogative Courts of Wales and York were obligated to proceed according to law, not according to "their private conceits and affections." Coke C.J. insisted that the King's reference to "according to their discretion" was an open-ended criterion and, therefore, contrary to the rule of law.

In addition to this general "rule of law" proposition, Coke C.J.'s judgment in the *Case of the Lords President of Wales and York* (1609) subjected the jurisdiction of the prerogative Councils to the fundamental rights embedded in the common law in several ways. In the first place, according to the Chief Justice, the King could not grant authority to the Councils to hear all real actions. Although the King could grant authority to hear *criminal* cases between the King and party "according to the law and custom of England," he could not grant authority to hear *civil causes* between party and party. Coke C.J. reasoned that with respect to the latter, the action had to commence by Royal writ. What was issued from the Councils of Wales and York was a Commission rather than a writ.[26] Coke C.J. tried to restrict the prerogative courts' jurisdiction in this case, in the second place, by holding that the King could not grant equitable jurisdiction to the Councils for otherwise the latter could not be controlled. Underlying this proposition there lay an important idea concerning fundamental rights: whereas with an equity court the subject had no *capacity to appeal* by writ of error, he did have such a capacity in the common law courts.[27] Finally, Coke C.J. attempted to limit potential abuses of fundamental rights incurred by the prerogative courts by holding that the common law courts could legitimately grant writs.[28] Coke C.J. reasoned that the King's Commission to the Councils of Wales and York referred to secret Instructions which, of course, were not part of the record. The "danger to the subject is great" if the Instructions were ever lost. If lost, all would be *coram non judice*. Furthermore, whereas the subject could challenge the jurisdiction of a common law court because all matters were a part of the record, he could not so question the Councils' jurisdiction where the law was "vague or uncertain" or where no one knew what that jurisdiction actually was.

One additional point should be stressed about Coke C.J.'s

18

"backward-looking" attempt to enlarge the scope of the subject's rights. A fundamental right had the legal consequence of rendering null and void any proclamation, statute or custom which conflicted with the right. Coke C.J. lay the groundwork for this proposition by his reliance upon the principle of *coram non judice*. An action was *coram non judice* if it had been determined before a person not a judge. Such a person would thereby be lacking in jurisdiction and his judgment would be void.[29] We have already seen how Coke C.J. applied this principle in *Prohibitions del Roy*.[30] In the *Case of Lords President of Wales and York*[31] Coke C.J. held that secret Instructions from the King to the prerogative courts would cause great danger to the subject if the Instructions were ever lost. For, if lost, all would be *coram non judice*. Finally, in the *Case of Prohibitions*,[32] Coke C.J. held that if a cause of debt were not legally within the jurisdiction of the Council of York, "all their proceedings were *coram non judice*, and then no rescous [that is, rescue] could be done."

During the year following these three cases (1610), the Chief Justice extended the principle of voidability from prerogative courts which adjudicated disputes to the legislation of the King himself. Coke C.J. held in the *Case of Proclamations*[33] that "the King cannot change any part of the common law, nor create any offence by his proclamation, which was not an offence before, without Parliament." Sir Edward attached a note to his report of the case, in addition, claiming that proclamations issued pursuant to the prerogative were "utterly against law and reason, and for that void; for *quae contra rationem juris introducta sunt non debent trahi in consequentiam*." Two years later (1612), Coke C.J. held in *Rowles* v. *Mason*[34] that the principles of the common law even prevailed over custom. In his words,

> Fortescue and Littleton and all others are agreed that the law consists of three parts. First, Common Law. Secondly, Statute Law, which corrects, abridges, and explains the Common Law; The third, Custom which takes away the Common Law: But the Common Law corrects, allows, and disallows both Statute Law and Custom, for if there be repugnancy in a statute, or unreasonableness in Custom, the Common Law disallows and rejects it as appears by Dr. Bonham's Case, and 8 Coke 27, H. 6 Annuity.[35]

The final chapter came when Coke C.J. held that fundamental rights embedded in the common law were paramount even over statutes of Parliament.

Chief Justice Coke's notion of the paramountcy of fundamental rights over Acts of Parliament found its most conspicuous expression in the infamous *Dr. Bonham's Case*, 1610.[36] Dr. Bonham, who had received his doctorate of medicine from Cambridge University, failed a medical examination administered by the Royal College of Physicians. The Royal College fined Dr. Bonham and ordered him not to practise medicine until he had passed the examination. The College threatened imprisonment for any future disregard of its order. Dr. Bonham continued to practise and refused to submit to re-examination. He was therefore imprisoned.[37] Dr. Bonham, in turn, sued the College for false imprisonment.

The Common Bench ruled in Dr. Bonham's favour. Five reasons were given, but the fourth was the relevant one for our purpose. Chief Justice Coke, Warburton, J. and Daniel, J. held that the Royal College of Physicians could not be "judges, ministers, and parties" in the same case. This basic principle of the common law separated the functions of judge, government official and party: "judges to give sentence or judgment, ministers to make summons, and parties to have the moiety of the forfeiture."[38] This common law principle should control the operation of the statute in this case because the Royal College was both a judge and a party in the dispute with Dr. Bonham. In Coke C.J.'s words:

> And ... in many cases, the common law will controul Parliament, and sometimes judge them to be utterly void: for when an Act of Parliament is against common right and reason, or repugnant, or impossible to be performed, the common law will controul it, and adjudge such act to be void; and, therefore, ... *Thomas Tregor's Case* ... saith, some statutes are made *against law and right*, which those who made them perceiving, would not put them in execution...[39]

Scholars have disagreed whether Coke C.J.'s position in *Dr. Bonham's Case* was that statutes were to be rendered void upon their being found to be inconsistent and repugnant with common law principles, or whether judges should merely construe statutes so as to be consistent with common law principles.[40] One need not resolve this issue, however, in order to appreciate the place of the case in the Chief Justice's overall thinking. Coke C.J.'s judgment in *Dr. Bonham's Case* illustrated his belief that the judge's role was to look *backward* into the legal tradition with a view to determine consistent, long-standing principles. Secondly, Coke C.J.'s own uncovering of precedents in *Dr. Bonham's Case* reflected how he *applied* his own theoretical perspective and how his application could aptly be described as "an antiquarian revival of obsolescent law with a view to applying it to current needs ..."[41] Finally, *Dr. Bonham's Case* provides some insight into Coke C.J.'s conception of fundamental law — whether the sources of the latter be judge-made or legislature-made — as a long-standing, relatively unchanging foundation for the legal order.

Notwithstanding Coke C.J.'s assertion in *Calvin's Case*[42] that the subject owed his allegiance to the King of England because the law of nature, which was an immutable part of England's municipal law, so demanded, it appears doubtful whether Coke C.J. himself believed in fundamental law solely or even primarily because of the theological relationship between human and natural law.[43] He undoubtedly revered what he believed to be the innate excellence of the principles of the common law for, as he asserted in the *Institutes*, their stability and fundamentalness lay in the fact that they were "the perfection of reason."[44] Sir Edward also strongly feared that any change in the principles of the common law would rock the foundation of society.[45] Whatever the precise motive, Coke C.J.'s theory of fundamental rights discoverable through "universal tradition and long practice" provided a framework for justifying the existence of fundamental rights and freedoms. Chief Justice Coke's fundamental rights were found, not created.

Section 2. Some Applications of Coke's Method for Justifying Fundamental Rights

Two late nineteenth century American decisions and one recent Canadian decision reflect how Chief Justice Coke's "backward-looking" method can be used to determine the meaning and scope of one's constitutional rights. In *Murray's Lessee* v. *Hoboken Land & Improvement Co.*[46] an executive order authorised confiscation of the property of a tax collector without a hearing. In resolving whether the lack of a hearing was consistent with due process of law, the United States Supreme Court held that the court must initially examine if the procedure was consistent with the express provisions of the U.S. Constitution. If not in conflict, the court "must look to those settled usages and modes of proceeding existing in the common and statute law of England, before the emigration of our ancestors, and which are shown not to have been unsuited to their civil and political condition by having been acted on by them after the settlement of this country ..." In his judgment Curtis J. indicated that due process had generally meant right to a notice and right to a hearing.

A second example is *Plessy* v. *Ferguson*[47] where the United States Supreme Court sustained an 1890 Louisiana statute requiring "equal but separate" accommodations for white and black railway passengers. The issue was whether this statute was contrary to the equal protection clause of the Fourteenth Amendment. The court held that this depended upon the reasonableness of the Louisiana statute. And, "in determining the question of reasonableness it [the legislature] is at liberty to act with reference to the established usages, customs, and traditions of the people ..." Gauged by this standard the statute was considered to be reasonable and, therefore, constitutional.

Probably the best example in American or Canadian law of how Chief Justice Coke's "backward-looking" method could be used to protect one's rights and liberties is that of the British Columbia Court of Appeal in *Rex* v. *Hess (No. 2)*[48] where O'Halloran, J. A. denied to Parliament the authority to authorise the detention of a person who had been acquitted on appeal, pending a further appeal to the Supreme Court of Canada. At issue was a Criminal Code provision which had enacted that an acquitted person could be detained within the time allowed for appeal or, if the appeal were taken, until its determination unless the Attorney-General gave written notice that he did not intend to appeal or unless the trial judge granted bail. O'Halloran J. A. held that Parliament could not oust the traditional judicial function of reviewing detention. "Long-established principles are unconcernedly infringed to a degree that I find it judicially impossible to attach to the assembled words any rational meaning ...,"[49] he declared.

The first part of his judgment emphasised the importance in the English common law of the principle of judicial independence:

> It is part of the common law of England that Parliament shall respect the decisions of the Courts. If Parliament may assume the power to set aside a decision of the Court or interfere with the enforcement of its judgments because it does not like a decision or a judgment ... [i]t would break down the independence of the judiciary and destroy the judicial system Canada and its common law provinces have inherited.[50]

O'Halloran J. A.'s "reading of constitutional history" led him to conclude that the Canadian Parliament did not possess the constitutional power to enact the Criminal Code provision. Quoting Coke C.J. O'Halloran J. A. stated that the High Commission's practice of arresting and imprisoning a person without proper trial was contrary to Magna Carta. O'Halloran J. A. continued to quote from Coke C.J. as follows:

> Now it is provided by Magna Carta and other statutes duly passed and assented to by the Crown, *quod tam majores quam minores justitiam habeant et recipiant in curia Domini Regis (viz,* "that all persons shall have and receive justice in Court of their Lord the King"). By 43 Edw. III, E.3 no man shall be put to answer without presentment before the

justices or *by due process according to the ancient law of the land*; and anything done to the contrary shall be void.[51]

After he examined Sir Edward Coke's 1628 speech in Parliament concerning *habeas corpus* as well as the Habeas Corpus Act, 1679, the Petition of Right, 1628 and the Act of Settlement, 1700-1, O'Halloran J. A. concluded that the criminal provisions at issue were

> all contrary to the written constitution of the United Kingdom, as reflected in *Magna Carta* (1215), the *Petition of Right* (1628), the *Bill of Rights* (1689) and the *Act of Settlement* (1700-01). I conclude further that the opening paragraph of the preamble to the BNA Act, 1867, which provided for a Constitution similar in Principle to that of the United Kingdom, thereby adopted the same constitutional principles, and hence s.1025a is contrary to the Canadian Constitution, and beyond the competence of Parliament or any provincial Legislature to enact so long as our Constitution remains in its present form of a constitutional democracy.[52]

Section 3. Some Problems with Coke's Method of Justifying Fundamental Rights

At first sight Chief Justice Coke's method of justifying fundamental rights would seem quite appealing. It worked well for Sir Edward himself in his skirmishes with the Stuart monarchy. One might even argue that his "backward-looking" method has adequately served the United Kingdom and Canadian courts in their defence of fundamental rights over the centuries. A case such as *Plessy* v. *Ferguson*, however, raises an intuitive suspicion that a "backward-looking" method of justifying the existence of fundamental rights can be counter-productive. I shall now give several reasons why the suspicion is more than intuitive and I shall show why these reasons are borne out by reference to the constitutional experience of the United Kingdom in Coke C.J.'s own time.

One of the more telling problems with Chief Justice Coke's "backward-looking" method is that Coke C.J. wished that it would secure a static, confining society. This, indeed, was the chief advantage which Sir Edward perceived in his approach: it ensured the ever-lasting stability of society — or, so he believed. In his discussion of one particular statute, for example, Sir Edward remarked that

> it is not almost credible to foresee when any Maxim or Fundamental Law of this Realm is altered (or elsewhere hath been observed) what dangerous inconveniences do follow, which most expressly appeareth by this most unjust and strange Act of 11 H.7...[53]

23

As we have seen in our discussion of *Rowles* v. *Mason*[54] and *Dr. Bonham's Case*,[55] judges were obligated to construe custom and legislative enactments in the light of the principles of the common law. The latter, he explained in the *Institutes*, were "the main pillars and supporters of the fabrick of the Commonwealth."[56] Common law principles had been "refined and approved by all the wisest men in former succession of ages, and proved and approved by continual experience."[57] It naturally followed, therefore, that

> ... the wisdome of the judges and sages of the law have always suppressed new and subtile inventions in derogation of the common law. And therefore the judges say in one booke, We will not change the law which always hath been used. And another saith, It is better that it be turned to a default, than the law should be changed, or any innovation made.[58]

Only with "great hazard and danger" could the fundamental principles be altered.

In addition to the static society which Coke C.J. intended his approach to secure, what Coke C.J.'s method really tells us is that, conceptually speaking, there will be very few fundamental freedoms or rights coincident with it, notwithstanding O'Halloran J. A.'s optimistic interpretation of English constitutional history. For, *if* there is a fundamental freedom or right it must have already existed in the law. In addition, it must have consistently persisted as a principle over a very long period of time.

This point has several negative consequences for any theory of fundamental rights. In the first place, if the legal tradition is silent on an issue, there will be no fundamental right. Secondly, there will be very few fundamental freedoms in any society which has evolved fairly rapidly. Thirdly, those fundamental freedoms which do exist have little possibility of growing in scope or number in the future for it is in the past, not the future, that we must look for their existence and weight. To freeze the meaning of a fundamental right to some "fixed stage of time or thought," Frankfurter once remarked, "is to suggest that the most important aspect of constitutional adjudication is a function for inanimate machines and not for judges ... Even cybernetics has not yet made that haughty claim."[59]

Fourthly, the uncovering of long standing principles can be a highly subjective pursuit. Despite O'Halloran J.A.'s pro-libertarian application of Chief Justice Coke's method of justifying the existence of fundamental rights in *Re Hess (No. 2)*, he found no difficulty in prohibiting the admission of William John Gordon Martin to the British Columbia Bar because Martin had adhered to

Marxist communism.[60] Martin had not been found guilty of any overt subversive conduct. Indeed, he had personally rejected subversive activity and the use of force against governmental institutions. The scope of freedom of conscience did not extend to Martin, in O'Halloran J. A.'s judgment.

Similarly, in *Miranda* v. *Arizona*,[61] Chief Justice Warren held for the U.S. Supreme Court that the prosecution could not use statements obtained from the accused through custodial interrogation unless it established effective procedural safeguards in order to secure the Fifth Amendment's privilege against self-incrimination. The accused, for example, had to be warned of the right to remain silent prior to any questioning. The Court's holding, the Chief Justice insisted, was "not an innovation in our jurisprudence, but is [was] an application of principles long recognised and applied in other settings." Mr. Justice Harlan, dissenting, documented how the Fifth Amendment's privilege against self-incrimination did not have any historical relation to extra-legal confessions. According to Mr. Justice Harlan, the two concepts differed by one hundred years in origin and derived through separate lines of precedents.

Two further consequences flow from the fact that Chief Justice Coke's approach requires that a right must have already existed in law and that it must have consistently persisted over a long period of time. First, Coke C.J.'s method of analysis could be consistently used to justify tyranny or slavery if the legal tradition lacked principles prohibiting either tyranny or slavery. Coke C.J.'s method is little help in a society lacking in libertarian traditions. Nor does it account for revolutionary leaders who are determined to institutionalise respect for fundamental rights in countries with autocratic traditions. Finally, Coke C.J.'s method provides little guidance in a complex legal system where, as in Canada, there are two very different legal traditions and where the country possesses multi-ethnic cultures. How would one resolve the situation where one legal tradition possessed a particular fundamental right but a second did not or where the scope of one right was narrower in one tradition than in the other?

A closer examination of Chief Justice Coke's contribution to English law shows how his "backward-looking" method of justifying the existence of fundamental rights could easily have led him to anti-libertarian positions. The English legal tradition was silent on many "civil liberties" issues in Coke C.J.'s day. If anything, that tradition had been one of strong authoritarianism for at least one hundred and twenty-five years. Freedom of dissent — religious or otherwise — was entirely alien to that tradition. Furthermore,

English society had rapidly evolved during the sixteenth century. The law suddenly had to cope with the new technology of the printing press.[62] And the skill of writing had become more common.[63] In addition, Coke C.J.'s unhistorical method combined with his ruthless ambition so as to display a highly subjective interpretation of English constitutional history. These factors worked to Coke C.J.'s advantage when, as Attorney-General and Chief State Prosecutor, he had exhibited an "unparalleled" "arrogance and brutality" towards the subject's liberties.[64]

These factors also provided the background for Sir Edward's own manipulation of legal history in his creation of the common law crime of seditious libel. His crime served as a wide-ranging instrument for a very repressive state. As Attorney-General, Sir Edward had initiated several prosecutions in the Star Chamber for criminal libel.[65] In those prosecutions, in his reporting of the *Case of de Libellis Famosis*,[66] in his participation and reporting of *John Lamb's Case*[67] and in his *Third Institute*,[68] Sir Edward argued and then definitively declared that seditious libel had *always* existed as a common law offence. It is important to note, however, that Sir Edward provided no authority for the common-law background to the crime until 1628 when, in his *Third Institute*, he resurrected two 1336[69] and 1344[70] decisions as well as *De Libellis Famosis* and *John Lamb's Case*. Neither of the "older two notable records"[71] provided any foundation for the crime. With respect to the first, the case of *Adam de Ravensworth*, Sir Edward mis-stated the facts and failed to clarify that there had been no specific offence named in the indictment. In addition, Irving Brant has pointed out that prevailing practices would have dictated that Adam de Ravensworth be charged with contempt of the King or even treason, but not seditious libel.[72] Professor Brant has successfully argued that the second "notable record", the case of *John de Northampton*, was equally inapplicable as an authority for the existence of a crime of seditious libel. Indeed, as Sir James Stephen wrote in his *History of the Criminal Law*,[73] the *Ravensworth* and *Northampton* decisions were "notable" in no way other than that Sir Edward alone mentioned them.

Sir James uncovered two earlier references to the seditious offences. Bracton mentioned them, according to Stephen, only "in the most cursory manner."[74] Secondly, the *Statute of Westminster the First*[75] forbade the citation or publication of "any false news or tales whereby discord or occasion of discord or slander may grow between the King and his people or the great men of the Realm." Sir James did not enlighten us, however, as to whether the courts had ever used this statutory provision. He did insist that under Henry VII, Edward VI, Mary and Elizabeth, any criticism of the government was brought within the crime of treason.[76] Thus, sedition did not appear as a separate common law crime until 1601 when Sir Edward Coke himself reported that seditious libel was a common law crime.

Sir Edward Coke's own role in the creation of the crime of seditious libel in English law as well as the non-libertarian legal tradition in Great Britain prior to Sir Edward's day demonstrate the problems which flow from Coke C.J.'s method of justifying the existence of fundamental rights. Notwithstanding his belated self-professed reliance upon the precedents of centuries past, Sir Edward exemplified how a prestigious, creative lawyer can manipulate legal history to support laws which are restrictive of fundamental rights. Furthermore, the legal tradition which Sir Edward inherited shows how a "backward-looking" method of justifying the existence of fundamental rights can lead to anti-libertarian positions if fundamental rights have not consistently persisted in the legal tradition over a long period of time. The Canadian constitutional experience verifies the contemporary seriousness of these problems.

Section 4. Would Chief Justice Coke's Method Lead to the Existence of Fundamental Rights in Canada?

One might respond to the above line of argument by suggesting that the problems flowing from Chief Justice Coke's method of establishing fundamental rights are conceptual problems, not realistic ones. In order to contend with this suggestion, therefore, I shall look to the Canadian constitutional experience with respect to the rights of political participation and religious conscience. The rights which I have chosen are the rights which one finds most commonly described by the Canadian judges, lawyers and legislators as fundamental rights. They are also rights which place Coke C.J.'s method of analysis in its most favourable light. If any rights were to be found embedded in Canadian legal history, one should think that these rights would be.

And yet, such is not in fact the case for the very reasons suggested in section 3 above.

a. *The right of political participation*

The right to participate in elections, for example, has been established only relatively recently, and by statute rather than by common law principles. If we amended Coke C.J.'s resource material for a legal tradition to include statutory and constitutional documents, we still would not be able to assert that freedom of political participation was established before the early twentieth century. The Bill of Rights, 1689, did contemplate that the Commons were elected, "that election of members of Parliament ought to be free," and that the House of Commons was "a full and free representative of this nation."[77] The subject did have the right "to petition the King, and all commitments and prosecutions for such petitioning are illegal." But only male subjects who owned a certain amount of land could vote. Furthermore, many Members of Parliament "represented" "rotten boroughs"; they were, in effect, appointed rather than elected.[78] The Great Reform Bill of 1832 enacted that non-landed property should be the basis of representation. The traditional connection between property and political power, however, remained. Between 1852-1860 four English statutes widened the property qualification and extended the franchise to educated persons.[79] Women were not given the franchise until shortly after World War I.[80] The conclusion seems warranted that even if there has been a right to political participation embedded in Canadian legal history, the right has been shared unequally.

If one looks backward into Canadian legal history, the most important document which is revealed is the *British North America Act, 1867.* Yet one can search in vain for some evidence of a right of political participation in that instrument. Section 17 sets out that "there shall be One Parliament for Canada, consisting of the Queen, an Upper House styled the Senate, and the House of Commons." Section 91 (1) provides that the House dies as a properly constituted authority after five years from the day of the return of the election writs unless "in time of real or apprehended war, invasion or insurrection" one-third of the members do not oppose an act of Parliament prolonging the House's life. The British North America Acts do not require that members of the House of Commons should be elected by universal suffrage. Furthermore, the persons in two of the three institutions composing Parliament (the monarchy and the Senate) receive their positions by heredity and appointment. The occupants of the two remaining institutions of government (the courts and the bureaucracy) are also appointed.

If the British North America Acts do not help us in establishing a right of political participation, can one find some common law principle embedded in our legal tradition which one might use to derive a right of political participation? There has been such a principle, the notion of legislative supremacy. The idea that the legislature is supreme has underlain the construction of statutes as well as the elaboration of the common law. Chapter II will show, however, why legislative supremacy does not, of necessity, support the existence of fundamental rights in general.

Briefly, fundamental rights can hardly be said to exist in the sense of being "at the root of the matter", "essential", "underlying", "formative" or "irreducible" if the legislature may create all rights, determine their meaning and scope, and legitimately abrogate them. The notion of legislative supremacy runs counter to the existence of a right of political participation, in particular, in that the prime source of political participation under the legislative supremacy perspective is the electoral process. But the electoral process is just that — a *process* which permits the citizen to approve or disapprove the performance of the legislature. Legislative supremacy does not contemplate that the citizen directly participate in the decisions which intimately affect his/her life. This point is verified by the fact that any attempt to by-pass the House of Commons, the monarchy or, possibly, the Senate in the legislative process, by a direct reference to the citizen's opinions in a plebescite, would likely be held unconstitutional in Canada.[81] Neither the British North America Act, 1867, nor the principle of legislative supremacy provide support for the existence of a right, let alone a fundamental right, of political participation in Canada. Even if a case could be made that the right of political participation inheres to our past, one could hardly suggest that English or Canadian legal history has compelled that the right be shared equally.

b. *The right of religious conscience*

As with the right of political participation, it appears difficult to justify the existence of a fundamental right of religious conscience in Canada if one follows the "backward-looking" method of analysis which Coke advocated and applied. Our legal history has not been silent with respect to the issue of the existence and scope of a right of religious conscience in Canada. United Kingdom statutes, the constitutional experience in the United Kingdom, a cluster of British and Canadian Government undertakings following the cession of Quebec to the British, Canadian statutes and judicial decisions provide ample resource material for a "backward-looking" inquiry. It is a moot issue, however, whether that constitutional history supports the existence of a fundamental right of religious conscience.

If the "backward-looking" method permits one to incorporate

English constitutional history into our inquiry, then the scales are weighed heavily against the existence of a fundamental right of religious conscience from the start. The Tudor monarchy used the ecclesiastical institutions and, in particular, the High Commission to persecute dissenters.[82] The Act of Supremacy, 1559, gave wide jurisdiction to the monarch, her heirs and successors to delegate authority to any person to regulate "all manner of jurisdictions, privileges and pre-eminences, in any wise touching or concerning any spiritual or ecclesiastical jurisdiction."[83] The Act of Supremacy went on to provide authority to the monarch's delegate

> and to visit, reform, redress, order, correct and amend all such errors, heresies, schisms, abuses, offences, contempts and enormities whatsoever, which by any manner of spiritual or ecclesiastical power, authority or jurisdiction, can or may lawfully be reformed, ordered, redressed, corrected, restrained or amended, to the pleasure of Almighty God, the increase of virtue, and the conservation of the peace and unity of this realm...

Whereas the Crown's authority to burden religious conscience had until 1559 been restricted by various principles surrounding the royal prerogative, this Act of Parliament constitutionalised and augmented the Crown's authority to invade religious conscience. The Act of Supremacy served as the constitutional basis for violent religious repression during the sixteenth and seventeenth centuries. The fact that the United Kingdom has had an official state religion since that time provides added weight for the non-existence of a fundamental right of religious conscience in Canada.[84]

On the other hand, this very persecution induced many settlers to leave the British Isles for North America in the hopes of finding freedom of religious conscience. We are required, as a consequence, to question whether early legal history in the Canadas provides institutional support for the existence of a fundamental right of religious conscience in contrast to the British inheritance.

The Articles of Capitulation of Quebec in 1760, the Articles of Capitulation of Montreal in 1760 and the Treaty of Paris, 1763 furnish weighty evidence of the existence of a preferred position for, if not a fundamental right of, the religious conscience of adherents to the major minority religion at the time (Roman Catholicism). These instruments are particularly compelling in that, according to constitutional law at the time of the cession of the French colonies in North America, all law-making authority in a conquered or ceded colony was subject to any reservations which might be undertaken in the Articles of Capitulation or a peace treaty. The general constitutional principle laid down that if the United Kingdom had acquired a colony by conquest or cession

30

and if the colony at the time of conquest had laws of its own, the laws of the conquered or ceded colony remained in force unless and until the Crown altered those laws.[85] This proposition, however, was *subject to two important qualifications* established by Lord Mansfield in *Campbell* v. *Hall* [86] In the first place, the articles of capitulation upon which the colony was surrendered and the treaty by which the colony was ceded were *sacred* and *inviolable*. Secondly, the Crown could not make any change in the laws of the conquered country "contrary to fundamental principles" (by which Lord Mansfield presumably meant the equitable principles of natural justice). Because the British acquired Quebec either by conquest or cession, rather than by settlement,[87] the terms of the Articles of Capitulation of Quebec and of Montreal in 1760 and the Treaty of Paris, 1763 are especially significant.

Most noteworthy are a cluster of obligations undertaken by the United Kingdom government to respect and protect the Roman Catholic religion. Article 6 of the Articles of the Capitulation of Quebec, 1759 guaranteed, for example, that

> the exercise of the Catholic, Apostolic, and Roman religion shall be preserved; that safe-guards shall be given to the houses of the clergy, to the monasteries and the convents, especially to His Lordship the Bishop of Quebec, who, full of zeal for religion and of love for the people of his diocese, desires to remain constantly in it, to exercise freely, and with the decency which has standing and the sacred mysteries of the Catholic, Apostolic, and Roman religion requires, his episcopal authority in the town of Quebec, whenever he shall think fit, until the possession of Canada has been decided by a treaty between his most Christian Majesty and his Britannic Majesty.
>
> Libre exercice de la religion romaine, sauves gardes accordées à toutes personnes religieuses ainsi qu'à Mr. l'évêque qui pourra venir exercer librement et avec decence les fonctions de son état lorsqu'il le jugera àpropos, jusqu'à ce que la possession de Canada ayt été decidée entre sa Majesté B. et S.M.T.C.[88]

According to William Houston, the draft Articles sent to Lieutenant de Ramzay from the Marquis de Vaudreuil had the following comment noted beside Article 6:

> Prouver que c'est "interest de S.M.B. dans le cas ou le Canada luy resteroit", et qu'en Europe touttes les conquettes que font les divers souverains, il ne changent point l'exercise de religion qu'autant que ces conquettes leur restent.[89]

The Article 6 pledge was supported by the general assurance in Article 2 that "the privileges" of the inhabitants were to be preserved. Article 2 safeguarded the effective exercise of Roman Catholicism in practice by providing that "the present capitulation shall be executed according to its form and tenor, without being subject to non-execution under pretext of reprisals or of the non-execution of some previous capitulation."

The Articles of Capitulation of Montreal, 1760 acknowledged British obligations toward the minority religion in even clearer language.[90] Article 27 expressly guaranteed the freedom of the Francophones to establish their Roman Catholic religion:

> The free exercise of the Catholic, Apostolic, and Roman religion shall subsist entire, in such manner that all classes and peoples of the towns and rural districts, places, and distant posts may continue to assemble in the churches, and to frequent the sacraments as heretofore, without being molested in any manner, directly or indirectly. These people shall be obliged by the English government to pay to the priests, who shall have the oversight of them, the tithes and all the dues they were accustomed to pay under the government of his Most Christian Majesty.
>
> Accordé our le libre exercise de leur Religion. L'obligation de payer la dixme aux prêtres dependra de la volonté du Roy.

Articles 28 to 35 went on to elaborate precise protections for the Roman Catholic clergy. Article 28, in particular, provided that "the Chapter, priests, cureo and missionaries shall continue with entire freedom of their parochial services and functions in the parishes of the towns and rural districts." Finally, one should read the Articles protecting Roman Catholicism in the light of Article 50 which provided generally that "the present capitulation shall be *inviolably executed* in *all* its articles, on *both* sides, and in good faith, notwithstanding any infraction and any other pretext with regard to preceding capitulations, and without resorting to reprisals."[91]

By the Treaty of Paris, 1763, the French government ceded her possessions over to the Crown of Great Britain "in the most ample manner and form, without restriction and without any liberty to depart from the said cession and guaranty, under any pretense, or to disturb Great Britain in the possessions..."[92] On the other hand, the Treaty did reflect a respect toward the religious freedom of Quebecois. Article 4 provided,

> but the King of Great Britain on his side agrees to grant the liberty of the Catholic religion to the inhabitants of Canada: he will consequently give the most precise and most effectual orders that his new Roman Catholic subjects may profess the worship of their religion, according to the rites of the Romish Church, *as far as the laws of Great Britain permit.*[93]

The latter clause differed from the undertaking in the Articles of Capitulation of Quebec and Montreal in that, although the Roman

Catholic religion occupied a protected position in the treaty, it was not acknowledged to be beyond legislative restriction. The phrase "as far as the laws of Great Britain permit" is not found in the Articles of Capitulation.

On the other hand, the institutional support for the protection of Roman Catholicism was not consistently embedded in the early constitutional experience of Quebec. As with other British colonies,[94] the authority of British administrators was set out in Royal Proclamations, Commissions and often secret Instructions. In the case of Quebec, the Treaty of Paris, 1763, was followed up with the Royal Proclamation, 1763,[95] the Commission of Governor Murray, 1763,[96] and the Instructions to Governor Murray dated 7 December 1763.[97] The latter three instruments gave wide authority for Governor Murray to introduce English laws into the colony and to encourage assimilation of the Francophone or, as the British described it, the Canadian community. The Proclamation, in particular, granted authority to the Governor with the consent of a Council and Assembly "to make, constitute, and ordain laws, statutes, and ordinances for the public peace, welfare, and good government of our said colonies, ... as near as may be, agreeable to the laws of England." The Instructions to Murray called for the demise of "the Canadian religion". According to Article 32,

> you are not to admit of any Ecclesiastical Jurisdiction of the See of Rome, or any other foreign Ecclesiastical Jurisdiction whatsoever in the Province under your Government.

The Instructions continued:

> 33. And to the end that the Church of England may be established both in Principles and Practice, and that the said Inhabitants may by Degrees be induced to embrace the Protestant Religion, and their Children be brought up in the Principles of it; We do hereby declare it to be our Intention... all possible Encouragement shall be given to the erecting Protestant Schools..., by settling, appointing and alloting proper Quanties of Land for that Purpose; and also for a Glebe and Maintenance for a Protestant Minister and Protestant School Masters; and you are to consider and report to Us ... by what other Means the Protestant Religion may be promoted, established and encouraged in Our Province under your Government.

Article 38 added that no person could teach without a licence from the Lord Bishop of London. It is difficult not to conclude that the intent of the 1763 Proclamation, Commission and Instructions was to stimulate the Canadian community to adopt the religious opinions and practices of the British.

On the other hand, Chief Justice Coke's "backward-looking" method of establishing fundamental rights would not permit one to stop with the Royal Proclamation, Commission and Instructions of 1763. We have already seen that the constitutional law of the period required that the terms of the Articles of Capitulation, 1760, and the Treaty of Paris, 1763, be "sacred and inviolable". The Royal Proclamation, Commission and Instructions of 1763 were thereby invalid to the extent that they contradicted the earlier undertakings by the British to protect freedom of religious conscience. In addition, Chief Justice Coke's "backward-looking" method of analysis requires that one read the 1763 Proclamation, Commission and Instructions in the light of other institutional history both before and after 1763. Although the 1763 instruments do provide evidence of the non-existence of any fundamental right of religious conscience even by Quebeçois, it is possible that the instruments were an aberration of an otherwise consistent recognition of the right.

It has already been shown that the Articles of Capitulation of Quebec and of Montreal in 1760 guaranteed the establishment and free exercise of Roman Catholicism without restriction. The Treaty of Paris, 1763, safeguarded its establishment and free exercise "as far as the laws of Great Britain permit." In addition, it appears that events subsequent to the Royal Proclamation, Commission and Instructions of 1763 rendered the latter invalid.

According to Sir J. G. Bourinot[98] and W. P. M. Kennedy,[99] there remained great uncertainty between 1763 and 1774 as to the nature and extent of British obligations toward the Canadians. This doubt presumably extended to the nature and scope of freedom of religious conscience. Furthermore, notwithstanding his Instructions, it is recorded that Governor Murray did not pursue the assimilationist policy expected of him.[100] Although the Commission and Instructions to him directed that he should summon a legislative assembly, Governor Murray did not do so for fear of placing political power in the hands of the English minority.[101] By late 1764 official Crown policy emanating from London also deviated from the 1763 instruments.[102] In 1766, for example, the Crown's legal officers expressly renounced the attempt by the Royal Proclamation of 1763 to abolish "all the usages and customs of Canada with the rough hand of a conqueror."[103]

Finally, in 1774, the Quebec Act expressly "revoked, annulled and made void" the Royal Proclamation of 1763, all Commissions and all Instructions to Governors.[104] The preamble to Section 4 acknowledged that the Royal Proclamation of 1763 as well as Commissions and Instructions to Governors Murray and Carleton "have been found upon experience to be inapplicable to the state and circumstances of the said Province." The preamble went on to explain why the 1763 instruments had been found inapplicable: namely, that at the time of the conquest, 65,000 inhabitants had professed Roman Catholicism. Also, these inhabitants had "for a long series of years" enjoyed "an established form of constitution and system of laws." Section 5 of the Quebec Act tried to recognise the religious fact by providing that persons

> professing the religion of the Church of Rome of and in the said Province of Quebec, may have, hold, and enjoy, the free Exercise of the Religion of the Church of Rome, *subject to the King's Supremacy, declared and established by an Act made in the first year of the Reign of Queen Elizabeth* [*i.e., the Act of Supremacy*].[105]

Section 15 followed this by providing that "no Ordinance touching religion... shall be of any force or effect until the same shall have received His Majesty's approbation."

Institutional support for the existence of a freedom of religious conscience for Roman Catholics can also be found in Section 2 of the Constitutional Act, 1791.[106] Section 2 required a "laying" procedure as a condition precedent for any statute which burdened religious practices. More particularly, "whenever any act or acts shall... in any manner relate to or affect the enjoyment or exercise of any religious form or mode of worship" the sovereign could assent to it only if the bill had previously been laid before the legislature and only if no single member had requested the withholding of assent. Section 42 of the *Act of Union, 1840* (Imp.) contained a similar provision.[107] Although the *Constitutional Act* and *Act of Union* anticipated legislative restriction upon religious freedom, the uncommon "laying" procedure did reflect a preferred constitutional position for religious freedom over other values. The statutes, in addition, widened the scope of religious freedom by apparently protecting all religions, not just Roman Catholicism.

Respect for religious freedom is echoed in several other constitutional and quasi-constitutional documents in Canadian legal history. In 1852 a statute of the legislature of Canada (which comprised present-day Ontario and Quebec) provided that

> whereas the recognition of legal equality among all Religious Denominations is an admitted principle of Colonial Legislation; And whereas... it is desirable that the same should receive the sanction of direct Legislative Authority, recognizing and declaring the same *as a fundamental principle* of our civil polity: Be it therefore declared... That the free exercise and enjoyment of Religious Profession and Worship, without

discrimination or preference, *so as the same be not made an excuse for acts of licentiousness...* is by the constitution and laws of this Province allowed to all Her Majesty's subjects within the same.[108]

Section 93 of the British North America Act, 1867, seems to imply the existence of at least a restricted right to establish a religion by providing that the legislatures shall not "prejudicially affect any Right or Privilege with respect to Denominational Schools which any Class of Persons have by Law in the Province at the Union."[109] Freedom of religion is, of course, recognised as a "fundamental freedom" and "human right" in the Canadian Bill of Rights, 1960.[110]

These constitutional and statutory undertakings by the British and Canadian governments seem to indicate that if one proceeds backward in an effort to inquire whether a fundamental right of religious conscience exists in Canada, religion occupies a preferred position. Several factors point to the conclusion, however, that the right is not a fundamental right and, secondly, that the right is very narrow in meaning and scope.

One is led to this assessment, in the first place, because the constitutional and statutory instruments most favourable to the existence of a freedom of religious conscience expressly contemplated that either the legislature or the executive arm of government may deny the right. The only exceptions to this point were the Articles of Capitulation of Montreal and of Quebec in 1760. Section 4 of the Treaty of Paris, 1763, guaranteed respect for Roman Catholic practices only "as far as the laws of Great Britain permit." Section 5 of the Quebec Act expressly provided that the free exercise of the Roman Catholic religion was "subject to the King's Supremacy, declared and established by [the Act of Supremacy, 1559]." But it has already been noted how the Act of Supremacy was used to sanction religious repression in Great Britain under the Tudors and Stuarts. Notwithstanding the uncommon "laying" procedure, the Constitutional Act, 1791, and the Act of Union, 1840, anticipated that legislatures could and would deny "the enjoyment or exercise of any religious freedom or mode of worship" after the "laying" requirement had been met. Similarly, because Sections 91 and 92 of the British North America Act, 1867 appear to exhaust all subject-matter, the Act does not contemplate any conceivable limit of the extent to which the right of religious conscience may be denied. Finally, the Canadian Bill of Rights itself expressly provides that the Canadian Parliament may deny the "fundamental" freedom of religion simply by introducing a statute with a "notwithstanding the Canadian Bill of Rights" clause. One can hardly suggest that this right of religious freedom is fundamental in the true sense of the word.

Just as important, there is little in our legal history to indicate that the right to religious conscience is shared equally amongst all persons. The thrust of the Articles of Capitulation, the Treaty of Paris, the Quebec Act, and the 1852 statute of the Canadian legislature is to protect only the Roman Catholic religion. Section 93 of the British North America Act merely assures the rights and privileges of denominational schools which existed in 1867. Precisely by assuring preferred protection of the Roman Catholic church the state treated religions unequally.

Finally, it is unclear from the constitutional and statutory instruments whether the protected right is really religious conscience. The documents appear to support the freedom to establish the Roman Catholic church. The record may, on its own terms, consistently protect the establishment of the Roman Catholic church on the one hand but not preclude the state from burdening or punishing a person because of his religious beliefs, thoughts or feelings on the other. The latter element relates to religious conscience whereas the former does not necessarily do so.

Chief Justice Coke relied upon judicial pronouncements as much as he did on statutory and constitutional documents as evidence of fundamental rights. As a consequence, a comprehensive examination of the right of religious conscience in Canada pursuant to Chief Justice Coke's method of analysis would require that one take account of judicial precedent. Three Canadian Supreme Court decisions have declared, in particular, that a fundamental freedom of religion has existed in Canada.

Rand J. recognized the preferred position of religious freedom, for example, in *Saumur* v. *City of Quebec*.[111] In *Saumur*, a by-law of the City of Quebec had provided that no book, pamphlet, booklet, circular or tract could be distributed without the written permission of the chief of police. According to the practice, a licence to distribute would be refused if the chief officer of the police department, acting with or without the city solicitor, believed that there was something objectionable in the tract and if the distributor refused to remove the objectionable part. Saumur argued that the by-law was beyond the legislative authority of the province.

After citing several of the above eighteenth and nineteenth century statutes Rand J. concluded that

> from 1760, therefore, to the present moment religious freedom has, in our legal system, been recognised *as a principle of fundamental character*; and although we have nothing in the nature of an established

church, that the untrammelled affirmations of religious belief and its propagation, personal or institutional, remain as of the greatest constitutional significance throughout the Dominion is unquestionable.[112]

The esteemed place of religious freedom in Canadian statutes and constitutional principles led Rand J. to conclude that

> strictly speaking, civil rights arise from positive law; but freedom of speech, religion and the inviolability of the person, are original freedoms which are at once the necessary attributes and modes of self-expression of human beings and the primary conditions of their community life within a legal order. It is in the circumstances of these liberties by the creation of civil rights in persons who may be injured by their exercise, and by the sanctions of public law, that the positive law operates. What we realize is the residue inside that periphery. Their significant relation to our law lies in this, that under its principles to which there are only minor exceptions, there is no prior or antecedent restraint placed upon them: the penalties, civil or criminal, attach to results which their exercise may bring about, and apply as consequential incidents. So we have the civil rights against defamation, assault, false imprisonment and the like, and the punishments of the criminal law; but the sanctions of the latter lie within the exclusive jurisdiction of the Dominion. Civil rights of the same nature arise also as protection against infringements of these freedoms.[113]

From this Rand J. reasoned that legislation "in relation" to religion was not a local or private matter: its dimensions were nationwide. Since the authority delegated to the chief officer was "in broad and general terms," the by-law could relate "indifferently to a variety of incompatible matters." The by-law did not "with sufficient precision" define the purpose of a refusal of distribution. Thus, the by-law related to a matter beyond the jurisdiction of the provinces.

Even though Rand J. accepted freedom of religion as an issue in *Saumur*, a close scrutiny of the above dictum as well as his judgment in *Henry Birks & Sons (Montreal) Ltd. v. Montreal and A-G of Quebec*[114] leads one to conclude that the freedom might not be fundamental. On the one hand, Rand J.'s "original freedom" perspective in the first sentence of his *Saumur* dictum quoted above seriously contemplates the existence of fundamental rights as opposed to the existence of mere rights. They are *original freedoms* "which are at once *the necessary attributes* and modes of self-expression of human beings and the *primary conditions* of their community life within a legal order." On the other hand, when one considers Rand J.'s statement in its context, one is led to see it simply as a re-statement of John Stuart Mill's principle of "self-regarding conduct". Accordingly, the state possesses authority to posit civil or criminal penalties if one's exercise of the "original freedoms" injures a second person. Rand J.'s pronouncement is subject to the same criticisms and weaknesses which we shall later level against Mill, not least of which is the fact it is difficult to conceive of any important conduct or thought which does not injure someone in some fashion. As a consequence, the state's "circumscription" — to use Rand J.'s term — of the "original freedoms" leaves very little room in which one can live freely.

Indeed, Rand J.'s dictum permits us to go one step further: there is no room in which one may operate freely without some sanction by the state. There is little doubt but that, for Rand J. "civil rights arise from positive law." The state creates civil rights so as to prevent the exercise of one's right from harming another. The state takes away civil rights for the same reason. This is why, according to Rand J. we possess "the civil rights" against defamation, assault, false imprisonment and criminal law penalties. Thus, the state not only potentially restricts the rights of the individual but it also creates his rights through positive law.

The conclusion that Rand J. left no room in which one could think or behave freely without the sanction of the state is consistent with Section 4 of the Treaty of Paris, 1763, Sections 5 and 15 of the Quebec Act, 1774, Section 2 of the Constitutional Act, 1791, Section 42 of the Union Act, 1840, the 1852 enactment of the Canadian Legislature, Section 92(13) of the British North America Act, 1867, and the Canadian Bill of Rights. The conclusion also flows from Rand J.'s own constitutional analysis in *Saumur.* We have seen how under each of the above legislative and constitutional documents the Crown or a legislature could deny the existence of religious freedom. And in *Saumur,* Rand J. assumed in his examination of the Quebec by-law that if one level of government did not have authority to restrict religious freedom, the other did have such jurisdiction. That is, Rand J. based his decision on a "division of powers" or federalism analysis rather than on the existence of individual or group rights per se.[115] Because legislation "in relation" to religion was not a local or private matter but, instead, involved something to which the "body politic of the Dominion" was more sensitive, the legislation fell under Section 91 rather than Section 92 of the B.N.A. Act. Quoting from Duff, C.J.C. in *Reference re Alberta Legislation,*[116] Rand J. confirmed that the British North America Act itself granted to Parliament what was not given to provincial legislatures.

Rand J. also followed a "division of powers" analysis in his 1955 *Henry Birks* judgment.[117] In that case a provincial statute had provided that "the municipal council may order, by by-law, that these stores be closed all day on New Year's Day, on the festival of the Epiphany, on Ascension Day, All Saints Day, Conception Day and on Christmas Day." Rand J. perceived the issue in terms of whether this enactment was a valid exercise of provincial jurisdiction. For many centuries, according to Rand J., English legislation had either forbade or compelled religious professions or celebrations on certain days. The law reserving Sunday as a day of rest went back to the reign of Edward III. After documenting extensive examples of similar legislation over the centuries, Rand J. held that these restrictions upon religious freedom were part of the English public law and were, therefore, brought within the federal criminal law power of the Canadian constitution. And yet, as Professor Noel Lyon and Mr. Ronald Atkey point out, [118] the framers of the British North America Act never intended to grant exclusive jurisdiction over fundamental rights to either the federal or provincial legislatures. The framers had not contemplated that the heads of legislative power would be used to protect fundamental rights. Even Section 92(13) ("civil rights in the province") was intended to refer to the private rights of property, contract and torts— not to "fundamental rights". Early constitutional documents preserving the civil rights of the colonies had used the term "property and civil rights" since the mid-eighteenth century. The mid-eighteenth century, however, was a period when the notion of fundamental rights was quite alien to the political-legal culture of the colonies of Upper and Lower Canada. Rand J.'s analysis appears to have been premised upon a constitutional framework which did not even contemplate the very existence of fundamental rights.

This *Birks* decision reflects a second limitation with respect to the application of Coke C.J.'s method for establishing the existence of a fundamental freedom of religion. Where the legislature allegedly infringes religious freedom, such an interference is valid if the court finds evidence of similar types of legislative interference in the past. If there is such evidence, then, for the purposes of the facts before the court, no freedom is threatened. We have noted how Rand J. was impressed by the fact that legislation compelling religious celebrations or forbidding the observance of certain religious practices on certain days or creating legal disabilities for religiously motivated conduct had had a continuous history since the reign of Edward III (1327-1377). For example, statutes dated 1354[119] and 1464,[120] which prohibited the sale of wool and shoes on Sunday, were repealed only in 1863. Enactments proscribing the holding of fairs and markets[121] and the holding of meetings "for any sports or pastimes whatsoever"[122] on Sundays had existed on the statute books since 1448 and 1625 respectively. The 1448 statute had, in addition, proscribed the holding of fairs and markets "upon high feast days." The requirement of the celebration of the principal Christian feast days still existed in Rand J.'s day. As a consequence of these examples, Rand held that the Montreal by-law was "in the same category" as the long-standing Sunday observance legislation.

Robertson and Rosetanni v. *The Queen*[123] also reflects this point. In that case the Supreme Court of Canada had to decide whether to uphold a conviction against the appellants for operating a bowling alley on a Sunday contrary to *The Lord's Day Act*, R.S.C. 1952, c. 171. Robertson and Rosetanni argued that this statute conflicted with the right to freedom of religion as protected in Section 1(c) of the Canadian Bill of Rights.[124] Ritchie J. noted that Section 1(c) was concerned with such "rights and freedoms" as they existed in Canada immediately prior to the enactment of the statute. After quoting Rand J.'s assertion in *Saumur* that religious freedom was of a "fundamental character" and "of greatest constitutional significance" in Canada, Ritchie J. went on to emphasise that fundamental freedoms were "freedoms of men living together in an organised society subject to a rational, developed and civilised system of law which imposed limitations on the absolute liberty of the individual." Various statutes had been enacted "since long before Confederation" "for the express purpose of safeguarding the sanctity of the Sabbath [i.e., Sunday]." Since the 1903 judgment of *Attorney-General of Ontario* v. *The Hamilton Street Railway Company*,[125] Ritchie, J. reasoned, such legislation had constituted a part of the criminal law. Parliament, therefore, could legitimately restrict religious freedom pursuant to Section 91(27) of the British North America Act. In his words,

> ... legislation for the preservation of the sanctity of Sunday has existed in this country from the earliest times and has at least since 1903 been regarded as a part of the criminal law in its widest sense. Historically, such legislation has never been considered as an interference with the kind of "freedom of religion" guaranteed by the Canadian Bill of Rights.[126]

As the dicta indicates, Ritchie J. had, in effect, fallen back upon Lord Coke's "backward-looking" analysis of the freedom of religion. But the approach had led him to conclude that because the legislation at issue had been on past statute books, there could not possibly be a fundamental freedom of religion in the circumstances before the court.

The shortcomings of Coke C.J.'s "backward-looking" method

of analysis pervade the most recent "freedom of religion case" before the Canadian courts. In *Re Essex County Roman Catholic Separate School Board and Porter et al*[127] a Catholic school board had employed Susan Porter and Patricia Podgorski under a "permanent teachers' contract" as prescribed by provincial regulations. Both employees were Roman Catholics. For undisclosed reasons they entered into civil marriages and, as a consequence, the Catholic school board dismissed them from their positions. The school board resolved that the two "by entering into a civil marriage has [have] publicly and seriously infringed" the denominational requirements of the school as protected by Section 93 of the British North America Act, 1867.

The issue was phrased in these terms: did Section 93(1) of the British North America Act, 1867 protect the Catholic school board's right to dismiss for denominational reasons. Section 93 provides that

in and for each Province the Legislature may exclusively make Laws in relation to Education, subject to and according to the following Provisions:
(1) Nothing in any such Law shall prejudicially affect any Right or Privilege with respect to Denominational schools which any Class of Persons have by Law in the Province at the Union:...

After a Board of Reference ordered their contracts to be continued, the Divisional Court held that the Catholic school board's right to dismiss for denominational reasons was a right or privilege with respect to denominational schools existing in 1867 and therefore protected by Section 93(1) of the British North America Act. The Divisional Court found Section 29 of the Schools Administration Act, R.S.O. 1970, c. 424, *ultra vires* Section 93(1) of the British North America Act in that Section 29 of the former authorised a continuance of a teacher's contract if a school board possessed insufficient grounds for dismissal even though the teacher's conduct or teaching was incompatible with his continued employment as a teacher in a Catholic school. The Ontario Court of Appeal held that, although the teachers still had "a right to resort to the courts and ask for damages on the basis that they were wrongfully dismissed if such was the case," the Board of Reference established to hear such an issue did not possess jurisdiction to hear any issue involving "the right to dismiss for denominational reasons."

Interestingly, Zuber J.A., speaking for the majority in the Court of Appeal, "[took] it to be obvious that if a school board can dismiss for cause, then in the case of a denominational school cause must include denominational cause." Zuber J.A. does not tell us why this is logically or necessarily so. Nor does he find it necessary to tell us what constitutes a "denominational cause". He does suggest, citing an analogous 1928 decision not directly on point, that

> serious departures from denominational standards by a teacher cannot be isolated from his or her teaching duties since within the denominational school religious instruction, influence and example form an important part of the educational process.

Zuber J.A. does not explain nor connect why a civil marriage is "a serious departure from denominational standards." Nor does he suggest why and how a civil marriage is directly or even tangentially related to "religious instruction, influence and example."

Be that as it may, Zuber J.A.'s method of analysis, which he believed the British North America Act required, dictated his conclusion.[128] Section 93 of the B.N.A. Act required that counsel and judge look backward into Ontario's legal tradition prior to 1867 in an effort to ascertain the nature and extent of the employee's rights. In Zuber J.A.'s words, "it is apparent [from Section 93 of the B.N.A. Act] that the starting point must be an inquiry into the rights and privileges with respect to separate schools in Ontario as of 1867." Section 7 of the Separate School Act, 1863, in turn, set out the law of 1867. It provided that the separate school trustees possessed the same authority as the common school trustees. Relying upon *Raymond* v. *School Trustees of the Village of Cardinal* (1887),[129] Zuber J.A. found that the pertinent statute (the Common Schools Act, 1859)[130] neither took away nor diminished the school board's common law rights as an employer.

Zuber J.A. did not indicate the nature of those common law rights of employment.[131] Certainly, being in the heyday of *laissez-faire* liberalism, the school board's authority to dismiss "for cause" would have been far more extensive than today. Indeed, it would be surprising to find that the school board needed "just cause" for dismissal in the common law prior to the mid-nineteenth century. It would be even more surprising to find that the common law supported a fundamental freedom of religious conscience for Mrs. Porter and Mrs. Podgorski prior to the mid-1800s.

By choosing the "backward-looking" method of analysis which he did, Zuber J.A. reached a conclusion which left no room for the existence of a freedom — let alone a fundamental freedom — of religious conscience for Mrs. Porter and Mrs. Podgorski.[132] His approach presumed a relatively static, confining society in that the fundamental rights of mid-nineteenth century Ontario would be the same fundamental rights of today. The rights would not grow in number nor in scope. Nor could their meaning alter over the decades.

Zuber J.A.'s method of argument determined his conclusion, in the second place, in that for Mrs. Porter and Mrs. Podgorski to possess a fundamental freedom of religious conscience, that freedom would have had to exist prior to 1867. I have shown earlier in this section that no such fundamental freedom of religious conscience can be found in the Canadian legal tradition. As a consequence, Zuber J.A.'s method of analysis alleviated the necessity of raising the very issue of whether a fundamental freedom of religious conscience exists in Ontario and, if so, whether it conflicts with and is paramount over the freedom to establish the Roman Catholic religion.

The Canadian constitutional experience with respect to the issues of political participation and religious conscience demonstrates the deeply unsatisfactory nature of Chief Justice Coke's "backward-looking" method for justifying the existence of fundamental rights. On the one hand, Chief Justice Coke found centuries-old precedents to support the principle of the "rule of law," the existence of specific fundamental rights, the legal fraternity's monopoly over the ascertainment of the existence of fundamental rights, and the voidability of conflicting Acts of Parliament, proclamations or customary rules. On the other hand, Sir Edward Coke's own manipulation of legal precedent to support the existence of the crime of seditious libel, hitherto unknown in English law, exhibited important problems which flowed from his method of argument. He intended his "backward-looking" method to secure a static, confining society. Furthermore, for a fundamental right to exist it had to have consistently persisted as a fundamental right over a long period of time. The crime of seditious libel served the conservative philosophy of the Stuart monarchy quite well. It is also understandable, given his method of amalysis, that Chief Justice Coke would support the existence of seditious libel in the light of the anti-libertarian legal tradition which he had inherited.

The Canadian constitutional experience demonstrates that if one analyzes the nature and scope of political participation and religious conscience in Canada as Coke C.J. would have us do, we could not sustain the existence of fundamental rights of political participation and of religious conscience in Canada. Our legal tradition was silent on the subject of political participation until the post-World War I period. The issue of political participation shows that Coke C.J.'s method of analysis does not, of necessity, justify

44

the existence of a fundamental right. And the legal tradition relating to religious conscience reflects how Coke C.J.'s method is inappropriate to a country where the legal tradition has favoured a minority religion over others and where that preferred position does not guarantee a freedom from the state's interference with religious conscience.

It may well be that contemporary society does not want to have fundamental rights. It may alternatively be the case that even if contemporary society believes that it is founded on fundamental rights, there may be no better method of establishing their existence than Chief Justice Coke's "backward-looking" method. My argument, however, begins with the claim accepted by our legislators, jurists and scholars; namely, that our societies are founded on the existence of fundamental rights. Looking backward into society's legal tradition provides one type of argument which common law lawyers have used to try to establish why certain rights are fundamental. This chapter has revealed why, with reference to the Canadian context, Chief Justice Coke's method of argument cannot support the existence of fundamental rights. It may well be the case, however, that the common law lawyer has not devised a better method of argument. It is to alternative approaches which I shall now turn in chapters II and III.

Notes

1. Bracton, *On the Laws and Customs of England*, trans. Samuel E. Thorne, (Cambridge, Mass.: Harvard U. Press, 1968), vol. 2, pp. 19,21.

2. *Harrison* v. *Carswell*, [1976] 2 S.C.R. 200, 62 D.L.R. (3d) 68, [1975] 6 W.W.R. 673, 25 C.C.C. (2d) 186.

3. G. B. Adams, *Constitutional History of England* (New York: Henry Holt, 1931), p. 246.

4. The worst form of maintenance, "the form that was most prevalent during the century that preceded Henry VII's succession, consisted in supporting unjust claims to land by violence or threat of violence and in deterring a litigant by similar means from seeking his just remedy in the law courts." C. G. Bayne, "Introduction," *Select Cases in The Council of Henry VII*, C. G. Bayne ed., Seldon Society, (London: Bernard Quaritch, 1958), vol. 75, p. cxi.

5. Retaining involved the medieval practice whereby a patron took a retainer under his protection in return for promises of support whenever he went to court or faced the army of his neighbour or King, ibid., p. cxix.

6. Embracery was the charge laid against the person who actually bribed the jury, ibid.

7. 1487, 3 Henry VII, c.1, as reprinted in G. B. Adams and H. M. Stephens, *Select Documents of English Constitutional History*, (hereinafter cited as *Select Documents*), (London: Macmillan & Co., 1929), p. 214.

8. A leading scholar of the Tudor period has written that the desire for "law and order" under the Tudors "was derived from the sense of the need of order, from the sense that the welfare and very existence of the Commonwealth was bound up with obedience to authority, from the sense of danger from foreign enemies; from, one might say, the common sense of the English people, or at least of its upper classes." J. W. Allen, *A History of Political Thought in the Sixteenth Century* (London: Methuen & Co., 1928), p. 132. See also J. N. Figgis, *The Divine Right of Kings* (New York: Harper Torch Books, 1965), p. 260.

9. See generally J. W. Allen, *A History of Political Thought in the Sixteenth Century* (London: Methuen & Co., 1928), pp. 121, 127, 128, 131. Also see J. N. Figgis, *The Divine Right of Kings* (New York: Harper Torch Books, 1965), p. 221 and idem, *Political Thought from Gerson to Grotius: 1414-1625* (New York: Harper Torch books, 1960, 1907), p. 74.

10. James I, *Trew Law of Free Monarchies* in *Political Works of James I* (Cambridge, Mass.: Harvard Univ. Press, 1918).

11. Ibid., pp. 63, 307. See also, J. W. Allen, *A History of Political Thought in the Sixteenth Century* (London: Methuen & Co., 1928), pp. 252 ff.; and F. J. C. Hearnshaw, "The Social and Political Problems of the Sixteenth and Seventeenth Centuries," in F. J. C. Hearnshaw, ed., *The Social and Political Ideas of Some Great Thinkers of the Sixteenth and Seventeenth Centuries* (New York: Barnes & Noble, 1926).

12. The jurisdiction of the Star Chamber pursuant to 1487, 3 Henry VII, c.1 is reprinted in the text, supra, between notes 3 and 8.

13. C. G. Bayne, "Introduction," *Select Cases in The Council of Henry VII*, supra, note 4, pp. cxlviii, cliii, cxi.

14. H. G. Richardson and G. Sayles, *The Early Statutes*, 200 L.Q.R. 540, p. 545 (1934); H. D. Hazeltine, "The Interpretation of Law by English Medieval Courts," in T. T. Plucknett, *Statutes and Their Interpretation in the Fourteenth Century* (Cambridge: Cambridge Univ. Press, 1922), p. xviii.

15. Joseph H. Smith, *Cases and Materials on the Development of Legal Institutions* (St. Paul, Minn.: West Publ. Co., 1965), (hereinafter cited as *Materials*), p. 335.

16. (1608), 12 Co. Rep. 63, 77 E.R. 1342 (K.B.).

17. Ibid., Co. Rep. 63, E.R. 1342.

18. Ibid., Co. Rep. 64, E.R. 1343.

19. Ibid.

20. Ibid.

21. Ibid., Co. Rep. 65, E.R. 1343.

22. Sir Rafe Boswell described the incident in this manner:

> After which [i.e. after Coke C.J.'s assertion] his majestie fell into that high indignation as the like was never knowne in him, looking and speaking fiercely with bended fist, offering to strike him etc. which the Lord Coke perceauing fell flatt on all fower; humbly beseeching his majestie to take compassion on him and to pardon him, if he thought zeale had gone beyond his dutie and allegiance. His Majesty not herewith contented, continued his indignation. Whereupon the Lord Treasurer, the Lord Cookes unckle by marriage, kneeled downe before his Majestie and prayed him to be favourable.

as quoted in R. G. Usher, "James I and Sir Edward Coke," 18 *Eng. Hist. Rev.* 664, p. 669 (1903) and reprinted in J. H. Smith, *Materials*, supra, note 15, p. 375.

23. *Prohibitions del Roy* (1608), 12 Co. Rep. 63, 64, 77 E.R. 1342, 1343 (K.B.).

24. Ibid.

25. (1609), 12 Co. Rep. 50, 77 E.R. 1331 (K.B.).

26. The significance of this reason, however, is unclear. For one thing, although the Chief Justice of the King's Bench did receive his authority over civil cases by a Royal writ in Coke C.J.'s day, most Justices received their authority by way of commission. Further, commissions were generally used to confer criminal jurisdiction with respect to only one case as with a commission for Oyer and Terminer. The commission to the Councils of Wales and York had conferred general jurisdiction. See generally, J. H. Smith, supra, note 15, p. 163.

27. On the other hand Coke C.J. seemed to have ignored the many commissions granting authority to boroughs to hear civil cases according to equity.

28. *Case of the Lords President of Wales and York* (1609), 12 Co. Rep. 50, 77 E.R. 1331 (K.B.).

29. Professor Joseph H. Smith defines the term in this manner: "An

action determined by a court lacking jurisdiction over the subject matter is *coram non judice* (before a person not a judge) and the judgment is void." J. H. Smith, *Materials*, supra, note 15, p. 715.

30. See text, supra, between notes 21 and 22 and 43 Edw. III, c.3:

> No man shall be put to answer without presentment before the justices, matter of record, or by due process, or by writ original, according to the ancient law of the land: and if anything be done against it, it shall be void in law and held for error. *Vide* 28 Edw. 3. c.3.; 37 Edw. 3.c.18. *Vide* 17 R.2. *ex rotulis Parliamenti in Turri*, art. 10.

31. See text, supra, note 28.
32. (1609), 13 Co. Rep. 30, 77 E.R. 1440 (K.B.).
33. (1610), 12 Co. Rep. 74, 77 E.R. 1352 (K.B.).
34. (1612), 2 Brownl. & Golds. 192, 198; 123 E.R. 892, 895 (C P.).
35. Ibid., E.R. 895.
36. (1610), 8 Co. Rep. 113b, 77 E.R. 638 (K.B.).
37. Dr. Bonham was imprisoned under authority of letters patent, dated 10 Henry VIII incorporating the Royal College of Physicians and under authority of statutes 14 and 15 Henry VIII, c. 1 and 1 Mar., c. 9.
38. *Dr. Bonham's Case* (1610), 8 Co. Rep. 113b, 118; 77 E.R. 638, 652 (K.B.).
39. Emphasis added. Coke misquoted *Thomas Tregor's Case* by adding the words "against law and reason." As a consequence, Coke C.J.'s statement of the principle in *Tregor's* case had a very different meaning from that originally intended. Indeed, Plucknett's thorough study of the authorities cited by Coke C.J. in *Dr. Bonham's* case led him to conclude that "the theory which he [Coke] believed to be their legal foundation must be credited to his own political thought rather than to that of his medieval predecessors upon the common bench." See T. F. T. Plucknett, *Bonham's Case and Judicial Review*, 40 Harv. L. Rev. 30, p. 45 (1926).
40. S. E. Thorne has argued, for example, that Coke C.J. simply applied ordinary rules of statutory construction accepted in his day and that he had not appealed to some unchangeable, higher natural law. See S. E. Thorne, *Dr. Bonham's Case*, 54 L.Q.R. 543 (1938). L. B. Boudin held a similar interpretation of *Dr. Bonham's* case in *Lord Coke and the American Doctrine of Judicial Power*, 6 N.Y. U.L.R. 223 (1929).
41. T. F. T. Plucknett, "Bonham's Case and Judicial Review," supra, note 39, p. 45.
42. (1608), 7 Co. Rep. 1a, 77 E.R. 377, 2 Brownl. 198, 265 Hard. 140, Howell 2 St. Tr. 638 (Exchequer Chamber). The issue there was whether the guardians of Robert Calvin, a Scotsman, could bring a real or personal action to recover any of Calvin's lands within England. Calvin had been born in Scotland after James I had acceded to the English throne. The defendants argued that they need not reply to Calvin's suit since Calvin was an alien born. Calvin demurred. The Exchequer Chamber held that Calvin was not an alien and, therefore, the defendant was compelled to reply. The Exchequer Chamber resolved the issue by relying upon feudal concepts and by treating the question in terms of the English law of real property. Since all of England

was in tenure any additions of property could be acquired by conquest, not by occupancy.

The case is important for our purposes because of Coke C.J.'s citation of numerous examples for his proposition that Parliament could not take from a man "that protection which the law of nature giveth unto him." For example, if an individual were convicted of felony or treason, he would lose the King's protection. But he would not lose

> that protection which by the law of nature is given to the King, for that is *indelebilis et immutabilis*, and therefore the King may protect and pardon him.

Similarly, a statute of Edward III expressly took an individual

> out of the King's protection generally if he is convicted of *praemunive*, yet this extendeth only to legal protection... for the Parliament could not take away that protection which the law of nature giveth unto him.

Co. Rep. 14a, E.R. 393. Coke asserted that "the law of nature itself was nor could be altered or changed." Co. Rep. 126, E.R. 391.

43. See generally R. A. Mackay, *Coke — Parliamentary Sovereignty or the Supremacy of the Law?* 22 Mich. L. Rev. 215 (1924) as well as T. T. Plucknett, "Dr. Bonham's Case and Judicial Review," supra, note 39 and G. H. Sabine, *A History of Political Theory*, 3rd. ed. (Toronto: Holt, Rinehart & Winston, 1961), pp. 451-454.

44. I *Coke Inst.* 976.

45. See text, infra, between notes 53 and 58. Also see T. T. Plucknett, *Statutes and Their Interpretation in the Fourteenth Century*, supra note 14, pp. 26-31; idem, *Concise History of the Common Law* 5th ed. (London: Butterworths & Co. Ltd. 1956), p. 336.

46. *Murray's Lessee* v. *Hoboken Land & Improvement Co.*, 18 How. 272 (1856).

47. *Plessy* v. *Ferguson*, 163 U.S. 537, 16 S. Ct. 1138 (1896).

48. *Rex* v. *Hess (No. 2)*, [1949] 4 D.L.R. 199, [1949] 1 W.W.R. 586 (B.C.C.A.).

49. Ibid., 202.

50. Ibid., 205.

51. Ibid., 207. O'Halloran J.A.'s emphasis. Halloran is quoting from Lord John Campbell, *The Lives of the Chief Justices of England*, rev. ed. (Long Island, N.Y.: Edward Thompson Co., 1894), vol. 1, p. 352.

52. *Rex* v. *Hess (No. 2)*, [1949] 4 D.L.R. 199, 204; [1949] 1 W.W.R. 586 (B.C.C.A.).

53. 4 *Coke Inst.* 41.

54. See text, supra, between notes 33 and 63.

55. See text, supra, between notes 35 and 42.

56. 2 *Coke Inst.* 74 as quoted in R. A. MacKay, "Coke — Parliamentary Sovereignty or the Supremacy of the Law," supra note 43, p. 231. The most

important pillar, of course, was Magna Charta, "being the fountaine of all the fundamental lawes of the realme" and *magnum in parvo*. 1 *Coke Inst*. 81b. Coke C.J. asserted that Magna Charta was "but a confirmation or restitution of the common law ..." ibid. Thus, "if any statute be made to the contrary of Magna Charta, it shall be holden for none." 3 *Coke Inst*. 111. As he explained in 2 *Coke Inst*. 51,

> I know that Prerogative in part of the Law, but Sovereign Power is no Parliamentary word: In my opninion, it weakens *Magna Charta*, and all our statutes; for they are absolute without any saving of Sovereign Power: and shall we now add it, we shall weaken the Foundation of Law, and then the Building must needs fall; take heed what we yield unto, Magna Charta is such a Fellow, that he will have no Sovereign. I wonder this Sovereign was not in Magna Charta, or in the Confirmations of it; If we grant this, by implication we give a Sovereign Power above all these Laws.

57. 4 *Coke Inst*. "Intro.," as quoted in C. H. McIlwain, *The High Court of Parliament* (New Haven: Yale U. Press), p. 86.

58. 1 *Coke Inst*. 282b.

59. *Rochin* v. *California*, 342 U.S. 165, 171; 72 S. Ct. 205 (1952).

60. *Martin* v. *Law Society of British Columbia*, [1950] 3 D.L.R. 173, [1949] 1 W.W.R. 993 (B.C.C.A.).

61. *Miranda* v. *Arizona*, 384 U.S. 436, 86 S. Ct. 1602, 16 L. Ed. 2d 694 (1966).

62. Printing did not become common in England until the mid-sixteenth century. See J. Stephen, *History of the Criminal Law* (London: MacMillan & Co., 1883), vol. 2, p. 309.

63. Writing had been a rare skill for centuries.

64. L. B. Boudin, "Lord Coke and the American Doctrine of Judicial Power," supra, note 40, p. 225 ff.

65. Hudson wrote that "in all ages libels have been severly punished in this court, but most especially they began to frequent about 42 and 43 Elizabeth [1600] when Sir Edward Coke was her attorney-general." See Hudson, *Treatise on the Star Chamber*, pp. 100-104 as quoted by Stephen, *History of Criminal Law*, supra note 62, p. 305.

66. *De Libellis Famosis* (1606), 3 Co. Rep. 254 (1826 ed.), 77 E.R. 250 (Star Chamber).

67. *John Lamb's Case* (1611), 5 Co. Rep. 108 (1826 ed.), 77 E.R. 822 (Star Chamber).

68. III *Coke Inst*. (6th ed., 1680) chap. 76, p. 174.

69. *Case of Adam de Ravensworth* (1336), Coram Rege Roll, no. 306, mem. 27 in Selden Society, *Select Cases in the Court of King's Bench Ed. III*, ed. Sayles, (London: Bernard Quaritch, 1958), vol. 76, p. 92.

70. *Archdeacon of Norfolk Case* 1315, Coram Rege Roll, no. 220, mem. 120 in Selden Society, *Select Cases in the Court of King's Bench, Edward IV*, ed. Sayles (London: Bernard Quaritch, 1958) vol. 74, p. 64.

71. This is Coke C.J.'s own phraseology in the *Third Institute*, supra, note 68.

72. I. Brant, *Seditious Libel: Myth and Reality*, 39 N.Y.U.L.R. 1, pp. 8, 9 (1964).

73. Stephen, *Criminal Law*, supra, note 62, vol. 2, p. 302.

74. Ibid., p. 301.

75. 1275, 3 Edw. I, c. 25, 26, 28.

76. Stephen, *Criminal Law*, supra, note 62, vol. 2, p. 303.

77. 1689, 1 Wm. and Mary, sess. 2, c. 2, as reprinted in C. Stephenson and F. G. Marcham, eds., *Sources of English Constitutional History*, rev. ed. (New York: Harper and Row, 1972), vol. 2, p. 599.

78. W. H. Machl, *The Reform Bill of 1832, Why Not Revolution?* (New York: Holt, Rinehart and Winston, 1967).

79. Sir David Lindsay Keir, *The Constitutional History of Modern Britain*, 8th ed. (New York: W. W. Norton and Co., 1966), pp. 466-473.

80. The Radicals unsuccessfully sought to have inserted provisions in favour of women's suffrage in the *Franchise Act*, 1884 (see Keir, ibid., p. 471). *The Representation of the People Act*, 1918, gave the vote to all women of at least thirty years of age who occupied, or whose husbands occupied premises to the annual value of £ 5 (ibid., p. 474).

In Canada, women in active military service were granted the right to vote in 1917 as were certain female relatives of men in the armed services. The federal franchise was granted to all women on May 24th, 1918. The right to vote in provincial elections was granted to women between 1916-1922 although Quebec did not follow suit until 1940 and Newfoundland did not grant the franchise on an equal basis with men until 1948. See generally, Margaret E. MacLellan, "History of Women's Rights in Canada," in *Cultural Tradition and Political History of Women in Canada*, Study No. 8, Royal Commission on the Status of Women in Canada (Ottawa: Information Canada, 1971), esp. pp. 12-18.

81. *In Re Initiative and Referendum Act*, [1919] A.C. 935, 943; 48 D.L.R. 18, 24 (P.C.), Viscount Haldane stated that "in accordance with the analogy of the British Constitution which the Act of 1867 adopted, the Lieutenant-Governor who represents the Sovereign is a part of the Legislature." As a consequence, any bill where the Lieutenant Governor has withheld his assent is not an act of parliament. See generally, William E. Conklin, *Pickin and its Applicability to Canada*, 25 U.T.L.J. 193, 201-204 (1975).

82. J. H. Smith, *Development of Legal Institutions*, supra, note 15, pp. 353-379.

83. 1559, 1 Eliz. I, c. 1.

84. *Act of Uniformity*, 1559, 1 Eliz. I, c. 2.

85. *Campbell* v. *Hall* (1774), 1 Cow p. 204, 98 E.R. 1048 (K.B.); *In Re Cape Breton* (1846), 5 Moo 259, 13 E.R. 489 (P.C.); *Kielly* v. *Carson* (1842), 4 Moo 63, 13 E.R. 225 (P.C.).

86. *Campbell* v. *Hall*, ibid.

87. There is a dispute, however, as to whether acquisition was by conquest or cession. See generally Anger and Honsberger, *Canadian Law of Real Property* (Toronto: Canada Law Book Co., 1959), chapt. 1; Armour, *A Treatise on the Law of Real Property* (Toronto: Canada Law Book Co., 1901), chapt. 2.

88. As reprinted in William Houston, *Documents Illustrative of the Canadian Constitution* (Hereinafter cited as *Documents*), 1970 reprint (New York: Books for Libraries Press, 1891), pp. 27 ff.

89. Ibid., p. 27.

90. As reprinted ibid., p. 33 ff.

91. Ibid., p. 55. Emphasis added.

92. As reprinted ibid., p. 61 ff. Emphasis added.

93. Ibid., p. 62. Emphasis added.

94. See generally, J. H. Smith, *Administrative Control of the Courts of the American Plantations*, 61 Col. L. Rev. 1210 (1961); and idem, *The English Legal System: Carry Over to the Colonies* (Univ. of Calif., 1975).

95. *The Royal Proclamation*, 7 October, 1763 as reprinted in W. P. M. Kennedy, *Documents of the Canadian Constitution, 1759-1915* [hereinafter cited as *Documents of the Canadian Constitution*], (Toronto: Oxford Univ. Press, 1918), pp. 18-21.

96. *Commission of Governor Murray*, 21 November, 1763 as reprinted in W. Houston, *Documents*, supra, note 88, pp. 74-78.

97. *Instructions to Governor Murray*, 7 December, 1763 as reprinted in Kennedy, *Documents of the Canadian Constitution*, supra, note 95, pp. 27-37.

98. Sir J. G. Bourinot, *A Manual of the Constitutional History of Canada from the Earliest Period to 1901* (Toronto: Copp, Clark, 1901), pp. 8, 9.

99. W. P. M. Kennedy, *The Constitution of Canada, 1534-1937*, 2nd ed. (Toronto: Oxford Univ. Press, 1938), pp. 48 ff.

100. George F. Stanley, *A Short History of the Canadian Constitution* (Toronto: Ryerson, Press, 1969), p. 27.

101. Though elected, one could not sit in the Assembly, according to the Instructions (Article 29), unless he swore an anti-Catholic oath. In addition, only "freeholders" could stand for election (Article 11).

102. *Ordinance Establishing Civil Courts, 1764* as reprinted in Kennedy, *Documents of the Canadian Constitution*, supra, note 95, pp. 37-40.

103. Letter from Governor Murray to the Lords of Trade dated October 29th, 1764 as reprinted in Kennedy, ibid., p. 41.

104. *The Quebec Act*, 1774, 14 Geo. III, c. 83, as reprinted in W. Houston, *Documents*, supra, note 87, pp. 90-96.

105. *Ibid*, p. 92. Emphasis added. See text, supra, between notes 82 and 84.

106. As reprinted in W. Houston, *Documents*, supra, note 88, pp. 112 ff.

107. 1840, 3 and 4 Victoria, c. 35, as reprinted in W. Houston, ibid., p. 149.

108. 1852, 14-15 Victoria (Canada), c. 175. Emphasis added.

109. See *Re Essex County Roman Catholic School Board and Porter et al.*, (1979) 21 O.R. (2d) 255 (Ont. C.A.). See discussion of case in text, infra, between notes 127 and 132. The argument for a freedom of religion by virtue of sect. 93 is suggested by D. A. Schmeiser, *Civil Liberties in Canada* (London: Oxford Univ. Press, 1964), p. 15.

110. R.S.C. 1970, App. 111. Sect. 1(c) of the Canadian Bill of Rights provides as follows:

1. It is hereby recognised and declared that in Canada there have existed and shall continue to exist without discrimination by reason of race, national origin, colour, religion. or sex, the following human rights and fundamental freedoms, namely.. :

(c) freedom of religion;

...

111. *Saumur* v. *City of Quebec*, [1953] 2 S.C.R. 299, [1953] 4 D.L.R. 641.

112. Ibid., 327. Emphasis added.

113. Ibid., 379.

114. *Henry Birks and Sons (Montreal) Ltd.* v. *Montreal and A.-G. of Quebec*, [1955] S.C.R. 199, [1955] D.L.R. 321.

115. For a criticism of the traditional federalism or 'division of powers' approach see generally, Noel Lyon and Ronald Atkey, *Canadian Constitutional Law in a Modern Perspective* (Toronto: Univ. of Toronto Press, 1972), pp. 370-377.

116. [1938] S.C.R. 100, 331; [1938] 2 D.L.R. 81.

117. *Henry Birks and Sons (Montreal) Ltd.* v. *Montreal and A.-G. of Quebec*, [1955] S.C.R. 199, [1955] D.L.R. 321.

118. N. Lyon and R. Atkey, *Canadian Constitutional Law in a Modern Perspective*, supra, note 115.

119. 1354, 28 Edw. III, c. 14.

120. 1464, 4 Edw. IV, c. 7.

121. 1448, 27 Henry VI, c. 5.

122. 1625, 1 Charles I, c. I. This enactment continues in the form of the *Lord's Day Act*, R.S.C. 1970, c. L-13.

123. *Robertson and Rosetanni* v. *The Queen*, [1963] S.C.R. 65, (1964) 41 D.L.R. (2d) 485.

124. See supra, note 110.

125. *Attorney-General of Ontario* v. *The Hamilton Street Railway Company*, [1903] A.C. 524, 20 W.W.R. 672 (P.C.).

126. *Robertson and Rosetanni* v. *The Queen*, [1963] S.C.R. 65, (1964) 41 D.L.R. (2d) 485.

127. (1979) 21 O.R. (2d) 255 (Ont. C.A.).

128. One should note that the factums of the parties also urged the Court to adopt a "backward-looking" method of analysis.

129. (1887), 14 O.A.R. 562.

130. 1859, 22 Vic. c. 65.

131. Interestingly, counsel for the appellants did argue in their factum that the Separate School Trustees did not have the right to dismiss teachers for denominational reasons in 1867. Counsel also argued that if such right could be found it did not extend to the dismissal of a teacher who had entered into a civil marriage.

132. This is not to suggest that there were not other fundamental rights at issue such as freedom of speech and academic freedom generally. The fact that the state has financially entangled itself with the Catholic school system adds further weight to civil liberties claims in this case.

Chapter II

The "Contemporary Values of Society" Argument

The common law lawyer has tried to establish the existence of fundamental rights from the context of a second, very different framework. Instead of looking backward to possible rights embedded in legal tradition, the lawyer has directed his attention to the content of society's contemporary values.

It is not surprising that lawyers in the Anglo-American-Canadian tradition should lean upon society's contemporary values as threshold criteria for the existence, nature and scope of fundamental rights. For one thing, weighty principles embedded in legal tradition may direct the lawyer to contemporary values. One of the most important principles in the Canadian legal tradition, for example, is legislative supremacy. The legislature, in turn, serves as a reflector of society's contemporary values. Secondly, conventional opinion equates democracy with the "will of the majority". Judicial deference to society's contemporary values coincides with what one might consider the proper judicial role in a democratic society. This inference has worked its way into the reasoning of the highest courts in Canada and the United States. The premise underlay legal arguments with respect to capital punishment, abortion, language rights in Canada, freedom of religion, emergency legislation, illegal conduct by the police and the like. Many jurists have assumed that issues involving liberty can, in a democratic society, be adequately resolved if one simply adopts that side of a debate to which over fifty percent of the citizenry adhere.

This chapter examines whether a "contemporary values" line of argument provides a satisfactory defence of fundamental rights. If a society professes to be founded upon fundamental rights, can the lawyer, consistent with their existence, content himself with questions directed to the "counting of heads"? That is, in a society founded upon fundamental rights, is there not a duty for legislators and judges to ascertain and apply the wishes of the majority of citizens?

I am not concerned here with whether capital punishment, for example, in fact acts as a deterrent against potential criminals nor whether the interest of the state necessitated the imposition of the War Measures Act in Canada in 1970. This chapter does not assess the criminological, security, medical or other data offered in support of the various positions taken on such complex issues as abortion, language rights or the like. Rather, even if one could scientifically prove that capital punishment (for example) deterred crime and even if the majority believed that capital punishment served such a function, the issue remains whether we can settle the moral-political problem on that basis. My focus, in other words, is not the intensity or extensiveness of the societal values, but rather the role of contemporary societal values in a society which claims to be founded upon the existence of fundamental rights.

It seems that the "contemporary values" method for establishing the existence of fundamental rights has taken three quite different forms in Anglo-Canadian-American legal literature. First, judges have oftentimes suggested that in a civil liberties case they should project into the record what they as judges consider to be the dominant contemporary values of society. This was Lord Devlin's idea of the "reasonable", "rightminded man". It also underlay some of the judgments of Mr. Justices Marshall, Cardozo, and Frankfurter. A second, Benthamite form of the "will of the majority" underlay the writings of some jurists. Gallup polls, plebescites, communications between politician and citizen, and the like have been used as indicia for the existence (or non-existence) of fundamental rights. A third, more traditional form has been the notion of the supremacy of the legislature. We shall examine each in turn.

The strength of each form as a defence of fundamental rights depends upon the merits of the arguments articulated in support of each form. By examining the arguments and ideas of the most forceful advocates of the "contemporary values" method for justifying the existence of fundamental rights, I wish to raise significant problems with the "contemporary values" method in general. As in the case of Sir Edward Coke's "backward-looking" method, I shall shift interchangeably from the constitutional experiences in one country to those of another in an effort to exemplify why the problems are so real and pressing in concrete cases.

It may well be that the theorists whom I have chosen have not all had the same problem before them. Some, such as Bentham, may have been more concerned with the role of a legislator whereas others, such as Lord Devlin of Mr. Justice Marshall, may have been more interested in the problems of adjudication. Their ideas, it might be suggested, are thereby taken out of context. There is, however, a wider context than the one which may have been consciously before them. What the theorists have sometimes had in common is an assumption that fundamental rights issues may be definitively resolved by reference to some form of society's contemporary values. This chapter attempts to question that very premise. What role the judiciary should play in adjudicating disputes is left for chapter VII.

Section 1. The "Shock the Conscience" Argument

a. *The Argument*

The first form of the "contemporary values" method of establishing the existence of fundamental rights can be detected in the writings of Lord Patrick Devlin and in the judgments of Justices Cardozo, Frankfurter and Marshall of the United States Supreme Court. The idea is that society's conscience determines whether fundamental rights are infringed in any particular case. Certain rights are fundamental because and to the extent that their infringement would shock the conscience of society.

Lord Patrick Devlin, Fellow of the British Academy and former Justice of Great Britain's highest court, argued in his famous lectures on *The Enforcement of Morals*[1] that neither philosophy nor reason will serve the lawmaker well in his quest for the moral principles which ought to underlie his society. Rather, he must look to the principles "which every right-minded person would accept as valid." And who was this "right-minded person"? Lord Devlin replied,

> it is the viewpoint of the man in the street — or to use an archaism familiar to all lawyers — the man in the Clapham omnibus. He might also be called the right-minded man. For my purpose I should like to call him the man in the jury box, for the moral judgment of society must be something about which any twelve men or women drawn at random might after discussion be expected to be unanimous.[2]

The "right-minded person" was "the reasonable man" who has for so long stood forth in common law judgments. But the "reasonable man" was not a rational man: "He is not expected to reason about anything and his judgment may be largely a matter of feeling." He did not philosophize for his was a "practical morality" which was based not on theological or philosophical foundations but "in the mass of continuous experience half-consciously or unconsciously accumulated and embodied in the morality of common sense."[3] Although a sense of right and wrong was essential

56

for a community to survive, that sense of right and wrong did not need to be "correct". It did not need to be "tested in the light of one set or another of those abstract propositions" peculiar to rationally or philosophically inclined men and women. Rather, the lawmaker was required merely to ascertain the *common*, as opposed to the *true*, beliefs of society.

But did Lord Devlin contemplate that these common beliefs should actually be representative of the majority's will? Unequivocally no. "The lawmaker's task, even in a democracy, is not the drab one of counting heads or of synthesizing answers to moral questions in a gallup poll,"[4] according to Lord Devlin. It would be "too much to require the individual assent of every citizen,"[5] he insisted. For Lord Devlin, democracy and universal suffrage required that the opinion of "the ordinary citizen" settle "matters of great moment."[6]

But how could Lord Devlin fall back upon the opinion of "the ordinary citizen" without appealing to the will of the majority or, for that matter, to philosophy? Lord Devlin's answer returned in a circular fashion to the "reasonable man" with which he began his discussion. What underlay society's moral values was the "ordinary man's" feelings of "intolerance, indignation and disgust."[7] For Lord Devlin, then, democratic theory required that the judge project into the record what the "man in the street" believed without actually polling that "man in the street" as to his own beliefs. And yet, Lord Devlin believed his approach to be non-elitist.[8]

Lord Devlin applied his method of argument to the issues of homosexuality and pornography. An interesting variation of his argument can also be found in the context of capital punishment and due process cases in the United States. One should note, in this regard, Mr. Justice Marshall's elaborate treatment of the Eighth Amendment's proscription against cruel and unusual punishment.

In *Furman* v. *Georgia* (1972)[9] the issue was whether a capital punishment enactment was "cruel and unusual". The Supreme Court found the existence of a fundamental right prohibiting cruel and unusual punishment by referring to the written Constitution.[10] It will be argued in chapter III that a written constitution with a bill of rights does not necessarily guarantee the existence of fundamental rights in concrete cases. In any case, even if a "written constitution" method of argument could adequately justify the existence of fundamental rights, the American Constitution does not direct one to conclude that capital punishment is contrary to any fundamental right concerning cruel and unusual punishment. Indeed, the Fifth Amendment contemplates capital punishment in three contexts: first, no person shall be held to answer for a *capital* crime unless...; secondly, no person shall be twice put in jeopardy "of *life* or limb"; and thirdly, no person shall be deprived of "*life*, liberty, or property without due process of law." Consequently, notwithstanding an entrenched Bill of Rights, an American court must still explain why cruel and unusual punishment is so fundamental and sufficiently wide in scope as to proscribe capital punishment. Mr. Justice Marshall attempted to provide such an explanation.

Mr. Justice Marshall began his judgment by examining the historical derivation and construction given to the Eighth Amendment in the past. He concluded his survey with an idea which resembled Lord Devlin's concern. The most important principle in analyzing "cruel and unusual punishment" issues, according to Justice Marshall, was that the Eighth Amendment "must draw its meaning from the evolving standards of decency that mark the progress of a maturing society."[11] Unless one could find a very recent decision, "*stare decisis* would bow to changing values, and the question of the constitutionality of capital punishment at a given moment in history would remain open."[12] Accordingly, the constitutionality of capital punishment would vary from one historical period to another.

Mr. Justice Marshall then proceeded to lay down four reasons which he believed would legitimately render a punishment cruel and unusual. First, did the punishment "inherently involve so much physical pain and suffering that civilized people cannot tolerate" it (for example, the use of the rack)? Secondly, was the punishment previously unknown as a penalty for a given offence (that is, unusual)? Thirdly, was it excessive and unnecessary? Fourthly, did popular sentiment abhor it? Mr. Justice Marshall's reasons for judgment relied upon the third and fourth standards. After holding that capital punishment was excessive and unnecessary because less severe penalties would satisfy the legitimate legislative purposes, he went on to conclude that even if capital punishment were not excessive, it was "morally unacceptable to the people of the United States at this time in their history."[13] As Mr. Justice Marshall noted, the very notion of changing values requires that the court recognise popular sentiment as a relevant consideration.

Unlike Lord Devlin's "ordinary man" terminology the constitutionality of capital punishment, according to Mr. Justice Marshall, turned on the opinion of an *informed* citizenry. Mr. Justice Marshall asserted that he was not interested in the question whether a

58

substantial proportion of American citizens would today, if polled, believe that capital punishment was barbarously cruel. Rather, Mr. Justice Marshall asserted that analysis should focus on the "predictable, subjective, emotional reactions of *informed* citizens."[14] By confining himself merely to the *informed* citizens, Mr. Justice Marshall stated that he had undercut the major argument against capital punishment: namely that the legislature, which was the voice of the people, had advocated retention. Indeed, deference to the legislature was "tantamount to abdication of our judicial roles."

Mr. Justice Marshall developed his perspective in *Gregg* v. *Georgia*.[15] In that case he held that the constitutionality of capital punishment was still inconclusive notwithstanding the fact that the legislatures of thirty-five states had subsequently enacted new statutes authorizing the death penalty for certain offences. Mr. Justice Marshall justified his position by claiming that few Americans had been exposed to the facts surrounding the capital punishment issue; lack of exposure likely led to an indifferent and uninformed citizenry; and this, in turn, resulted in the preservation of the status quo. In *Gregg* v. *Georgia* Mr. Justice Marshall referred to a recent study[16] which confirmed that the American people knew very little about the death penalty, and that the opinions of an informed public would differ significantly from the "ordinary" — to use Lord Devlin's term — public.

Mr. Justice Marshall's judgments concerning cruel and unusual punishment lie in a long tradition of American Supreme Court judgments which have attempted to explain the meaning of a constitutional right in terms of a "shock" to contemporary values. An early variant on the theme was Mr. Justice Cardozo's judgment in *Palko* v. *Connecticut*.[17] In *Palko*, Mr. Justice Cardozo reasoned that due process of law had not been violated since the legal procedures which had been followed in *Palko* did not shock society's conscience. The defendant had initially been sentenced to imprisonment for life on being found guilty of murder. When the state appealed, a new trial was ordered. Palko was re-tried and sentenced to death. Mr. Justice Cardozo held that the fact that Palko had been re-tried and eventually sentenced to death did not deprive him of life without due process of law. Certain freedoms such as the freedoms of the press, religion, peaceable assembly and the right of counsel were required of the states pursuant to the due process clause of the Fourteenth Amendment, according to Mr. Justice Cardozo, because those freedoms were "implicit in the concept of ordered liberty." The "rationalizing principle" emerging from the cases, he asserted, was whether a particular practice in a particular case was "of the very essence of a scheme of ordered liberty." That is, did any particular practice violate a "principle of justice so rooted in the traditions and conscience of our people as to be ranked as fundamental."[18] In the *Palko* facts Mr. Justice Cardozo posed the crucial test this way:

> Is that kind of double jeopardy to which the statute has subjected him a hardship *so acute and shocking* that our policy will not endure it? Does it violate those "fundamental principles of liberty and justice which lie at the base of all our civil and political institutions"? [19]

Mr. Justice Frankfurter attempted to apply Mr. Justice Cardozo's "shocking the conscience" definition of "due process of law" in the so-called "incorporation" cases. The central issue facing the court in these cases concerned the meaning of he Fourteenth Amendment as it applied to the states. In particular, did the "due process of law" clause of the Fourteenth Amendment incorporate the first eight Amendments so as to apply to the states as well as to the federal government? At issue in *Adamson* v. *California.* [20] for example, was a California statute which permitted the court or even the opposing counsel to comment upon the failure of a defendant to explain or to deny certain evidence. Mr. Justice Frankfurter believed that the due process clause of the Fourteenth Amendment only required that the states comply with the "fundamental principles of liberty and justice." Although this test made judicial discretion inescapable the judiciary's function, according to Mr. Justice Frankfurter, was merely to ascertain whether the California statute "offended those canons of decency and fairness which express the notions of justice of English-speaking peoples even toward those charged with the most heinous offences." Mr. Justice Frankfurter believed this test to be very different from the "merely subjective test" which automatically incorporated those provisions of the first eight Amendments which the individual Justice conceived to be "indispensable to the dignity and happiness of a free man." And yet, Mr. Justice Frankfurter admitted that canons of "decency and fairness" were not authoritatively formulated anywhere.

In *Rochin* v. *California*,[21] Mr. Justice Frankfurter further elaborated his test by suggesting that the requisite issue was whether a particular proceeding (in that case, forced stomach-pumping in order to obtain state evidence) "shocks the conscience" or "is bound to offend even hardened sensibilities." The police, he held, must respect "certain decencies of civilized conduct," "the community's sense of fair play and decency." Rather than drawing on "our merely personal and private notions," the decencies of civilized conduct were "deeply rooted in reason and in the compelling traditions of the legal profession."

b. *Some Problems*

The first problem with the "shock the conscience" analysis of a fundamental right is that the determination and scope of a freedom is highly subjective and discretionary. As Mr. Justice Black emphasised in his dissenting opinion in *Rochin*, Mr. Justice Frankfurter's test of "the community's sense of fair play and decency" was a "nebulous" standard which legitimised an "unlimited power" to invalidate laws. Mr. Justice Frankfurter had not really informed us as to how "to discover 'canons' of conduct so universally favoured." As a consequence, Mr. Justice Black continued, the "accordion-like qualities of this philosophy must inevitably imperil all the individual liberty safeguards specifically enumerated in the Bill of Rights."

The "accordian-like" quality of Mr. Justice Frankfurter's version of the "shock the conscience" test for fundamental rights is exemplified in his dissenting opinion in *Irvine* v. *California* (1954).[22] In that case the petitioner had been convicted of gambling offences partially because of incriminating statements gathered through a listening device installed in the petitioner's home. The decisive element here, as in *Rochin*, according to Mr. Justice Frankfurter, was the "additional aggravating conduct which *the Court* finds *repulsive*." [emphasis added]

Even Mr. Justice Marshall's reliance upon the values of the "informed citizen" is a highly subjective judicial determination. This test could well allow the judge to project his own subjective values into his assessment of what constitutes the values of the informed citizen. Walter Lippman in his classic work *Public Opinion*[23] made a persuasive argument that politicians and interest groups have used the term "public opinion" as just such a cloak. This conclusion is all the more apparent when one comes to terms with Mr. Justice Marshall's claim that the Justice's role is not to assess the principled reasons of an informed citizen's judgment in the manner which Ronald Dworkin[24] or John Stuart Mill[25] might have considered essential for a valid moral position. Rather, a Justice should inquire into "the predictable, *subjective, emotional* reactions of informed citizens."

Lord Devlin's analysis also fails to escape from the criticism made above concerning the highly subjective judicial determination of the existence and scope of our fundamental rights. Lord Devlin tells us that the opinion of "the man on the street" is not to be assessed in any quasi-scientific manner. The judge need not provide any philosophical or religious grounds for his conclusions about the common man's opinion. Indeed, he need not give *any* reasons for his determination. Nor need contemplation nor deep analysis be involved in the judge's task. For, the "man on the street" is the "right-thinking" man whose moral opinions are those of "a reasonable civilized man or a reasonable Englishman."[26] The "right-thinking" man's feelings of "intolerance, indignation and disgust" lie at the basis of our legal order. Lord Devlin's pivotal test for the judicial determination of society's moral judgments is intuitive, tautological and deceptively simple. It is as if Lord Devlin actually believed that the opinion of "the man on the street" was something "out there" in the objective world to be gathered only for the asking. One need not to be a sophisticated psychologist to perceive that Lord Devlin's test is little more than a very crude tool to rationalise the judge's own political-moral preconceptions, premises and prejudices.

This leads to a second limitation of the "shock the conscience" method for justifying the existence and scope of a fundamental right. A "fundamental" right established by this method is an *ad hoc* right, one which may exist one day in a given circumstance but not the next in a similar circumstance. The "predictable, subjective, emotional reactions" of Mr. Justice Marshall's "informed citizen" will vary over time: the citizen's emotional reactions are entirely relative to the cultural values of the society being assessed. Similarly, the Justices Cardozo-Frankfurter "shock the conscience" technique of defining the content of the due process clause in the Fourteenth Amendment in the "incorporation" cases must proceed on a case by case basis. Whereas stomach-pumping was held to "shock the conscience" in *Rochin*,[27] the gathering of incriminating evidence through a concealed listening device in *Irvine*[28] was held to involve merely a trespass to property plus eavesdropping. Without explanation, the Supreme Court seemed to believe that the latter constituted a value of lesser importance than the coercion by a physical assault upon the person in *Rochin*. Without some explanation, how could a competent lawyer advise a client as to whether the client possessed a fundamental right in any particular case? Counsel would have to be capable of predicting whether the repulsiveness of the procedure at hand had already entered into the conscience of mankind as the personalities on the court would interpret that conscience. Such well-known advocates of the "rule of law" as Bracton, Coke and Dicey would certainly have shuddered if one were to claim that this legal process constituted the rule of law.

Thirdly, the "shock the conscience" method for justifying the nature of a fundamental right would be inapplicable in a country such as Canada which possesses a variety of cultures, each having centuries-old conflicting legal traditions. There are important value differences among the cultures, differences which conflict. Any appeal to "shocking the conscience" of society would not provide a rational response where values do conflict. Nor would the conscience of society be ascertainable. Indeed, Mr. Justice Marshall's "informed citizen" and Lord Devlin's "reasonably civilized man" standards themselves reflect the values of particular segments of particular societies in particular historical periods.[29] Their tests provide the court with the opportunity of imposing the subjective, culturally induced values of the dominant elite upon the cultural sub-groups within society. A right held to be fundamental might in effect be fundamental merely to that elite.

The central problem of the "shock and conscience" justification of fundamental rights is that it provides us with no principled criteria for deciding which rights are fundamental and which are not.[30] We are still not told why "fundamentality" is at issue in one set of circumstances and not in another. And where fundamentality is at issue, the lack of principled criteria leaves us with little indication as to the nature and scope of the fundamental right. Furthermore, the "shock the conscience" method of argument provides us with little guidance as to how the court or the legislature is to resolve a conflict between one "fundamental" value and another. The roots of fundamental freedom are left unanswered once again.

Section 2. The "Majority Will" Argument

a. *The Argument*

Common law lawyers in Great Britain, the United States and Canada have taken a second tack in their attempt to ascertain the contemporary values of society. Instead of asking whether particular conduct by the state "shocked the conscience", we have been directed to ask what constituted the "will of the majority" in any particular case. The issue which must be faced is as follows: if the "majority's will" resolved important moral-political issues in society, what consequences would flow for the existence and scope of fundamental rights?

At first glance, this method of argument would overcome several of the objections encountered above with respect to "shocking the conscience of society". For one thing, assuming that one could scientifically ascertain the "will of the majority", one could no longer allege that adjudication provides judges with the opportunity of inculcating their own moral-political values. Nor could one even suggest that the legislature itself would impose its own values over those of the majority. Furthermore, unlike the "shock the conscience" approach, the "majority will" provides a principled criterion for distinguishing fundamental rights from non-fundamental rights in that reference would always be made to one principle: the majority's will. Finally, adjudication of apparent conflicts between one fundamental right and another would be quite simplified. Instead of attempting to ascertain the conscience of the "ordinary man" or the "informed citizen", the court would need only be required to calculate how fifty per cent of the citizenry felt toward each prospective right. The interminable question of why fundamental rights are fundamental would seemingly be finally resolved. Those rights would be fundamental if the majority for whatever reason, philosophic or otherwise, so declared.

One of the foremost theorists on the subject of the "will of the majority" was Jeremy Bentham. Bentham announced the general outline of his utilitarian perspective in his works, *A Fragment on Government*[31] and *An Introduction to the Principles of Morals and Legislation.*[32] The *Fragment* was a critique of the *Commentaries of the Laws of England* which, in turn, had been written by Bentham's former professor, Sir William Blackstone. In contrast to Blackstone, Bentham believed that the true function of jurisprudence was not just to describe how people do in fact behave but also to examine how they *ought* to behave. The latter pursuit, which he called censorial jurisprudence,[33] required an ethical standard by which one would be able to evaluate human behaviour. Bentham believed that he had discovered such a standard. His standard was utility.

As to the descriptive aspect of his jurisprudence, Bentham insisted that "nature has placed mankind under the governance of two sovereign masters, pain and pleasure." These two forces "govern us in all we do, in all we say, in all we think: every effort we can make to throw off our subjection, will serve but to demonstrate and confirm it."[34] Pleasure and pain naturally conflicted within each individual as well as amongst individuals. Bentham emphasised that each person sought to maximize the greatest quantum of pleasure over pain that he could possibly muster. This amalgam of pleasure and pain was what Bentham meant by the word utility. In his words:

> By utility is meant that property in any object, whereby it tends to produce benefit, advantage, pleasure, good or happiness, (all this in the

present case comes to the same thing) or (what again comes to the same thing) to prevent the happening of mischief, pain, evil, or unhappiness to the party whose interest is considered...[35]

In the same way that utility was supposed to describe how people *actually* behaved so also was it supposed to provide the only intelligible *goal* for an individual or, indeed, for society as a whole. "The general object which all laws have, or ought to have, in common," he wrote, "is to augment the total happiness of the community and therefore, in the first place, to exclude, as far as may be, everything that tends to subtract from that happiness: in other words, to exclude mischief."[36] As he asserted earlier in the *Introduction*, the total happiness of the community constituted "the *sole* end which the legislator ought to have in view."[37] Each individual, he continued, "ought, as far as depends upon the legislator, to be *made* to fashion his behaviour" in conformity with this "sole standard" of the total happiness of individuals. Thus, one measured the utility of any proposed law by its tendency to bring happiness or to diverge from happiness.[40]

Bentham defined happiness as "benefit", "advantage", "pleasure" or "good".[41] The legislator should aim to add and subtract the pleasures and pains of each citizen so as to produce an outcome which accurately corresponded to the greatest happiness of the greatest number in society.[42] Bentham believed that this calculation was possible in practice. And he believed that it ought to be used so as to resolve all moral-political issues of the day.

Bentham's elaborate theory of the "majority will" would appear to provide us with a method to establish the existence of fundamental rights. The legislator need only accurately measure the pleasures and pains of the total populace. The judiciary need merely apply and enforce the legislator's calculation. Bentham went so far as to explain how the legislator should add and subtract the pleasures and pains so as to produce an outcome which accurately corresponded to the greatest happiness of the greatest number. In fact, he defined fourteen different pleasures and twelve different pains.[43] Of the pleasures he listed sense, wealth, skill, amity, a good name, power, piety, benevolence, malevolence, memory, imagination, expectation, association and relief. Of the pains he set out privation, senses, awkwardness, enmity, ill name, peity, benevolence, malevolence, memory, imagination, expectation and association. He described the nature of each of these pleasures and pains[44] as well as the relevant factors which altered them.[45] He even devised seven "dimensions of value" which the legislator was to use as standards in measuring the pleasures and pains: intensity, duration, certainty or uncertainty, propinquity or remoteness, fecundity,[46] purity,[47] and extent.[48]

Bentham's lifetime work was remarkable for its sophistication and its thoroughness. He translated his philosophic perspective into concrete legislative and constitutional proposals. Despite this philosophical and practical endowment, serious problems remain with his approach if we want to use it as a method of argument for justifying the existence of fundamental rights.

b. *Problems with the "Majority Will" Argument*

The first problem is a practical, not a theoretical one. We know now that it is very difficult, if not impossible, to calculate society's total happiness in practice. How would the legislator objectively quantify and compare the citizenry's feelings toward such seemingly unquantifiable moral-political values as free speech, freedom of religious conscience, the right to privacy or the right to political participation? Are such rights and freedoms quantifiable in the same manner that one quantifies monetary, statistical or material objects?

An extended complication originates with the initial issue of ascertaining an agenda of possible rights from which the citizenry are to choose. Is the legislator obliged to provide a "carte blanche" in the voting booth so that the citizenry can register their own opinions as to what possible rights should be on the list? If so, who is to decide what rights should be on the initial agenda? How are we to arrive at an agenda if no consensus forms amongst the citizenry as to what should compose the agenda? Even if these problems were surmountable, who is to say what issues should go to the public for decision? Again, strictly speaking, the "will of the majority" theory would suggest that the citizenry register their opinions as to the critical issues on a "carte blanche". But would over fifty per cent of the citizenry in any country ever agree as to the key issues facing the country?

These practical problems lead into a more theoretical question. Why is fifty per cent the magic number for determining the "majority"? Why not choose, say, sixty-six per cent or seventy-five per cent? Can a majority of fifty per cent decide *that* initial question? If so, why?

Even if we could intelligently explain why fifty per cent is the magic number, even if over fifty per cent of the citizenry agreed to the central issues and the agenda of fundamental rights, and even if we could quantify those rights, a further practical problem remains. How would the legislator or the adjudicator measure the intensity of each individual's opinion on each issue? And even if the legislator could measure the intensity of persons' opinions, would not such an accounting militate against the very "will of the majority" that the legislator or adjudicator is aiming to ascertain? The latter would appear to arise in that, because of varying intensities, the opinions of some individuals would be given more weight than others.

These practical problems force us to remain sceptical of any self-professed claim by any politician, political party or interest group that he, she or it represents the "majority will" on any particular issue. These problems also require that the citizen scrutinize whether a political leader's electoral victory does in fact permit him to use the "majority will" as an excuse to restrict liberty or to fail to ensure social equality. We can certainly remain sceptical of any judge's claim that he is justified in resolving a civil liberties dispute in a certain direction because the "will of the majority" corresponded with his conclusion on the particular issue. Indeed, if the "will of the majority" does not and cannot exist in fact, then continued reference to the "will of the majority" may be misdirected.

In addition to the above set of practical problems, there is a second pertinent reason why the "will of the majority" cannot be used to establish the existence of fundamental rights. As with the "shock the conscience" form of ascertaining society's contemporary values, there would be no theoretical limit upon which the majority may restrict the rights of individual citizens. The majority may take away one's freedom to speak on any issue, to practise a particular religion, to join a particular political association, even to think certain thoughts. Similarly, the majority may legitimately practise discrimination or permit the practice of discrimination according to race, sex, colour, creed and national origin. Racial segregation and apartheid would not be precluded. Indeed, the majority may metaphysically create the existence of a religious, racial or political group even though that group does not in fact exist much, as Jean-Paul Sartre argued, the anti-Semites had done with respect to the Jews.[49] Finally, there would be no conceivable limit to the repression of fundamental rights in that the "majority will" could consistently sustain grotesque social and economic inequalities except, possibly, an equality amongst the members of the majority. The majority could legitimately legislate the worst forms of tyranny and slavery known to mankind just as individuals and minorities have perpetrated in the past.

This point is borne out by a close look at our theorist of the "majority will". Bentham in his *Introduction* makes it quite clear that the state could make any conduct a crime so long as to do so would create the greatest happiness of the greatest number. As he wrote,

> any act *may* be an offence, which they whom the community are in the habit of obeying shall be pleased to make one: that is, any act which they shall be pleased to prohibit or to punish. But, upon the principle of utility, such acts alone *ought* to be made offences, as the good of the community requires should be made so.[50]

Furthermore, once the state had created a crime, the courts could determine the nature and severity of a sentence by reference to the greatest happiness of the greatest number.[51] Bentham advocated equality merely in the numerical sense that each person's happiness was to be given equal weight. Mill attributed to Bentham the dictum that "everybody to count for one, nobody for more than one."[52] For Bentham, laws "gently favouring" economic equality were to be preferred because at a certain point greater happiness would result from granting wealth to a poor person than to an already wealthy person. Bentham's theory of the greatest happiness of the greatest number left little room for either liberty or equality as independent moral considerations. They were valued only to the extent that they increased the overall total happiness of the greatest number.[53]

This leads us to a third limitation of the "will of the majority" method for establishing the existence of fundamental rights. As with the "shocking the conscience" method, rights will be *ad hoc* rights. They may exist one day in a given circumstance with respect to a particular issue but not the next in a similar circumstance. There is no principled reason why the majority should be consistent over an extended period of time. Indeed, to the extent that one's values reflect the environment in which one is raised from childhood, one's values will change as the environment changes. The repurcussions for the legislative and adjudicative process would be severe. Government would repeatedly be required to amend legislation in order to take account of varying public perceptions of the agenda of fundamental rights. Counsel would be obliged to predict the extent and intensity of the majority's repulsiveness toward any proposed legal action.

The fourth and final problem is that we may seriously question whether the rights in a "will of the majority" society are fundamental in a real sense of the word. In the Introduction to this book I noted that our dictionaries define the word "fundamental" as "the root of the matter", "essential", "indispensable", "the groundwork of a system", "basic", "underlying", "primary", "formative" or "irreducible". In the light of the above problems incurred in a "will of the majority" method for establishing the existence of fundamental rights, the notion of a right in a "will of the majority" context could hardly be said to satisfy the definition of fundamental in even a remote sense. So long as there is no theoretical limit to the extent to which the state may restrict one's rights, it is difficult to describe one's rights as fundamental rights. Rather, the "will of the majority" more accurately meets that definition. As we have seen, the non-existence of rights is quite consistent with the majority's will.

Bentham's own discussion of the nature of a right verifies the non-fundamental nature of a right in the "will of the majority" method of argument. A "right", for Bentham, was something which *ought to be done*. Freedom of speech was a right, for example, if the freedom was the right or proper conduct to follow. As he explained in *An Introduction*,

> Of an action that is comfortable to the principle of utility, one may always say either that it is one that ought to be done, or at least that it is not one that ought not to be done. One may say also, that it is right it should be done; at least that it is not wrong it should be done: that it is a right action; at least that it is not a wrong action. When thus interpreted, the words *ought*, and *right* and *wrong*, and others of that stamp, have a meaning; when otherwise, they have none. [54]

Bentham defined a right in *Anarchical Fallacies* in similar terms:

> That in proportion as it is *right* or *proper*; i.e., advantageous to the society in question, that this or that right — a right to this or that effect — should be established and maintained, in that same proportion it is *wrong* that it should be abrogated. [55]

But what constituted right (or proper) conduct? That conduct which increased the community's overall happiness. [56] If a right was advantageous to society as a whole, the state should establish, maintain and protect the right. If a right contributed disadvantages to the community, the state should abrogate the right. In this manner, the individual's rights were conflated into the *felicitic calculus* of "the greatest happiness of the greatest number". One's rights were not "essential" or "irreducible". The forcefulness, indeed, the very existence of one's rights were entirely contingent upon the "greatest happiness of the greatest number".

A right, for Bentham, was a social concession or, to use the words of one of Bentham's disciples (John Austin), "a simple permission" granted to the subject by the state. [57] "That which has no existence cannot be destroyed — that which cannot be

69

destroyed cannot require anything to preserve it from destruction," Bentham reasoned. "*Natural rights* is simply nonsense: natural and imprescriptible rights, rhetorical nonsense — nonsense upon stilts...," he continued.[58] A real right came from real laws enacted by the state in the name of the majority. "Imaginary" or fundamental rights came from "imaginary" laws "invented by poets, rhetoricians, and dealers in moral and intellectual poisons." The advocates of natural rights were "the mortal enemies of law, the subverters of government, and the assassins of security."[59] John Austin described them as "the ignorant and bawling fanatics who stun you with their pother about liberty."[60] Given their "will of the majority" frame of reference it is understandable why Bentham and his follower would react so strongly against the notion of a stronger — if not fundamental — sense of rights.

Section 3. The "Supremacy of the Legislature" Argument

a. *The Argument*

We have now examined two forms of the "contemporary societal values" argument which jurists have used in an effort to establish the existence of fundamental rights. The first form questioned whether a particular state practice shocked society's conscience. Lord Devlin ascertained society's conscience by reference to "the ordinary man on the street" and Mr. Justice Marshall did so in terms of the "informed citizen". The second form of the "contemporary values" argument has looked to the "will of the majority" for the expression of society's contemporary values. The third, a constitutionally more acceptable form in Canada and the United Kingdom, is by reference to the "will of the legislature". Unlike the first two perspectives, the idea underlying the "will of the legislature" is that legislation is, in Edmund Burke's words, a matter "of reason and judgment, and not of inclination."[61] Burke has posed this question: "and what sort of reason is that in which the determination precedes the discussion, in which one set of men deliberate and another decide, and where those who form the conclusion are perhaps three hundred miles distant from those who hear the arguments?" Accordingly, legislators were not delegates of the constituents. Rather, legislators were an elected elite who arrived at their own judgments after due consideration and argument.

According to the doctrine of legislative supremacy, a right is fundamental if the majority in the legislative chamber believe it to be fundamental. In its strictest sense the court's task is simply to

70

apply and enforce the legislature's determination. The court must accept the legislative enactment at face value, without second thoughts about the motives, wisdom or reasons for the legislature's decision.[62] Nor may the court scrutinize the legislative process in order to assure itself that facts have not been misrepresented to the legislature.[63] The legislature, furthermore, may not bind itself into the future: what the legislature deems fundamental on one occasion it may undo on another.[64] This principle of legislative supremacy provides the central pillar underlying the Canadian legal system.[65]

Probably the foremost contemporary advocate of this third form of the "contemporary values" argument has been Mr. Justice Pigeon of the Canadian Supreme Court. In his dissenting judgment in *R. v. Drybones*[66] Pigeon J. held that the *Canadian Bill of Rights* could not be used to render another legislative enactment inoperative. One "compelling reason" for his decision, according to Pigeon J., was

> the presumption against implicit alteration of the law, Parliament must not be presumed to have intended to depart from the existing law any further than expressly stated (Maxwell, etc.). In the present case, the judgments below hold in effect that Parliament in enacting the *Bill* has implicitly repealed not only a large part of the *Indian Act* but also the fundamental principle that the duty of the courts is to apply the law as written and they are in no case authorized to fail to give effect to the clearly expressed will of Parliament. It would be a radical departure from this basic British constitutional rule to enact that henceforth the courts are to declare inoperative all enactments that are considered as not in conformity with some legal principles stated in very general language . . . .[67]

According to Pigeon, J. the meaning of such expressions as freedom of religion and freedom of speech were "in truth largely unlimited and undefined." Their actual content expanded and varied over time. But, "in the traditional British system that is our own by virtue of the British North America Act, 1867, the responsibility for updating the statutes in this changing world rests exclusively upon Parliament."[68] The Canadian Bill of Rights embodied this "traditional principle". Accordingly, the principle of legislative supremacy explained why Parliament had declared the enacted "human rights and fundamental freedoms" to have existed in the past and to continue to exist in the future. The human rights had existed in the past because and only to the extent that Parliament had declared that they so existed.

Pigeon J. adopted his *Drybones* reasoning in *A.-G.Canada v. Lavell; Isaac v. Bedard*.[69] Indeed, he claimed that the majority in

Lavell had finally realised the implication of legislative supremacy for the construction of Canadian Bill of Rights.[70] Pigeon J. again adopted the principle of "legislative supremacy" as the central element in his reasons for judgment in *The Queen* v. *Burnshine*[71] and *A. G. Canada* v. *Canard*.[72]

Pigeon J. has not been alone in his utilisation of the principle of "legislative supremacy" so as to restrict the effect of the alleged fundamental rights in the Canadian Bill of Rights. His dissenting judgment in *Drybones* was accompanied by Abbott J. Abbott J. relied upon the principle of "legislative supremacy" as the sole reason for overriding the supposed fundamental rights in the Canadian Bill of Rights. Justice Abbott held that

> the interpretation of the *Bill of Rights*, adopted by the courts below, necessarily implies a wide delegation of the legislative authority of Parliament to the courts. The power to make such a delegation cannot be questioned but, in my view, it would require the plainest words to impute to Parliament an intention to extend to the courts, such an invitation to engage in judicial legislation. I cannot find that intention expressed in s.2 of the *Bill*.[73]

What is most important in understanding Justice Ritchie's majority judgments in *Lavell* and *Regina* v. *Miller and Cockriell*[74] as well as the "frozen meaning" doctrine more generally is the connection between the "frozen meaning" doctrine, on the one hand, and legislative supremacy on the other. The principle underlying certain elements in Ritchie J.'s judgments in *Lavell* and *Miller and Cockriell* is that the courts possess a duty to follow whatever the legislature declares so long as the legislature has legislative authority pursuant to Sections 91 and 92 of the British North America Act, 1867. The notion of legislative supremacy lies behind Ritchie J.'s exclamation in *Lavell*, for example, that

> to suggest that the provisions of the Bill of Rights have the effect of making the whole Indian Act inoperative as discriminatory is to assert that the Bill has rendered Parliament powerless to exercise the authority entrusted to it under the Constitution of enacting legislation which treats Indians living on reserves differently from other Canadians in relation to their property and civil rights.[75]

Ritchie J. went on to return approvingly to the *Drybones* dicta of Justice Pigeon that

> If one of the effects of the *Canadian Bill of Rights* is to render inoperative all legal provisions whereby Indians as such are not dealt with in the same way as the general public, the conclusion is inescapable that Parliament... has also made any future use of federal legislative authori-

ty over them [i.e., Indians] subject to the requirement of expressly declaring every time "that the law shall operate notwithstanding the Canadian Bill of Rights." I find it very difficult to believe... one would have expected this important change to be made explicitly not surreptitiously so to speak.[76]

Ritchie J. used this dicta to rebut the contention that the alleged fundamental rights in the Canadian Bill of Rights should override special legislation.[77]

In the more recent case of *Regina* v. *Miller and Cockriell*[78] Ritchie J. confronted counsel's argument that the mandatory death penalty was cruel and unusual punishment contrary to Section 2(b) of the Canadian Bill of Rights. Justice Ritchie, who delivered the main majority judgment, repeated the familiar "frozen meaning" doctrine.[79] He held that the meaning of "cruel and unusual punishment" was the meaning which it bore when the Canadian Bill of Rights was enacted; namely, 1960. In 1960 "there did not exist and had never existed in Canada the right not to be deprived of life." Parliament could not possibly have intended to abolish the death penalty "by such an oblique method" as proscribing "cruel and unusual punishment" in the Canadian Bill of Rights.

Ritchie J. gave a great deal of weight to the fact that Parliament had seen fit to retain the death penalty pursuant to certain Criminal Code amendments *after* the passage of the Canadian Bill of Rights. Accordingly, the Criminal Code Amendments constituted "strong evidence" of the nature and scope of the individual's right not to be subjected to "cruel and unusual punishment". Although the Court did not have an explicit duty to assess current community standards of morality, Justice Ritchie believed that the Court was directly doing so by relying heavily upon Parliament's latest enactments. In his words, current community standards of morality were "essentially questions of policy and as such they were of necessity considerations effecting the decision of Parliament as to whether the death penalty should be retained.'[80] Ritchie J.'s frame of reference clearly contemplated that Parliament quite properly functioned as the dictator and evaluator of Canada's fundamental rights because, in contrast to the court, Parliament more accurately reflected the contemporary values of the Canadian society.

Justices Pigeon, Abbott and Ritchie have been accompanied by Martland, J., Laskin C.J.C. and others in their reliance upon the principle of legislative supremacy as their method for establishing the meaning, scope and effect of the fundamental rights set out in the Canadian Bill of Rights. Justice Martland explained his majority judgment in *Burnshine* on the ground that when the Canadian Bill of Rights was enacted, the concept of "equality before the law" could not possibly have been wider in scope than at the time of the *Burnshine* case because such a meaning "would have involved a substantial impairment of the sovereignty of Parliament in the exercise of its legislative powers under Section 91 of the British North America Act and could only have been created by constitutional amendment, or by statute.'[81] Martland J. went on to emphasise that *"it is not the function of this Court,* under the Bill of Rights, to prevent the operation of a federal enactment, designed for this purpose, on the ground that it applies only to one class of persons, or to a particular area."[82]

Chief Justice Laskin has invariably dissented from the orthodoxy expressed by Justices Pigeon, Abbott and Martland. And yet, he too has used legislative supremacy as a pivotal factor in his own method for establishing the meaning, scope and effect of fundamental rights as set out in the Canadian Bill of Rights. In dicta which Laskin C.J.C. laid down in *Curr* v. *The Queen*[83] and which the majority of the Supreme Court subsequently adopted in *Burnshine*,[84] Laskin C.J.C. announced that whether Section 1(a) of the Canadian Bill of Rights or, indeed, any other provision of the Bill controlled substantive federal legislation "did not directly arise in *R.* v. *Drybones.*" Laskin continued that when substantive — as opposed to procedural — law was at stake,

> compelling reasons ought to be advanced to justify the Court in this case to employ a statutory (as contrasted with a constitutional) jurisdiction to deny operative effect to a substantive measure duly enacted by a Parliament constitutionally competent to do so, and exercising its powers in accordance with the tenets of responsible government, which underlie the discharge of legislative authority under the *British North America Act, 1867.*

Chief Justice Laskin's respect for legislative supremacy was reflected, once again, when he went on to assert in *Curr* that the American experience with the "due process" clause had little application to Canada because, in Canada, *"the major role is played by elected representatives of the people."*[85] Laskin C.J.C. developed his analysis of the effect of the "fundamental" rights by emphasizing in *Burnshine* that "the primary injunction of the Bill" was

> to determine whether a challenged measure is open to a compatible construction that would enable it to remain an effective enactment. If the process of construction in the light of the Bill yields this result, it is unnecessary and, indeed, it would be *an abuse of judicial power to sterilize the federal measure.*[86]

74

b. *Some Problems with the "Legislative Supremacy" Form of the "Contemporary Values" Argument*

As with the "shock the conscience" and the "will of the majority" forms, so also "legislative supremacy" suffers from important practical and theoretical limitations as a method of argument in support of the existence of fundamental rights. It was argued above that certain practical factors render a sense of mythology to the use of the term "will of the majority". The impossibility of quantifying and comparing the citizenry's feelings toward different possible rights; the difficulty of obtaining a consensus with respect to an agenda of potential fundamental rights; the problem of a consensus with respect to the critical issues; the statistical difficulty of measuring the intensity of opinions; and, finally, the issue of deciding what per cent should constitute "the majority": these factors suggest that one should be sceptical of the claim by any politician, political party, interest group or judge that the "will of the majority" justifies restrictions upon liberty or social justice. These obstacles also confront any "will of the legislature" method of ascertaining society's contemporary values.

An additional set of problems with respect to the latter method could be appreciated if we could speculate as to how a judiciary would deal with a statute which had expressly created and delineated specified fundamental rights. Alas, speculation is unnecessary, for the Parliament of Canada enacted such a statute in 1960[87] and, as we have seen, the supremacy of Parliament has been a central factor in the judicial construction of the statute.

The long title, Section one and the preamble of the Canadian Bill of Rights all describe the enacted rights as *human* rights and the freedoms as *fundamental* ones. The preamble provides that by enacting the Bill the Canadian Parliament was affirming that the Canadian Nation was founded upon human rights and fundamental freedoms. Parliament's directive was emphatic: the rights and freedoms had existed and *"shall* continue to exist"; and *every* law in Canada *"shall* be construed and applied so as not to abrogate, abridge or infringe these rights and freedoms." Parliament believed the rights and freedoms so fundamental that they were to prevail over any conflict with *any* statutory, judicial, customary or regulatory rule unless Parliament "expressly declared" that the latter conflicting rule was to operate "notwithstanding the Canadian Bill of Rights." *No court* had authority to restrict a right or freedom unless Parliament had prefaced such a restriction with a "notwithstanding" clause.

Despite the clear, imperative nature of Parliament's directive in the Canadian Bill of Rights, the Canadian judiciary has still been required to construe the meaning and scope of the rights in concrete circumstances. And the courts have had available ample techniques with which to construe the rights and freedoms narrowly. As Professor Willis once argued in his important essay "Statute Interpretation in a Nutshell,"[88] there are three different techniques for determining legislative intent (the "literal", "absurdity" and "mischief" approaches), all equally valid. Each technique can lead to a different conclusion. Contemporary Canadian decisions reflect the continued validity of his thesis.[89] Even if, by a combination of the three approaches, one "purpose" could be obtained, our courts have ample devices to avoid, enlarge and restrict the "purpose" of a statutory enactment. Statutory presumptions are but one example.[90]

And so, for example, the Supreme Court of Canada has very narrowly construed the "fundamental freedom" of "equality before the law" as guaranteed by Section 1(b) of the Canadian Bill of Rights. Adopting Dicey's 1885 definition of "legal equality" from the *Law of the Constitution*,[91] the *Lavell* Court[92] defined the term as "equality in the administration and application of the law by the law enforcement authorities and the ordinary courts of the land." The majority of the Supreme Court again confirmed this construction in *Burnshine*.[93] The consequence of this "equal application" construction is, of course, that "equality before the law" is consistent with both a society of slaves and a government of tyranny. According to the Supreme Court's definition of "equality before the law", the judiciary's function is not to scrutinize the moral content of legislation. Rather, the court need merely ensure the equal application of the law within any class of persons created by the legislature. The most arbitrary forms of racial or religious discrimination and the most authoritarian, oppressive regimes could be consistently justified pursuant to this construction so long as our laws were evenly applied.

Similarly, Parliament expressly provided in the Canadian Bill of Rights that due process of law and the right to counsel shall be fundamental freedoms in Canada.[94] Despite the clarity and imperativeness of Parliament's direction, the Canadian Supreme Court has so narrowly construed these rights that it is difficult to suggest that they are fundamental in any real sense. By virtue of *Curr*,[95] the right to counsel is limited only to persons who explicitly request the right. According to the majority in *Brownridge* v. *The Queen*[96] the request must be made *bona fide* rather than "for the purpose of delay or for some other improper reason." The individual must sufficiently inform himself of Canadian law that

76

he knows that his right to counsel is fundamental. The Supreme Court held in *O'Connor* v. *The Queen* that the circumstances must be such that the exercise of the right would have actually made a practical difference to the disposition of the accused's case.[97] And, as the facts in *Hogan* v. *The Queen* demonstrate, the individual who wishes to exercise his right must be of unusual fortitude.[98]

In addition to construing the meaning and scope of fundamental freedoms narrowly, the Canadian courts have scrutinized alleged infringements of the freedoms with the same strictness as if fundamental freedoms were not at issue. We shall shortly see in chapter III that the level of judicial scrutiny of legislation which allegedly infringes a fundamental right is a crucial determinant of the outcome in any case. The *Burnshine*[99] and *Canard*[100] decisions illustrate that the Supreme Court has been quick to find some hypothetical reason for the statutory classification allegedly infringing "equality before the law". Indeed, the level of judicial scrutiny in the *Burnshine* case was something less than a diluted "minimum rationality" test in that Burnshine was required to establish "compelling reasons" why the statutory classification was not related to the statutory purpose.[101]

The majority of our Supreme Court justices believe that they have been construing and applying the "fundamental" freedoms and "human" rights in the manner Parliament really intended. If we grant the belief of the majority and if its construction of the Canadian Bill of Rights is what Parliament in fact intended, then the use of "legislative supremacy" as the method for establishing the existence and scope of fundamental rights rests upon sandy ground. The Canadian experience demonstrates that, where the roots of fundamental rights are considered to be the contemporary values of society as reflected in the notion of "legislative supremacy", those roots can be quite weak in practice.

The disappointing Canadian experience points to the important conceptual weakness of the "will of the majority" and "legislative supremacy" methods of establishing the existence of fundamental rights. How can a right be considered fundamental if the legislature creates all rights, determines their meaning and scope, and possesses the authority to destroy them? Whether an individual possesses a right depends entirely upon the beliefs of the legislative majority at any particular moment in history. The legislative majority could enslave a minority of the total populace. Indeed, the legislative majority could conceivably enslave a majority of the populace for political judgments are left to the legislature, not to the citizenry. There would be little to prevent the legislative majority from legislating and even adjudicating indeterminate sentences upon political dissidents. What is more, the legislative majority could legitimately withhold a right whenever it so desired, in which case the right would simply be explained away as no longer fundamental. The "tyranny of the majority" which Mill so feared would remain a conceptual possibility. There would be no immunity from the legislative denial of our rights and freedoms. There would, therefore, be no rights and freedoms which we could accurately describe as "the root of the matter", "essential", "indispensable", "irreducible" or fundamental.

Unlike the "will of the majority" analysis, however, the notion of legislative supremacy suffers from an added limitation. It lacks the important participatory element found in democratic thought. One common element in the meaning of democracy has been the idea of participation in political decision-making by the people. The prime source of participation under the legislative supremacy framework has been the electoral process. The electoral process is just that — a *process* which permits the citizen to approve or disapprove the performance of the legislator. The citizen is given the opportunity to determine which elite is to be permitted to participate in the actual political decision-making. By contributing campaign funds, writing editorials or, possibly, by playing the role of an "apparachiki", the citizen may even influence the actual composition and direction of a political elite. But it would be difficult to suggest that legislative supremacy by itself contemplates that the citizen directly, let alone intimately, participates in the decisions which affect his/her life. For, in theory at least, deliberation and decision are left to the legislature.

This latter point is confirmed by a further limitation of "legislative supremacy" as a method of argument. It is difficult to speak of legislative supremacy as a realistic viable form of ascertaining society's values when political scientists in Canada[102] and Great Britain[103] no longer consider the legislature to be the supreme political institution in the body politic. Statutes and even more so, the statutory instruments made thereunder, are no longer the true product of society's contemporary values — at least as the values are reflected by society's representatives in the House of Commons. Other sources of power have gradually arisen relative to the role Parliament used to play in the legislative process when the courts acknowledged legislative supremacy as the fundamental principle of the Constitution.[104] Large party machines have arisen with positive and negative sanctions (for example, patronage, withdrawal of election funds, withdrawal of official support in the elections, and the like.) The political parties have influenced the

78

voting patterns of Members of Parliament as well as the type of candidate likely to stand for election. The choice of issues in election campaigns emanate from central party headquarters. Major policy initiatives came to be made initially by the Cabinet (after the 1880s) and eventually (especially after World War II) by a large, complex bureaucracy. Political power is not exercised so much when the Cabinet approves the various alternatives presented to it but rather when senior public servants determine the issues and articulate what they consider to be the realistic alternatives.

Political scientists have documented how, indeed, the initiation of legislative policy rarely proceeds from the Commons itself.[105] Even in the case where a Minister himself initiates a legislative policy it is a bureaucrat — the draftsman — who rounds out the policy and who decides the "practicality" of implementing the legislative policy.[106] Once the proposed bill reaches the floor of the House, party discipline within the majority party as well as House Standing Orders militate against any substantial amendment to a bill either from opposition members or backbenchers of the majority party. The dialectical debate within the Chamber possesses an air of unreality except in those relatively rare circumstances when a minority government exists.

The relations between the Commons and the Crown's advisers have been transformed to such an extent since Parliament became the supreme political institution in 1689 that to hang upon the legislature the existence, meaning or scope of a freedom is nothing less than judicial abdication of responsibility. Whereas the constitutional principle of "legislative supremacy" arose over a century after the legislature had, in fact, become the supreme political institution in the body politic of Great Britain, Canadian courts have retained the legal principle even though the legislature is no longer the supreme political institution.[107] The constitutional principle but political fiction of "legislative supremacy" provides a weak foundation for the existence of fundamental rights. Indeed, the very political subordination of the legislature in the legislative process in Canada and England provides a significant consideration in favour of Professor Lusky's thesis that the court ought to possess a special role in protecting "discrete and insular minorities" and in preventing "legislative" interference with such traditionally considered fundamental rights as political expression, political assembly and religion.[108]

c. *The Problem of Legislative Supremacy in the United Kingdom and Canadian Constitutions*

On the other hand, one might suggest that I have entirely ignored the importance of the principle of legislative supremacy in the United Kingdom and Canadian constitutions. It might be submitted that the concerns raised above, though accurate, are entirely academic for our courts are obligated to follow the Constitution and *the Constitution* requires that the legislature be supreme. One can reply to this submission only by examining why it is supposed that our Constitution requires that the legislature be supreme.

What is meant by the term "legislative supremacy"? Notwithstanding his exposition of the relationship between human laws and the law of nature in the first ninety-two pages of his *Commentaries*,[109] Sir William Blackstone took the position that "The power and jurisdiction of Parliament is so transcendent and absolute, that it cannot be confined either for causes or persons, within any bounds."[110] He continued,

> it hath sovereign and uncontrollable authority in making, confining, enlarging, restraining, abrogating, repealing, reviving and expounding of laws, concerning matters of all possible denominations, ecclesiastical and temporal, civil, military, maritime or criminal: this being the place where absolute despotic power, which must in all governments reside somewhere, is entrusted by the constitution of these kingdoms. ...
> it can, in short, do everything that is not naturally impossible; and therefore some have not scrupled to call its power the omnipotence of parliament. True is that what the parliament doth, no authority upon earth can undo...

By the time that Dicey had studied the concept of legislative supremacy in the mid-nineteenth century, he had recognised an important problem.[111] On the one hand, he acknowledged that Parliament's authority was unlimited. On the other hand, he believed that Parliament was not supreme in actual power. The real sovereign power, Dicey believed, was with the will of the people. Dicey thought that he could escape from the dilemma by distinguishing between legal and political sovereignty.

Professor Heuston has restricted the term even more so by suggesting that "the courts will accept as finally authoritative any document which is in truth the authentic expression of the sovereign's will."[112] Accordingly, the courts would possess authority to scrutinize whether any document is, indeed, an "authentic expression". J. B. Mitchell, on the other hand, seems to contemplate a wider definition by describing legislative supremacy as "the absence of any *legal* restraint upon the legislative power of the

United Kingdom Parliament."[113] This absence of legal restraint has two elements:

> The positive one would mean that Parliament is competent to legislate upon any subject-matter, and the negative aspect implies that once Parliament has legislated no court or other person can pass judgment upon the validity of the legislation.

Professor H. W. R. Wade, for his part, has concluded that the English doctrine of legislative supremacy centers upon three propositions: first, that the Houses of Parliament alone can exercise control over their internal proceedings; secondly, that statutes are conclusive in the sense that courts have no jurisdiction to examine the legislative process lying behind the enactment on a statute; and thirdly, that Parliament may not bind itself into the future.[114]

However refined one's definition of "legislative supremacy" the question remains. *Why* may no authority on earth "undo" what the Parliament doth? Why will the courts accept as "finally authoritative" any document which is in truth the authentic expression of the legislature's will? Why is the legislature "competent to legislate upon any subject-matter"? Why may Parliament not "bind itself" into the future?

The traditional response in Canada would be, of course, that the British North America Act, 1867, so declares. But in what Section(s) of the British North America Act does one find the above propositions? Do Sections 91 and 92 enact that the federal and provincial legislatures may legislate upon *all* subject-matters? What Section of the British North America Act provides that Canadian courts may pass judgment only upon jurisdictional disputes involving Sections 91 and 92? Section 17 enacts that "there shall be One Parliament for Canada."[115] Other provisions of the Act require a time limit for the calling and dissolution of Parliament.[116] These provisions, however, in no way require that the legislatures are supreme in any of the senses elaborated by leading jurists. Nor do the provisions relating to the Judicature[117] proscribe the courts from passing judgment upon enactments of the legislatures, nor for that matter, do the Judicature provisions direct the courts to accept as finally authoritative any expression of the legislature's will. One might finally resort to the preamble of the British North America Act according to which Canada is to have a Constitution "similar in principle to that of the United Kingdoms." By virtue of the preamble, it might be submitted, Canada had adopted the principle of legislative supremacy in the 1867 United Kingdom Constitution.[118] Unfortunately, interpretation principles in the United Kingdom require that one may use a preamble only to resolve an ambiguity or incongruity within the existing enacting portion of a statute.[119] There is no such ambiguity or incongruity within the British North America Act, 1867.

Let us assume that the British North America Act did require that Parliament be supreme. The issue would remain, why are the Canadian courts obligated to follow the British North America Act? A student of law would answer that the British North America Act was a duly enacted instrument of the United Kingdom Parliament. But why, in turn, should the Canadian courts follow the United Kingdom Parliament? Again, the student would have a reply. Canada was, at the passing of the British North America Act, subject to the United Kingdom Parliament and, in addition, the United Kingdom Parliament had duly enacted the British North America Act according to the proper manner and form requirements at the time.

This line of response leads us back to the orginal question. For, what gives the "manner and form" requirements their authority? One can trace the statutory, common law or customary basis of "manner and form" requirements in Canada and Great Britain only so far until one returns to the issue originally posed. If the courts will obey any legal rule which alters a "manner and form" requirement itself, we must ask this question: what institution can alter the "manner and form" requirement and why should the courts obey the new rule?

It is submitted that Professor Wade pointed in the right direction when he suggested that the courts obey statutes not because of any legal rule but because of political history.[120] That is, the source of the constitutional obligation of courts lies in the world of political norms, not the Austinian world of legal rules. Quoting approvingly from Salmond, Wade explained,

> all rules of law have historical sources. As a matter of fact and history they have their origin somewhere, though we may not know what it is. But not all of them have legal sources. Where this so, it would be necessary for the law to proceed *ad infinitum* in tracing the descent of its principles. It is requisite that the law should postulate one or more first causes, whose operation is ultimate and whose authority is underived. ... The rule that a man may not ride a bicycle on the footpath may have its source in the by-laws of a municipal council; the rule that these by-laws have the force of law has its source in an Act of Parliament. But whence comes the rule that Acts of Parliament have the force of law? This is legally ultimate; its source is historical only, not legal. ... It is the law because it is the law, and for no other reason that it is possible for the law itself to take notice of. *No statute can confer this power upon Parliament, for this would be to assume and act on the very power that is to be conferred.*[121]

The principle of legislative supremacy has its authority, in other words, with the Revolutionary Settlement of 1688.

The implications of Wade's important point are clear. First, the question rises to the fore as to whether or not the important political facts and vaules which led the courts to adopt the principle of legislative supremacy have undergone sufficient change since 1688 to justify a new or amended *grundnorm*, a new constitutionally binding principle.

Secondly, the law student's reliance upon the Canadian Constitution is not the ultimate rebuttal to the problems which I have raised in this chapter with respect to the "legislative supremacy" argument for the existence of fundamental rights. The reason why "the Constitution" inadequately rebuts the problems raised above is that the Constitution itself rests upon *normative*, political assumptions. As a consequence, the student is required to question whether "legislative supremacy" *ought to* provide the political assumption underlying the elaboration of the meaning and scope of our fundamental rights by the judiciary. That is, the very nature of constitutional obligation in Canada begs that the student (and the lawyer) ask normative questions as a legitimate inquiry in Canadian constitutional analysis. The judge, lawyer or law student who uses the constitutional principle of "legislative supremacy" as the reason to discard normative questions as merely academic questions is himself making a value judgment in the world of political norms.

This would seem to suggest that counsel[122] and judge alike have avoided their duties during recent years when they have elaborated the principles of the common law, as in the "abuse of process" cases,[123] without addressing normative or "ought" questions. This also suggests why counsel and judge alike have lived in an "Alice in Wonderland" world of "make-believe" when they have tried to construe and apply statutes in the light of the Canadian Bill of Rights without asking normative or "ought" questions.[124] The irony is that the approaches of Justices Pigeon, Ritchie and Martland, as described earlier in this chapter for example,[125] appear to contradict Parliament's own instruction in the Canadian Bill of Rights that *the Courts*, as well as Parliament, have the responsibility of actively protecting our fundamental rights by making moral-political judgments concerning the meaning and scope of our fundamental rights.[126] Our Supreme Court has incorporated its own moral-political values into its judgments by assuming that the Court could consistently remain "apolitical" by leaving the moral-political issues to Parliament and the Government.

A third implication flows from the source of constitutional obligation in Canada. "Legislative supremacy" is a mere conception, not a perception.[127] It is a real constitutional principle because it is deeply believed in. The "constitutional" obligation thrust upon Canadian courts that they have a duty not to restrain the legislature is real because the participants (that is, the lawyers, judges, and legislators) act *as if* that obligation were real.

These three implications which flow from the nature of constitutional obligation are confirmed when one appreciates the historical time lapse between the rise of the political supremacy of the United Kingdom Parliament, on the one hand, and the court's eventual acknowledgment of that supremacy, on the other. English courts did not displace Chief Justice Coke's theory of fundamental rights immediately after the Glorious Revolution of 1688. In *King* v. *Earl of Banbury* (1694)[128] and *The City of London* v. *Wood* (1701)[129] for example, Chief Justice Holt relied upon *Dr. Bonham's Case*[130] as authority for the proposition that judges "construe and expound Acts of Parliament, and adjudge them to be void." In the 1754 judgment of *McKenzie* v. *Stewart*[131] Lord Hardwicke L.C. asserted that he would never have followed a particular statute had it ever been suggested that the statute had been obtained by fraudulent means. Later House of Lords decisions of *Biddulph* v. *Biddulph* (1790)[132] and *Green* v. *Mortimer* (1861)[133] similarly contemplated a more active judicial approach than the doctrine of legislative supremacy holds. It does not seem to be until the second quarter of nineteenth century at the earliest that English courts began to accept the constituent elements of legislative supremcy.

More particularly, we have already noted that Professor Wade has suggested that the English doctrine of legislative supremacy centers upon three propositions: first, that the Houses of Parliament alone can exercise control over their internal proceedings; secondly, that statutes are conclusive in the sense that the courts have no jurisdiction to examine the legislative process lying behind the enactment of a statute; and thirdly, that Parliament may not bind itself into the future.[134] Although the first principle was laid down in Section 9 of the Bill of Rights, 1689, the English courts did not definitively accept the principle that the Houses of Parliament alone could control their internal proceedings until *Stockdale* v. *Hansard* (1839).[135] The English courts did not accept the second, "conclusiveness of statutes" proposition until the 1835 decision of *The Proprietors of the Edinburgh and Dalkeith Ry. Co.* v. *John Wauchope*.[136] Even then, however, the *Wauchope* court's statement of the proposition of the "conclusiveness of statutes" was mere *obiter dicta* limited, in addition, to facts involving private rather than public bills.[137] United Kingdom and Canadian courts repeated the dicta until 1974 when the House of Lords finally adopted the principle as the *ratio* of its decision.[138] Interestingly, it does not appear to be before 1914 that English or Canadian courts adopted the third element of "legislative supremacy" (that is, that the legislature may not bind itself into the future).[139]

The history of the rise of "legislative supremacy" in English and Canadian constitutional law leads one to conclude that the second and third elements of the constitutional principle of "legislative supremacy" were judicial, rather than legislative, creations. And yet, these very judicially created propositions underlie the repeated explanations, by counsel and judiciary alike, for judicial passivity toward legislative infringements of fundamental rights.

But why is this so? How can the courts create two principles and then religiously follow them as if they were part of the constitution? The explanation lies in the world of normative political values, not in law. The two judicially created principles merely represented the judiciary's recognition of the political norm or desire that Parliament (and, in particular, the Commons) *ought* to be supreme over all other institutions in the body politic. Political supremacy was finally established with the Bill of Rights, 1689. The judiciary's recognition of the political reality took another century and a half.

But if this is so, if normative political values underlie Canadian and English judicial passivity in the protection of fundamental rights, counsel may legitimately insist that the judiciary re-examine the traditional character of argument which has been used to support the existence, meaning and scope of fundamental rights. Indeed, counsel has a duty to insist upon such a re-examination in the light of the problems encountered above with the "backward looking" and "contemporary societal values" arguments. The very nature of constitutional obligation in the United Kingdom and Canada requires that counsel search beyond the traditional resource material of the law for his arguments in support of fundamental rights. I shall begin to make such an inquiry in chapters IV to VI.

1. Lord Patrick Devlin, *The Enforcement of Morals*, (New York, Toronto: Oxford Univ. Press, 1965).

2. Ibid., p. 15.

3. Ibid.

4. Ibid., p. 94.

5. Ibid., p. 15.

6. Ibid., p. 91.

7. Ibid., p. 17.

8. Ibid., pp. 91-92.

9. 408 U.S. 238, 92 S. Ct. 2726, 33 L. Ed. 2d 346 (1972).

10. The Eighth Amendment reads, "Excessive bail shall not be required nor excessive fines imposed, nor cruel and unusual punishments inflicted."

11. Quoting from Chief Justice Warren in *Trop* v. *Dulles*, 356 U.S. 86, 101, 78 S. Ct. 590, 2 L. Ed. 2d 630 (1958).

12. *Furman* v. *Georgia*, 408 U.S. 238, 330, 92 S. Ct. 2726, 33 L. Ed. 2d 346 (1972).

13. Ibid., 360 ff.

14. Ibid., 362.

15. 428 U.S. 153, 232, 96 S. Ct., 2621, 2973 (1976).

16. Austin Sarat and Neil Vidmar, *Public Opinion, The Death Penalty, and the Eighth Amendment: Testing the Marshall Hypothesis*, Wisc. L. Rev. 171 (1976).

17. 302 U.S. 319, 58 S. Ct. 149, 82 L. Ed. 288 (1937).

18. Quoting from *Snyder* v. *Mass.*, 291 U.S. 97, 54 S. Ct. 67 (1934).

19. Quoting from *Hebert* v. *Louisiana*, 272 U.S. 312, 47 S. Ct. 103 (1926).

20. 332 U.S. 46, 67 S. Ct. 1672, 91 L. Ed. 1903 (1947).

21. *Rochin* v. *California*, 342 U.S. 165, 72 S. Ct. 205, 96 L. Ed. 183 (1952).

22. *Irvine* v. *California*, 347 U.S. 128, 74 S. Ct. 381, 98 L. Ed. 561 (1954).

23. Walter Lippmann, *Public Opinion* (New York: Free Press, 1965).

24. Ronald Dworkin, "Lord Devlin and the Enforcement of Morals", 75 *Yale L.J.* 986 (1961). Dworkin argued that for one to take a valid moral position he must be able to give a reason for it. But not every reason will do. Reasons which do not count are those of prejudice, personal emotional reaction, patently false propositions of fact (that is, they challenge "the minimal standards of evidence and argument I generally accept and impose upon others"), and the "parroting" or simple citation of other persons' beliefs.

25. John Stuart Mill, *On Liberty*, ed. Mary Warnock (London: Fontana, 1962), p. 131:

> ...but an opinion on a point of conduct, *not supported by reasons*, can only count as one person's *preference*; and if the reasons when given, are a mere appeal to a similar preference felt by other people, it is still only many people's liking instead of one. [emphasis added]

26. Lord Devlin, supra note I, p. 15.

27. *Rochin* v. *California*, 342 U.S. 165, 72 S. Ct. 205, 96 L. Ed. 183 (1952).

28. *Irvine* v. *California*, 347 U.S. 128, 74 S. Ct. 381, 98 L. Ed. 561 (1954).

29. It has been argued, for example, that the North American lawyer's belief in "reasoned elaboration" of an opinion has been only one phase — and a passing phase at that — in the evolution of legal academic thinking in North America. See generally, White, *The Evolution of Reasoned Elaboration: Jurisprudential Criticism and Social Change*, 59 Va. L. Rev. 279 (1973).

30. The importance of principled criteria underlying a body of law has been emphasized by Herbert Wechsler in *Toward Neutral Principles of Constitutional Law*, 78 Harv. L. Rev. 1 (1959). Whether or not "neutral" principled criteria are possible is another question. See, e.g., Arthur S. Miller and Ronald F. Howell, *The Myth of Neutrality in Constitutional Adjudication*, 27 U. Chi. L. Rev. 661 (1960); Louis H. Pollak, *Racial Discrimination and Judicial Integrity: A Reply to Professor Wechsler*, 108 U. Pa. L. Rev. 1 (1959). I have argued elsewhere that, notwithstanding his desire to separate his personal moral-political values from his judicial decisions, Mr. Justice Holmes could not succeed in doing so. William E. Conklin, *The Political Theory of Mr. Justice Holmes*, 26 Chitty's L.J. 200 (1978).

31. Jeremy Bentham, *A Fragment on Government*, ed. F. Montague (Oxford: Clarendon Press, 1891) [hereinafter cited as *A Fragment*].

32. Jeremy Bentham, *An Introduction to the Principles of Morals and Legislation*, ed. L. J. Lafleur (New York: Hafner, 1948) [hereinafter cited as *An Introduction*].

33. A book of jurisprudence can have but one or the other of two objects: 1. To ascertain what the *law* is. 2. To ascertain what it ought to be. In the former case it may be styled a book of *expository* jurisprudence; in the latter, a book of *censorial* jurisprudence; or, in other words, a book on the *art of legislation*. Jeremy Bentham, ibid., p. 324.

34. Jeremy Bentham, ibid., chap. 1, para. 1.

35. Jeremy Bentham, ibid., chap. 1, para. 3.

36. Jeremy Bentham, ibid., chap. 13, para. 1.

37. Jeremy Bentham, ibid., chap. 3, para. 1. In his *Principles of Judicial Procedure* Bentham asserted that

of the substantive branch of the law, the only defensible object, or say end in view, is the maximization of the happiness of the greatest number of the members of the community in question. ... Consistently with the nature of man, and the preservation of his species, no other could any extensive body of law have had for its end in view.

as reprinted in *Works of Jeremy Bentham*, ed. J. Bowring, 11 vols. (New York: Russell & Russell Inc., 1962) vol. 2, p. 6 [hereinafter cited as Bentham, *Works*].

38. Emphasis original.

39. Jeremy Bentham, *An Introduction*, supra, note 32, chap. 3, para. 1.

40. Jeremy Bentham, *An Introduction*, supra, note 32, chap. 1, paras. 2, 6, 7; *A Fragment*, supra, note 32, chap. 1, para. 45.

41. Jeremy Bentham, *An Introduction*, supra, note 32, chap. 1, para. 3.

42. As Bentham himself explained in *Securities Against Misrule*,

[G]overnment is good in proportion as it contributes to the greatest happiness of the greatest number; namely, of the members of the community in which it has place. Rule may therefore come under the denomination of misrule in either of two ways; either by taking for its object the happiness of any other number than the greatest, or by being more or less unsuccessful in its endeavours to contribute to the greatest happiness of the greatest number.

as reprinted in Bentham, *Works*, supra, note 37, vol. 8, p. 558.

43. Jeremy Bentham, *An Introduction*, supra, note 32, chap. 5, para. 2,3.

44. Jeremy Bentham, ibid., chap. 5, paras. 4 to 33.

45. Jeremy Bentham, ibid., chap. 6.

46. "Fecundity" meant the chance which a pleasure (or pain) had of being followed by sensations of the *same* kind. J. Bentham, ibid., chap. 6, para. 5.

47. "Purity" meant the chance of a pleasure not being followed by a sensation of pain and vice versa. J. Bentham, ibid., chap. 6, para. 6. Thus, a pleasure would have high fecundity if there were a great chance of it being followed by another pleasure; and it would be very pure if there were little chance of it being followed by a pain.

48. "Extent" refers to the number of persons who are affected by a pleasure or pain.

49. Jean-Paul Sartre, *Anti-Semite and Jew*, trans. by George J. Becker, (New York: Schocken Books, Inc., 1965).

50. Jeremy Bentham, *An Introduction*, supra, note 32, chap. 16, para. 1.

51. Jeremy Bentham, ibid., chap. 15, para. 2; chap. 13, paras. 1-3. Note also his explanation for the defences of consent, infancy, insanity and intoxication, *ibid.*, chap. 13, paras. 4, 9.

52. John S. Mill, *Utlitarianism* in *Essential Works of John Stuart Mill*, ed. Max Lerner, (New York, Toronto, London: Bantam Books, 1961), p. 246.

53. See generally Jeremy Bentham's discussion of the distribution of wealth in *Pannomial Fragments* as reprinted in Bentham, *Works*, supra, note 37, vol. 3, pp. 228-230; and in *Logical Arrangements*, ibid., pp. 293-294.

For his connection of inequality to the greatest happiness of the greatest number see generally, *The Constitutional Code*, ibid., vol. 9, pp. 14-18; and *Leading Principles of the Constitutional Code, for any State*, ibid., vol. 2, pp. 271-272.

54. Jeremy Bentham, *An Introduction*, supra, note 32, chap. 1, para. 10.

55. Jeremy Bentham, *Anarchial Fallacies*, *Works*, supra note 37, vol. 2, p. 520. Emphasis original.

56. See generally, Jeremy Bentham, *An Introduction*, supra, note 32.

57. J. Austin, *Lectures on Jurisprudence*, 2nd. ed. (1861; reprint ed.,

New York: Lennox Hill Co., 1970), vol. 1, p. 242 [hereinafter cited as Austin, *Lectures*].

58. Jeremy Bentham, *Anarchial Fallacies, Works*, supra, note 37, vol. 2, p. 501.

59. Jeremy Bentham, *ibid.*, p. 523.

60. John Austin, *Lectures* supra, note 57, p. 242.

61. Edmund Burke, "Speech to the Electors of Bristol," November 3rd, 1774, as reprinted in B. W. Hill's *Edmund Burke: On Government, Politics and Society* (Harvester Press Ltd., 1975), p. 157.

62. See, for example, *Labrador Company* v. *The Queen*, [1893] A.C. 104, 123 per Lord Hannen (P.C.); *Hoani te Heuhen Tukino* v. *Aotea District Maori Land Board*, [1941] A.C. 308, 322 per Viscount Simon L. C. (P.C.).

63. See generally, *The Proprietors of the Edinburgh and Dalkeith Ry. Co.* v. *John Wauchope* (1842), 8 Cl. & Finn. 710, 8 E.R. 279 (H.L.); *Lee* v. *Bude and Torrington Junction Ry. Co.* (1871), 6 L.R. 576 (C.P.); and *British Railways Board* v. *Pickin*, [1974] A.C. 765, [1974] 2 W.L.R. 208 (H.L.) reversing [1972] 3 All E.R. 923, [1973] Q.B. 219, [1972] 3 W.L.R. 824 (C.A.).

64. This notion has a long history and, as a result, is deep-rooted. See generally, *Duke of Argyle* v. *Commissioners of Inland Revenue*, [1914] L.T. 893 (K.B.); *Vauxhall Estates Ltd.* v. *Liverpool Corp.*, [1932] 1 K.B. 733, 743, 745, per Avory J. (K.B.); *Ellen Street Estates Ltd.* v. *Minister of Health*, [1934] 1 K.B. 590, 595, 597 per Scrutton, L.J. and Maugham, L.J. (C.A.); *British Coal Corp.* v. *The King*, [1935] A.C. 500, [1935] All. E.R. 139, [1935] 3 D.L.R. 401 (P.C.). But see *Blackburn* v. *A.-G.*, [1971] 1 W.L.R. 1037, [1971] 2 All. E.R. 1380 (C.A.).

65. The notion of legislative supremacy underlies the interpretation principle that later statutes prevail over conflicting, earlier statutes (see ibid.). In addition, it pervades the elaboration of the common law. See, e.g., the judicial treatment of the criminal defence of "abuse of process" in *R.* v. *Wray*, [1971] S.C.R. 272, 295-296, 299-300, 11 D.L.R. (3d) 673, 11 C.R.N.S. 235, [1970] 4 C.C.C.1 per Martland and Judson J.J. (S.C.C.); in *R.* v. *Osborn*, [1971] S.C.R. 184, 190-191, 15 D.L.R. (3d) 85, 12 C.R.N.S. 51, 1 C.C.C. (2d) 482 per Pigeon J. (S.C.C.); and in *Rourke* v. *The Queen*, [1978] 1 S.C.R. 1021, 1045, (1977), 38 C.R.N.S. 268, 35 C.C.C. (2d) 129 per Pigeon J. (S.C.C.).

66. *R.* v. *Drybones*, [1970] S.C.R. 282, 9 D.L.R. (3d) 473, 71 W.W.R. 161, 10 C.R.N.S. 334, [1970] 3 C.C.C. 355 per Pigeon J. (S.C.C.).

67. *R.* v. *Drybones*, ibid., 305.

68. *R.* v. *Drybones*, ibid., 306.

69. *A.-G. Canada* v. *Lavell*; *Isaac* v. *Bedard*, [1974] S.C.R. 1349, (1973) 38 D.L.R. (3d) 481, 23 C.R.N.S. 197, 11 R.F.L. 333 (S.C.C.).

70. *A.-G. Canada* v. *Lavell*, ibid., 1390, per Pigeon J.:

> I agree in the result with Ritchie J. I certainly cannot disagree with the view I did express in *R.* v. *Drybones*... Assuming the situation is such as Laskin J. says, it cannot be improper for me to adhere to what was my dissenting view, when a majority of those who did not agree with it in

respect of a particular section of the Indian Act, R.S.C. 1970, c. 1-6, now adopt it for the main body of this important statute.

71. *The Queen* v. *Burnshine*, [1975] 1 S.C.R. 693, 708-709, 44 D.L.R. (3d) 584, [1974] 4 W.W.R. 49, 25 C.R.N.S. 270 (S.C.C.).

72. *A.-G. Canada* v. *Canard*, [1976] 1 S.C.R. 170, (1975), 52 D.L.R. (3d) 548, [1975] 3 W.W.R. 1.

73. *R.* v. *Drybones*, [1970] S.C.R. 282, 299, 71 W.W.R. 161, 9 D.L.R. (3d) 473, 10 C.R.N.S. 334, [1970] 3 C.C.C. 355 (S.C.C.).

74. *R.* v. *Miller and Cockriell*, [1977] 2 S.C.R. 680, 70 D.L.R. (3d) 324, 11 N.R. 386, [1976] 5 W.W.R. 510 (S.C.C.).

75. *A.-G. Canada* v. *Lavell*; *Isaac* v. *Bedard*, [1974] S.C.R., 1349, 1359, (1973), 38 D.L.R. (3d) 481, 23 C.R.N.S. 197, 11 R.F.L. 333 (S.C.C.).

76. Ibid., 1361-1362.

77. Ibid., 1361.

78. *Regina* v. *Miller and Cockriell*, [1977] 2 S.C.R. 680, 70 D.L.R. (3d) 324, 11 N.R. 386, [1976] 5 W.W.R. 510 (S.C.C.).

79. According to the "frozen meaning" doctrine all of the human rights and fundamental freedoms set out in the Canadian Bill of Rights had existed and were protected under the common law. The Canadian Bill of Rights did not purport to define new rights nor to enlarge the scope of the existing meaning of the rights. The Bill merely reaffirmed the existence of the rights in a statute.

One can trace this notion back to Mr. Justice Ritchie's judgment in *Robertson and Rosetanni* v. *The Queen*, [1963] S.C.R. 651, 654 ff., to Mr. Justice Pigeon's dissenting opinion in *R.* v. *Drybones*, [1970] S.C.R. 282, 305 and to Mr. Justice Ritchie's majority decision in *Curr* v. *The Queen*, [1972] S.C.R. 889, 916. The "frozen meaning" doctrine has been approved and applied in *A.-G. Canada* v. *Lavell*; *Isaac* v. *Bedard*, [1974] S.C.R. 1349 (S.C.C.) per Ritchie J., and in *The Queen* v. *Burnshine*, [1975] 1 S.C.R. 693 (S.C.C.) per Martland J. as well as in *R.* v. *Miller and Cockriell*, [1977] 2 S.C.R. 680 (S.C.C.) per Ritchie J.

For some problems with the "frozen meaning" doctrine see generally, William E. Conklin and Gerald A. Ferguson, *The Burnshine Affair: Whatever Happened to Drybones and Equality before The Law*, 22 Chitty's L.J. 303, pp. 305-307 (1974).

80. *R.* v. *Miller and Cockriell*, [1977] 2 S.C.R. 680, 705-6, 70 D.L.R. (3d) 324, 11 N.R. 386, [1976] 5 W.W.R. 510 (S.C.C.).

81. *The Queen* v. *Burnshine*, [1975] 1 S.C.R. 693, 705, 44 D.L.R. (3d) 584, [1974] 4 W.W.R. 49, 25 C.R.N.S. 270 (S.C.C.).

82. Ibid., 707. Emphasis added.

83. *Curr* v. *The Queen*, [1972] S.C.R. 889, 899, (1972), 26 D.L.R. (3d) 603, 18 C.R.N.S. 281, 7 C.C.C. (2d) 181.

84. *The Queen* v. *Burnshine*, [1975] 1 S.C.R. 693, 707, 44 D.L.R. (3d) 584, [1974] 4 W.W.R. 49, 25 C.R.N.S. 270 per Martland J. (S.C.C.).

85. *Curr* v. *The Queen*. [1972] S.C.R. 889, 900-902, (1972), 26 D.L.R. (3d) 603, 18 C.R.N.S. 281, 7 C.C.C. (2d) 181. Emphasis added.

86. *The Queen* v. *Burnshine*, [1975] 1 S.C.R. 693, 714, 44 D.L.R. (3d)

584, [1974] 4 W.W.R. 49, 25 C.R.N.S. 270, 286 (S.C.C.). Emphasis added.

87. Canadian Bill of Rights, 1960, (Can.) c. 44; R.S.C. 1970, Appendix.

88. 16 Can. Bar. Rev. 1 (1938).

89. For examples of the "literal" approach see *Murray* v. *West Vancouver*, [1937] 3 W.W.R. 269 (B.C.S.C.); *Magor & St. Mellons Rural District Council* v. *Newport Corp.*, [1952] A.C. 189, [1951] 2 All. E.R. 839 (H.L.). For an example of the "absurdity" approach see *R.* v. *Mojelski*, 65 W.W.R. 565 (Sask. C.A. 1963) revg 60 W.W.R. 355 (Sask. Q.B. 1967); for an example of the "mischief" approach see *McBratney* v. *McBratney* [1919], 59 S.C.R. 550, 50 D.L.R. 132, [1919] 3 W.W.R.1.

90. For other examples see Elmer A. Driedger *The Construction of Statutes* (Toronto: Buttonworths, 1975).

91. A. V. Dicey, *An Introduction to the Study of the Law of the Constitution*, intro. by E. C. S. Wade, 10th ed. (1885; reprint ed., Toronto: Macmillan & Co., 1962). Dicey considered "equality before the law" synonymous both with "legal equality" (ibid., p. 193) and "the equal subjection of all classes to the ordinary law... administered by the ordinary courts" (ibid., p. 202). Dicey asserted that "legal equality" required *the same ordinary courts* to administer the law without partiality as between governmental officials and ordinary citizens. That is, there should be no special judicial tribunals with special jurisdiction over officials, as in the France of Dicey's time (ibid., p. 195). Furthermore, the ordinary courts should administer the same law universally to all classes, without being influenced by political or economic favoritism (ibid., p. 193-194, 301).

For the inapplicability of Dicey's definition to the Canadian Bill of Rights see William E. Conklin and Gerald Ferguson, *The Burnshine Affair: Whatever Happened to Drybones and Equality before the Law*, 22 Chitty's Law Journal 303 (1974). Also see, Walter Tarnopolsky, *The Canadian Bill of Rights and the Supreme Court Decisions in Lavell and Burnshine: A Retreat from Drybones to Dicey?*, 7 Ott. L. Rev. 1 (1974).

92. *A.-G. Canada* v. *Lavell*; *Isaac* v. *Bedard*, [1974] S.C.R. 1349, (1973) 38 D.L.R. (3d) 481, 23 C.R.N.S. 197, 11 R.F.L. 333 (S.C.C.).

93. *The Queen* v. *Burnshine*, [1975] 1 S.C.R. 693, 704-705, 44 D.L.R. (3d) 584, [1974] 4 W.W.R. 49, 25 C.R.N.S. 270 (S.C.C.).

94. According to Sect. 1(a) the following "human rights and fundamental freedoms" exist:

"a) the right of the individual to life, liberty, security of the person and enjoyment of property, and the right not to be deprived thereof except by due process of law."

Section 2 provides that "... no law of Canada shall be construed or applied so as to...

c) deprive a person who has been arrested or detained... (ii) of the right to retain and instruct counsel without delay, or...

d) authorize a court, tribunal, commission, board or other authority to compel a person to give evidence if he is denied counsel protection against self-incrimination or other constitutional safeguards;

e) deprive a person of the right to a fair hearing in accordance with the principles of fundamental justice for the determination of his rights and obligations; ..."

95. *Curr* v. *The Queen*, [1972] S.C.R. 889, 26 D.L.R. (3d) 603, 18 C.R.N.S. 281, 7 C.C.C. (2d) 181.

96. *Brownridge* v. *The Queen*, [1972] S.C.R. 928, 28 D.L.R. (3d) 1, 18 C.R.N.S. 308, 7 C.C.C. (2d) 417 per Ritchie J. (S.C.C.).

97. *O'Connor* v. *The Queen*, [1966] S.C.R. 619, 57 D.L.R. (2d) 123, 48 C.R. 270, [1966] 4 C.C.C. 342.

98. *Hogan* v. *The Queen*, [1975] 2 S.C.R. 574, 48 D.L.R. (3d) 427, 26 C.R.N.S. 206, 18 C.C.C. (2d) 65, 9 N.S.R. (2d) 145, 2 N.R. 343.

99. *The Queen* v. *Burnshine*, [1975] 1 S.C.R. 693, 44 D.L.R. (3d) 584, [1974] 4 W.W.R. 49, 25 C.R.N.S. 270 (S.C.C.).

100. *A.-G. Canada* v. *Canard*, [1976] 1 S.C.R. 170, (1975), 52 D.L.R. (3d) 548, [1975] 3 W.W.R. 1.

101. See generally, William E. Conklin, *The Utilitarian Theory of Equality before the Law*, 8 Ott. L. Rev. 485, pp. 499-501, (1976).

102. See generally, W. A. Matheson, *The Prime Minister and the Cabinet* (Toronto: Methuen, 1976); House of Commons and Senate (Canada), Standing Joint Committee on Regulations and Other Statutory Instruments, *Second Report*, 2nd sess., 30th Parl. (Ottawa: Queens Printer, 1976-77); T. A. Hockin, *Apex of Power* (Scarborough: Prentice-Hall, 1971); C. E. S. Frank "The Dilemma of the Standing Committee of the Canadian House of Commons," 4 *Can. J. Pol. Sc.* 1, (1971); T. d'Aquino, "The Prime Minister's Office: Catalyst or Cabal? Aspects of the Development of the Office in Canada and some thoughts about its future," 17 *Can. Pub. Adm.* 55 (1975); D. Smith, "Comments on 'The Prime Minister's Office: Catalyst or Cabal'? 17 *Can. Pub. Adm.* 80 (1974); House of Commons (Canada), Special Committee on Statutory Instruments, *Third Report*, 1969; J. E. Kersell, *Parliamentary Supervision of Delegated Legislation* (London, 1960); G. Bruce Doern and Peter Aucoin, eds., *The Structures of Policy-Making in Canada* (Toronto: Macmillan, 1971).

103. R. H. S. Crossman, "Introduction" in Walter Bagehot's *The English Constitution* (London: Fontane, 1963); S. Walkland, *The Legislative Process in Great Britain* (London: George Allen & Unwin, 1968); H. V. Wiseman, ed., *Parliament and The Executive* (London: Routledge & Kegan Paul, 1966); R. M. Punnett, *Front-Bench Opposition* (London: Heinemann, 1973); J. P. Mackintosh, *The British Cabinet* 2nd ed. (London: Methuen, 1968) esp. pp. 73-218 and 567-577.

104. As argued below, the United Kingdom courts did not accept legislative supremacy as the fundamental principle of the Constitution until the second quarter of the nineteenth century. See text infra, between notes 130 and 136.

105. Walkland, *The Legislative Process in Great Britain*, supra, note 103.

106. E. Driedger, "The Preparation of Legislation," 31 *C.B.R.* 33 (1953); *The Composition of Legislation*, "Preface" (Ottawa: Queen's Printer, 1957).

107. As to the extended time lag before the English courts translated the political reality into constitutional principles see text, infra, between notes 130 and 136.

108. Louis Lusky, *By What Right?* (Charlottesville, Virginia: The Michie Co., 1975).

109. William Blackstone, *Commentaries on the Laws of England*, 1st ed., 4 vols., (1765; reprint ed., London: Dawsons of Pall Mall, 1966) vol. 1, p. 39 (hereinafter cited as *Commentaries*).

Blackstone began his *Commentaries* with a theological discussion of the nature of the universe. "Man," he wrote, "must necessarily be subject to the laws of his creator, for he is entirely a dependent being. ... And consequently as man depends absolutely upon his maker for everything, it is necessary that he should in all points conform to his maker's will."

When God created the earth out of nothing, "He impressed certain principles upon that matter, from which it can never depart, and without which it would cease to be." Ibid., p. 38. Being dictated by God, these principles were "superior in obligation to any other [law] ... binding all over the globe, in all countries, at all times. Ibid., p. 69.

110. William Blackstone, Ibid., vol. 1, p. 156.

111. A. Dicey, *An Introduction to the Study of the Law of the Constitution*, intro. by E. C. S. Wade, 10th ed. (1885; reprint ed., London: Macmillan & Co., 1962).

112. R. F. V. Heuston, *Essays in Constitutional Law*, 2nd ed. (London: Stevens & Sons, 1964), p. 7.

113. J. B. Mitchell, *The Sovereignty of Parliament — Yet Again*, 79 L.Q.R. 196, p. 197 (1963).

114. E. C. S. Wade, "Introduction" to the 10th ed. of Dicey's *An Introduction to the Study of the Law of the Constitution*, supra, note 98.

115. See also, for example, Sections 69 and 71.

116. Sections 20, 91(1) and 85.

117. Sections 96-101.

118. The latter submission is historically inaccurate. See generally, text infra, between notes 130 and 136.

119. *A.-G. v. Ernest Augustus (Prince) of Hanover*, [1957] A.C. 436 (H.L.).

120. E. C. S. Wade, *The Basis of Legal Sovereignty* [1955] Cambridge L.J. 172.

121. Dr. Glanville Williams, ed., *Salmond on Jurisprudence*, 10th ed., p. 155 as quoted by Wade, ibid., p. 187. Emphasis added.

122. One should note in this regard Beetz J.'s recent comment in *Dupond* v. *City of Montreal* (1978), 19 N.R. 478, 496 that counsel were apparently unprepared to articulate any content to their submission on behalf of the fundamental freedom of association "couched" as it was "in such general terms". Beetz J. asked:

> What is it that distinguishes a right from a freedom and a fundamental freedom from a freedom which is not fundamental? Is there a correlation between freedom of speech and freedom of assembly on the one hand and, on the other, the right, if any, to hold a public meeting on a highway or in a park as opposed to a meeting open to the public or

private land? How like or unlike each other are an assembly, a parade, a gathering, a demonstration, a procession?

Beetz J. then went on to stress that "modern parlance has fostered loose language upon lawyers." A close look at the factums of recent Supreme Court of Canada civil liberties cases would appear to verify Beetz J.'s concern. See, for example, the factum submitted in *Regina v. Miller and Cockriell*, [1977] 2 S.C.R. 680, 70 D.L.R. (3d) 324, 11 N.R. 386, [1976] 5 W.W.R. 510 (S.C.C.) where appellant counsel submitted in their factum, vol. 2, p. 281, that the death penalty was cruel and unusual punishment because it was unusually severe and its severity degraded the dignity and worth of the human being. Counsel made this submission without explaining what they meant by the words "dignity" and "worth". Nor did counsel show why the dignity of the accused outweighed the dignity of the victim or, at least, why the dignity of the victim could be ignored.

Given the inability of counsel to deal with the moral-political issues involved in *Dupond*, Justice Beetz admittedly found it necessary to elaborate his own personal normative or "ought" propositions (or, more accurately, his "preferences") without authority and without reasoning (except for proposition number 4, p. 497).

123. See, for example, *R. v. Wray*, [1971] S.C.R. 272, 11 D.L.R. (3d) 673, 11 C.R.N.S. 235, [1970] 4 C.C.C. 1 (S.C.C.); *R. v. Osborn*, [1971] S.C.R. 184, 15 D.L.R. (3d) 85, 12 C.R.N.S. 51, 1 C.C.C. (2d) 482; and *Rourke v. The Queen*, [1978] 1 S.C.R. 1021, (1977) 76 D.L.R. (3d) 193, 38 C.R.N.S. 268, 35 C.C.C. (2d) 129, [1977] 5 W.W.R. 487, 16 N.R. 181 (S.C.C.).

124. See text, supra, between notes 65 and 87.

125. Ibid.

126. See text, supra, between notes 86 and 88.

127. Hamish Gray describes sovereignty as "a metaphysical conception" in *The Sovereignty of Parliament Today*, 10 U. of Tor. L.J. 54, 54 (1953). See also, K.W.B. Middleton, *Sovereignty in Theory and Practice*, 64 *Juridicial Review* 35 (1952).

128. (1694) Skinner 517, 526 (K.B.).

129. (1701), 12 Mod. 669, 88 E.R. 1592.

130. *The Case of the College of Physicians* or *Dr. Bonham's Case* (1610), 8 Co. Rep. 114a, 2 Brown 1. 255, 77 E.R. 646 (C.B.). See text supra, chap. 1, between notes 35 and 42.

131. (1754), 9 Mor. Dict. 7443 (H.L.).

132. (1790), 5 Cru. Dig. (4th edn.) 26, 40 Digest (Repl.) 487 (H.L.).

133. (1861), 3 L.T. 642, 35 (Repl.) 324, 348 (H.L.).

134. E. C. S. Wade, "Introduction", supra, note 114.

135. (1839), 9 Ad. & E. 1, 8 L.J.Q.B. 294, 112 E.R. 1112.

136. (1835), 8 Cl. & Fin. 710, 8 E.R. 279.

137. See, for example, *Gallant v. R.*, [1949] 2 D.L.R. 425 (S.C.P.E.I.); *R. v. Irwin*, [1926] Ex. C.R. 127 (Ex. C.); and *Drewery et al. v. Century City Developments Ltd. et al. (no. 1)* (1975), 6 O.R. (2d) 288 (Ont. H.C.).

138. *British Railways Bd. v. Pickin*, [1972] 2 W.L.R. 208 (H.L.) reversing

[1972] 3 All. E.R. 923, [1973] 1 Q.B. 219, [1972] 3 W.L.R. 824 (C.A.).

For an analysis of this case as well as the propositions set out in text, supra, between notes 134 and 138 see generally, William E. Conklin, *Pickin and its Applicability to Canada*, 25 Univ. Tor. L.J. 193 (1975).

139. See generally, *Duke of Argyle* v. *Commissioners of Inland Revenue*, [1914] L.T. 893 (K.B.); *Vauxhall Estates Ltd.* v. *Liverpool Corporation*, [1932] 1 K.B. 733, 743, 745 per Avory J. (K.B.); *Ellen Street Estates Ltd.* v. *Minister of Health*, [1934] 1 K.B. 590, 595, 597 per Scrutton L.J. and Maugham L.J. (C.A.); *British Coal Corp.* v. *The King*, [1935] A.C. 500, [1935] All. E.R. 139, [1935] 3 D.L.R. 401, [1935] 2 W.W.R. 564, 64 C.C.C. 145 (P.C.). But see, *Blackburn* v. *A.-G.*, [1971] 1 W.L.R. 1037, [1971] 2 All. E.R. 1380 (C.A.).

95

Chapter III

The "Entrenched Bill of Rights" Argument

We have now examined the character of the arguments traditionally made in support of the existence of fundamental rights in the United Kingdom and in Canada. The character of the one method of argument is backward-looking. The other relies upon society's contemporary values. Counsel and judge have sometimes, as in the case of Chief Justice Coke, employed the one method of argument. On other occasions, counsel and judge have imperceptibly shifted from the one to the other in hopes of solidifying their conclusions. I have raised serious shortcomings in the character of the two arguments and I have used United Kingdom, Canadian and American constitutional experiences to substantiate the serious nature of those weaknesses. One is warranted in concluding that counsel and judge cannot consistently support the existence of fundamental rights by the character of argument examined in chapters I and II. No matter how vocal their self-professed beliefs in fundamental rights, no matter how sincere their submissions, the direction of a "backward-looking" or a "contemporary societal values" argument runs counter to the very existence of fundamental rights.

As a consequence, the student at law watches with interest as the federal government of Canada repeatedly attempts to entrench a Bill of Rights in the Canadian Constitution. The Canadian Government has claimed that the entrenchment of a Bill of Rights in a written constitution will guarantee the existence and protection of fundamental rights.[1] By placing a Bill of Rights beyond statutory or constitutional amendment, it is claimed, the Canadian judiciary as well as government officials would finally be convinced that the fundamental rights are intended to override all inconsistent legislation, common law principles, or administrative conduct.[2] Fundamental rights would no longer "float around", protected on some days and abrogated on others. Rather, our fundamental rights would always exist because, to quote from Section 5 of the federal government's latest draft Bill of Rights, the rights would "be incapable of being alienated by the ordinary exercise of such legislative or other authority as may be conferred by law on its respective institutions of government."[3]

The lawyer's role would be relatively simple. He could ascertain fundamental rights with certainty. Whereas an unwritten constitution is largely judicially created and thereby lends more legitimacy to an inquiry into the normative political presuppositions underlying each constitutional principle, a written constitution with an entrenched Bill of Rights would seem to release counsel from the necessity of asking hard moral-political questions about the nature and meaning of fundamental rights. The latter questions would already have been expressly contemplated and their resolution incorporated into the terms of the written constitution. The problems I elaborated in chapters I and II with respect to the traditional modes of argument in support of fundamental rights would no longer persist. Or, so the argument would go.

I now wish to question the above line of argument. Whether or not entrenchment would in fact convince the judiciary and government officials that fundamental rights are to override all conflicting legislation, common law principles or government conduct is, it is submitted, a very debatable question. The arguments raised in the Appendix at the end of this book suggest otherwise with respect to the Canadian Government's latest proposal for an entrenched Bill of Rights (Bill C-60).[4] What I wish to show is that even if entrenchment had such an effect, important problems remain which lend scepticism to the seeming definitiveness of an "entrenched Bill of Rights" argument for the establishment of fundamental rights.

An "entrenched Bill of Rights" argument still requires that important moral-political issues be asked. Both counsel and judge must be prepared to face these issues in order to determine the meaning and scope of the entrenched rights, the priority scale of entrenched rights when one conflicts with the other, and the level of judicial scrutiny over legislation, common law principles, or government conduct which allegedly infringes the rights. The necessity of asking moral-political questions is so important as to render an "entrenched Bill of Rights" argument, of itself, inadequate as an argument in support of the existence and nature of fundamental rights.

Section 1. The Meaning and Scope of the Terms of an Entrenched Bill of Rights

The exigency of asking moral-political questions can be most perceptibly appreciated when one examines the American constitutional experience with an entrenched Bill of Rights. The first set of considerations which the American experience raises is that even an entrenched Bill of Rights still requires that a court make normative political judgments about the meaning and scope of the specific, express guarantees.

This is so, in part, because of the "open texture of law" — to use H. L. A. Hart's term.[5] The application of words at some point prove indeterminate, Hart explained. Such is especially the case where, as here, general terms such as "freedom of speech", "due process of law" and the like are used. There are additional reasons why counsel and court must make normative political judgments. For one thing, once the meaning of a term has been determined, there may be occasions when one entrenched right conflicts with another. For example, freedom of speech conflicts with the right to a fair hearing in the common constructive contempt cases. Presumably it might be possible for an entrenched Bill of Rights to provide that one freedom — say, freedom of speech — shall be the paramount freedom in all such circumstances. On the other hand, the courts would still have to define the scope of the paramount freedom. Such a pursuit would require some evaluative balancing of freedoms on the part of the courts. Furthermore, draftsmen are mere human beings, not omniscient gods. It is very difficult to conceive that, after defining the scope of various freedoms, any human being could foresee all the very different possible combinations of conflicts between the various guarantees in future cases. Finally, even if conceivable, it is difficult to believe that the constitution framers would want to foreclose the possibility that there might in the future arise new moral-political arguments as to why a conflict should be resolved in a manner different from the specific intent of the original draftsmen of the Bill of Rights.

Again, the explicit entrenchment of rights and freedoms in the American Constitution still leaves open the question of the meaning and scope of the fundamental freedoms. The Fourteenth Amendment, for example, provides that "nor shall any State deprive any person of life, liberty, or property, without due process of law." But as Mr. Justice Harlan quickly pointed out in his dissenting judgment in *Duncan* v. *Louisiana*,[6] the constitutional restrictions upon state action in the Fourteenth Amendment are couched in very broad and general language. This generality has forced the U.S. courts during the past one hundred years to engage in a very difficult pursuit which Justice Harlan called "the search for intermediate premises".[7] The courts must still give content to such terms as "life", "liberty", "property" and "due process of law". And before they can elaborate the required "intermediate

98

premises", the courts must have some notion of the criterion or criteria for determining why fundamental rights are fundamental. We saw in chapter II that society's conscience does not provide us with such a criterion. We shall now see that an entrenched Bill of Rights also fails to provide us with such a criterion.

Mr. Justice Black believed that he had found an answer to the question of why fundamental rights are fundamental. To the issue of "what is the context of the due process clause" of the Fourteenth Amendment, Mr. Justice Black responded in *Adamson* v. *California*[8] that the due process clause incorporated all of the existing "specific" guarantees of the Bill of Rights. He strongly objected to Justice Frankfurter's "natural law — due process" approach to the problem of the meaning of the Fourteenth Amendment's "due process" clause. We have seen that, according to Justice Frankfurter, the "due process" clause required that the states merely comply with the "fundamental principles of liberty and justice" accepted by English-speaking peoples.[9] Justice Black replied that Justice Frankfurter's formula degraded the constitutional safeguards of the Bill of Rights and, at the same time, appropriated on an *ad hoc* basis a broad power to the courts "to roam at large in the broad expanse of policy and morals and to trespass, all too freely, on the legislative domain."[10] In *Duncan*,[11] Justice Black repeated that both the "fundamental fairness" test and the test of "shocking the Court's conscience" depended "entirely on the particular judge's idea of ethics and morals instead of requiring him to depend on the boundaries fixed by the written words of the Constitution."[12] The inevitable judicial discretion involved in construing the express words of the written constitution appeared to Justice Black to be a very different type of discretion than Justice Frankfurter's "natural law — due process" formula.[13]

But does Justice Black's theory of total incorporation really provide us with adequate guidelines for explaining the meaning of the due process clause? The first point to note is that Justice Black's total incorporation viewpoint, as well as the prevailing perspective of selective incorporation, do not provide principled guidelines to the question of why fundamental rights are fundamental.[14] For one thing, as Justice Harlan points out in his dissenting judgment in *Duncan*,[15] neither the wording of the Constitution nor the Fourteenth Amendment's history indicates that the Bill of Rights should be incorporated into the due process clause of the Fourteenth Amendment. Justice Harlan considered that "the overwhelming historical evidence" demonstrates that "the Congressmen and state legislators who wrote, debated, and ratified the 14th Amendment did not think they were 'incorporating' the Bill of Rights."[16] Because of the breadth and generality of the Fourteenth Amendment's wording, the framers could not possibly have intended that the meaning of such terms as "liberty" and "due process of law" be limited to mid-nineteenth century conceptions. Rather, the framers must have contemplated that "the increasing experience and evolving conscience of the American people" would add new "intermediate premises." That selective or total incorporation could not have been the framers' intent becomes clear when one realizes the absurd consequence of restricting the meaning of "due process of law" to the first eight amendments: the Seventh Amendment's requirement of a right to trial in all civil suits over $ 20 would be included in "due process of law". If Justice Harlan is correct that "neither history nor sense" support Justice Black's total incorporation theory, then Justice Black was compelled to face the issue of why he believed the freedoms and rights in the first eight amendments to be more fundamental than other freedoms and rights.

The contemporary judicial approach of "selective incorporation" also fails to confront the latter issue. According to the theory of "selective incorporation", some of the first eight amendments apply against the states and, if an amendment does apply, it has the same impact and force as if it applied against the federal executive or legislature. Mr. Justice White, who delivered the majority opinion in *Duncan*, held that the test of whether a right was selectively incorporated depended upon whether it was among those

> fundamental principles of liberty and justice which lie at the base of all our civil and political institutions, *Powell* v. *Alabama*, 287 U.S. 45, 67 (1932); whether it is "basic in our system of jurisprudence", *In Re Oliver*, 353 U.S. 257, 273 (1948); and whether it is "a fundamental right, essential to a fair trial", *Gideon* v. *Wainwright*, 372 U.S. 335, 343-44 (1963); *Malloy* v. *Hogan*, 378 U.S. I, 6 (1964); *Pointer* v. *Texas*, 380 U.S. 400, 403 (1965).[17]

Justice White noted in a footnote that, whereas in prior cases the court had asked whether "a civilized system could be imagined that would not accord with the particular protection," the recent cases questioned whether "a particular procedure is fundamental — whether, that is, it is a procedure necessary to an Anglo-American regime of ordered liberty."[18]

In the *Duncan* case the appellant had requested a trial by jury for a misdemeanor. The Louisiana Constitution granted jury trials only in cases where capital punishment or imprisonment at hard labour were imposed. Applying the test of fundamentality cited above, Justice White held that

> because we believe that trial by jury in criminal cases is fundamental to the American scheme of justice, we hold that the Fourteenth Amendment guarantees a right of jury trial in all criminal cases which — were they to be tried in a federal court — would come within the Sixth Amendment's guarantee.[19]

He concluded that

> in the American States, as in the federal judicial system, a general grant of jury trial for serious offences is a fundamental right, essential for preventing miscarriages of justice and for assuring that fair trials are provided for all defendants.[20]

Professor Henkin has documented how, as in the case of "total incorporation", there seems little historical, textual or precedential authority for the selective incorporation of particular provisions of the Bill of Rights into the "due process" clause.[21] In addition, it is difficult not to agree with Justice Harlan's remark in *Duncan* that the selective incorporation process lacks the internal consistency which total incorporation at least provides.[22]

Accordingly, the reason for and nature of the relevance of the Bill of Rights must still be articulated. Neither the "total" nor the "selective incorporation" approaches no less than the Frankfurter-Harlan "ordered liberty" approach to the meaning of "due process of law" (or, for that matter, "life", "liberty" or "property") can avoid the basic issue of why fundamental rights are fundamental. With total and selective incorporation, in Justice Harlan's words, "the court has justified neither its starting place nor its conclusion."[23] According to Justice Harlan, the court provides "no real reasons" why one right should be "in" and another "out". The selective incorporationists define "fundamental" in terms of "old", "much praised" and "found in the Bill of Rights". The process of reasoning of incorporationist doctrine is that the Bill of Rights is incorporated into the due process clause because the Bill's provisions are fundamental, and the Bill's provisions are fundamental because they are in the Bill of Rights. As Justice Harlan rightly points out, "the definition of 'fundamental' thus turns out to be circular"[24] and, one might add, highly subjective. The inevitable issue of why fundamental rights are fundamental remains unresolved.

A second important point with respect to the incorporationist perspective is that, even if it explained why some rights are more fundamental than others, the court would still have to define the meaning and scope of the incorporated provisions. But the court could not adequately seek out definitions without, once again, elaborating and applying some "fundamentality" notion. What, for example, is an "unreasonable" search and seizure as guaranteed in the Fourth Amendment? What does "just compensation" mean in the Fifth Amendment? What does "the Assistance of Counsel" mean in the Sixth Amendment? What is the scope of the freedoms of "religion", "speech", or "assembly" as protected in the First? What do the terms "cruel and unusual" mean in the Eighth? And how does one resolve a conflict between one guarantee and another? Each of these questions requires that counsel and court be prepared to inquire into political philosophy. The simple entrenchment of the rights and freedoms is not enough.

The capital punishment cases of *Furman* v. *Georgia* (1972)[25] and *Gregg* v. *Georgia* (1976)[26] exemplify why counsel and judge must, of necessity, be prepared to examine moral-political philosophy even in a jurisdiction with a written entrenched Bill of Rights. Two of the majority in *Furman* (Justices Stewart and Douglas) concerned themselves with the risks of arbitrary and unequal application of capital punishment because of its infrequent imposition. Infrequent application of capital punishment inferred that the penalty was unusual. Justice Stewart concluded that the Eighth Amendment would not tolerate a legal system which permits "this unique penalty" of death "to be so wantonly and so freakishly imposed." Justice Douglas stressed that "implicit in the ban on 'cruel and unusual' punishment was the incompatibility of the risk of discrimination and arbitrariness in broad sentencing discretion." He held it "cruel and unusual" to apply capital punishment selectively to weak and unpopular minorities.

Justice White, interestingly, expressly adopted a utilitarian standard for assessing whether the death penalty was cruel and unusual. He believed the death penalty had ceased "realistically to further these (social) purposes."[27] It had "only marginal contributions to any discernible social or public purposes." Justice Brennan, on the other hand, began with human dignity rather than the social welfare as his starting point of analysis: "death," he held, "is an unusually severe and degrading punishment." As we have already seen in chapter II, Justice Marshall believed that the Eighth Amendment required the court to discern "the predictable subjective, emotional reactions of informed citizens."[28] Justice Powell, in dissent, believed that the Eighth Amendment required the court to consider whether the death penalty fell outside "the likely legislative intent" in creating the particular crime. Chief Justice Burger's dissent reflected due deference to the legislature's own judgment.

In *Gregg* v. *Georgia* Justice Marshall retained his "informed citizens" test; Justice Brennan fell back upon "the principle of civilized treatment guaranteed by the [cruel and unusual punishment] clause," and the majority (per Justices Stewart, Powell and Stevens) held that, in the light of *Furman*, the Eighth Amendment only required that death not be imposed in "an arbitrary or capricious manner". Justice White (with Chief Justice Burger and Justice Rehnquist) also considered the prime issue to be whether the discretion to sentence an accused to death was standardless or discriminatory.

The judgments in *Furman* v. *Georgia* and *Gregg* v. *Georgia* beg inquiry into moral-political philosophy. If counsel or judge adopt a utilitarian framework of analysis, as did Justice White in *Furman*, does that framework militate against the very existence of a fundamental right against cruel and unusual punishment? [29] If counsel or judge use "human dignity" as the threshold criterion for the meaning of "cruel and unusual" as did Justice Brennan in both cases, how can counsel or judge adequately connect "cruel and unusual" with "human dignity" without articulating some content in the latter notion? We have seen in chapter II, for example, that it would not be adequate to equate "human dignity" with what shocks the community's conscience. Must counsel consider the dignity of the victim and, if so, why does the dignity of the murderer outweigh the dignity of the victim? Similarly, if counsel or judge rely upon the "likely legislative intent" to define the meaning of "cruel and unusual" as did Justice Powell and Chief Justice Burger in *Furman*, why should we choose the legislature's intent to ascertain the meaning of a fundamental right? We have already seen in chapter II, for example, that legislative supremacy is not, of necessity, consistent with the existence of fundamental rights. Rather than settling constitutional issues, the propositions and tests put forward in *Furman* and *Gregg* beg inquiry into moral-political philosophy in order to grapple with the meaning and scope of enumerated rights.

Section 2. The Standard of Judicial Scrutiny

The American experience with an entrenched Bill of Rights raises a second reason why an "entrenched Bill of Rights" argument does not, of necessity, establish nor guarantee the existence of fundamental rights. Even if the meaning and scope of the guarantees in the Bill were clear, counsel and court would still be required to ascertain the level of judicial scrutiny required of legislation or administrative conduct allegedly infringing a fundamental right. Should the court, for example, scrutinize the purpose of the legislation? If so, may the court hypothesize possible legitimate purposes of the statute or must the court limit itself to the "purpose" of the statute as reflected from within the four corners of the Act? Alternatively, may the court examine the true motive of the legislation and pronounce upon its legitimacy? If counsel or judge resolve these issues, they must then question whether the statutory purpose is served by compelling state interests or, alternatively, by any state interests. Should the court contemplate whether the state could have accomplished the same purpose by less onerous alternative means? Does the state possess a heavier burden when some fundamental rights are burdened in contrast to others? If so, which rights and why? In addition, are the fact categories to which a statute is to apply immediately suspect and, if so, why? Are classifications suspect because the group within it has been disadvantaged in the past, because it has not been represented very well in the political process in the past or because the stigma is attached to the group? Whether an individual finds himself/herself within a suspect category depends upon the reason why the court considers the group category suspect. In turn, if the court considers a classification immediately suspect, a higher level of judicial scrutiny of the legislation will be triggered.

The American experience indicates that an "entrenched Bill of Rights" argument in support of fundamental rights does not answer these questions in simple terms. Judicial legislation appears necessary but principled reasons of judgment will be forthcoming only after counsel and judge have tried to respond to our interminable question: namely, why are fundamental rights fundamental? This point is especially clear when one examines the "reasonable relationship" and "compelling state interest" analysis of the equal protection clause of the Fourteenth Amendment.

The above point can be restated as follows. An entrenched Bill of Rights does not provide definitive answers to civil liberties problems. In particular, the outcome of any civil liberties issue will be determined in large measure by the level of scrutiny which the court pursues toward an allegedly harmful statute or regulation. And yet, entrenched Bills of Rights do not necessarily indicate what level of judicial scrutiny should be exercised in particular cases when the legislature has allegedly infringed one of the entrenched rights. In those constitutions where one might argue that a certain level of judicial scrutiny has been contemplated,[29] the level of scrutiny appears to be the very weak "reasonable relationship" test discussed below. The American experience shows that

such a test has not successfully supported the existence of fundamental rights in practice.[30]

With respect to the American experience, the Warren court was
criticised for sacrificing analysis of fundamental rights in that the
Court would choose a level of scrutiny which reached the result
which the Warren court itself found desirable in any particular
case. The Warren court's approach was both *ad hoc* and "all or
nothing". The traditional reasonable relationship test, for example, would invariably confirm the constitutionality of any statute
but the "strict scrutiny" test would invariably result in the invalid-
ity of a statute. The Warren court did not adequately analyze why
or when one test should be applied rather than another.

In the aftermath of the Warren court, Professor Gerald Gunther
developed a "means-oriented test with bite"[31] and Mr. Justice
Marshall advocated a "sliding-scale" test.[32] It seems that the effect of the Gunther and Marshall tests is to provide the scale of
judicial review but only *after* the important issue has been resolved
as to why a fundamental right is fundamental. The tests do not
provide principled criteria to indicate what level of scrutiny is
applicable in any particular case. It is submitted that the tests lack
such principled criteria because they do not ask the moral-political
question of why a fundamental right is fundamental. In other
words, the application of any particular test of judicial scrutiny is
inadequate *unless and until* counsel and the courts face the issue as
to why fundamental rights are fundamental. An entrenched Bill of
Rights does not provide an answer to that issue.

a. *The Reasonable Relationship Test*

The Warren court developed the "compelling state interest" test in
order to provide strict judicial scrutiny of legislation infringing
upon "fundamental interests" or rights and "invidiously discriminatory" classifications. The pre-Warren court had applied a "reasonable relationship" test pursuant to which the court assessed
whether there was a reasonable (sometimes, rational) connection
between the classification in the statute and the statute's overall
purpose. An early American Supreme Court decision defined the
test in this manner:

> 1. The equal-protection clause of the Fourteenth Amendment does
> not take from the state the power to classify in the adoption of police
> laws, but admits of the exercise of a wide scope of discretion in that
> regard, and avoids what is done only when it is *without any reasonable
> basis*, and therefore is *purely arbitrary*. 2. A classification having some

reasonable basis does not offend against that clause merely because it is not made with mathematical nicety, or because in practice it results in some inequality. 3. When the classification in such a law is called in question, if any state of facts reasonably can be conceived that would sustain it, the existence of that state of facts at the time the law was enacted must be assumed. 4. One who assails the classification in such a law must carry the burden of showing that it does not rest upon any reasonable basis, but is essentially arbitrary.[33]

This summary merely begs the question: what is an "essentially arbitrary" classification? Tussman and tenBroek responded in their classic essay that a classification was reasonable if it succeeded in the similar treatment of persons similarly situated.[34] To determine whether persons were similarly situated, one merely had to look at the purpose of the statute that set up the classification.

This "reasonable relationship" examination had three important elements: the legislative classification, the statutory purpose, and the relationship between the classification and that purpose. The correspondence between the classification and purpose was *prima facie* unreasonable, according to Tussman and tenBroek, in three situations. First, the classification might be under-inclusive: that is, the legislature should have included other persons in the class. Secondly, it could be over-inclusive: the legislature should have excluded some of the persons it had brought within the class. Thirdly, it could be both under- and over-inclusive: the legislature should have included some persons and excluded others. Tussman and tenBroek described the internment of the Japanese Americans as an instance of the third relationship. The classification of "American citizens of Japanese ancestry" was under-inclusive because it excluded American citizens of German and Italian ancestry who were arguably under the same suspicion of disloyalty. On the other hand, the classification was over-inclusive because not all Americans of Japanese ancestry were disloyal.

Simple under- or over-inclusiveness did not, however, in itself result in unconstitutionality. The classification was only *prima facie* unreasonable and could be sustained if "supportable by reasoned considerations."[35] Over time, the "reasonable classification" test subtly evolved into a "rational relationship" or "minimum rationality" test with the consequence that, as Professor Goodpaster has explained,[36] the courts virtually abdicated judicial review. This development prevailed particularly with respect to social and economic legislation.[37] The courts, for example, developed a very strong presumption that a statute satisfied the constitutional requirement of "equal protection".[38] Similarly, the courts came to ask merely whether "any state of facts

106

reasonably may be conceived to justify [the classification]."[39] Another way of putting this point is that the courts were quick to cite any purpose which might justify the classification rather than the particular purpose articulated in the statute. Furthermore, the most probably "reasoned consideration" was naturally conceived to be the one which supported the statute's constitutionality.[40] This was especially so in emergency conditions.[41] Finally the courts found it sufficient that an under-inclusive classification only partially remedy the alleged mischief leading to the enactment of the statute.[42] So long as the classification had "some reasonable basis", the court would sustain it, even though "it [was] not made with mathematical nicety" or "in practice... results in some inequality."[43] As a consequence of these factors, the United States Supreme Court sustained the constitutionality of all but one state statute challenged between 1937 and 1970 on "reasonable relationship" grounds under the "equal protection" clause.[44] In effect, therefore, a decision to proceed under the "reasonable relationship" test virtually determined the result without analysis as to the nature of the fundamental rights allegedly infringed or the extent to which they were burdened.

b. *The "Compelling State Interest" Test*

The Warren court developed the "compelling state interest" test in order to provide stricter judicial scrutiny of legislation infringing upon "fundamental interests" and "invidiously discriminatory" classifications than the court had usually given. In contrast to the "reasonable relationship" test, the court looked closer at the legitimacy of the state's purpose. Secondly, the court considered whether the purpose could be more adequately served by some "less onerous alternative". Thirdly, the Court weighed the importance of the purpose as against the undesirability of the classification: only compelling state purposes could sustain the constitutionality of a statute subject to the "compelling state interest" test.

The test, which received its first judicial acknowledgement in Justice Stone's famous footnote in the 1938 Supreme Court decision of *United States* v. *Caroline Products Co.*,[45] encompassed two forms of legislation. The first involved classifications which "invidiously discriminated": race was an example. Other classifications sometimes considered suspect have been wealth,[46] sex[47] and illegitimacy of birth.[48] The second type of proscribed legislation involved "fundamental interests" or "fundamental rights". Those interests generally thought to be "fundamental" have been the right to appeal,[49] right to counsel,[50] the right to interstate travel,[51] and the right to vote.[52] In *San Antonio Independent School Dist.* v. *Rodriquez*[53] counsel unsuccessfully argued that the right to an education was also fundamental. Generally the court has denied that a fundamental interest was at issue where social or economic legislation was involved.[54]

The "compelling state interest" test shares a common problem with other aspects of the third major form of argument in support of fundamental freedom: namely, one must go into the world of political norms in order to decide whether an interest is fundamental. In *Skinner* v. *Oklahoma* Mr. Justice Douglas considered marriage and procreation "one of the basic civil rights of man", "fundamental to the very existence and survival of the race".[55] In *Griffin* v. *Illinois* Justice Frankfurter held that denial of a free trial transcript to an indigent imposed a condition which "offend[ed] the deepest presuppositions of our society."[56] In *Boddie* v. *Connecticut*, Justice Harlan held that because the marriage relationship occupied a "basic position" "in this society's hierarchy of values" and because the state monopolized the sole means of divorce, court fees amounting to $60 for indigents could not be required.[57] The right to a divorce was "the exclusive precondition to the adjustment of the fundamental human relationship." Justice Brennan held in *Shapiro* v. *Thompson* that "the nature of our Federal Union and our constitutional concepts of personal liberty unite to require that all citizens be free to travel throughout the length and breadth of our land uninhibited by statutes..."[58] Quoting from *U.S.* v. *Guest*,[59] Justice Brennan believed that "it suffices" that the right to interstate travel "occupies a position fundamental to the concept of our Federal Union." The right need not be explicitly mentioned in the Constitution because it was "so elementary," such a "necessary concomitant of the stronger Union the Constitution created." Similarly, in *Reynolds* v. *Sims*[60] Chief Justice Warren held the right to vote freely to be fundamental because it was "of the essence of a democratic society"; it was "individual and personal in nature"; and it was "preservative of other basic civil and political rights".[61] These explanations of the fundamentality of the franchise were repeated and adopted in *Harper* v. *Virginia Bd. of Elections.*[62] The majority in *Kramer* v. *Union Free School Dist. No. 15* emphasised the rationale that the right to vote is "preservative of other basic civil and political rights."[63] In *Kramer* Chief Justice Warren explained that the presumption of constitutionality and the traditional rationality test "are based on an assumption that the institutions of state government are structured so as to represent fairly all the people." And "when the challenge to the statute is in effect a challenge of this basic assumption, the assumption can no longer serve as the basis for preserving constitutionality."[64]

But do these justifications for the preservation of these fundamental freedoms really tell us much? First, why are the freedoms "so elementary", "of the essence of a democratic society"? The criterion that a right be "of the essence of democracy" tells us very little, for example: it simply begs the question as to why the right is of the essence of democracy. Similarly, the criterion that a fundamental right must be "preservative of other basic civil and political rights", does not tell us what a "basic" civil and political right is. These questions, as well as the judicial propositions from which they are derived, are questions about political philosophy.

Secondly, the requirement that a fundamental right be preservative of other basic civil and political rights would exclude from our list some rights which we traditionally consider to be fundamental. For this reason it is somewhat suspect. Such a criterion would presumably preclude the right to counsel, due process of law, the presumption of innocence and other traditional civil rights from the list of fundamental rights. Some very important political rights such as the various freedoms of expression, could exist without the right to counsel, due process and the like. The right to counsel, that is, is not necessarily preservative of freedom of speech, the press or religion. Although not conclusive, this factor may be some cause to suspect the applicability of the requirement to a context other than the right to vote.

Thirdly, do the justifications really give us any principled guidance as to why one right is fundamental and another is not? Why, for example, did the Supreme Court rule unconstitutional the franchise qualifications of ownership of realty or custody of schoolchildren in school district elections as a violation of the fundamental right to vote in *Kramer* whereas in the same year the court unanimously held that imprisoned voters could be legitimately denied an absentee ballot when the ballots were provided to other classes of persons?[65] Is it enough for the court to assert that the issue was "only a right to an absolute ballot, not an impact on 'the fundamental right to vote' "? Justice Harlan seemed to be on point when he suggested in *Griffin* (dissenting) that the majority's holding there was "simply an unarticulated conclusion that it [i.e., the state] violates 'fundamental fairness.' "[66] In *Harper* Justice Harlan suggested that the basis of the court's determination of the right to vote as fundamental was "highly subjective". The court had employed "wholly inadequate", "captivating phrases" and "political doctrines popularly accepted at a particular moment of our history."[67]

But when Justice Harlan in *Boddie*[68] considered that the marriage relationship occupied a "basic position" in "this society's scale of values," how did he determine that marriage occupied such a position? Did he unconsciously use Justice Marshall's "informed citizen" approach? Did he unconsciously look to legal tradition as Chief Justice Coke would have him do? Or, did he merely give his own intuitive subjective political judgment of the scale of values in American society? Whatever the method, it was inarticulated and, in his case, tautological. To suggest as does Justice Brennan that the right of inter-state travel flows from "personal liberty" merely begs the question "what does this thing 'personal liberty' mean"? Tautological circular assertions have hardly been known to be "sufficient" explanations despite what Justice Brennan might have thought to the contrary. The compelling state interest test is found wanting because the court, in its application of the test, has failed to justify why a fundammental interest is indeed fundamental. And until we find such a criteria, we will not know the level of scrutiny to expect of our courts in their review of legislation.

The problem is compounded when we consider how the court has examined social and economic legislation. Two good examples are the *Dandridge* v. *Williams*[69] and *Rodriquez*[70] decisions. We shall examine *Dandridge*.

In *Dandridge*, Maryland's welfare scheme granted a maximum of $ 250 per familly, regardless of size or need. Appellants argued that the scheme discriminated among welfare recipients merely on the basis of the size of the family. Subsistence benefits were paid to some needy dependent children whereas other children similarly needy but in a larger family received less. The Supreme Court, per Justice Stewart, applied the traditional rationality test. Stewart J. conceded that if this had been a case where the government allegedly infringed the First Amendment, then the court would have applied a compelling state interest test. The crucial distinction, according to the Justice, was that "here we deal with state regulation in the social and economic field."[71] To invalidate state social or economic regulation would be far too reminiscent of another era despite the factual difference that former precedents dealt with state regulation of business or industry whereas this case admittedly involved "the most basic economic needs of impoverished human beings."[72]

But is the reminiscence of a former era a sufficient reason for not imposing stricter scrutiny? In *Reynolds* v. *Sims* the court expressed concern about the "debasement or dilution of the weight of a citizen's vote."[73] In *Harper* the court realized that economic factors were relevant to that dilution.[74] In *Kramer* the Court feared "the danger of denying some citizens any effective voice in the governmental affairs which substantially affect their lives."[75] In other words, the issue for the court in the voting cases was not whether liberty had been denied but rather whether the worth of liberty was being undermined. The court overcame the traditional liberal distinction between liberty and the worth of liberty. The issue which the *Dandridge* case poses is this: is the worth of liberty being respected if "the most basic economic needs of impoverished human beings" is not met. In such a circumstance how can American citizens possess "an equally effective voice" in the election of legislators "[as] the Constitution demands" — to use the words of the Chief Justice in *Reynolds* v. *Sims?*[76]

c. *The Gunther Model of Judicial Scrutiny*

Two other approaches have been advocated with respect to the level of scrutiny which the court should adopt. Both have been put forth in an effort to avoid the judicial arbitrariness of deciding which classifications are inherently discriminatory and which interests are fundamental ones. Professor Gunther's model would require, first, that there be a "substantial" connection between the classification and the legislative ends and, secondly, that only articulated rather than hypothetical purposes be considered.[77] The court would concern itself solely with means, not ends, and would supposedly thereby avoid ultimate value judgments about the legitimacy and importance of legislative purposes.[78] The only limitation upon judicial scrutiny along these lines would appear to be judicial competence:

> when the Court cannot confidently assess whether the means contribute to the end because the data are exceedingly technical and complex; or when a "myriad" of claimants upon the legislature permits wide range of responses, with any one as "reasonable" an allocation decision as any other.[79]

This "means-oriented" test would not mean an end to the compelling state interest test. The latter test would still be required "when classifications such as race or interests such as speech" were involved.[80] Gunther's test, on the other hand, would apply in "a wide range of statutes, including the social and economic regulatory legislation."[81] The wide gap between the compelling state interest and rationality tests would be thereby closed, as would the traditional dichotomy between property and liberty.

But has Professor Gunther finally found an answer to the issue of what level of scrutiny a court should exercise over a fundamental interest? Several reasons indicate a negative response.

In the first place, Professor Gunther contemplated that the courts would continue to employ the "compelling state interest" test in the context of fundamental interests and suspect classifications. Gunther did not believe that the court would expand the list of fundamental interests and suspect classifications. Nevertheless, he did advocate a stricter level of scrutiny for such cases in comparison to ordinary cases. Gunther's model left unanswered why the present fundamental interests were fundamental and why the present suspect categories were suspect. In other words, Gunther left by default the explanation as to why the "compelling state interest" test should be used in judicial practice. But is that all that fundamentalness means?

Secondly, Gunther advocated that for many, if not most, cases the court should use the old "reasonable relationship" test with a new "bite". The court should follow the new "bite" test in a wide range of statutes, including social and economic regulatory legislation. The only criterion which Gunther offered for not following his means-oriented test was judicial competence. Judicial manageability of any issue thereby became the sole criterion for employing a "reasonable relationship" as opposed to a "reasonable relationship" test with a "bite". But is judicial competence a truly satisfactory basis to justify the level of scrutiny of any legislation? Justice Harlan reminded us in another context (*Oregon* v. *Mitchell* concerning whether certain provisions of the Voting Rights Act Amendments, 1970, constituted a constitutional exercise of Congressional power) that constitutional issues surrounding the equal protection clause are inappropriately characterised as "factual": "Where the balance is to be struck," he held, "depends ultimately on the values and the perspective of the decision-maker."[82] Professor Gunther's argument, therefore, is misdirected for he assumes that Congress is more competent than the judiciary to make independent determinations of fact. But constitutional issues invariably depend upon values as well as "objective facts".

Finally, except for the already established fundamental interests and suspect categories, the judiciary's function, for Gunther, is to scrutinize the means used in the legislation. In most cases, that is, the legislative "purpose" is given. It is quite possible that the legislature may restrict a fundamental right but, because judicial the court is obliged to accept the legislature's purpose as legitimate. Except for the rights already deemed fundamental, the court must accept a legislature's declaration that a particular enactment does not infringe a fundamental right. As a consequence, Professor Gunther leaves the crucial determination of the fundamentality of fundamental rights in the great number of cases to the legislature. He thereby opens up his approach to the same criticisms already levied against the "legislative supremacy" method for determining and explaining the fundamentality of fundamental rights and freedoms.

d. *Justice Marshall's Model of Judicial Scrutiny*

In contrast to Professor Gunther's three-tier approach, Mr. Justice Marshall has advocated a "spectrum of standards" for reviewing legislation. In *Dandridge*[83] and *Massachusetts Bd. of Retirement v. Murgia,*[84] the Justice held that emphasis should be placed upon three factors: the character of the classification in question, the relative importance to individuals in the class discriminated against of the governmental benefits that they do not receive, and the state interests asserted in support of the classification. The first and third factors are already familiar. The second factor was particularly important in a case such as *Dandridge*, according to Justice Marshall. Since the challenged legislation imposed a "maximum grant" limit of 250 dollars per month per family, regardless of the family's size or needs, the majority classified the legislation as social and economic. Accordingly, the appropriate test was "reasonable relationship". But Justice Marshall pointed out that this case was far removed from the area of business regulation since it involved the "literally vital interests of a powerless minority — poor families without breadwinners." The individual interests here at stake involved "the stuff that sustains those children's lives: food, clothing, shelter." Marshall J. insisted that rather than defining a right, fundamental or otherwise in an a priori fashion, the Court should concentrate upon the relative importance of not receiving the governmental benefits to the individuals in the class.

In *Rodriquez*[85] Justice Marshall eliminated the second consideration. Instead, he focused upon the "recognised invidiousness" of the classification and "the constitutional and societal importance of the interest adversely affected." What did Justice Marshall mean by the term "constitutional and societal importance"? According to Marshall J., it would not do to suggest that the "answer" to whether a particular interest is fundamental must lie in the explicit or implicit guarantees of the Constitution. Nevertheless, the determination of the issue must be "firmly rooted" in

113

the text of the Constitution. The crucial judicial task, therefore, was to examine whether the constitutionally guaranteed rights were dependent upon interests not mentioned in the Constitution and, if so, to what extent. He explained that "as the nexus between the specific constitutional guarantee and the nonconstitutional interest draws close, the nonconstitutional interest becomes more fundamental and the degree of judicial scrutiny applied when the interest is infringed on a discriminatory basis must be adjusted accordingly." In *Murgia*, Justice Marshall described these nonconstitutional interests as "vital to the flourishing of a free society:"

> there remain rights, not now classified as "fundamental", that remain vital to the flourishing of a free society, and classes, not now classified as "suspect", that are unfairly burdened by invidious discrimination unrelated to the individual worth of their members. Whatever we call these rights and classes, we simply cannot forego all judicial protection against discriminatory legislation bearing upon them, but for the rare instances when the legislative choice can be termed "wholly irrelevant" to the legislative goal.[86]

The *Rodriquez* case reflects how Justice Marshall would apply his "sliding scale" approach. At issue in *Rodriquez* was the Texas system of financing public education. It had relied heavily upon local property taxes with consequential substantial interdistrict disparities in per-pupil expenditures. Mexican-American parents brought a class action on behalf of children of poor families residing in districts having a low property tax base. Justice Marshall rejected the rigidified two-tier analysis of a lenient standard of rationality and strict scrutiny. The central consideration in a case like *Rodriquez*, according to Justice Marshall, was the constitutional and societal importance of the interest adversely affected and the recognised invidiousness of the classification. The court, in the past, had held some interests as fundamental even though they were not mentioned in the Constitution. The right to procreate, the right to vote in state elections, and the right to an appeal from a criminal conviction exemplified how the court would display a strong concern with legislation due to the importance of the interests at stake even though the Constitution did not mention such rights, according to Marshall J. They were important because they were, to some extent, interrelated with constitutional guarantees. So, for example, the right to vote in state elections was closely tied to the freedoms of expression in the First Amendment. The right to appeal in criminal cases enhanced the integrity of the range of rights implicit in the Fourteenth Amendment's due process of law clause. Similarly Justice Marshall held, education directly affected the ability of a child to exercise his First Amendment rights and his participation in the political process. The importance of the relationship was marked when disadvantaged or powerless minorities were involved. Although personal wealth was not a permanent disability and although it did not share the same general irrelevance as race or nationality, personal wealth was very relevant to the interest of education. Group wealth, in particular, represented a serious basis of discrimination because the disadvantaged individual had no significant control over it. Rather, governmental action was the sole cause of the wealth classification in this case.

Justice Marshall's "sliding-scale" test makes a major contribution to the discussion of fundamentality in that it emphasises the crucial importance of the nexus between the effective use of constitutional rights, on the one hand, and the constitutional rights themselves, on the other. Or, to use terminology from John Rawls,[87] Justice Marshall's test contemplates the relevance of the *worth* of liberty in a democratic society. Poverty, ignorance, and a general lack of social and economic means affect the worth of liberty or the value to the individual of a constitutional right. A person with greater economic, social or political power will possess greater ability to influence public opinion, to affect public officials and to select political candidates than less fortunate members of society. Indeed, traditionally considered fundamental freedoms such as speech, the press, assembly, political participation and the like may be virtually meaningless for poorer citizens who could not affect the political process even if they so desired. Nor are such freedoms of high value if the citizenry are ignorant, through lack of education or by governmental design, of political events.

On the other hand, Justice Marshall's perspective leaves some of the seemingly interminable issues unanswered. In the first place, although the express provisions of the written Constitution provide the critical source of the Justice's assessment of the articulated state interests involved, the question which we have already experienced remains: why does fundamentality lie in the express words of the written Constitution? Why is a court obligated to follow the express words of a written Constitution? The fact that the Constitution may require such still leaves the question unanswered, unless we are to adopt circular reasoning. For the resolution of the issue we must, as with the principle of legislative supremacy, go to political history and to the political norms reflected in that history. Secondly, as to his reliance upon the express constitutional provisions as the source of his assessment of the articulated state interests, we are still left with the immense problems of construing the meaning and scope of the express provisions.[88] Thirdly, Justice Marshall does not elaborate how we are to determine "the relative importance to individuals in the class" of a lack of receipt of governmental benefits. Nor, finally, does he explain on what basis a court should scrutinize "the character of the classification in question". Should the court ask whether the classification is based on an immutable trait such as race or sex? If so, religious, political and wealth classifications would be less suspicious than, say, sex classifications. Or, does Justice Marshall mean to focus upon another possible criterion such as whether the classificatory trait is completely irrelevant to a citizen's abilities or person, or whether the trait stigmatises him or whether he belongs to a group which has been historically politically powerless or disadvantaged?

At the beginning of this chapter I noted the popular claim that an entrenched Bill of Rights will guarantee the existence of fundamental rights. I have now tried to show that at least two obstacles stand in the way of that claim. Notwithstanding the apparent simplicity and clarity of an "entrenched Bill of Rights" argument, counsel, judges, legislators and bureaucrats will still be compelled to make normative political judgments. They will be required to make normative political judgments about the meaning and scope of the enumerated rights. They will also be required to make normative political judgments about the very nature of fundamental rights themselves. This latter requisite will flow from the necessity to ascertain a standard of judicial scrutiny appropriate to the existence of fundamental rights.

The American constitutional experience demonstrates that traditional legal resources will not resolve the above two problems. Written constitutions, statutes, regulations and judicial decisions can take the common law lawyer only so far. At some point he must make normative political judgments concerning the meaning of the enumerated rights and, secondly, the standard of scrutiny connected with any alleged burdening of the rights. Counsel is compelled to do more than make normative political judgments, however. He must be prepared to elaborate justifications for his normative political judgments from the world of political philosophy. He must do so in order that his judgments possess a principled, consistent basis. I shall now attempt such a task in chapters IV to VI. In chapter VII I shall return to constitutional analysis with a view to resolving the issues which the common law lawyers' arguments have left unanswered.

116

1. See, e.g., Government of Canada, *The Constitutional Amendment Bill: Text and Explanatory Notes*, (Ottawa: Information Canada, 1978) p. 4; idem, *The Constitutional Amendment Bill, 1978: Explanatory Document*, (Ottawa: Information Canada, 1978) pp. 8-12; idem, *A Time For Action: Highlights of the Federal Government's Proposals for the Renewal of the Canadian Federation*, (Ottawa: Information Canada, 1978) pp. 2, 9.

Also see, e.g., idem, *Proposal for a Constitutional Charter of Human Rights*, (Ottawa: Queen's Printer, 1968); idem. *The Constitution and the People of Canada* (Ottawa: Queen's Printer, 1969), pp. 16, 18; Special Joint Committee of Senate and House of Commons on Constitution of Canada, *Final Report*, 4th sess., 28th Parl. (Ottawa: Information Canada, 1972) pp. 18-19.

2. For this point of view see, e.g., the testimony of Professor Walter S. Tarnopolsky before the Special Joint Committee of the Senate and House of Commons on the Constitution of Canada, May 11th, 1970, in *Proceedings*, 3rd sess., 28th Parliament, vol. 8, pp. 7-9, and on Sept. 12th, 1978 in *Proceedings*, 3rd sess., 30th Parliament, vol. 12, pp. 8-9.

3. Canada, House of Commons, 3rd sess., 30th Parliament, 26-27 Eliz. II, 1977-78, *Bill C-60: Constitutional Amendment Act, 1978*, Sect. 5.

4. Appendix, William E. Conklin, "Some Problems concerning the Bill of Rights Provisions of Bill C-60," a brief submitted to Special Joint Committee of Senate and House of Commons on the Constitution of Canada, Sept. 15th, 1978.

5. Hart, H. L. A., *The Concept of Law* (Oxford: Oxford U. Press, 1961), pp. 120 ff.

6. Justice Harlan (joined by Justice Stewart) dissenting, 391 U.S. 145, 88 S.Ct. 1444, 20 L. Ed. 2d 491 (1968).

7. Ibid., 175.

8. 332 U.S. 46, 67 S. Ct. 1672, 91 L. Ed. 1903 (1947). Justice Black dissenting.

9. See text supra, chapter II between notes 19 and 22.

10. *Adamson* v. *California*, 332 U.S. 46, 90, 67 S. Ct. 1672, 1696.

11. *Duncan* v. *Louisiana*, 391 U.S. 145, 88 S. Ct. 1444, 20 L. Ed. 2 d 491 (1968).

12. Joined by Justice Douglas, ibid., 168-169.

13. Aside from this policy difference, Justice Black believed that his theory of incorporation received both historical and legal support. His argument was that the due process clause should be read in the context of the Fourteenth Amendment as a whole. The second sentence of the Fourteenth Amendment provided that "No State shall make or enforce any law which shall abridge the privileges or immunities of citizens of the United States." "What more precious 'privilege' of American citizenship could there be," he asked, "than that privilege to claim the protections of our great Bill of Rights?" He reasoned that an absurd consequence would result if the court

read the "privileges and immunities" clause so as to exclude the safeguards of the Bill of Rights to state conduct. Ibid., 166-167.

14. This is also the thrust of Professor Louis Henkin's essay, *"Selective Incorporation" in the Fourteenth Amendment*, 73 Yale L. J. 74 (1963-64) [hereinafter cited as *Selective Incorporation*]. The term "fundamentality" is his.

15. *Duncan* v. *Louisiana*, 391 U.S. 145, 88 S. Ct. 1444, 20 L. Ed. 2d 491 (1968).

16. Ibid., 174.

17. Ibid., 148-149.

18. Ibid., 149, footnote 14.

19. Ibid., 149.

20. Ibid., 157-158.

21. Louis Henkin, *Selective Incorporation*, supra, note 14.

22. *Duncan* v. *Louisiana*, 391 U.S. 145, 176, 88 S. Ct. 1444, 1463, 20 L. Ed. 2d 491, 511.

23. Ibid., 181.

24. Ibid.

25. *Furman* v. *Georgia*, 408 U.S. 238, 92 S. Ct. 2726, 33 L. Ed. 2d 346 (1972).

26. *Gregg* v. *Georgia*, 428 U.S. 153, 96 S. Ct. 2909, 49 L. Ed. 2d 859 (1976).

27. *Furman* v. *Georgia*, 408 U.S. 238, 312, 92 S. Ct. 2726, 2764.

28. See generally, text, supra, chap. II between notes 11 and 17.

29. Each of the draft entrenched Bills of Rights which the Canadian Government has placed before the public has expressly adopted the "reasonable classification" standard of judicial scrutiny. The "Victoria Charter", after "guaranteeing" the traditional civil and political rights in Articles 1 and 2, provided in Article 3 that

> nothing in this Part shall be construed as preventing such limitations on the exercise of the fundamental freedoms as are reasonably justifiable in a democratic society in the interests of public safety, order, health or morals, of national security, or of the rights and freedoms of others, whether imposed by the Parliament of Canada or the Legislature of a Province, within the limits of their respective legislative powers, or by, the construction or application of any law.

The Special Joint Committee of Senate and House of Commons on the Constitution of Canada recommended in its *Final Report*, 4th sess., 28th Parl. (Canada), (Ottawa: Information Canada, 1972):

> 21. The rights and freedoms recognized by the Bill of Rights should not be interpreted as absolute and unlimited, but should be exercisable to the extent that they are reasonably justifiable in a democratic society.

Article 25 of the Canadian Government's latest proposals for an entrenched Bill of Rights provides:

25. Nothing in this Charter shall be held to prevent such limitations on the exercise or enjoyment of any of the individual rights and freedoms declared by this Charter as are justifiable in a free and democratic society in the interests of public safety or health, the interests of the peace and security of the public, or the interests of the rights and freedoms, of others, whether such limitations are imposed by law or by virtue of the construction or application of any law.

(Bill C-60, 3rd. sess., 30th Parliament (Canada), 26-27 Eliz. II, 1977-78). For comment on Article 25 see Appendix, infra.

Also see the Constitutions of Bangladesh (Article 47 and Part IXA), Barbados (Chap. III), Botswana (Sects. 8(5), 9(2), 11(5), 12(2), 14(3), 16, 17), Cyprus (Sects. 13(1), 15(2), 18(6), 19(3), 20(1), 21(3), 23(3), 27(1)), Guyana (Chap. II), India (Sects. 19(2), (3), (4), (5), (6)), Jamaica (Chap. III), Kenya (Sects. 70-86), Malta (Sects. 33-48), Mauritius (Sects. 3-19), Nauru (Sects. 3-15), Sri Lanke (Sect. 18(2)), Uganda (Sect. 14), and Western Samoa (Part II).

30. See text, infra, between notes 32 and 45. Also see, William E. Conklin, *The Utilitarian Theory of Equality before the Law*, 8 Ott. L. Rev. 485, 485-503 (1976).

31. See text, infra, between notes 76 and 83.

32. See text, infra between notes 82 and 89.

33. *Lindsley* v. *Natural Carbonic Gas Co.*, 220 U.S. 61, 78-79, 31 S. Ct. 337, 340 (1911) [emphasis added].

34. Joseph Tussman and Jacobus tenBroek, *The Equal Protection of the Laws*, 37 Calif. L. Rev. 341 (1949).

35. See generally Charles L. Black, *The Lawfulness of the Segregation Decisions*, 69 Yale L. J. 421, p. 486 (1960).

36. Gary S. Goodpaster, *The Constitution and Fundamental Rights*, 15 Ariz. L. Rev. 479, p. 486 (1973).

37. See, for example, *Daniel* v. *Family Security Life Ins. Co.*, 336 U.S. 220 (1949); *Kotch* v. *Board of River Pilot Comm'rs.*, 330 U.S. 552 (1947); *Williamson* v. *Lee Optical Co.*, 348 U.S. 483 (1955); *McGowan* v. *Maryland*, 366 U.S. 420 (1961); *Railway Express Agency Inc.* v. *New York*, 366 U.S. 106, 69 S. Ct. 463 (1949).

38. See, e.g., *McDonald* v. *Bd. of Election Comm'rs.*, 394 U.S. 802, 809, 89 S. Ct. 1404, 1408 (1969).

39. *McGowan* v. *Maryland*, 366 U.S. 420, 426, 81 S. Ct. 1101, 1105 (1961). See also *McDonald* v. *Bd. of Election Comm'rs.*, ibid., U.S. 809, S. Ct. 1408; *Flemming* v. *Nestor*, 363 U.S. 603, 611-12, 80 S. Ct. 1367, 1372-73 (1960).

40. See generally, Note, *Developments in the Law in Equal Protection*, 82 Harv. L. Rev. 1065, 1078 (1969).

41. See, e.g., *Hirabayashi* v. *United States*, 320 U.S. 81, 63 S. Ct. 1375 (1943); *Korematsu* v. *United States*, 323 U.S. 214, 65 S. Ct. 193 (1944).

42. *Williamson* v. *Lee Optical of Oklahoma*, 348 U.S. 483, 75 S. Ct. 461 (1955); *West Coast Hotel Co.* v. *Parrish*, 300 U.S. 379, 57 S. Ct. 578 (1937).

43. *Lindsley* v. *Natural Carbonic Gas Co.*, 220 U.S. 61, 78, 31 S. Ct. 337, 340.

44. Richard Fielding cites the single anomalous case as *Morey* v. *Doud*, 354 U.S. 457, 77 S. Ct. 1344 (1957). Richard Fielding, *Fundamental Personal Rights: Another Approach to Equal Protection*, 40 U. Chi. L. Rev. 807, p. 811 (1973).

45. 304 U.S. 144, 152-53, footnote 4, 58 S. Ct. 778, 783-84, footnote 4 (1938):

> There may be narrower scope for operation of the presumption of constituitonality when legislation appears on its face to be within a specific prohibition of the Constitution, such as those of the first ten Amendments, which are deemed equally specific when held to be embraced within the Fourteenth...
>
> It is unnecessary to consider now whether legislation which restricts those political processes which can ordinarily be expected to bring about repeal of undesirable legislation, is to be subjected to more exacting judicial scrutiny under the general prohibitions of the Fourteenth Amendment than are most other types of legislation... Nor need we enquire whether similar considerations enter into the review of statutes directed at particular religious ... or national ... or racial minorities... whether prejudice against discrete and insular minorities may be a special condition, which tends seriously to curtail the operation of those political processes ordinarily to be relied upon to protect minorities, and which may call for a correspondingly more searching judicial inquiry....

46. In *Harper* v. *Virginia Bd. of Elections*, 383 U.S. 663, 668, 86 S. Ct. 1079, 1082 (1966), Justice Douglas asserted that "wealth, like race, creed, or color, is not germane to one's ability to participate intelligently in the electoral process."

47. In *Frontiero* v. *Richardson*, 411 U.S. 677, 93 S. Ct. 1764 (1973) Justice Brennan held sex to be a suspect category.

48. In *Levy* v. *Louisiana*, 391 U.S. 68, 88 S. Ct. 1509 (1968) Justice Douglas, speaking for the majority, held that a Louisiana statute "invidiously discriminated" when it allowed legitimate, but not illegitimate, children to recover damages for the wrongful death of their mother.

49. *Griffin* v. *Illinois*, 351 U.S. 12, 76 S. Ct. 585, 100 L. Ed. 891 (1956).

50. *Douglas* v. *California*, 372 U.S. 353, 83 S. Ct. 814, 9 L. Ed. 2d 811 (1963).

51. *Shapiro* v. *Thompson*, 394 U.S. 618, 89 S. Ct. 1322, 22 L. Ed. 2d 600 (1969).

52. *Harper* v. *Virginia Bd. of Elections*, 383 U.S. 663, 86 S. Ct. 1079, 16 L. Ed. 2d 169 (1966).

53. 411 U.S. 1, 98 S. Ct. 1278, 36 L. Ed. 2d 16 (1973). But see Mr. Justice Marshall's (Justice Douglas concurring) dissenting opinion.

54. See, e.g., *Daniel* v. *Family Security Life Ins. Co.*, 336 U.S. 220 (1949), *Kotch* v. *Board of River Pilot Comm'rs.*, 330 U.S. 552 (1947), *Williamson* v. *Lee Optical Co.*, 348 U.S. 483 (1955), *McGowan* v. *Maryland*, 366 U.S. 420 (1961), *San Antonio Independent School Dist.* v. *Rodriquez*, 411 U.S. 1, 98 S. Ct. 1278 (1973) per Justice Powell.

55. 316 U.S. 535, 541, 62 S. Ct. 1110, 1113 (1942).

56. 351 U.S. 12, 22; 76 S. Ct. 585, 592; 100 L. Ed. 891 (1956).

57. 401 U.S. 371, esp. 374-377, 91 S. Ct. 780, esp. 784-785, 28 L. Ed. 2d 113 (1971).

58. 394 U.S. 618, 629; 89 S. Ct. 1322, 1329; 22 L. Ed. 2d 600 (1969).

59. 383 U.S. 745, 757-758; 86 S. Ct. 1170, 1178; 16 L. Ed. 2d 239 (1966) per Stewart J. as quoted in *Shapiro*, ibid., U.S. 630, S. Ct. 1329, L. Ed. 2d 613.

60. 377 U.S. 533, 84 S. Ct. 1362, 12 L. Ed. 2d 500.

61. Ibid., U.S. 555, 561, 562; S. Ct. 1378, 1381, L. Ed. 2d 527.

62. 383 U.S. 663, 667-668; 86 S. Ct. 1079, 1082; 16 L. Ed. 2d 169 (1966) per Justice Douglas.

63. 395 U.S. 621, 626; 89 S. Ct. 1886, 1089; 23 L. Ed. 2d 583, 589 (1969). See also *Yick Wo* v. *Hopkins*, 118 U.S. 356, 370; 6 S. Ct. 1064, 1071; 30 L. Ed. 220 (1886).

64. Ibid. U.S. 628, S. Ct. 1890, L. Ed. 2d 590.

65. *McDonald* v. *Bd. of Election*, 394 U.S. 802, 89 S. Ct. 1404 (1969) per Warren C. J.

66. *Griffin* v. *Illinois*, 351 U.S. 12, 36; 76 S. Ct. 585, 598-599; 100 L. Ed. 891 (1956).

67. *Harper* v. *Virginia Bd. of Elections*, 383 U.S. 663, 683; 86 S. Ct. 1079, 1090; 23 L. Ed. 2d 169, 182 (1966).

68. *Boddie* v. *Conn*, 401 U.S. 371, 91 S. Ct. 780, 28 L. Ed. 2d 113 (1971).

69. 397 U.S. 471, 90 S. Ct. 1153, 25 L. Ed. 2d 491 (1970).

70. *San Antonio Independent School Dist.* v. *Rodriquez*, 411 U.S. 1, 98 S. Ct. 1278, 36 L. Ed. 2d 16 (1973).

71. *Dandridge* v. *Williams*, 397 U.S. 471, 484; 90 S. Ct. 1153, 1161; 25 L. Ed. 2d 491, 502 (1920).

72. Ibid.

73. 377 U.S. 533, 563-568; 84 S. Ct. 1362, 1382-1385; 12 L. Ed. 2d 500.

74. *Harper* v. *Virginia Bd. of Elections*, 383 U.S. 663, 668; 86 S. Ct. 1079, 1082; 16 L. Ed. 2d 169, 173 (1966).

75. *Kramer* v. *Union Free School District No. 15*, 395 U.S. 621, 626-627; 89 S. Ct. 1886, 1089-1090; 23 L. Ed. 2d 583 (1969).

76. 377 U.S. 533, 565; 84 S. Ct. 1362, 1383; 12 L. Ed. 2d 500. For other criticisms of the court's treatment of socio-economic legislation, see R. G. McCloskey, *Economic Due Process and the Supreme Court: An Exhumanation and Reburial*, 1962 Sup. Ct. Rev. 34; Van Alstyne, *The Demise of the Right-Privilege Distinction in Constitutional Law*, 81 Harv. L. Rev. 1438 (1968); Charles A. Reich, *Individual Rights & Social Welfare: The Emerging Legal Issues*, 74 Yale L.J. 1245 (1965); Richard Funston, "The double standard of Constitutional Protection in the Era of the Welfare State," 90 *Pol. Sc. Q.* 261 (1975); Henry J. Abraham, " 'Human' Rights vs. 'Property' Rights; A Comment on the 'double standard,' " 90 *Pol. Sc. Q.* 288 (1975); Note, *The Supreme Court, 1975 Term*, 90 Harv. L. R. 50, pp. 86 ff. (1976).

77. Gerald Gunther, *Foreward: In Search of Evolving Doctrine on a Changing Court: A Model for a Newer Equal Protection*, 86 Harv. L. Rev. 1, pp. 20-21 (1972).

78. Ibid., pp. 22-23.

79. Ibid., p. 24.

80. Ibid.

81. Ibid.

82. 400 U.S. 112, 206; 91 S. Ct. 260, 306; 27 L. Ed. 272, 328 (1970).

83. *Dandridge* v. *Williams*, 397 U.S. 471, 521; 90 S. Ct. 1153, 1180; 25 L. Ed. 2d 491 (1970).

84. 427 U.S. 307, 318; 96 S. Ct. 2562, 2569; 49 L. Ed. 2d 520 (1976).

85. *San Antonio Independent School Dist.* v. *Rodriquez*, 411 U.S. 1, 98 S. Ct. 1278, 36 L. Ed. 2d 16 (1976).

86. *Massachusetts Bd. of Retirement* v. *Murgia* 427 U.S. 307, 320; 96 S. Ct. 2562, 2570; 49 L. Ed. 520 (1976).

87. See text, infra, chap. V between notes 60 and 67.

88. See text, supra, between notes 24 and 29.

Part Two

The Moral-Political Foundation
of Fundamental Rights

Chapter IV

The Principle of "Self-Regarding" Conduct and the Utilitarian Perspective

I have now examined three forms of argument which have been used to try to establish the existence of fundamental rights. The arguments arose from the resource material traditionally available to the common law lawyer: judicial decisions, statutes, regulations, legal writings and constitutions. Our discussion in chapters I to III raised important shortcomings with each form of argument. We were led to the conclusion that one could not overcome the problems within the common law lawyer's traditional resource material. The problems raised in chapters II and III, in particular, suggested that the lawyer must be prepared to make inquiries into the world of political philosophy if he wishes to make a consistent and adequate defence of fundamental rights. Chapters IV to VI will begin such an inquiry.

My inquiry is merely a beginning because I confine myself to liberal political theorists such as Jeremy Bentham, John Stuart Mill, John Rawls, Isaiah Berlin, and T. H. Green. Liberal political theory is a useful starting point, in turn, because there is a good chance that an awareness of the liberal political theory of rights will help make the lawyer more conscious of the political presuppositions of the law which he is advocating. In addition, the shortcomings and inconsistencies of the liberal political theory of rights may provide a needed perspective for the common law lawyer to appreciate in a deeper sense why the traditional forms of argument elaborated in chapters I to III proved inadequate as arguments for the existence of fundamental rights. Although my starting point is liberal political theory, the possibility is not foreclosed that one could make a consistent argument for the existence of fundamental rights by working within the framework of some other political theory. Nor is the possibility precluded that one might work within another political perspective, and yet come to support an argument for the existence of fundamental rights similar to that which I shall elaborate in chapter VI.

One idea which seems to have been particularly close to the Anglo-American notion of liberty is the concept of the "inner sphere of life". There is, it has been claimed, an inner sphere of life over which neither society nor the state may interfere. The individual's thoughts and actions reign uncontrolled and uncontrollable within that inner sphere. This idea that the inner sphere of life ought to be protected underlies much of the contemporary dialogue concerning such issues as obscenity, censorship, abortion, drugs, electronic surveillance and suicide. The idea plays an important role in liberal political and legal theory. It deserves our attention.

The idea of the "inner sphere of life" appears to have found clear expression in John Stuart Mill's classic essay *On Liberty*.[1] Mill began his essay by stressing that the central problem for liberty in his day was not political oppression by government but rather "social tyranny" by "the most active part of the people".[2] His society had devised various ways to protect liberty from political oppression. Political liberties or rights protected the citizen from government regulation, he claimed. Breach of those rights justified "specific resistance, or general rebellion". Secondly, society had established constitutional checks which set out minimum conditions for a governmental act to be valid. But, according to Mill, these two methods of protecting liberty were insufficient to protect a minority from an oppressive majority. Social tyranny was more formidable than many kinds of political oppression because it "leaves fewer means of escape, penetrating much more deeply into the details of life, and enslaving the soul itself," according to Mill. Society tended to impose its own ideas and practices as rules of conduct upon dissenters, thereby fettering the development of individuality. As with political authority, there needed to be a limit to the legitimate interference of collective opinion upon the individual's independent thought and conduct. Mill sought a test which would demarcate that limit.

The core to Mill's *On Liberty* was his belief in the distinction between two spheres of life. On the other hand, according to Mill, there was an inner sphere of life which "affects only himself, or if it also affects others, only with their free, voluntary, and undeceived consent and participation."[3] Society possessed, if any, only an indirect interest in this inner sphere. The inner sphere was, for Mill, "the appropriate region of human liberty." As he wrote in another work,

> whatever theory we adopt with respect to the foundation of the social union, and under whatever political institutions we live, there is a circle around every individual human being, which no government, be it that of one, of a few, or of many, ought to be permitted to overstep: there is a part of the life of every person who has come to years of discretion,

126

within which the individuality of that person ought to reign uncontrolled either by any other individual or by the public collectivity. That there is, or ought to be, some space in human existence thus entrenched around, and sacred from authoritative intrusion, no one who professes the smallest regard to human freedom or dignity will call in question.[4]

In all cases in which a person's conduct affected only his own interests, he asserted in *On Liberty*, "there should be perfect freedom, legal and social, to do the action and stand the consequences".[5]

If we could successfully construct an argument to justify why society and the state ought not to penetrate the "inner sphere of life" and if we described rights as the foundation-stones which entrenched the boundaries of that sphere, we could quite legitimately describe the rights as fundamental rights. The number and scope of the fundamental rights, of course, would depend upon what we meant by the term "the inner sphere of life". Although we shall examine below what Mill himself meant by the term, the "inner sphere of life" would *prima facie* seem to be bound up with a fundamental right of political and religious conscience.

The rights which delineated and entrenched the "inner sphere of life" would be at "the root of the matter", "essential", "basic", "underlying", "primary", "formative", or "irreducible". The rights would not be created by the state. Nor would the state be able to deny their existence. This is because the rights would be "original rights", to use the term of Mr. Justice Rand.[6] They would be original in the sense that they would be the formative, underlying building-block of the politico-legal system from which all civil institutions — including the state — would be derived.

The threshold problem is to construct an argument as to why neither the state nor society ought to penetrate, burden, harm or monitor "the inner sphere of life." Since the idea is his, it might be a useful starting point to see what John Stuart Mill meant by the term "the inner sphere of life" and then to question whether the utilitarian political tradition or Mill himself could consistently support the claim that neither the state nor society ought to penetrate the "inner sphere of life".

Section 1. Mill's Principle of "Self-Regarding" Conduct

Mill believed that he had discovered "one very simple principle", a practical principle, which delineated the boundary between legitimate societal intervention upon the individual and the individual himself. His principle, he thought, governed society's relationship with the individual in all cases. The thrust of it was that "the sole end for which mankind [were] warranted, individually or collectively, in interfering with the liberty of action" of any individual was self-defence or, to use his term, "self-protection". That is, society might rightfully exercise authority over an individual against the latter's will only for one reason: to prevent harm to others. Individuality ought to remain uncontrolled in all other circumstances. As Mill asserted, "in the part which merely concerns himself, his independence is, of right, absolute. Over himself, over his own body and mind, the individual is sovereign."[7] The latter circumstances Mill described as "self-regarding"; the former as "other-regarding".

What specific elements composed the "inner sphere of life", according to Mill? In the first place, the "inner sphere" comprised "the inward domain of consciousness" from which Mill derived liberty of conscience "in the most comprehensive sense", liberty of thought and feeling, and absolute freedom of opinion on all subjects. The freedom of expressing and publishing opinions, though "other-regarding", rested upon similar reasons and was "practically inseparable" from the inward liberty of thought. Secondly, the inner sphere of life required liberty of tastes and pursuits unless such liberty harmed others. Thirdly, there flowed the freedom of association "for any purpose not involving harm to others." No society was "completely free" unless these three freedoms were "absolute and unqualified."[8]

On the other hand, the outer sphere of life involved one's direct interventions with other persons. Mill's essay indicated two kinds of such interactions. First, there was activity "hurtful to others". We have seen that Mill incorporated this category of "other-regarding" conduct into his initial statement of the principle. He curiously added a second category, however.

On several occasions Mill stated that one may harm the interests of another not only through his acts but also through his omissions. In his "Introduction", after setting out his principle, Mill stated that there is a *prima facie* case to punish a person who fails to perform "many positive acts for the benefit of others, which he may rightfully be compelled to perform."[9] Mill's examples were such duties as the giving of evidence in court, the bearing of one's "fair share in the common defence, or in any other joint work necessary to the interest of the society of which he enjoys the protection," and the performance of "certain acts of benefience, such as saving a fellow creature's life, or interposing to protect the defenceless against ill-usage, things which *whenever it is obviously a man's duty to do*..."[10] When Mill re-stated his principle of "self-regarding" conduct in chapter IV he asserted that although society is not founded on a social contract,

> every one who receives the protection of society owes a return for the benefit, and the fact of living in society renders it indispensible that each should be *bound to observe a certain line of conduct* towards the rest.[11]

This "line of conduct" entailed not only the maxim that one ought not to harm the interests of another but also that every person should bear "his share (to be fixed on some equitable principle) of the labours and sacrifices incurred for defending society or its members from injury and molestation." The latter involves an issue of "duty", we are told, and the duty is violated when "a distinct and assignable obligation to any other person or persons" is infringed.[12]

What examples did Mill provide of "self-regarding" conduct?[13] Muslims, he claimed, expressed moral outrage towards Christians who ate pork simply because of the personal tastes and other self-regarding concerns of Christians. According to Mill, Southern Europeans believed married clergy to be irreligious, unchaste, indecent, gross and disgusting. And, the Spanish state in Mill's day prohibited all forms of non-Roman Catholic public worship. Similarly, the Puritans in New England and Great Britain had succeeded in pressuring their respective governments to enact statutes which preserved the Sabbath as a day of rest for *all*, prohibited the sale of liquors except for medical purposes, and endeavoured to repress all public as well as private amusements — including music, the theatre and dance. These cases Mill found to be clear examples of "self-regarding" conduct. Despite the fact that a strong case could be made for prohibiting such personal "immoralities", the consequence of so doing would be that society would adopt the logic of persecutors. We would be "admitting a principle of which we should resent as a gross injustice the application to ourselves."[14] The conduct in these examples, according to Mill, was individual, not social.

Mill admitted that the principle of "self-" and "other-regarding" conduct was not entirely clear-cut. "No person is an entirely isolated being," he recognised.[15] It is "impossible for a person to do anything seriously or permanently hurtful to himself, without mischief reaching at least to his near connections, and often far beyond them," he continued. Having recognised the overlap between the two concepts, what then did Mill mean by "self-regarding" conduct?

One should bear in mind at least three aspects of Mill's own analysis of "self-regarding" conduct. In the first place, Mill emphasized the difference between direct and indirect effects. "Self-regarding" conduct was that activity with which society had only an *indirect* interest. That is, it affected the individual "directly and in the first instance".[16] If the conduct affected others, it did so "only with their free, voluntary, and undeceived consent and participation." So, for example, a person "of ripe years" should be permitted to choose his own life style because he alone was "the person *most interested* in his own well-being..."[17] The interests of his parents or any other person, except in the cases of strong personal attachment, was "fractional", "altogether indirect" and "trifling, compared with that which he himself has."

Secondly, John Rees has clarified an important point with respect to Mill's notion of "self-regarding" conduct. The division between "self-" and "other-regarding" acts occurred where one's behaviour interfered with the *interests* of others, not where his conduct *merely affected* others.[18] Mill went to some effort in *On Liberty* to use the term "interests" when he stated his principle. In chapter IV, in particular, Mill continually referred to the *interests* of the individual and society.

Rees' point is important because, without the notion of interests, Mill's principle would be primarily concerned with the subjective feelings of the members of society. Whether or not an individual's conduct was "self-regarding" would depend upon how *the others* in the society perceived the effect of the individual's conduct upon them. When one brings the notion of "interests" into the discussion, the opportunity arises for a wider examination of whether the effects upon the society of the individual's conduct also infringe the *interests* of society. The latter inquiry permits an assessment of the issue "from the outside", as it were. As a consequence, the interests of society are not necessarily what the members of society declare to be their interests. Indeed, Mill meant to assert such when he emphasized that the society could intervene upon the individual's conduct only when it had become established that the individual had violated a "distinct and assignable obligation". The individual, in other words, had to have done more than simply affect other persons. For this reason, Fitzjames Stephen misdirected his critique of Mill's principle when Stephen asserted that "there is hardly a habit which men in general regard as good which is not acquired by a series of more or less painful and laborious acts."[19]

So, for example, an obscene periodical or film may well affect the reader physically, emotionally and physiologically. It might excite others or incite revulsion amongst them. Most readers would be hard pressed not to admit and even to insist upon that. But whether or not the reading of the book or the viewing of a film affects society's interests is another matter. It might be in society's interest that the free flow of obscene materials be permitted, for otherwise the desire of others to write and publish, say, politically motivated pamphlets might also tend to be more rigorously scrutinized by the authorities. It might also be in society's interest that the obscene materials be published or produced because, to use Mill's argument, there may be some truth to the opinions or ideas expressed. The individual would thereby be "deprived of the opportunity of exchanging error for truth."[20] On the other hand, the obscene materials might falsely portray the role of sex in human life. In such circumstances, the individual would lose "what is almost as great a benefit, the clearer perception and livelier impression of truth, produced by its collision with error."[21] The latter might arguably be the circumstance where, for example, films and publications portray sexual displays of animals and adults with children. Such expression, it would seem, would impress upon the observer the pivotal importance of human dignity in our sexual relationship with other humans — a dignity which is denied in such expression. For this and other reasons, obscene materials might affect others but not necessarily harm their interests.

This leads to a third point which was, it is submitted, central to Mill's analysis. Conduct was "self-regarding" if, even though it harmed others, it did so only because of the "preferences" which others held of the individual's acts. Mill defined the term "preference" in this manner:

> People are accustomed to believe, and have been encouraged in the belief by some who aspire to the character of philosophers, that their feelings, on subjects of this nature, are better than reasons, and render reasons unnecessary... but an opinion on a point of conduct, not supported by reasons, can only count as one person's preference; and if the reasons, when given, are a mere appeal to a similar preference felt by other people, it is still only many people's liking instead of one.[22]

Mill readily acknowledged that "self-regarding" conduct affect the feelings of others.[23] One could, for example, cause feelings of admiration. Or, one could become the object of distaste or even contempt because of his own "self-regarding" conduct. Although the individual was, in a sense, thereby penalized by his conduct, according to Mill, "he suffer[ed] these penalties only in so far as they [were] the *natural* and, as it were, the *spontaneous* consequences of the faults themselves." The penalties were indirect and were not "purposely inflicted on him for the sake of punishment".[24]

Society might express its distaste and ostracise the individual; society could remonstrate, reason, persuade, or entreat him; society could caution others not to associate with him. But society could not legitimately inflict pain for the express purpose of punishment if the individual's conduct merely contravened society's "preferences". Not even "one's own good, either physical or moral" was "a sufficient warrant" to penalise him. Something more was required than that society's "preferences" had been violated. The individual must have actually caused harm to others. But even that was not enough. The harm must have been caused to the interests of others and their interests could not possibly include their "preferences". One was not liable to others if his acts would not have harmed others, in other words, but for the beliefs which others held of his conduct. The harm must have been related to a distinct, definite duty which the individual owed to others. And that duty must have been specifically assigned to the particular individual.

Section 2. Benthamite Utilitarianism and the Protection of "Self-Regarding" Conduct

We have now shown that Mill defined the "inner sphere of life" in terms of "self-regarding conduct" and we have elaborated the central elements of the latter notion. It is appropriate, therefore, that we consider whether it is possible to construct an argument for the protection of such conduct within the prevailing philosophic tradition of the Englishspeaking world.

Bentham's theory of utilitarianism would, at first sight, appear to provide an answer to the problem of determining what conduct is "self-regarding" and what is "other-regarding". The reason why Bentham's theory would seem to provide an answer is that his approach would apparently provide the ideal legislator with a perspective from which he could actually calculate *when* an individual's conduct infringed the *interests* of society. Although John Stuart Mill clearly amended Bentham's theory so as to focus primarily upon the "higher pleasures" of the "developing individual" rather than more hedonistic pleasures, it might help to clarify our thoughts by examining the kinds of factors which a Benthamite legislator might take into account when faced with the issue whether "self-regarding" conduct ought to be protected.

How, then, would a Benthamite legislator approach the many diverse instances where it is alleged that one's conduct interferes with the interests of others either through acts or omissions to act? Let us deal with three general types of behaviour in hopes that we can cast some insight upon the considerations which a Benthamite would take into account with respect to other examples. The three general kinds of behaviour which I have in mind are as follows. First, there is conduct which "interferes" with others because of the widespread *feelings* of "reprobation" and "disgust" of other persons toward the conduct. Obscene publications or homosexuality would be examples of this first category. Secondly, there is behaviour where the individual is inducing self-inflicted harm. Here the community intervenes presumably in order to protect the individual from harm. As examples, we would have attempted suicide or a contract into slavery. The third, closely related class of cases involves conduct which the community infringes largely because of a paternalistic concern that the individual might at some future time harm himself. As examples, there are requirements that an individual wear a helmet when he is driving a motorcycle, that a driver of an automobile and his passengers use seat-belts, or that persons be forbidden to swim at a public beach unless a lifeguard is on duty.

Each of these three types of interference with "self-regarding conduct" is sufficiently complex to warrant an essay in itself.[25] On the other hand, any argument which attempted to support the protection of "self-regarding conduct" would be both incomplete and inadequate were it not to raise some of the important factors which the argument would take into account in the above general categories of cases.

Bentham's utilitarianism seemed to have been premised on at least three assumptions. First, he assumed that each individual behaved in his own self-interest. This assumption was particularly reflected in his discussion of cases where punishment was groundless.[26] Although an individual A's conduct may have been "mischievous or disagreeable" upon B, B may have consented to the conduct. As long as the consent was "free and fairly obtained", it provided the best proof that A inflicted no real harm upon B.

But why was this so? Because, Bentham told us, "no man can be so good a judge as the man himself, what it gives him pleasure or displeasure."[27] Not only did the individual act according to his own self-interest, he alone was the best judge of his own interests. This second assumption, interestingly, is reflected in much of Mill's *On Liberty*.[28]

Thirdly, Bentham assumed that a legislator could accurately measure and compare one person's pleasures against another's pains. Indeed, he went so far as to elaborate how the legislator could add and subtract the pleasures and pains amongst many individuals so as to produce an outcome which corresponded with the greatest happiness of the greatest number. We have seen in chapter II of this book that Bentham defined fourteen different pleasures and twelve different pains.[29] Of the pleasures he listed sense, wealth, skill, amity, a good name, power, piety, benevolence, malevolence, memory, imagination, expectation, association and relief. Of the pains he set out privation, senses, awkwardness, enmity, ill name, piety, benevolence, malevolence, memory, imagination, expectation and association. Bentham described the nature of each of these pleasures and pains[30] as well as the relevant factors which altered them.[31] Bentham then devised seven "dimensions of value" which the legislator was to use as standards in measuring the pleasures and pains: intensity, duration, certainty or uncertainty, propinquity or remoteness, fecundity,[32] purity,[33] and extent.[34]

How would an advocate of Bentham's utilitarianism have approached each of the three general classes of behaviour raised above? A Benthamite would appeal directly to the measurement of pleasures and pains between the parties in any particular case. If the second party to an act were the society, then the Benthamite would weigh the pleasures (and possible pains) which the society would gain by interfering with the conduct as against the pains which the individual would experience from the intervention. The Benthamite would also assess the pains (and possible pleasures) society would experience by *not* interfering in the conduct as against the pleasures such non-intervention would produce for the individual concerned. The Benthamite would then compare the result of the above two inquiries. He would favour a decision which produced, in total, more pleasures than pains.

When Mill pronounced that society possessed jurisdiction to interfere with an individual's conduct whenever that conduct was "hurtful to others", what type of harm would a Benthamite utilitarian include within his calculations and how would he measure that harm? Would he consider only bodily harm or would he contemplate "emotional harm"? If the latter, would a Benthamite acknowledge that "emotional harm" could conceivably be inflicted upon the community when, for example, two homosexuals held hands while striding down Broadway or when obscene material was sold at a public newstand? Bentham left little doubt but that his ideal legislator would be obliged to take psychological harm into account.

Bentham expressly considered harm to be of the "psychological" variety in that all the pains which he elaborated were pains of the psyche: "piety", "benevolence", "malevolence", "memory", "imagination", "expectation", and "association". Homosexual behaviour in public or the sale of obscene material — to take two examples of our first category of cases — might well inculcate in the majority feelings of "indignation and disgust", to use Lord Devlin's words.[35] Such conduct would no doubt create pleasure for the homosexuals or salesmen of obscene pamphlets, the more so that the community became disgusted. But the community would suffer pain simply because it believed the behaviour immoral. A Benthamite, therefore, would have to weigh the homosexuals' or salesmen's pleasureable responses as against the community's moral reaction. Although admittedly speculative, common sense would seem to lead one to conclude that the physical and emotional intensity in addition to the certainty of the pleasures could conceivably be quite high with respect to the two homosexuals. In psychiatric circles it is accepted that the pleasures of the homosexuals would be of short duration, low fecundity and low purity.[36] Any love relationship is accompanied with painful experiences. The extent of the homosexuals' pleasures would obviously be minimal since usually there are only two homosexuals involved at any one time.

From the viewpoint of the passers-by on Broadway, on the other hand, the pains might conceivably be equally intense, of possibly longer duration, low remoteness, high fecundity, high purity and certainly of great extent (since many persons would observe the couple on a street such as Broadway). In contrast, the "passers-by" would possess a smaller quantum of pains if the homosexual couple paraded, say, in Greenwich Village. Indeed, the pains would conceivably be minimal if the couple walked and lived amongst homosexuals themselves. Thus, although the Benthamite legislator would protect the "self-regarding conduct" of the homosexuals in the latter circumstances, he would not in the former.

We have, in this example, raised circumstances when a Benthamite legislator would not always protect "self-regarding" conduct. Indeed, with respect to the first class of cases of which homosexuality and obscenity are examples, a Benthamite utilitarian could not even afford a *prima facie* presumption in favour of the protection of "self-regarding" conduct. The examples also reflect how difficult it would be for a legislator to measure accurately the pleasures and pains between two individuals. It would be even more difficult to measure them between one individual and the society as a whole. What standard of comparison could the Benthamite legislator use? The most that we as commentators can do is, using our own admittedly subjective and speculative imagination, attempt *to conceive* various *fact situations* in which homosexuality might be at issue within a community and then to question whether in any of these circumstances the Benthamite legislator would not wish to protect "self-regarding" conduct.

The second type of "self-regarding" conduct involves cases where the society might want to intervene in order to protect an individual from harming himself through suicide or the signing of a contract of slavery. It might well be that the community as a whole would greet such conduct with abhorrence and possibly disgust. This would be particularly so if the community mores were supported by a strong religious code which prohibited such conduct in absolute and damnifying terms. *If* such were the case, then our calculations would be similar to those raised above with respect to the homosexual example. It is conceivable, on the other hand, that the community would not respond to an attempted suicide or contract into slavery with moral abhorrence. In that case the community would be less of a "party" to the conduct. Our calculations would, therefore, focus more upon the pleasures and pains which the suicidal victim or the contractee himself would experience from the conduct. We would also confine our calculation to the pains and pleasures experienced by immediate friends and relatives.

As in the case of the homosexuality example, the results of our calculations for a successfully executed suicide would vary cor-

	Pleasures to victim *	*Pains to society*
intensity	high	variable
duration	short	variable
certainty	high	variable
propinquity	close	variable
fecundity	nil	variable
purity	low**	variable
extent	low	variable

* These calculations do not estimate what pleasures and pains the individual would have if he continued living. Though of crucial importance, this factor would appear to be impossible to measure.

** The pleasure of suicide to the victim would probably be impure as it would be likely that pain would flow to relatives and friends as a consequence of the suicide. This would not always appear to be the case.

responding to the facts of the case. The included diagram demonstrates those factors which would vary with the circumstances. It would seem that, in our example, the only certainty would be the pleasures of the act of suicide to the victim himself.

The Benthamite utilitarian would let the community interfere with the suicidal victim's "self-regarding" act only if the "pains" of the loss of life were quite high. One factor, very difficult to calculate, would be the pleasures and pains which the potential suicide victim would experience had he continued living. Another important factor would be whether the victim was surrounded by close friends and relatives who greatly loved him. A further complicating factor would be whether his friends, relatives or even the community as a whole were politically, culturally or financially dependent upon the victim. Thus, a Benthamite utilitarian could justify interference with an attempt of suicide if the suicidal individual were young in years, a financially successful businessman, the president of a country, a Minister of Defence in wartime, or a "family man" with emotionally dependent relatives and friends. Affluence, social status or political success are, of course, no guarantee that the individual would experience overwhelming happiness had he continued living. When he began the act of suicide, the suicidal victim presumably contemplated that he would not experience such happiness in the future. Nevertheless, even if his pains greatly outweighed his pleasures had he continued living, the chances are very high that the pains of his loss to the community could be overbearing if he had become "indispensable" to his family, friends or the community as a whole.

Other circumstances can be conceived when the Benthamite legislator would be unwilling to interrupt the act of suicide. Sometimes elderly citizens possess few friends and have few, if any, family members financially dependent on them. In North American society an argument could be made that elderly ladies have an even lower economic worth. If the person is suffering from, say, a terminal or otherwise painful disease such as rheumatism, the continued sight of the elderly person may bring intense distress and anxiety to family members and friends. In addition, the family and community may actually gain benefit from the elder's death through inheritance and death duties (if the elder were a wealthy individual). In these circumstances, although the intensity and duration of the "pleasure" derived from his death may be minimal, the act of death would have high levels of certainty, fecundity and extent. The act of death would, therefore, be very impure, the death being followed by pleasure in the community and amongst the few relatives. The Benthamite utilitarian would be led to accept passively the suicide of a suffering elderly person. The Benthamite would be hard pressed to permit the suicide, on the other hand, if the gentleman were a learned scholar, writer or artist and if he were capable of continuing his work despite his illness.

Another example of the class of "self-inflicted" harms occurs where one voluntarily contracts himself into slavery. Although "liberty" is certainly a pleasure and its loss a pain, other factors might come into play. The slave and his ancestors might have been in dire poverty for many years. The prospect of regularly having food and lodging for the prospective slave and his family might be a pleasure of immense intensity, long duration, great certainty, low remoteness and high fecundity. Only its purity would be low since the consequence of the contract will be loss of liberty. But that impurity is relatively minor if compared to the advantages gained from the contract. For the Benthamite, therefore, a contract into slavery is clearly justifiable in the circumstances contemplated. Such a contract might not be justifiable in a society where the opportunities for economic betterment are profuse and social welfare is secure.

Similar considerations enter the picture when the Benthamite is faced with the third group of cases: that is, where the question arises whether to protect an individual out of fear that he might harm himself in the future. Let us assume, for example, that a policeman sees a young man, James, getting onto his motorcycle without a helmet. Let us also assume that the law authorizes the policeman to impound the motorcycle until James purchases a helmet and promises to wear it. Would a Benthamite permit the policeman to intervene upon James' "self-regarding" conduct? The policeman receives little pain and probably a small amount of pleasure from the interference. To all intents and purposes, therefore, we need only focus upon the pleasures and pains of one person, James.

Our results could conceivably read as follows:

	Pleasures	Pains
intensity	variable	low
duration	variable	short
certainty	variable	variable
propinquity	variable	variable
fecundity	variable	low
purity	variable	high
extent	variable	low

138

As in the above cases, a Benthamite would react differently when faced with different circumstances. The certainty of pain, for example, would be high if James used his motorcycle for his livelihood and if he could not afford a helmet. The propinquity of the pain would be very close if, in addition, James' family were economically dependent upon him. Unlike the other two cases discussed above, however, this is a case where "pain" will result from both a decision to intervene and not to intervene. As Professor Greenawalt reminds us,[37] "reducing losses" may be as much a contribution to the greatest good as increasing gains. An important variable, therefore, is the statistical risk that James will have a motorcycle accident within his lifetime and the additional risk that he will be killed or severely injured from such an accident as a result of his not wearing a helmet. If the risks were very low then the pains of interference might outweigh the pains of not interfering. Such would probably be the case, for example, if James had a very small motorcycle and if there were no larger "carriers" in his daily travels. But as these circumstances are unlikely today, a Benthamite could justifiably intervene to restrict "self-regarding" conduct in this third class of cases.

From the examples in the three classes of cases involving "self-regarding" conduct, it would seem that a Benthamite utilitarian could not always justify the protection of "self-regarding" conduct. Indeed, he could not even accept a *prima facie* presumption that such conduct should be protected. If anything, a Benthamite utilitarian would support a presumption that society ought to intervene upon self-regarding conduct in all cases of self-inflicted harm (e.g., suicide and contracts into slavery) if the individual were making or had the propensity to make a significant economic or cultural contribution to society.

Generally, the outcome of the Benthamite calculation varies directly with the circumstances of the case. Facts can be conceived whereby society should intervene upon "self-regarding" conduct in each of the three classes of cases. Although we have seen how difficult it is for a Benthamite legislator to compare the pleasures and pains accurately between an individual and society and to calculate the pleasures and pains of a suicidal victim if he had continued to live, the fact that the ultimate outcome of the utilitarian calculation hinges upon the facts of any case leads us to the conclusion that a Benthamite utilitarian could not support an argument for the inviolability of "self-regarding" conduct.

It is clear that Mill would have been shocked at these conclusions. Either he was not a Benthamite utilitarian or, if he was, he did not comprehend the direction into which this brand of utilitar-

139

ianism would lead him. We have seen in our discussion of the term "preferences" that Mill believed, for example, that the state could not legitimately interfere with A's conduct simply because of the intensity of B's belief that A's conduct was immoral or insane.[38] In another context in *On Liberty* Mill wrote that:

> his own good, either physical or moral, is not a sufficient warrant. He cannot rightfully be compelled to do or forbear because it will be better for him to do so, because it will make him happier, because, in the opinions of others, to do so would be wise, or even right. — In the part which merely concerns himself, his independence is, of right, absolute. Over himself, over his own body and mind, the individual is sovereign.[39]

In the same vein, Mill believed that society did not even have the authority to intervene on B's behalf in order to protect him. Society, for example, had no authority to prevent an individual from drinking alcohol.[40] Nor had society the right forcibly to prevent an individual from harming himself as in the case of someone about to jump off a bridge,[41] or in the case of continual drunkenness (unless, of course, the drunkard were shirking his duties toward his family).[42] On the other hand, society did have authority to prevent an individual from voluntarily contracting himself into slavery because, contrary to the viewpoint of a Benthamite utilitarian, slavery was such a harmful evil that under no conditions could it ever have benefits.

Section 3. Rule Utilitarianism and the Protection of "Self-Regarding" Conduct

Mill's position with respect to "self-regarding" conduct can be better understood, it is submitted, by distinguishing between two versions of utilitarianism which have been rigorously developed by moral philosophers during the past quarter century.[43] The one, known as "act" or "extreme" utilitarianism, examines the consequences of a particular action on the welfare of all human beings. No reference is made to other cases. Rather, one determines the utility of *each particular action or practice*. Bentham's theory was a fairly simplified version of act utilitarianism. In contrast, according to the second version of utilitarianism known as "rule" (or "restricted") utilitarianism, one initially determines whether a particular act relates to some general moral or legal rule. After weighing the advantages and disadvantages of that particular rule, one then compares the utility of following that rule in comparison with other possible rules. At issue is whether the rule is justifiable

140

in the great majority of cases in terms of its long term as well as short term consequences on the general welfare. Once one has chosen the rule of greatest utility for the general welfare in most cases, the particular conduct is then assessed by its conformity to that rule.

So, for our purposes, what appears to be a "self-regarding" act must initially be related to some rule which would protect such an act. Although the protection of the conduct might be justifiable in the particular circumstances, one must still go on to examine whether such a rule had advantageous long term consequences upon other rules, principles or policies of the society at large. The rule utilitarian, in other words, will assess the "pleasures" and "pains" which a general *rule* permitting or prohibiting interference upon the conduct will have for the society in similar or even relatively dissimilar cases.[43]

Richard Wasserstrom,[45] J. J. C. Smart[46] and others[47] have made what appears to be a persuasive argument that it is difficult to detect any important theoretical distinctions between act and rule utilitarianism. The rule utilitarian could revise any rule so as to take account of a new rule more coincident with the general welfare. One could thereby take into account exceptions to the original rule. And the same factors which would lead the act utilitarian to break a rule would also lead a rule utilitarian to amend the rule. Thus, as long as there were no theoretical limit to the number of rules which could be introduced, it would be difficult to foresee a case in which the rule utilitarian would of necessity come to a different outcome than would an act utilitarian.

Notwithstanding the likelihood that both versions of utilitarianism would theoretically lead one to the same result, with respect to any case of "self-regarding" conduct, rule utilitarianism does provide a more sophisticated perspective with which we can better isolate the factors surrounding the advisability of protecting "self-regarding" conduct in any particular set of circumstances. In particular, rule utilitarianism directs concentration on long term consequences and, in addition, on the repercussions of those consequences for other societal practices, rules, principles and policies. As Wasserstrom comments, although a careful act utilitarian would also theoretically take these factors into account, a rule utilitarian would more easily be led to consider such factors as necessarily relevant.[48] A rule utilitarian perspective is also worthwhile for our purposes in that Mill's *On Liberty* and his *Utilitarianism* seem to reflect that Mill himself perceived some validity to the distinction.

Mill defended liberty primarily upon rule utilitarian grounds.[49]

Chapter 3 of *On Liberty* begins, for example, with very strong words in favour of "the free development of individuality" and "individual spontaneity" as the "end of man". Upon realizing that "spontaneity forms no part of the ideal of the majority of moral and social reformers," Mill fell back upon the utilitarian value of von Humbolt's general rule that "freedom" and "variety of situations" were required. Von Humbolt's rules were required because society needed "strong natives" who had strong characters.[50] In addition, when a person developed his individuality, he became, as a rule, more valuable to himself and to society: "there is a greater fulness of life about his own existence, and when there is more life in the units there is more in the mass which is composed of them...", Mill argued.[51]

In chapter 4 of *On Liberty*, Mill elaborated the "self-regarding — other-regarding" distinction in terms of the utilities of a general rule of protection. He stressed, for example, that a social rule punishing grown persons for not taking proper care of themselves would have negative long-term consequences for the society because such persons would eventually "grow up mere children incapable of being acted on by rational consideration of distant motives."[52] Furthermore, "the odds are" that when society interferes with "self-regarding" conduct,

> it interferes wrongly, and in the wrong place. On questions of social morality, of duty of others, the opinion of the public, that is, of an overwhelming majority, though often wrong, is likely to be still oftener right; because on such questions they are only required to judge of their own interests; of the manner in which some mode of conduct, if allowed to be practiced, would affect themselves. But the opinion of a similar majority, imposed as a law on the minority, on questions of self-regarding conduct, is quite as likely to be wrong as right...[53]

Finally, Mill's arguments for liberty of thought and discussion in chapter 2 of *On Liberty*, although not directly relevant to his principle of "self-regarding" conduct, similarly reflected a rule utilitarian perspective. To silence a dissenting opinion was to claim infallibility for the opinion of the day, according to Mill. But, since infallibility was impossible, it was always conceivable that the silenced opinion might add something to the public knowledge. Government benefited by synthesizing the opinions of all persons. To the claim that governments had the duty to uphold certain useful beliefs Mill replied that the usefulness of an opinion was itself a matter of opinion. Thus, to deny the expression of an opinion was to obstruct the general welfare of society.[54]

If we keep Mill's considerations in mind, it becomes clear that whereas act utilitarianism might easily justify interference with "self-regarding" conduct in a variety of circumstances, a general rule permitting such intervention in all similar cases might be more difficult to justify. For example, instead of weighing the complex pleasures and pains of an ostracized homosexual couple on the one hand and the feelings of reprobation and disgust by the public on the other hand, a rule utilitarian would be obliged to assess the long-term consequences of a rule prohibiting homosexual behaviour in public. Negative long-term consequences of such a rule are conceivable. It might be impossible to administer such a rule equally or effectively. In addition, enforcement of such a rule might lead to serious political dissatisfaction within the homosexual community as against law enforcement officers. Indeed, if the rule were enforced rigorously, such enforcement might cause disrespect towards the law generally not only by practising homosexuals but also by the liberal-minded members of the community. Furthermore, as Rolf Sartorius suggests,[55] the utilitarian must take account of the interests of future generations who in all probability are unlikely to hold strong beliefs against homosexuality.

On the other hand, a rule utilitarian would also be required to examine whether the non-existence of such a rule would gravely loosen the moral fabric of society. If that fact were proven by reference to history or sociology then a revised rule which permitted interference with "self-regarding" conduct might in some communities (e.g., a very religious one with strong moral values) be justifiable. If the latter case could not be established, the rule utilitarian would be obliged to protect the homosexuals' "self-regarding" conduct. In either case, the community's moral "preferences" of reprobation would not, of themselves, be sufficient grounds to prohibit homosexual conduct. The community's moral "preferences" would be only one relevant consideration which ought to be given due weight. The weight would depend on whether the particular moral rule was "essential to [society's] existence" — to use Lord Devlin's phrase.[56]

In the second class of cases (that is, where the community interferes with behaviour which involves self-inflicted harm), the conclusion appears warranted that a rule utilitarian could justify an infringement of self-regarding conduct by some means but not by others. The social and economic costs might be too high, for example, for any rule which required that all suicidal "patients" be sent to a mental institution. The costs would include the loss of economic contribution by the individual to the community, a grave financial burden upon the community, and financial and emotional losses to the individual's dependents and family. In addition, such a rule would deflate respect for privacy which, as Mill argued, is an important value contributing to the social good.[57] A rule utilitarian would find it easier to accept a rule which offered state-financed psychiatric therapy on an "outpatient" basis for persons with suicidal tendencies.

Aside from costs, Professor Greenawalt has suggested three other considerations which we might take into account in this context.[58] First, if a rule allowed for severe sanctions (such as involuntary detention in a mental institution) against the participant of self-inflicted harm, the rule would probably require that officials ascertain facts concerning the individual's state of mind as well as the surrounding circumstances.[59] But, in the case of an allegedly mentally ill patient, such an examination of the facts would be very difficult. For example, the examination would require a scrutiny of the individual's sexual pattern, work atmosphere, religious training, childhood, adolescent problems as well as the psychological and social make-up of the individual's immediate relatives and peer group. This uncertainty in the ascertainment of facts would amount to a negative long term consequence of applying the initial rule. In order to avoid this empirical uncertainty, the state might amend the rule so as to take the individual's behaviour (attempted suicide) as definitive evidence of the unstable mind. This amended rule would not suffer from uncertainty of facts, nor would the immediate privacy of the individual and his family be subject to public scrutiny. On the other hand, the amended rule would be introduced at the sacrifice of a major bulwark of liberty: the social value of *mens rea* as a required element of an offence. This loss could have "gravitational force" with long-term repercussions for the use of *mens rea* in other contexts.

Secondly, Professor Greenawalt mentions that one should take account of the methods available to induce compliance to a rule.[60] The threat of commission to a mental institution or the fact that a contract into slavery will be declared illegal with a sanction of imprisonment may not induce compliance in a society which sees nothing morally wrong with suicide or disguised forms of slavery. There may be available other means which have better chances to induce compliance with fewer costs. Commission to a mental institution might well aggravate the individual's psychological state. Similarly, imprisonment might simply reaffirm the prospective slave's conviction that slavery is a preferable life-style to that of a "free man" in an economically deprived environment. Compulsory psychiatric, psychological and social therapy on an outpatient basis might provide a better method to induce compliance to a moral rule which deals with attempted suicides. Similarly, state economic incentives, social security, due process protections and reformed laws (e.g., debtor-creditor, landlord and tenant) might be more successful at inducing compliance to a moral rule which proscribed contracts into slavery.

Thirdly, we must consider the nature of a rule itself.[61] If it is uncertain whether an individual is subject to a rule, the rule may have little utility in terms of its long-term social consequences. For example, some health authorities recognize more subtle forms of attempted suicide. Notable instances occur when an individual wants — consciously or not — to die and follows through with his desire by drinking himself to death or by taking continuous high dosages of anti-depressants.[62] An even more subtle example arises when a person who desires death develops a psychosomatic disease (as, for example, ulcers, some intestinal diseases such as Krone's Disease, or some forms of heart and respiratory diseases). This is not to suggest that these latter diseases are commonly caused by a death wish, although psychiatric opinions differ on this point.[63] My point is simply that at times persons do desire death and that it would be difficult for one to know whether any moral rule prohibiting attempted suicide was intended to include such subtle, timely and complex forms of "attempted suicide". As a consequence, a rule utilitarian might well conclude that a rule prohibiting attempted suicide was unjustifiable because of the very complexity of the behaviour which the rule was intended to control.[64]

Professor Greenawalt's considerations also provide insight into the question of how a rule utilitarian would face the third class of cases: that is, where the community interferes with the individual's behaviour out of paternalistic concern that he might injure himself at some future time as, for example, by not wearing a motorcycle helmet. As with the case of homosexuality, a rule utilitarian would weigh the alternative means available to a rule which required a policeman to confiscate a motorcycle whenever the driver was not wearing a helmet. The rule utilitarian must weigh the economic and value costs as well as the effectiveness of various alternatives. Enforcement of the initial rule, for example, might alienate the class of motorcyclists from the law. A particular motorcyclist might require his motorcycle for his livelihood; in such a case, the initial rule would be enforced with heavy personal and economic costs. The rule utilitarian, therefore, might consider whether an advertising campaign would be more appropriate. Or, if this were unsuccessful, a motorcyclist who needed his motorcycle for his livelihood might be prohibited from driving it on evenings and weekends.

The above examples reflect the complex considerations which a rule utilitarian must take into account. This very complexity, supported by the notion of fallibility, provides some support to Mill's assertion that society's assessment of the utilities of a rule "is quite as likely to be wrong as right."[65] On the one hand, it is questionable whether "freedom" and "variety of situations" produce persons of strong character. It does seem also debatable whether a general rule protecting "self-regarding conduct" may necessarily have beneficial consequences for society's economic and political welfare as in the case of attempted suicide or a contract into slavery.

On the other hand, a presumption in favour of self-regarding conduct would force a rule utilitarian to consider all available and appropriate means to the fulfillment of a societal goal. Such a presumption would oblige the rule utilitarian to examine the uncertainty of facts, the effectiveness of inducing compliance and the nature of rules, as the cases of suicide and contracts into slavery exemplify. These three factors may have significant consequences for society's welfare. Finally, as in the homosexuality and motorcycle helmet cases, such a presumption would encourage a rule utilitarian to assess the social and economic costs of an alternative rule permitting interference with "self-regarding" conduct.

Where a rule utilitarian would appear to disagree with Mill is in the absolute inviolability of "self-regarding" conduct. A rule utilitarian just could not accept the proposition that in all cases the individual ought to reign uncontrolled in the "inner sphere" of his life. The general rule directing the protection of self-regarding conduct would have to be amended so as to allow for exceptions as in the case where it could be established that the public display of homosexual conduct would gravely loosen the moral fabric of society. Our discussion concerning attempted suicide showed that, contrary to what Mill believed, one's own good, both physical and moral, could be a sufficient warrant to intervene in some cases by some means but not by others. Again contrary to Mill's views, society's "preferences" or deep-felt feelings of disgust would be a relevant consideration to be taken into account if those feelings were "essential to [society's] existence."

Section 4. Mill's Arguments for the Protection of "Self-Regarding" Conduct

i. *Some Weaknesses in His Arguments*

We have seen that neither a Benthamite utilitarian nor a rule utilitarian would be able to support an argument for the protection of "self-regarding" conduct in the sense which Mill intended the term. Let us return, therefore, to Mill's own arguments for the protection of "self-regarding" conduct in order to see whether his arguments are more satisfactory.

One of Mill's central arguments for "self-regarding" conduct was that, if conduct neither violates a specific duty to an assignable person nor causes harm, "the inconvenience [of protecting "self-regarding" conduct] is one which society can afford to bear, for the sake of the greater good of human freedom."[66] If society attempted to coerce a vigorous and independently-minded individual, the latter would rebel for he would never feel that others had the right to control his conduct. The independent individual, in other words, would *naturally* support the principle of "self-regarding" conduct.

But is that really so? Is it not possible that such a person would prefer that society prohibit him from freely purchasing certain drugs without a prescription, for example, so that he could devote his time and energies for issues he considered more important? Does not some societal interference alleviate some anxiety which any independently-minded citizen would face if he had to decide whether to choose a certain line of conduct in so many contexts in this complex life? Would he not contribute more to the general welfare by reserving his mental and psychic energies for more important matters rather than by examining in detail the probable consequences of pursuing various courses of action?

Secondly, assuming that the independently-minded individual did naturally support the principle of "self-regarding" conduct, why does it follow that he would respect the "self-regarding" conduct *of others*? Would he not, believing his actions righteous, more naturally expect that others follow his example and would he not thereby tend to interfere with other "self-regarding" conduct?

Thirdly, the pursuit of "self-regarding" conduct might "naturally" lead to a non-vigorous individualist as in the case of someone who, upon taking drugs, becomes addicted and transformed into a passive "vegetable". Indeed, the pursuit of "self-regarding" conduct might "naturally" lead to a non-individualist as in the case of someone who, in a rational state of mind, proceeded to commit suicide. Thus, not only would a vigorous individualist not necessarily want the "self-regarding" principle nor respect it in others, but the principle might consistently support the existence of a non-vigorous, passive, person. The principle itself, if applied rigorously, could in some circumstances produce the very character which Mill least respected.

A second argument for "self-regarding" conduct, which Mill believed to be the stronger, was that "when it [the public] does interfere, the odds are that it interferes wrongly, and in the wrong place."[67] Whereas the majority are usually right when the issue is one of "other-regarding" conduct since the majority in such cases are required to judge their own interests, their opinion is quite as likely to be wrong as right when they decide what is in the best interests of a minority.

This argument, however, assumes that there are such things as "rightness" and "wrongness". This assumption seems to coincide with a utilitarian perspective in that the rightness of an action is gauged by its utilitarian relationship to the general welfare. But could not a stronger argument be made that, with respect to "self-regarding" conduct, an individual's conception of rightness is just as valid as society's because we simply do not know what is right or wrong in such contexts? The objection which we should have toward the Puritans who prohibited music, dance or theatre and the objection which we should have toward the Spain of Mill's day which enforced a state religion is not, in other words, that society may more often be wrong than right. Rather, the objection is that, with respect to such matters, we just do not know what is wrong or right and, therefore, the dissenter's position is just as valid as the Puritan's or the state's.

The latter point may well be what Mill actually intended to argue for it underlies one of his three arguments for freedom of thought and discussion. Mill argued that to silence discussion assumes infallibility on the part of the silencer. "To refuse a hearing to an opinion because they are sure that it is false," Mill argued, "is to assume that *their* certainty is the same thing as *absolute* certainty."[68] The dominant beliefs in other countries, sects and periods of history have differed greatly from the dominant opinions of North American society at any particular point in time. Who is to suggest that the former were wrong and that the dominant opinion today is right? What criterion of validity can be employed? Is not any criterion culturally-laden? These issues underlie Mill's second argument for freedom of thought and discussion.

Mill's arguments in support of "self-regarding" conduct can be more fully appreciated when one understands the philosophic perspective from which he wrote. Mill grew up in an intellectual environment premised upon the validity and applicability of utilitarianism to social, political and moral problems. Taught by his father, nurtured by the Mills' neighbour and his father's best friend, Jeremy Bentham, and schooled in law under the guidance of John Austin, Mill's formative years were steadfastly secured in the utilitarian tradition. His *On Liberty* both preceded and followed his explicit expositions in utilitarian theory. Notwithstanding Gertrude Himmelfarb's assertions to the contrary,[69] Mill's *On Liberty* was written from a utilitarian perspective. This point is confirmed when one reads an essay which he wrote at the same time, *The Subjection of Women.*[70] We have already seen how rule utilitarianism is reflected in the very nature of Mill's own arguments for "self-regarding" conduct and freedom of discussion.[71]

It seems, upon reflection, that Mill advocated the protection of "self-regarding" conduct not because of the intrinsic worth of the individual but because of the instrumental value of "self-regarding" conduct to the greater welfare of society. He argued the point expressly, for example, when he asserted that "the inconvenience [of protecting "self-regarding" conduct] is one which society can *afford* to bear, for the sake of the *greater good* of human freedom."[72] Although one owed a duty of respect and development to himself, according to Mill, one was not accountable to society to satisfy those duties. One was unaccountable to society to comply with a duty of respect to oneself because it was not for "the *good of mankind* that he be held accountable to them."[73] And again, when society does interfere with purely personal conduct, "the odds are that it interferes wrongly, and in the wrong place."[74] Society is, as a consequence, so much more the loser, Mill reasoned. Mill expressly forewent any justification of "self-regarding" conduct which gave liberty an abstract validity, independent of utility. He seemed to preclude the possibility that the protection of "self-regarding" conduct might ever contradict the social welfare although, as we have seen above,[75] his notion of utility was quite different from Bentham's. Utility was, for Mill, the highest level principle from which he derived the principle of "self-regarding" conduct. The latter did not possess intrinsic merit nor was it independently binding.

The primacy of the social welfare in Mill's *On Liberty* appears even clearer when one reads his argument for "self-regarding" conduct in the context of his justification for freedom of expression. In one infamous passage Mill argued that the greater social good required that society not silence even one person:

> The peculiar evil of silencing the expression of an opinion is, that it is robbing the human race; posterity as well as the existing generation; those who dissent from the opinion, still more than those who hold it. If the opinion is right, they are deprived of the opportunity of exchanging error for truth: if wrong, they lose, what is almost as great a benefit, the clearer perception and livelier impression of truth, produced by its collision with error.[76]

Mill's other arguments for freedom of expression also appealed to the community's happiness. In the first place, he argued that to silence a dissenting opinion was to claim infallibility for the opinion of the day. But, since infallibility was impossible, the possibility always existed that the silenced opinion might add something to public knowledge. Secondly, the best government was one capable of synthesizing the opinions of dissenters. This was so because only by the collision of adverse opinions would the true opinions be extracted. Of course "no belief which is contrary to truth can be really useful."[77] Thirdly, whether or not an opinion would prove useful to society was itself a matter of opinion, "as disputable, as open to discussion, and requiring discussion as much, as the opinion itself."[78] But there could be "no fair discussion of the question of usefulness, when an argument so vital may be employed on one side, but not on the other."[79]

Mill's final argument for free expression was that free expression was essential for the full development of the individual. Although this would seem to indicate a shift from social happiness to individuality as an ultimate good, Mill quickly emphasised that individuality was "one of the principal ingredients of human happiness, and quite the chief ingredient of individual and social progress."[80] More precisely, "[in] proportion to the development of his individuality, each person becomes more valuable to himself, and is therefore capable of being more valuable to others. There is a greater fulness of life about his own existence, and when there is more life in the units there is more in the mass which is composed of them."[81] A spontaneous, creative, fully developed individual had an especially great utility to society "when the opinions of masses of merely average men are everywhere become or becoming the dominant power."[82] Thus, John Stuart Mill even justified freedom of expression in terms of its instrumental or utilitarian connection to the achievement of social happiness.

iii. *Some Conceptual Problems with a Utilitarian Argument*

Mill's utilitarian perspective raises an important conceptual weakness in his arguments for the protection of "self-regarding" conduct. The reason why Benthamite and rule utilitarianism could not support the absolute inviolability of the "inner sphere of life" lies in the fact that the ultimate norm in utilitarianism is "the greatest happiness of the greatest number" or, if you will, the social welfare. This ultimate norm provides the vantage point from which both an act and a rule utilitarian must assess all behaviour. Utilitarian theory, therefore, contemplates any infringement of "self-regarding" conduct whenever *society* calculates such infringement as necesssary for the greatest happiness of the parties or, in the case of rule utilitarianism, for the greatest happiness of the greatest number. Sir James Fitzjames Stephen pushed this perspective to its logical conclusion when he asserted that the state could legitimately coerce the "inner sphere of life" whenever society deemed such coercion necessary to establish and maintain a religion, to establish and maintain a moral code, to alter an existing form of government or to protect the state itself.[83] We have seen that a Benthamite utilitarian could justify the most outrageous forms of intervention with self-regarding conduct: slavery and tyranny. A rule utilitarian would have to limit himself to the issue of the means employed (that is, slavery and tyranny) to further the welfare of the greatest number.

We have seen in our elaboration of Mill's principle that Mill meant the term "self-regarding" to include three types of conduct: conduct which had only indirect effects for society, conduct which did not affect the interests of society, and conduct whose harm to society was unsupported by reasons. We have also seen that Mill believed that most of the examples of which he spoke did not qualify as "other-regarding" under his understanding of the term. Notwithstanding Mill's intent, his acceptance of the greatest social welfare as the pivotal norm in his perspective opens up his argument to the charge that the social welfare might not of necessity require the protection of "self-regarding" conduct. Despite his desire to support the inviolability of the "inner sphere of life", as a consequence of his adoption of utilitarianism, he valued "self-regarding" conduct because of its instrumental relationship to the greater social welfare rather than because of the intrinsic worth of the individual himself.

We have perceived this conceptual limitation in Mill's own justificatory framework for the protection of "self-regarding" conduct. The conceptual limitation can also be seen by a close look at Mill's very conception of the principle of "self-regarding" conduct. Despite Mill's professed support of "self-regarding" conduct and despite the fact that he addressed his essay in reaction to the phenomenon of the "tyranny of the majority", he hung the implementation of his "one very simple principle" upon the majority or, more accurately, upon the chief spokesmen of society's majority. As soon as a person's conduct prejudically affected the interests of others, society possessed jurisdiction. Whether or not society could intervene then depended upon the issue of whether such interference promoted the general welfare.[84] As he explained,

> as soon as any part of a person's conduct affects prejudicially the interests of others, *society has jurisdiction* over it, and the question whether the *general welfare* will or will not be promoted by interfering with it, becomes open to discussion...[85]

Indeed, Mill went further by suggesting in another passage that society had a *prima facie* right to intervene once any person had harmed another. In such circumstances the onus of proof shifted from the society to the advocate of "self-regarding" conduct.[86] The only requirement for this shifting of the burden of proof appears to be that an individual simply allege that he or society had been harmed. It is initially for society to determine what constitutes harmfulness. And it is initially for the society or any "self-styled" representative of society to adjudicate whether certain allegedly harmful conduct or an accompanying rule protecting that conduct might or might not contribute to society's welfare. We have already examined the practical outcome of that question. The important conceptual point, however, is that society possesses jurisdiction over an individual's conduct if and when society alone deems that its own general welfare is at issue.

The primacy of the social welfare leads into a second, related conceptual problem with utilitarian theory. When Mill re-stated his "self-regarding" principle in chapter 4 of *On Liberty* he explained that, although society was not founded on a social contract, "every one who receives the protection of society owes a return for the benefit, and the fact of living in society renders it indispensable that each should be *bound* to observe a certain line of conduct towards the rest."[87] Mill later called this a "distinct and assignable obligation". From this obligation Mill derived two maxims: first, that one ought not to harm the interests of others; and, secondly, that each person owed a duty to society to bear "his share (based on some equitable principle) of the labours and sacrifices incurred for defending the society or its members from injury and molestation."[88] We have already seen that Mill provided as examples such duties as the giving of evidence in court, the bearing of one's fair share "in the common defence or in any other joint work necessary to the interest of the society," and the performance of "certain acts of benefience such as saving a fellow creature's life or interposing to protect the defenceless against ill-usage, things which *whenever it is obviously a man's duty to do...*"[89]

But whence comes the "distinct and assignable obligation"? Does it arise from social custom? This could hardly be the case in the light of Mill's own strong criticism of social custom.[90] Does the society itself have the authority to impose obligations. If so, what implication does this have for the notion that there is such a thing as "self-regarding" conduct which ought to be protected? Or, does the obligation arise internally within the individual? If the latter, would that not result in social chaos?

This is a central issue which one must face if an argument is to be made in favour of the protection of "self-regarding" conduct. The problem is that, again notwithstanding his intent to support the inviolability of the "inner sphere of life", the implication of Mill's arguments is to leave it to society to impose the initial obligation. That is, the initial obligation comes *from without* rather than from within the individual, although there may have been limits in Mill's own mind as to what society could properly make an obligation. Ironically, this external source of the "distinct and assignable obligations" invites the very tyranny of the majority which Mill so dreaded. Furthermore, the scope of protection posited by a majority to a "self-regarding conduct" will vary from one society to another, and from one historical period to another. Finally the external source leads us to the conclusion that the scope of "self-regarding" conduct will, as Wollheim suggests, "only with difficulty be enlarged for its enlargement will depend upon a corresponding shift in public norms."[91]

We have already seen some evidence for the conclusion that society posits the obligations in Mill's elaboration of the nature of an "other-regarding" act.[92] Mill quite explicitly singled out the external source of the obligation when he asserted, for example, that

> it makes a vast difference both in our feelings and in our conduct towards him whether he displeases us in things in which *we* think we have a right to control him, or in things in which *we* know that we have not...[93]

On another occasion, he stated that the individual is accountable to society "if society is of opinion that the one (that is, social punishment) or the other (that is, legal punishment) is requisite for its protection."[94] Mill's application of his basic principle of "self-regarding" conduct in chapter 5 of *On Liberty*, finally, reflected his perception of the source of the obligation. More particularly, society could legitimately intervene where an instigator of "self-regarding" conduct "derives a personal benefit from his advice" because "he makes it his occupation, for subsistence or pecuniary gain, to promote *what society and the State consider to be an evil*."[95] Similarly, there was a "right *inherent in society* to ward off crimes against itself by antecedent precautions" such as the internment of a drunkard who had on an earlier occasion been convicted of causing violence to others under the influence of alcohol.[96]

These first two conceptual problems with utilitarianism (the primacy of the community welfare and the source of obligation) appear to be inconsistent with Mill's own theme of the integrity of self-regarding conduct. In one passage, for example, Mill asserted that society had authority to impose obligations *only* with respect to "other-regarding" conduct.[97] In another passage he emphasized that "a person's taste is as much his own peculiar concern as his opinion or his purse."[98] Indeed, the first two conceptual limitations of utilitarian theory appear to run counter to Mill's important focus on the absolute character of the inner sphere of life as outlined in part one of this chapter.

How can this apparent inconsistency be resolved? One avenue might be to examine Mill's definition of an "other-regarding" act. We have already seen that Mill believed that whether an act was other-regarding depended upon whether it violated "a distinct and assignable obligation". But this approach is entirely circular: "other-regarding" conduct exists only when an obligation is violated, and the obligation is applied only to the "other-regarding" conduct. One way out of this dilemma might be to focus upon the source of the duties which an individual owes to society. We shall turn to this focus in chapter VI.

1. John Stuart Mill, *On Liberty*, ed. Mary Warnock (Glasgow: William Collins Sons & Co., 1962), p. 129. All further references will be to this edition.

2. Ibid., p. 137.

3. Ibid.

4. John Stuart Mill, *Principles of Political Economy*, ed. Donald Winch (London: Penguin, 1970), p. 306.

5. Mill, *On Liberty*, supra, note 1, p. 206.

6. *Saumur v. City of Quebec*, [1953] 2 S.C.R. 299, 379; [1953] 4 D.L.R. 641. See text, supra, chap. I, note 113.

7. John Stuart Mill, *On Liberty*, supra, note 1, p. 135.

8. See generally, ibid., p. 138.

9. Ibid., p. 136.

10. Ibid., emphasis added.

11. Ibid., p. 205. Emphasis added.

12. Ibid., p. 212.

13. See generally, Ibid., pp. 215-225.

14. Ibid., p. 218.

15. Ibid., pp. 210-211.

16. Ibid., p. 137.

17. Ibid., p. 206. Emphasis added.

18. John C. Rees, "A Re-Reading of Mill on Liberty," in P. Radcliffe, ed., *Limits of Liberty: Studies of Mill's "On Liberty"* (Belmont, California: Wadsworth, 1966), p. 87. Also see John C. Rees, "Was Mill for Liberty?" 14 *Political Studies* 72 (1966) and Maurice Cowling, "Mill and Liberalism," in J. B. Schneenwind, ed., *Mill: A Collection of Critical Essays* (London: U. of Notre Dame Press, 1968).

19. Sir James Fitjames Stephen, *Liberty, Equality and Fraternity*, ed. R. J. White (London: Cambridge University Press, 1967), p. 57.

20. See generally, Mill, supra, note 1, pp. 142-147.

21. Ibid., p. 143.

22. Ibid., p. 131.

23. Ibid., p. 207.

24. Ibid., p. 208. Emphasis added.

25. Each of these examples has, indeed, been the subject of an essay in itself. For contracts into slavery, for example, see Joel Feinberg's "Legal Paternalism," 1 *Canadian Journal of Philosophy* 105, pp. 105-124; (1971); for homosexuality, see Lord Devlin, "Morals in the Criminal Law," *The Enforcement of Morals* (London: Oxford U. Press, 1965) and H. L. A. Hart, *Law, Liberty and Morality* (Stanford: Stanford U. Press, 1963).

26. Jeremy Bentham, *The Principles of Morals and Legislation*, ed. L. J. Lafleur (New York: Hafner, 1948), chap. 13, sect. 2, pp. 171 ff.

27. Ibid., p. 172.

28. "But neither one person, nor any number of persons," for example, "is warranted in saying to another human creature of ripe years, that he shall

not do with his life for his own benefit what he chooses to do with it," because "he is the person most interested in his own well-being: the interest which any other person,... can have in it is trifling...," Mill, *On Liberty*, supra note 1, p. 206.

29. Jeremy Bentham, *The Principles of Morals and Legislation*, ed., L. J. Lafleur (New York: Hafner, 1948), chap. 5, paras. 2 & 3, p. 33.

30. Ibid., chap. 5, paras. 4-33.

31. Ibid., chap. 6.

32. "Fecundity" meant the chance which a pleasure (or pain) has of being followed by sensations of the *same* kind. Bentham, ibid., para. 5.

33. "Purity" meant the chance of a pleasure not being followed by a sensation of a pain and vice versa. Bentham, ibid., para. 6. Thus, a pleasure has high fecundity if there is a great chance of it being followed by another pleasure; and it is very pure if there is little chance of it being followed by a pain.

34. "Extent" refers to the number of persons who are affected by a pleasure or pain.

35. Lord Patrick Devlin, "Morals in the Criminal Law," in *The Enforcement of Morals* (London: Oxford U. Press, 1965), p. 17.

36. For the meaning of these terms see supra, notes 32 and 34.

37. Kent Greenawalt, "Some Related Limits of Law," in J. Roland Pennock and John W. Chapman, ed., *The Limits of Law: Nomos XV* (New York: Atherton Press, 1973).

38. See text, supra, between notes 21 and 25.

39. Mill, *On Liberty*, supra, note 1, p. 135.

40. Ibid., p. 220.

41. Ibid., p. 229.

42. Ibid., p. 230.

43. See generally, M. O. Bayles, ed., *Contemporary Utilitarianism* (N.Y.: Anchor, 1968); D. H. Hodgson, *Consequences of Utilitarianism* (Oxford: Clarendon, 1967); A. Quinton, *Utilitarian Ethics* (N.Y.: St. Martin's Press, 1973); and J. J. C. Smart & Bernard Williams, *Utilitarianism For and Against* (Cambridge: Cambridge U. Press, 1973).

44. For an example of the latter see infra, note 55 and accompanying text.

45. Richard Wasserstrom, *The Judicial Decision* (Stanford: Stanford U. Press, 1961), chap. 6.

46. J. J. C. Smart, "An Outline of a system of Utilitarian Ethics," in J. J. C. Smart and Bernard Williams, *Utilitarianism For and Against* (Cambridge: Cambridge U. Press, 1973).

47. David Lyons, *The Forms and Limits of Utilitarianism* (London: Oxford U. Press, 1965). Also see citations in Smart, ibid., note 4.

48. Richard Wasserstrom, *The Judicial Decision*, supra, note 45, p. 136.

49. This conclusion appears to differ from Sartorius' in *The Enforcement of Morality*, 81 Yale L.J. 891, pp. 901 ff. (1972), although Sartorius was less concerned with the applicability of the "label" "act utilitarianism" to Mill per se than he was in establishing a general utilitarian case for the protection of "self-regarding" acts. In addition to the references to Mill already cited my

conclusion is consistent with a passage in Mill's *Utilitarianism*, ed. Mary Warnock (Glasgow: William Collins Sons & Co., 1962), pp. 225-6:

> There is no difficulty in providing any ethical standard whatever to work ill... but... mankind must by this time have acquired positive beliefs as to the effects of some actions of their happiness; and the beliefs which have thus come down are *the rules of morality for the multitude*... But to consider the rules of morality as improvable, is one thing; to pass over the intermediate generalisations entirely, and endeavour to test each individual action directly by the first principle, is another. It is a strange notion that the acknowledgement of a first principle is inconsistent with the admission of secondary ones... Whatever we adopt as the fundamental principle of morality, we require subordinate principles to apply it by;...

And at p. 278.:

> We must remember that only in these cases of conflict between secondary principles is it requisite that first principles should be appealed to. There is no case of moral obligation in which some secondary principle is not involved...

50. Mill, *On Liberty*, supra note 1, p. 189.
51. Ibid., p. 192.
52. Ibid., p. 213.
53. Ibid., p. 215.
54. Ibid., p. 148.
55. Ralf Sartorius, *The Enforcement of Morals*, 81 Yale L.J. 891, pp 909-910 (1972).
56. Lord Devlin, "Morals in the Criminal Law," in *The Enforcement of Morals* (London: Oxford U. Press, 1965), p. 11.
57. See text, supra, corresponding to notes 50-54.
58. Kent Greenawalt, "Some Related Limits of Law," supra note 37.
59. Ibid., p. 126.
60. Ibid., p. 126-7.
61. Ibid., p. 127-8.
62. This suggestion, like other empirical observations in this chapter, is based on my own observations of friends and relatives, as well as conversations with psychiatrists, introspection and general reading.
63. Note the Freudian notion of a "death wish".
64. Similarly, a rule utilitarian might conclude that a general rule prohibiting a contract of slavery may be so vague or ambiguous that prospective parties are uncertain whether the rule is supposed to cover them. For example, a Canadian farmer may be uncertain whether he would come within the scope of such a rule if he were to contract to provide food, lodging and security of tenure for life to West Indian or Portuguese workers in exchange for sixty hours of conscientious work for one dollar per hour.
65. Mill, *On Liberty*, supra note 1, p. 215.
66. Ibid., p. 213.
67. Ibid., pp. 214-215.

68. Ibid., p. 143.

69. Gertrude Himmelfarb, *On Liberty and Liberalism: The Case of John Stuart Mill* (N.Y.: Knopf, 1974). Miss Himmelfarb is not alone in interpreting Mill's *On Liberty* from a "self-development" rather than a utilitarian perspective. See, for example, David Spitz, "Freedom and Individuality: Mill's Liberty in Retrospect", in *Liberty: Nomos IV*, ed. J. W. Chapman & J. R. Pennock (N.Y.: Atherton, 1962); Richard B. Friedman, "A New Exploration of Mill's Essay *On Liberty*," 14 *Political Studies* 281 (1966); Albert W. Levi, "The Value of Freedom: Mill's Liberty," 70 *Ethics* 37 (1959); C. B. Macpherson, *The Life and Times of Liberal Democracy* (Oxford, London, New York: Oxford U. Press, 1977), pp. 50 ff.; idem, *Democratic Theory* (London: Oxford U. Press, 1973) pp. 31-32.

70 John Stuart Mill, *The Subjection of Women* (1869) reprinted in Alice S. Rossi, ed., *Essays in Sex Equality* (Chicago: U. of Chi. Press, 1970).

71. See text, supra, between notes 48 and 55.

72. Mill, *On Liberty*, supra, note 1, p. 213. Emphasis added.

73. Ibid. p. 209. Emphasis added.

74. Ibid. p. 214.

75. See text, supra, between notes 48 and 55.

76. Mill, *On Liberty*, supra note 1, p. 142.

77. Ibid., pp. 148-149, 171.

78. Ibid., p. 148.

79. Ibid., p. 149.

80. Ibid., p. 185.

81. Ibid., p. 192.

82. Ibid., p. 196.

83. Sir James F. Stephen, *Liberty, Equality and Fraternity*, supra, note 19, p. 61.

84. Mill, *On Liberty*, supra, note 1, p. 205.

85. Ibid., p. 205. Emphasis added.

86. Ibid., p. 136.

87. Ibid., p. 205. When Mill initially laid down his principle of "self-regarding" conduct he asserted at p. 136 that a person may be compelled "to bear his fair share in... any... joint work necessary to the interests of the society of which he enjoys the protection."

Similarly, in chap. 4 of his *Utilitarianism* reprinted in supra, note 49, p. 304 he asserted that

> it is a part of the notion of Duty in every one of its forms, that a person may rightfully be compelled to fulfill it. Duty is a thing which may be *exacted* from a person, as one exacts a debt. Unless we think that it may be exacted from him, we do not call it his duty. Reasons of prudence, or the interest of other people, may militate against actually exacting it; but the person himself, it is clearly understood, would not be entitled to complain. [emphasis added]

Also note another of Mill's passages in "Auguste Comte and Positivism," in J. S. Mill, *Essays on Ethics, Religion and Society* in *Collected Works* (Toronto: U. of Tor. Press, 1969), vol. 10, pp. 337-338:

There is a standard of altruism to which all should be required to come up... It is incumbent on every one to restrain the pursuit of his personal objects within the limits consistent with the essential interests of others... The proper office of those sanctions is to enforce upon every one, the conduct necessary to give all other persons their fair chance: conduct which chiefly consists in not doing them harm... we are bound to keep our promise. And inasmuch as everyone, who avails himself of the advantages of society, leads others to expect from him all such positive good offices and disinterested services as the moral improvement of mankind has rendered *customary*, he deserves moral blame if, without just cause, he disappoints that expectation. Through this principle the *domain of moral duty*, in an improving society, *is always widening*. [emphasis added]

88. Mill, *On Liberty*, supra, note 1, p. 205.
89. Ibid., p. 136. Emphasis added.
90. Ibid., p. 197-204.
91. Richard Wollheim, "John Stuart Mill and the Limits of State Action," 40 *Social Research* 1, p. 6 (1973).
92. Text, supra, at note 85.
93. Mill, *On Liberty*, supra, note 1, p. 210.
94. Ibid., p. 226.
95. Ibid., p. 231. Emphasis added.
96. Ibid., p. 230. Emphasis added.
97. Ibid., p. 131.
98. Ibid., p. 215.

Chapter V

John Rawls' Theory of Fundamental Rights

Our initial excursion into liberal political theory has met with serious obstacles. If either Benthamite or rule utilitarianism could have consistently supported an argument for the inviolability of the "inner sphere of life", we would have ascertained a starting-point with which to elaborate a defence of fundamental rights. Neither Benthamite nor rule utilitarianism could consistently sustain the inviolability of the "inner sphere of life". Nor, for that matter, could Mill's own arguments. The explanation lay in the sometimes implicit, oftentimes explicit reliance upon the "greatest happiness of the greatest number" or some similar term as the ultimate political goal for society. The societal source of one's obligations toward others also served as a reason for the short-comings of the utilitarian perspective.

It might be beneficial, at this stage of our study, to come to terms with John Rawls' important contribution, *A Theory of Justice*[1]. Rawls set out determined to overcome the contradictions and inherent problems with utilitarianism. At the same time, Rawls worked within the liberal political tradition. Although he did not confine himself to the issue of the "inner sphere of life", Rawls' *A Theory of Justice* does reflect a continuity with Mill's general concern for liberty.

I have chosen Rawls' political theory over that of other political theorists, such as John Locke, T. H. Green or Immanuel Kant, for additional reasons.[2] For one thing, there arises from Rawls' theory a series of issues which any contemporary political theory of fundamental rights should face. Although Rawls does not resolve the issues, the issues crystallize in his work with unusual clarity. In addition, Rawls himself suggests why fundamental rights (he calls them "basic liberties") are fundamental. He argues that the rights flow from the freedom of religious conscience and from the primary good of self-respect. As a consequence, it is in our interest to scrutinize his arguments. Finally, Rawls brings a remarkable comprehensive outlook to the problems of utilitarianism and funda-

160

mental rights in general. This very comprehensiveness makes his theory of fundamental rights worthy of our consideration.

Section 1. Outline of Rawls' Theory

The general outlines of Professor Rawls' theory of justice are no doubt familiar to the reader. In an attempt to find ideal principles of justice which a well-ordered society ought to have — normatively, that is — he proceeds according to the social contract methodology adopted by Locke and Rousseau. The purpose of the initial contract is to set out the principles of justice which are to regulate all future agreements in perpetuity. The initial "Original Position" is not an actual historical state of affairs; it is a purely hypothetical situation. The parties to it are "free and rational" and "concerned to further their own interests."[3] They are all equal "as moral persons, as creatures having a conception of their good and capable of a sense of justice:" they "all have the same rights in the procedure for choosing principles."[4]

Most important is the fact that in this Original Position the parties face a veil of ignorance: no one knows his/her place in society, his class, his fortune, his natural abilities, his intelligence or the like. No one even knows his conception of the good. Further, the parties do not know the economic, political, cultural or other circumstances of their particular society.[5] On the other hand, they do understand political affairs, economic theory, human psychology, and the basis of social organization. That is, they understand "the general facts about human society."

But why should the parties face the veil of ignorance? Because the veil of ignorance provides the precondition for a fair agreement: all parties to the agreement are similarly situated and no one is able to design the principles so as to favour his particular condition. Thus, "justice as fairness"[6] means that the principles of justice are chosen in an initial position which is in itself fair. Once chosen, the principles will be used as guide-posts to choose a constitution and to enact legislation. The principles of justice will be of universal and timeless validity: there will be no second chance. The parties will choose "once and for all the standards which are to govern [their] life prospects."[7]

And which principles would the parties choose in the Original Position? Rawls suggests two principles.[8] The first principle — and the principle with which we will be primarily concerned — is that

> each person is to have an equal right to the most extensive total system of equal basic liberties compatible with a similar system of liberty for all.

161

The second principle is that

> social and economic inequalities are to be arranged so that they are both:
>
> a) to the greatest benefit of the least advantaged, consistent with the just savings principle, and
>
> b) attached to offices and positions open to all under conditions of fair equality of opportunity.

Several questions should be faced by way of explication of Rawls' first principle:
1. what does he mean by the term "the most extensive total system"?
2. what are the "basic liberties"?
3. when would one detect whether the system is incompatible with "a similar system of liberty for all"?

Rawls ranks the first principle in priority over the second. He initially argues, furthermore, that liberty can be restricted only for liberty. Liberty may be justifiably restricted for the sake of liberty according to two criteria:
a) a less extensive liberty must strengthen the total system of liberty shared by all;
b) a less than equal liberty must be acceptable to those with the lesser liberty.

Rawls really outlines two theories of justice.[9] According to the "special conception of justice," the most extensive total system of basic liberties will not be compromised for greater social and economic advantages. As he explains, "beyond some point it becomes and then remains irrational from the standpoint of the original position to acknowledge a lesser liberty for the sake of greater material means and amenities of office." Rawls leaves it ambiguous as to how we will detect when that "some point" is. We are told that the priority of liberty prevails in a society where "the basic wants of individuals can be fulfilled"[10] and when social conditions allow "the effective establishment of fundamental rights."[11] Rawls certainly seems to consider the magic point to be coincident with a certain level of economic development. An important issue for our purposes is whether there are any problems with Rawls' priority rule.

a. *The Most Extensive Total System of Basic Liberties*

What does Rawls mean when he claims that every person is to have "an equal right to the most extensive total system of equal basic liberties"? Rawls' idea is that one basic liberty may be weighed as against another so as to produce "the best total system of equal liberty."[12] That is, one basic liberty may be traded off with another. So, for example, political liberties may be weighed against liberty of conscience and freedom of the person "up to the point where the danger to liberty from the marginal loss in control over those holding political power just balances the security of liberty gained by the greater use of constitutional devices."[13] The "most extensive total system" of basic liberties contemplates the "weighing against one another small variations in the extent and definition of the different liberties," the "marginal exchanges within the system of freedom."[14] One could conceivably have a combination of basic liberties whereby the most extensive system of A's liberty equalled B's liberty despite the fact that A, being a politician, had more political freedom than B but B possessed greater freedom of conscience. Rawls' point is not that a party to the Original Contract might prefer more of a particular liberty but rather that he not prefer a greater *system* of liberty *as a whole*.

b. *What are the Basic Liberties?*

In this initial statement of the two principles of justice,[15] Rawls sets out that the basic liberties are "roughly speaking" as follows:

> political liberty (the right to vote and to be eligible for public office) together with freedom of speech and assembly; liberty of conscience and freedom of thought; freedom of the person along with the right to hold (personal) property; and freedom from arbitrary arrest and seizure as defined by the concept of the rule of law.

In his later more detailed elaboration of the equal liberty principle, however, Rawls focuses only on political liberty, freedom of conscience and the rule of law.[16] Rawls' rule of law, a term said to lie at the foundation of the English and Canadian constitutions,[17] contains the familiar Diceyan principle that there should be no offence without a law and that laws must be impartially administered. Rawls adds to Dicey's list [18] the principles that ought implies can, that similar cases must be treated similarly and that the law should be administered according to natural justice. "Ought implies can" means that laws be of such a nature that men can reasonably be expected to follow or to avoid them.[19] In addition, legislators and administrators must act in good faith. Finally, "ought implies can" necessitates that impossibility of performance be a defence.

One should note several points with respect to the constituent elements of Rawls' basic liberties. First, although Rawls admits his list to be "roughly speaking," the liberties he cites are sharply distinguished from other values in that "liberty can be restricted only for the sake of liberty."[20] That is, liberty may not be sacrificed for other social or economic goods.

Secondly, Rawls does not state whether the right to own private property is a "basic liberty". He does assert, as we have seen,[21] that "the right to hold [personal] property" is a basic liberty. He insists, however, that the means of production may or may not be privately owned. A market economy is common to both private property and socialist regimes.[22] According to Rawls, whether a society adopts a private property or socialist regime depends upon the traditions, institutions, historical circumstances and social forces of the country.

Thirdly, Rawls' list of basic liberties focuses on the political and civil aspects of the liberty traditionally accepted amongst liberal political and legal theorists[23] in contrast to social and economic aspects of freedom traditionally identified as a socialist concern. One can also appreciate that Rawls separates socio-economic factors from his conception of basic liberties by looking closely at his second principle of justice. In particular, the second principle contemplates social and economic inequality so long as the inequality is to the advantage of the least favoured.[24] The primacy of the political-civil aspects of liberty over socio-economic elements is similarly evidenced in Rawls' priority principle that liberty may be restricted only for the sake of liberty.

Rawls attempts to explain his exclusion of economic and social rights from the content of his basic liberties *by distinguishing between liberty and the worth of liberty*.[25] Poverty, ignorance and a lack of means generally, he asserts, affect "the worth of liberty, the value to individuals of the rights that the first principle defines."[26] A person with greater authority and wealth will have greater means to achieve his ends. He will have greater ability to influence public officials, to affect public opinion and to select candidates than "the less fortunate members of society." The worth of liberty will be unequal. But all citizens will have the equal liberty to vote. As a consequence, compensating steps must be taken. For example, in a private property society political parties must be made independent from private economic interests.[27] Property and wealth must be widely distributed, and government must regularly subsidize free public discussion. An important issue for any political theory of fundamental rights is whether the theory can properly omit socio-economic elements from the content of the rights.

c. *Compatibility with a Similar System of Liberty for All*

Rawls acknowledges that liberties could collide with one another. Where they conflicted, the delegates to the constitutional convention would be required to limit their scope of the liberties according to two criteria: first, restrictions may have to be imposed equally upon all individuals as, for example, in a law against murder. In that case the relevant vantage point would be that of the representative equal citizen.[28] Secondly, restrictions may have to be levied upon some particular individuals. In that case the unequal treatment must be in the interests of the least favoured.[29] Rawls exemplifies this second type of restriction by reference to Mill. Mill was persuaded that the least advantaged would benefit from a system of government where persons with greater intelligence and education had extra votes. It was in each citizen's interest for the wiser and more knowledgeable to govern. According to Rawls, Mill should have explicitly asserted that, as a consequence of a franchise weighted in favour of the more advantaged, the gain to the uneducated was in terms of a larger security to their other liberties.[30] Neil MacCormick gives as an example of this second type of restriction the special privileges of free speech, freedom from arrest and the like traditionally preserved for Members of Parliament.[31] These privileges tend to protect and strengthen the political institutions and, as a result, the overall system of liberties for all.

Rawls tries to apply his priority principle that liberty may be restricted only for the sake of liberty in his section on "Toleration and the Common Interest."[32] In his analysis of toleration Rawls asserts that liberty of conscience may be limited "by the common interest in public order and security." When the state acts to protect the public order, it is doing so as the citizens' agent. One can justify restrictions upon liberty of conscience by reference to the original contract, according to Rawls, because in the Original Position each party realizes that the disruption of public order is a danger to the liberty of all. The public order is "a necessary condition for everyone's achieving his ends whatever they are (provided they lie within certain limits) and for his fulfilling his interpretation of his moral and religious obligations."[33]

But does Rawls provide any limitation to the use of the term "public order" as a justification for restrictions upon liberty? The common interest, Rawls suggests, is determined by reference to the "representative equal citizen." The state may not restrict basic liberties unless, from the viewpoint of the "representative equal citizen," there is a reasonable expectation that the state's failure to proscribe certain conduct will damage the public order.[34] The reasonable expectation must be based on evidence and reasoning acceptable to all. The threat to the public order must be "not merely possible or in certain cases even probable, but reasonably certain or imminent." There must be "a reasonably certain interference with the essentials of public order."[35]

Section 2. Some Unresolved Issues with Rawls' Theory

The problems which one encounters in Rawls' theory of justice are not uncommon in liberal legal and political theory. Most notable is Rawls' failure to acknowledge the complex considerations involved in assessing whether the most extensive system of basic liberties of one person is compatible with that of another.

a. *Compatibility with a Similar System of Basic Liberties for All*

According to Rawls, the aggregation of different liberties takes place not in the working out of the original contract but in the deliberations of the constitutional convention or the legislature.[36] Since Rawls is primarily concerned with determining the principles of justice in the Original Position, he finds it unnecessary to guide us as to the relative values of the several liberties. He defines liberty in this way: "this or that person (or persons) is free (or not free) from this or that constraint (or set of constraints) to do (or not to do) so and so." But this does not tell us very much. Indeed, he admits that he will "try to bypass the dispute about the meaning of liberty."[37] We have already perceived that Rawls recognizes that liberties will conflict with each other.[38] And his common example is that freedom of speech loses its value if everyone talks at once.[39] He does tell us that the participants in the constitutional convention and the legislature will elaborate the meaning and scope of the basic liberties. They will do so from the viewpoint of the "representative equal citizen."[40] But "ideally these conflicts (among liberties) will not occur and it should be possible, under favourable conditions anyway, to find a constitutional procedure that allows a sufficient scope for the value of participation (say) without jeopardizing the other liberties."[41]

Rawls' optimism underestimates the difficulty of the problem. Unfortunately he finds it unnecessary to elaborate priority rules in the weighing of conflicting rights and freedoms — assuming such priority rules could be elaborated.

What, for example, does Rawls mean by the term "freedom of the person"? Does he have in mind some notion of privacy or

166

autonomy? If so, how does justice as fairness help us to resolve the many and various instances of conflicts between freedom of speech and assembly on the one hand, and freedom of the person on the other? Does "freedom of the person" protect an individual from being libelled and, if so, why? Does it include "security of the person" and, if so, at what point does a speech threaten that security? Must "speech" actually entail spoken words or may it include behaviour such as the wearing of a swastika in a Jewish community meeting? And the questions can go on.

This leads into a second problem with respect to Rawls' treatment of the "total system of the most extensive liberty." Part of the explanation as to why Rawls does not pay more attention to the problem of conflicts of rights is that he seems to treat the basic liberties as something which one can measure mathematically. He is not alone in this perspective. Brian Barry,[42] in his critique of Rawls, goes so far as to plot liberty and wealth on either side of an indifference curve familiar in micro-economic theory.

Michael Lessnoff makes several pertinent points in this context.[43] First, one just cannot quantify restrictions on such freedoms as free speech and the right to vote in terms of some common measuring rod. Secondly, even if one could measure such freedoms, there is no reason to expect that a trade-off between wealth and speech on the one hand would be the same as that between wealth and enfranchisement on the other. Thirdly, the innumerably diverse fact situations involving restrictions upon free speech and the franchise complicate the issue even further: free speech or the right to vote is simply not a single quantifiable commodity. One might add that this complication arises with more intensity when one begins to focus on "the worth of liberty" as opposed simply to liberty itself.

Rawls leaves us with the same citicism he made of intuitionism.[44] Rawls had contended that intuitional theory provided no explicit method, nor priority rules for weighing several first principles when they conflicted. The intuitionist resolved a conflict by striking a balance via intuition, "by what seems to us most nearly right"[45] "unguided by constructive and recognizably ethical criteria."[46] Although Rawls recognized that "any conception of justice will have to rely on intuition to some degree,"[47] he believed that his explicit priority principles would alleviate our reliance on intuitive judgments to a great extent. First principles would, therefore, not have to be balanced by intuition.[48] Rawls believed that if he could defend his priority rules his theory would be superior to intuitionism:

> The assignments of weights is an essential and not a minor part of a conception of justice. If we cannot explain how these weights are to be determined by reasonable ethical criteria, the means of rational discussion have come to an end. An intuitional conception of justice is, one might say, but half a conception.[49]

To the extent that the meaning and scope of his basic liberties are left unarticulated and to the extent that Rawls does not provide a procedure whereby he could resolve conflicts amongst basic liberties in concrete cases, to that extent his theory of justice succumbs to the very criticism he made of intuitionism. It is not without reason that is was a lawyer — H. L. A. Hart — who emphasised the complexity involved in applying Rawls' principles.[50] Rawls' concern with only the extent or amount of liberty conceals and misrepresents the character of all but the simplest conflicts. In Feinberg's words,

> At best, "priority rules" in such contexts are useful rules of thumb, telling us that in general one kind of element should be weighted more than another kind, but not *how much* more, nor even that it *invariably* weighs more.[51]

Rawls does not even provide a "rule of thumb."

b. *The Priority Rule*

One "rule of thumb" Rawls'does provide, however, is that it can never be justifiable to restrict liberty for the sake of some economic or social advantage in the special conception of justice. In any concrete case, according to Rawls, the first principle must be initially satisfied before one addresses social and economic matters. Presumably slavery would be ruled out, for example, if the motive for slavery were more economic wealth amongst society's masses, although slavery for that reason would not be ruled out under the "general conception" of justice. Norman Daniels is quick to point out that Rawls' "special conception" implies an assumption common to Hobbes, Locke and John Stuart Mill: namely, that political liberty is compatible with significant social and economic inequalities.[52]

One should note, to begin with, that Rawls treats the package of basic liberties as an all-or-nothing affair. Either socio-economic conditions allow for the effective establishment of the rights or socio-economic conditions do not do so.[53] If the former, then our material devices would never make it rational for parties in the original contract to agree to greater economic benefit at the cost of a lower total system of basic liberties. Even the smallest increase in the total system of basic liberties is to be preferred over a large increase in material wealth. Why must liberty and equality be an all-or-nothing affair? Why must they be presumed to be contradictory?

Secondly, when and where is the cut-off point between the general and special conception of justice? Rawls suggests in one context that the general conception shifts into the special conception of justice at that point when social conditions are such that the basic rights can be "effectively established" or admit of "effective realization."[54] Towards the end of his book, he returns to the distinction between the two conceptions of justice.[55] He asserts that "eventually there comes *a time in the history* of a well-ordered society beyond which the special form of the two principles takes over and holds from then on." A "certain level of wealth" will have to be attained.[56] It may be necessary "to raise *the level of civilization* so that *in due course* these freedoms can be enjoyed." But when does that time come? How does one "know" it? He clearly states that all material wants are not satisfied in the special conception.[57] If the two principles of liberty and equality are contradictory as Rawls assumes, then such vague phrases as "effectively established", "a time in history", a "certain level of wealth", "in due course" provide an inadequate basis to call the priority rule into operation.

Thirdly, Professor Rawls' distinction between the first and second principle of justice is just too simple. P. H. Nowell-Smith reminds us that, historically speaking, societies have not always postponed their socio-economic interests in favour of the basic liberties.[58] On the other hand Nowell-Smith's criticism, which is ever so true today, does not reach Rawls' distinction between the first and second principles because the criticism rests on a descriptive assessment of the "real world" rather than on a criticism of the distinction on normative grounds.[59] More telling is H. L. A. Hart's criticism that the parties in the Original Position just cannot give a determinate answer to a concrete case of conflict between the two principles unless the veil of ignorance is lifted.[60] Why would parties in the original position prefer free intellectual inquiry over the necessities of housing, food and an education for example? Why would it be irrational for a person in the lowest economic level, just prosperous enough to permit Rawls' priority rule to operate, to prefer greater material security over freedom of speech?

A final problem with Rawls' priority principle is that liberty and equality may not be so contradictory as Rawls and the liberal tradition have invariably assumed. As mentioned above, although

Rawls insists that the basic liberties must be held equally, equality in the *worth* of these basic liberties is not required.[61] By "worth" Rawls means "the value to individuals of the rights that the first principle defines." One seems warranted in concluding that inequalities in the worth of basic liberties is justifiable in Rawls' scheme in that inequalities in wealth, income and power are permitted under the second principle so long as the inequalities advantage the worst-off representative members of society moreso than do other alternatives.[62] And the worth of basic liberties varies with one's economic, intellectual, social or political ability to take advantage of his basic liberties. Rawls sets no absolute limits to the distribution of "fair" inequalities. Clearly, unequal inheritance of wealth would be justifiable under Rawls' theory.

Normal Daniels, however, makes a very strong argument that we should not accept the unequal worth of liberty in the Original Position.[63] The priority of basic liberties over other social goods is "a hollow abstraction lacking real application"[64] unless we can *effectively* exercise those basic liberties. It is not very useful to speak of equal political liberty, for example, if the wealthy have a greater ability to select candidates, influence public opinion, influence elected officials, and possess more access and control over the media. Similarly, clear inequality in the right to a fair trial exists if the poor cannot afford legal counsel, let alone better legal counsel, at trial or on appeal, or if the wealthy possess better opportunities to legislate laws which favour their interests.

Furthermore, Daniels continues, inequality in the worth of one basic liberty (for example, the right to vote) has a multiplying effect upon the worth of other basic liberties. If the wealthy, for example, have more effective access to the political process, there is a greater chance that the wealthy will gain greater influence over the media as well as the curriculum of the schools. This latter consequence, in turn, increases the worth of their freedom of expression. Even freedom of conscience on some occasions may be effectively restrained by economic circumstances. Daniels cites as one example religions which impose pilgrimages as the test of the truly faithful. Pilgrimages are, of course, expensive, time-consuming acts. Economic factors also enter the picture for religious adherents whose religious obligations preclude military service. The wealthy are in a better position to practise their religion because of the necessary legal costs and harsh employer practices against pacifists. Indeed, Rawls himself acknowledged in an earlier article that the most extensive liberty required equality in the distribution of wealth and power.[65] In "Justice as Fairness" Rawls set up a society whose members "are sufficiently equal in power and ability to guarantee that in normal circumstances none is able to dominate the others."[66]

c. *The Common Interest Principle*

We have seen that Rawls believed that he could resolve some conflicts of basic liberties by his principle that liberties could only be limited for the sake of the total system of basic liberty itself. The priority rule precluded the possibility that liberty necessitated equality. Rawls rigidly separated the two concepts. But Rawls contemplated a second circumstance when basic liberties might be restricted. This arose out of his principle of "the common interest". He defined the "common interest" principle in this way:

> According to this principle institutions are ranked by how effectively they guarantee the conditions necessary for all to further their aims, or by how efficiently they advance shared ends that will similarly benefit everyone. Thus reasonable regulations to maintain public order and security, or efficient measures for public health and safety, promote the common interest in this sense. So do collective efforts for national defense in a just war.[67]

One issue with respect to Rawls' "common interest" principle is whether the principle encompasses any conceptual limit to restrictions upon basic liberties. As Thomas Scanlon points out, the "common interest" principle could be used to justify restrictions with respect to time, place and manner of political demonstrations, parades, placing of posters, and the use of loudspeakers.[68] The "common interest" principle incorporates non-basic liberties (such as uninterrupted sleep or undefaced buildings) into the calculation of restricting the basic liberties.

Rawls' theory of the "common interest" suffers from the same weakness as that raised above with respect to the lack of priority rules for weighing conflicts of basic liberties. What criteria does Rawls provide to guide us in deciding when the common interest necessitates restrictions upon the basic liberties? First, he tells us that there must be "a reasonable expectation" that a failure to maintain "public order and security" will in fact damage the public order.[69] Secondly, the expectation "should not be merely possible or in certain cases even probable, but reasonably certain or imminent." Thirdly, this reasonably certain or imminent expectation must be based on evidence and ways of reasoning acceptable to all. That is, "it must be supported by ordinary observation and modes of thought (including the methods of rational scientific inquiry where these are not controversial) which are generally recognized as correct." This criterion, Rawls repeats, "appeals to what everyone can accept." It represents an agreement to limit liberty only by reference to "a common knowledge and understanding of the world."

But are these criteria adequate? As in the case of conflicts among liberties, Rawls' generalities are so vague that whether any society will in fact follow the principles of justice in concrete cases will be very difficult to determine. Indeed, one could go so far as to suggest that Rawls' doctrine of the "common interest" provides so little guidance in concrete cases that it renders his overall theory of justice invalid in the sense of being contrary to an important element of his own conception of the rule of law: that is, "that laws be known and expressly promulgated, that their meaning be clearly defined..."[70] Rawls virtually admits this to be the consequence of his doctrine when, after setting out the above three criteria, he states that whether "other forces will be called into play that work to preserve the justice of the whole arrangement" presents "a practical dilemma which philosophy alone cannot answer."[71] The resolution of the dilemma, he continues, "depends on the circumstances." The theory of justice, he assures us, "only characterizes the just constitution" — the inference being that how and when the criterion is to be applied is beyond the scope of his inquiry.

But is it? What does Rawls mean by the term "ordinary observation and modes of thought"? He suggests that the modes must be non-controversial. But in at least one case in recent history when the government used "the common interest" to justify restrictions on basic liberties of all citizens (the FLQ crisis in Quebec, 1970-71), an important unresolved issue was precisely that: what constitutes agreed-upon methods of rational scientific inquiry. The government's method of inquiry into the facts was controversial and to this day the issue has not been resolved.[72] Must the evidence of a threat to the public order be admissible in a court of law? Can restrictions upon liberties be imposed on the basis of hearsay: of newspaper reports or the distribution of radical pamphlets by university students?[73] May restrictions upon liberties be justified on the basis of a prediction of a Gallup poll that the majority of the populace in the next election will vote against a present municipal government in favour of a loose coalition of "left-wing" personalities? Further, if it is the government which assesses the evidence of a threat to public order, must the government expose those facts to the public? Must it justify its actions? May a court look behind a government proclamation in order to scrutinize the facts so as to assure itself that the circumstances

172

actually necessitated the restrictions of basic liberties? [74] These are important legal issues which ultimately determine when the "common interest" may be invoked in order to restrict the basic liberties. And yet, Rawls gives little guidance as to how these issues should be resolved.

A second issue with respect to Rawls' "common interest" doctrine arises out of the question, *who* is to determine when a threat to the public order is reasonably expected? Rawls is not entirely clear on this point. He does assert on several occasions that it is *the government's right* to maintain public order and security.[75] But the government has "neither the right nor the duty to do what it or a majority (or whatever) wants to do in questions of morals and religion."[76] The government's duty is simply to underwrite the conditions necessary for everyone's pursuit of his interests. And the members of the government fulfill this function by placing themselves in the position of "the representative equal citizen."[77] Rawls gives us little indication of the nature of this "representative equal citizen" nor how the members of the government or the majority of society can dissociate their own interests from those of "the representative equal citizen." Indeed, the latter dissociation is particularly difficult in the light of Rawls' own conception of individuals in the Original Position. The individual pursues his own self-interest. He is unwilling to accept a basic political position "merely because it maximized the algebraic sum of advantages (to society) irrespective of its permanent effects on his own basic rights and interests."[78]

In fact, when Rawls tries to apply his common interest doctrine to a concrete problem (the toleration of the intolerant),[79] he seems ultimately to leave the resolution of the issue in the hands of those in power. The tolerant, he asserts, have the right to restrict the behaviour and beliefs of the intolerant when they (that is, the "tolerant") "sincerely and with reason believe that intolerance is necessary for their own security." This right of repression follows "readily enough" because in the Original Position each person agrees to the right of self-preservation. More precisely, when "liberty itself *and their own freedom*" are in danger, the "just citizen" "can properly force the intolerant to respect the liberty of others."[80] Or, as Rawls put it two paragraphs later, the intolerant sect should be restricted "only when the tolerant *sincerely* and with reason believe that *their own security* and that of the institutions of liberty are in danger."[81] For this reason, Rawls' introduction of the notion of the "common interest" is at odds with his initial desire to think of each member of the just society as having "an inviolability founded on justice or, as some say, on natural right, which even the welfare of everyone else cannot override."[82]

Thus, because Rawls has provided little guidance as to *who* determines when a threat to public order is reasonably expected, the determination is in effect left to the persons in power. As noted, the persons in power represent "the representative equal citizen".[83] But they also have the right to preserve their own power position.[84] In addition, the justification for restricting basic liberties depends on the *sincerity* of the powerholders' beliefs as well as on their reasoning ability. Rawls' doctrine of the common interest thereby provides the conceptual framework for an authoritarian government.

A third issue with respect to Rawls' doctrine of the "common interest" is that the notion of the "common interest" introduces a new norm to which liberty and equality are subject. Liberty is no longer paramount as in his earlier proposition that liberty could be restricted only for the sake of liberty. Now we find that the state may infringe liberty for the sake of the "common interest". The "common interest", in turn, is assessed and determined by the persons in power. The "common interest" is directly related to the stability of a well-ordered society.[85] The basic liberties are conditioned by the public order and security because, as we have seen,[86] Rawls calls for restrictions upon liberty whenever a threat to the public order is reasonably expected.

This interpretation of the priority of public order and security in Rawls' thinking is not a misreading of his writings. In his first important essay on the subject of liberty,[87] Rawls defined the principle of equal liberty as merely a presumption from which the state may justifiably depart in order to protect public order and security.[88] "Liberty," he told us, "means that... there is freedom of religious belief, worship, and conduct save as limited by the state's interest in public order and security..."[89] And, again, "liberty of conscience is limited, everyone agrees, by the state's interest in public order and security!" In *A Theory of Justice* Rawls tries to make the principle of equal liberty more than a mere presumption: he places the two principles of justice in serial or lexical order so that we must supposedly satisfy the first principle in the ordering before we can move on to any other.[90]

Nevertheless, Rawls' principles are not the independent guideposts which he set out to establish in *A Theory of Justice*. Rawls makes it quite clear in his initial introduction to *A Theory of Justice* that it is a stable well-ordered society with which he is concerned. The parties in the Original Position are to choose prin-

174

ciples of justice only for the governance of a "well-ordered society." As David Lyons points out,[91] Rawls' aim of a well-ordered society is one of several features which seem to restrict the applicability of the principles of justice initially chosen in the Original Position. Indeed, public order and security are so important to Rawls that he devotes one of his nine chapters attempting to establish why his principles of justice provide for more stability than utilitarianism and other conceptions of justice.[92] The "common interest" doctrine is simply one example of the importance played by public order and security in Rawls' writings.

This raises a fourth issue with respect to Rawls' "common interest" doctrine. Rawls believes his justification for freedom of conscience can be extended for other liberties generally.[93] It would seem, therefore, that his doctrine of the "common interest" is similarly applicable to liberties other than freedom of conscience. Indeed, Rawls does extend the common interest doctrine to freedom of speech restrictions: his continual reference to the need for reasonable procedures of inquiry and debate reflects his concern for public order in a free speech context. On the other hand, this latter example is not of the same nature as political restrictions upon freedom of speech. More precisely, Rawls improperly extends his rules of debate analogy to freedom of speech generally. As a consequence, an assumption pervades: when the threat of political instability is imminent, there is a real and direct relationship between the existence and utilization of basic liberties on the one hand, and political instability on the other. It is one thing for Rawls to assume that there is a relationship between freedom of speech on the one hand, and two speakers talking at the same time in a public meeting on the other. It is quite another thing for Rawls to assume that there is a causal relationship between the general exercise of freedom of speech or freedom of conscience generally and political instability.

But there is little empirical evidence which demonstrates that the exercise of Rawls' basic liberties has any causal relationship to political instability.[94] Although the onus is on Rawls to substantiate his assumption, he will find little evidence for it in the studies of the political instability during the mid-1960s in such countries, for example, as the Phillipines, Indonesia, Cambodia, South Vietnam or Thailand.[95] If anything, restrictions upon the basic liberties stimulated the crystallization of political disaffection in these and other countries. Two contemporary examples of the latter point are referred to daily in our newspapers: the political opposition to Madame Ghandi in India and the growing basis of the Parti

Quebecois in Quebec in the early 1970s were ignited in no small way by the total withdrawal of Rawls' basic liberties in the two societies in the recent past.

The sources of political instability in any society are complex and the exercise of basic liberties is rarely one of them. As the U.S. National Advisory Commission on Civil Disorders pointed out,[96] the causes of racial disorders in the United States in the mid-1960s were "imbedded in a massive tangle of issues and circumstances — social, economic, political and psychological — which arise out of the historical pattern of Negro-White relations in America." Some of those factors were pervasive discrimination and segregation, black migration to major cities and white exodus therefrom, black ghettos, frustrated hopes, the legitimation of violence by state and local officials and the feeling of powerlessness of many blacks in the white "power structure." The withdrawal of basic liberties would not have erased any of those complex factors. Indeed, the withdrawal of basic liberties would have ignited the political disaffection even more so than the United States actually experienced.

Hannah Arendt's distinction between violence and power impresses upon us the lack of a causal relationship between the exercise of basic freedoms and political instability.[97] "Power," she says, "corresponds to the human ability not just to act but to act in concert."[98] Power belongs to the group, not to the individual. As soon as the group, from which the power originated, disappears, the "powerful" person also disappears. The hallmark of "authority" is "unquestioning recognition by those who are asked to obey; neither coercion nor persuasion is needed." Consequently "to remain in authority requires respect for the person or the office."[99] The government's superiority in any confrontation lasts only as long as the power structure of the government remains intact: "that is, as long as commands are obeyed and the army or police are prepared to use their weapons." When power rules absolutely, violence is absent since power and violence are opposites. But when the power behind a government's use of violence breaks down, revolution or rebellion is ushered in. The abruptness with which the situation may change reflects how civil disobedience — to laws, rules and institutions — is "but the outward manifestation of support and consent."

In this way, although power as reflected through support and consent is essential for any government, violence is not. Nor are the more sophisticated trappings of violence such as the withdrawal of basic liberties. According to Hannah Arendt, the cost of substituting violence for power is the government's own loss of power to the point of impotency. That is, "violence appears where power is in jeopardy, but left to its own course it ends in power's disappearance."[100] Thus, the exercise of such basic liberties as freedom of speech or of assembly may well reflect a lack of support and consent for a government; it may well reflect a lack of authority on the part of the government. But restrictions upon the exercise of those basic liberties do not remove the sources of the lack of support. Such restrictions can only usher in further diminution of a government's power and further political instability. Such restrictions, in other words, can only be contrary to the common interest if by the "common interest" we mean a well-ordered society.

d. *The Self-Contained Nature of Rawls' System of Basic Liberties*

I have raised several unresolved issues encompassed in Rawls' theory of liberty: first, the compatibility of one's liberty with a similar system of basic liberties for all; secondly, the priority of basic liberties over social and economic inequalities; and thirdly, the common interest principle. Each of these three issues raises a final common problem. Rawls seems to assume that we can weigh and restrict the most extensive system of basic liberties in a self-contained fashion without reference to any further outside values.

We have seen, for example, that Rawls found it unnecessary to guide us as to the relative weight of the different liberties.[101] But as H. L. A. Hart pointed out, we need some criterion of the value of the different liberties in order to resolve conflicts among them.[102] In order to resolve conflicts we must consider the relative weight of different modes of behaviour in concrete situations as well as the extent or amount of freedom. But, according to Hart, an analysis of the relative weight of modes of behaviour must appeal to much more than "a greater liberty." Similarly, Professor Charles Frankel has reminded us that, according to Rawls, we can choose the basic liberty package over equality in the Original Position without making any decision about the relative worth of different parties' conceptions of the good.[103] Rawls' treatment of the basic liberties package as an all-or-nothing affair over socio-economic considerations[104] his failure to indicate the cut-off point more precisely between the general and special conception of justice[105] the simplicity of his distinction between the first and second principle[106] and his distinction between liberty and the worth of liberty:[107] Rawls assumes that each of these issues can be resolved without appeal to some ultimate norms which are either initially brought into the Original Position or are outside of it.

This point is particularly reflected in Rawls' treatment of the "common interest". We have seen how Rawls leaves some important issues unanswered. The criteria by which the common interest may be used to justify restriction of the basic liberties are left open-ended.[108] The decision to restrict basic liberties is left to the members of the government.[109] Although the government is to speak for "the representative equal citizen" Rawls defines the latter in terms of one's own self-interest in the Original Position. That self-interest includes the right of self-preservation. But because the interests of different people and their own perceptions of those interests will diverge, so too will the relative value placed upon the conflicting liberties and the common interest diverge amongst different persons. Conflicts between liberties and conflicts between liberties and the common interest cannot be resolved without some reference either to utilitarian considerations or, alternatively, "to some conception of what all individuals are morally entitled to have as a matter of human dignity or moral right," to use the words of H. L. A. Hart.[110]

What we still need is some principled criterion to determine why fundamental rights are fundamental. The basic liberties are not undifferentiated. Nor can they be added and subtracted mathematically. When one liberty conflicts with another we must have some guideline, some criterion to gauge why one liberty is more basic or more fundamental than another. If liberty can be distinguished from the worth of liberty, we must know why liberty is more important than the worth of liberty. That is, we must know why we should be willing to scrutinize liberty more closely than restrictions upon the socio-economic conditions making up the worth of liberty. We must, in other words, determine whether Rawls' principles of justice rest upon an a priori ontological hypothesis concerning what Rawls believes to be important to human beings.

Section 3. Rawls' Arguments for the Existence of the Basic Liberties

Rawls does provide some indication as to why the basic liberties are basic. This hint protrudes from his two arguments showing why basic liberties must be distributed equally. The one argument begins with liberty of conscience.[111] The second is concerned with the principle of self-respect.[112]

178

Rawls' argument for liberty of conscience proceeds as follows. Because of the veil of ignorance in the Original Position, the parties do not know the particular content of their religious convictions nor do they know whether their religious or moral beliefs will be shared by the majority or the minority.[113] The parties will opt for equal liberty of conscience because they just cannot take chances with their liberty by agreeing to let the dominant religious faction persecute or suppress others if it wishes.[114] In addition, because the initial contract is final and absolutely binding in perpetuity, greater social and economic benefits will inadequately suffice to justify a less than equal liberty. "The reasoning in this case," Rawls informs us, "can be generalized to apply to other freedoms, although not always with the same force."[115]

The first problem with this argument is that if the initial contract is final and binding, *why* does Rawls begin with freedom of conscience rather than, say, equality as the paramount basic liberty? Rawls does not explain why. He can only offer the assertion that "the question of equal liberty of conscience is settled. It is one of the fixed points of our considered judgments of justice."[116] And, toward the end of the book when he sets out the "Grounds for the Priority of Liberty," all he can suggest is that "as the general level of well-being rises... only the less urgent wants remain to be met by further advances... At the same time... a growing insistence upon the right to pursue our spiritual and cultural interests asserts itself."[117]

But why? Why is liberty of conscience the starting point? Why do spiritual and cultural interests assert themselves "beyond some point"? Because of intuition? Because our cultural traditions have said so? Because our conscience is the most "personal" thing which a human being will ever possess? Is liberty of conscience a fixed point because privacy is so important in a just society? If so, then why does Rawls so obscurely leave his explanation in the air? Without telling us why, we will not know why liberty of conscience is basic. Nor will we ever have a criterion to assess which liberties are more basic than others. Nor will we ever be able to determine the scope of the basic liberties when they conflict with each other.

If we grant for the moment that spiritual and cultural interests do assert themselves "beyond some point," is it true that "the reasoning in this case can be generalized to apply to other freedoms"? By the very fact that Rawls places an incomparably higher value on religious liberty and thereby excludes other social goods such as, say, security of the person, liberty of assembly and the like, from consideration, how can his reasoning extend so as to justify the latter liberties? The latter are already secondary in importance to liberty of conscience by definition. As Brian Barry explains, Rawls' argument for liberty of conscience cannot be generalized to other liberties because liberty of conscience depends "essentially on a claim about the distinctive features of religious and moral convictions *as against* other interests. It therefore hardly lends itself to being generalized *to* other interests."[118]

Norman Daniels suggests a further weakness in Rawls' attempt to extend his arguments for liberty of conscience.[119] Religious toleration is fairly harmless if it is narrowly construed. But when we bring into consideration moral or political obligations of a "non-religious" character, the risk arises that the liberty of these moral and political obligations may affect and harm others to an undesirable extent. Can non-religious political and moral wants, beliefs and preferences claim the same importance as a justificatory basis of freedoms of speech, assembly, political participation and personal freedoms in contrast to freedom of conscience? Are not arguments for the latter far more complex and difficult than any argument for freedom of conscience?

b. *The Principle of the "Self-respect" Argument*

Rawls' second, more far-reaching argument for the priority of the basic liberties derives from the extreme importance he places upon self-respect. To begin with, he indicates that self-respect is important in his initial elaboration of the two principles of justice.[120] Rawls places self-respect along with rights and liberties, powers and opportunities, and income and wealth as the chief primary goods in society. By the time that Rawls decides to elaborate the "grounds for the priority of liberty,"[121] he is prepared to assert that it is "perhaps" the main primary good. He defines self-respect as having two aspects: first, "it includes a person's sense of his own value, his secure conviction that his conception of his good, his plan of life, is worth carrying out;" secondly, it "implies a confidence in one's ability, so far as it is within one's power, to fulfill one's intentions."[122] Self-respect is a primary social good because "without it nothing may seem worth doing, or if some things have value for us, we lack the will to strive for them. All desire and activity becomes empty and vain, and we sink into apathy and cynicism."[123] This is why Rawls believes that we place such great significance with respect to how we think others value us.[124]

Accordingly, liberty is fundamental because it is the most effective social basis for self-respect. This relationship between liberty and self-respect exists because "the need for status is met by the public recognition of just institutions, together with the full and diverse internal life... that equal liberty allows."[125] In one of the most significant passages in his book, Rawls goes on to assert that

> the basis for self-esteem in a just society is not then one's income share but the public affirmed distribution of fundamental rights and liberties. And this distribution being equal, everyone has a similar and secure status when they meet to conduct the common affairs of the wider society. No one is inclined to look beyond the constitutional affirmation of equality for further political ways of securing his status. Nor, on the other hand, are men disposed to acknowledge a lesser than equal liberty.

To accept a lesser than equal liberty would "have the effect of publicly establishing their inferiority." It would "indeed be humiliating and destructive of self-esteem."

From this we can see that liberty meets the need for status. An additional consequence is that liberty must be distributed equally, otherwise the holder of a less than equal liberty would be publicly humiliated.

But why does liberty fulfill the need for self-respect whereas wealth does not? Rawls explains that if material wealth were the basis of self-respect, not everyone could possess the highest status.[126] Each man's gain would be another's loss. Self-respect, in other words, could not be distributed equally. But because of the pre-eminence of this primary good (that is, self-respect), the parties in the Original Position would not want this situation. But why would the parties not agree to equal wealth? Because, Rawls believes, this would be "irrational in view of the possibility of bettering everyone's circumstances by accepting certain inequalities."[127] Rawls' compromise solution is "to support the primary good of self-respect as far as possible" by assigning equal basic liberties and giving them priority over the relative shares of material means.

Rawls applied his self-respect argument for basic liberties to the right of equal participation in government. The latter principle requires that "all citizens are to have an equal right to take part in, and to determine the outcome of, the constitutional process that establishes the laws with which they are to comply."[128] As a consequence each vote should have approximately the same weight,[129] and all citizens should have an equal access "at least in the formal sense" to public office. This principle of equal political liberty, Rawls asserts, "is bound to have a profound effect on the moral quality of civic life" partially because one citizen's relations to another's are given a secure basis. More importantly, equal political rights "enhance the self-esteem and the sense of political competence of the average citizen."[130] Having political opinions leads to the development of one's intellectual and moral faculties. Men and women acquire "an affirmative sense of political duty and obligation" because they must explain and justify their views by appealing to principles that others can accept. Thus, political freedoms "strengthen men's sense of their own worth, enlarge their intellectual and moral sensibilities, and lay the basis for a sense of duty and obligation upon which the stability of just institutions depend."[131]

We have now seen that in order to understand why the parties to the Original Contract would choose the primacy of the basic liberties we could not remain within the logical framework of the Original Position.[132] Rawls' own failure to go outside of the initial tenets of his contract analysis provides insight to some problems which are internal to his own argument. Once we tried to determine whether Rawls' principles rested on *a priori* ontological hypotheses we found liberty of conscience and, now, self-respect as just such hypotheses. Liberty of conscience suffers from major limitations. On the other hand, one element common to liberty of conscience and self-respect is the importance of an impenetrable inner sphere of life encircling the individual.

Self-respect, of course, means much more than personal autonomy. Self-respect provides a far sounder basis for understanding why liberties and freedoms are truly fundamental. Rights, freedoms and interests are fundamental if there exists "an indispensable nexus" — to use Mr. Justice Marshall's term[133] — between the right and the moral-political norm of self-respect.

Rawls' notion of self-respect may finally suggest a principled criterion for which we have been searching to explain why fundamental rights are fundamental. The traditional juristic arguments failed to support consistently the existence of fundamental rights. We also found wanting the various brands of utilitarianism. Even John Stuart Mill's arguments for the protection of "self-regarding" conduct suffered from serious conceptual difficulties. Rawls' political theory of liberty also possesses shortcomings, not least of which is the self-contained nature of the most extensive system of basic liberties. Hidden within the internices of Rawls' complex exposition, on the other hand, we have found an argument which, at face value, appears to support the existence of fundamental rights in a consistent manner. In the next chapter I shall take up his idea and use it as a basis to elaborate my own argument for the existence of fundamental rights.

1. John Rawls, *A Theory of Justice* (Cambridge: Harv. Univ. Press, 1971).

2. Ronald Dworkin might also be noted. Although Dworkin has, on a few occasions, suggested what his own political theory would entail, his writings have for the most part focused on the legal implications of a liberal theory of rights. For that reason I examine his contribution in chapter VII.

3. John Rawls, *A Theory of Justice*, p. 13.

4. Ibid., p. 19.

5. Ibid., p. 137.

6. Ibid., p. 12.

7. Ibid., p. 176.

8. Ibid., p. 302.

9. Ibid., pp. 62 ff.

10. Ibid., p. 543.

11. Ibid., pp. 152, 542.

12. Ibid., p. 203.

13. Ibid., p. 230.

14. Ibid.

15. Ibid., p. 61.

16. Ibid., chap. 4.

17. See text, supra, chap. II between notes 90 and 93.

18. See supra chap. II, note 91.

19. John Rawls, *A Theory of Justice*, p. 237.

20. Ibid., p. 302.

21. Ibid., p. 61.

22. Ibid., p. 273.

23. See, for example, John Locke, *Treatise on Civil Government* (N.Y.: Appleton-Century-Crofts, 1937), pp. 18 ff. Robert Paul Wolff also makes this point in *Understanding Rawls* (Princeton: Princeton U. Press, 1977), p. 88.

24. John Rawls, *A Theory of Justice*, p. 303.

25. Ibid., pp. 203 ff.

26. Ibid., p. 204.

27. Ibid., p. 225.

28. Ibid., p. 229.

29. Ibid., p. 231.

30. Ibid., p. 233.

31. Neil MacCormick, *Justice According to Rawls*, 89 L.Q.R. 393, p. 409 (1973).

32. John Rawls, *A Theory of Justice*, section 34.

33. Ibid., p. 213.

34. Ibid.

35. Ibid., p. 215.

36. Ibid., pp. 196-197.

37. Ibid., p. 201.

38. See text, supra, corresponding to notes 28-35.

39. John Rawls, *A Theory of Justice*, p. 203.

40. Ibid., p. 204.

41. Ibid., p. 230.

42. Brian Barry,, *The Liberal Theory of Justice* (Oxford: Clarendon Press, 1973), pp. 62 ff.

43. Michael Lessnoff, "Barry on Rawls' Priority of Liberty," 4 *Phil. Pub. Affairs* 100, pp. 113 ff. (1974).

44. John Rawls, *A Theory of Justice*, sections 7 and 8.

45. Ibid., p. 34.

46. Ibid., p. 40.

47. Ibid., p. 41.

48. Ibid., p. 43.

49. Ibid., p. 41.

50. H. L. A. Hart, *Rawls on Liberty and Its Priority*, 40 Univ. of Chicago L. Rev. 534, p. 550 (1973).

51. Joel Feinberg, *Justice, Fairness and Rationality*, 81 Yale L. J. 1004, p. 1007 (1972).

52. Normal Daniels, "Equal Liberty and Unequal Worth of Liberty," in Daniels, ed., *Reading Rawls: Critical Studies on Rawls' "A Theory of Justice"* (Oxford: Basil Blackwell, 1975), p. 253.

53. John Rawls, *A Theory of Justice*, pp. 152, 542, 543.

54. Ibid., p. 153.

55. Ibid., p. 542.

56. Ibid., p. 542. Emphasis added.

57. Ibid., p. 543.

58. P. H. Nowell-Smith, "A Theory of Justice?" 3 *Phil. Soc. Sci.* 315, p. 322.

59. One should note, however, that at least one African leader has written that even if a high level of economic development were reached, his country should prefer economic and social equality over basic liberties. See, generally, Kaunda, Dr. K., *Letter to My Children* (Longman, 1973), *Humanism in Zambia and a Guide to its Implementation* (Lusaka: Zambia Info. Sevices, 1967), *Zambia's Guideline for the Next Decade* (Lusaka: Zambia Info. Services, 1968) esp. at p. 16. Note how Kaunda translates the principle of self-respect and human dignity into social policy.

60. H. L. A. Hart, supra, note 50, p. 544.

61. Text, supra, corresponding to notes 25-27.

62. John Rawls, *A Theory of Justice*, p. 278.

63. Norman Daniels, supra note 52.

64. Ibid., p. 278.

65. John Rawls, "Justice as Fairness," in Peter Laslett and W. G. Runciman, ed., *Philosophy, Politics and Society, Second Series* (Oxford: Oxford U. Press, 1962), pp. 138, 139 as noted by C. B. Macpherson, *Democratic Theory: Essays in Retrieval* (Oxford: Clarendon Press, 1973), p. 92.

66. John Rawls, "Justice as Fairness," in Peter Laslett and W. G. Runciman, ed., *Philosophy, Politics and Society, Second Series* (Oxford: Oxford U. Press, 1962), p. 138.

67. John Rawls, *A Theory of Justice*, p. 97.

68. T. M. Scanlon, *Rawls' Theory of Justice*, 121 U. of Penn. L. Rev. 1020 (1973).

69. John Rawls, *A Theory of Justice*, p. 213.

70. Ibid., p. 237.

71. Ibid., p. 219.

72. See generally, Dennis Smith, *Bleeding Hearts... Bleeding Country: Canada and the Quebec Crisis* (Hurtig, 1971).

73. Unfortunately, the Official Secrets Act prevents me from elaborating upon the nature of the "evidence" which the government had at its disposal concerning the threat to the public order. I was required to examine two of the three files on the FLQ crisis when I was an articling student at the Department of Justice, Government of Canada, 1971-72. One should also note that of the several hundreds of citizens detained pursuant to the Public Order Regulations and the Public Order (Temporary Measures) Act, 1970, during the FLQ Crisis only 62 persons were charged. D. Schmeiser, *Control of Apprehended Insurrection: Emergency Measures vs. the Criminal Code*, 4 Man. L. J. 359 (1971). With respect to those 62 persons, all charges, except one were dropped. The latter person was acquitted.

74. Montgomery, J. A. held in *Gagnon & Valieres* v. *R.* (1971), 14 C.R.N.S. 321, (1971) Que. C.A. 454 that the Canadian courts had no such jurisdiction. The issue has been the subject of a great deal of litigation in Canada. *Ft. Francis Pulp and Paper Co., Ltd.* v. *Manitoba Free Press Co. Ltd.*, [1923] A.C. 695, 706, *Ref re Validity of the Wartime Leasehold Regs.*, [1950] S.C.R. 124, *In re George Gray* (1919), 57 S.C.R. 153, *Ref re Regs re Chemicals*, [1943] 1 D.L.R. 248. *Re Bd. of Commerce Act*, [1922] A.C. 191, 197-198, *Co-operative Committee on Japanese Canadians* v. *A.-G. Canada*, [1947] A.C. 87, 101-102. See generally, William E. Conklin, *Pickin and its Applicability to Canada*, 25 Univ. of Tor. L. J. 193, 198-200 (1975).

75. John Rawls, *A Theory of Justice*, p. 213.

76. Ibid., p. 212.

77. Ibid., p. 213.

78. Ibid., p. 14.

79. Ibid., pp. 206 ff.

80. Ibid., p. 219. Emphasis added.

81. Ibid., p. 220. Emphasis added.

82. Ibid., p. 28.

83. Ibid., p. 213.

84. Ibid., pp. 213, 219, 220.

85. Ibid., p. 219.

86. Ibid., p. 213.

87. John Rawls, "Constitutional Liberty and the Concept of Justice," in C. J. Friedrich and J. W. Chapman ed., *Justice: Nomos VI* (New York: Lieber-Atherton, 1974).

88. See especially ibid., pp. 101, 118.

89. Ibid., p. 118.

90. John Rawls, *A Theory of Justice*, pp. 42 ff.

91. David Lyons, "Rawls vs. Utilitarianism," 69 *J. Phil.* 535, p. 540 (1972).

92. John Rawls, *A Theory of Justice*, chap. 8.

93. Ibid., p. 209.

94. On the subject of the causes of political instability generally see C. E. Black, *The Dynamics of Modernization, A Study in Comparative History* (London: Harper and Row, 1966), Peter Calvocoress, *New States and World Order* (London: Chatto and Windus, 1962), S. E. Finer, *The Man on Horseback* (London: Pall Mall Press, 1962), F. E. Von der Menden, *Politics of Developing Nations* (New York: Prentice-Hall, 1964); and Barrington Moore Jr., *Social Origins of Dictatorship and Democracy* (London: Penguin, 1966).

95. Michael Breecher, *The New States of Asia* (London: Oxford Univ. Press, 1963), esp. pp. 1-88; A Vandenbosch, and R. Butwell, *The Changing Face of South East Asia* (Louisville: Kentucky Press, 1967); Barrington Moore Jr., *Social Origins of Dictatorship and Democracy* (London: Penguin, 1966), esp. chap. 9.

96. National Advisory Commission on Civil Disorders, *Report* (New York: Bantam Books, 1968), esp. pp. 203-206.

97. Hannah Arendt, *On Violence* (N.Y.: Harcourt, Brace and World, 1969, 1970), pp. 40-56.

98. Ibid., p. 44.

99. Ibid., p. 45.

100. Ibid., p. 56.

101. See text, supra, between notes 36-51.

102. H. L. A. Hart, supra note 50, p. 543.

103. Charles Frankel, "Justice, Utilitarianism, and Rights," 3 *Social Theory Practice* 27, p. 40 (1974).

104. See text, supra, at note 53.

105. See text, supra, between notes 54-57.

106. See text, supra, between notes 54-56.

107. See text, supra, between notes 61-66.

108. See text, supra, between notes 67-71.

109. See text, supra, between notes 75-82.

110. H. L. A. Hart, supra note 50, p. 545.

111. See generally, John Rawls, *A Theory of Justice*, pp. 205-211.

112. See generally, ibid., pp. 543-548. Rawls writes at p. 543 that "One reason for this [i.e., the priority of liberty] I have discussed in connection with liberty of conscience and freedom of thought. And a second reason is the central place of the primary good of self-respect and the desire of human beings to express their nature in a free social union with others."

113. Ibid., p. 206.

114. Ibid., p. 207.

115. Ibid., p. 206. Also see Ibid., p. 209.

116. Ibid., p. 206.

117. Ibid., pp. 542-543.

118. Brian Barry, supra, note 42, p. 38. Emphasis original.

119. Norman Daniels supra, note 52, p. 267.

120. John Rawls, *A Theory of Justice*, sect. 11. For an excellent sum-

.mary of Rawls' reasoning on this point see H. Shue, "Liberty and Self-Respect," 85 *Ethics* 195 (1974-75).

121. John Rawls, *A Theory of Justice*, sect. 82.
122. Ibid., p. 440.
123. Ibid.
124. Ibid., p. 544.
125. Ibid.
126. Ibid., p. 545.
127. Ibid., p. 546.
128. Ibid., p. 221.
129. Ibid., p. 223.
130. Ibid., p. 234.
131. Ibid.
132. See text, supra, between notes 110-111.
133. See text, supra, between notes 195-199.

Chapter VI

An Argument in Support of Fundamental Rights

Chapter IV elaborated John Stuart Mill's notion of "self-regarding" conduct. We saw that the core to his notion was his distinction between an inner and outer sphere of life. Society could interfere with one's conduct only when the conduct harmed the interests of others. That harm could arise out of one's acts or omissions. But upon what basis did one possess a duty to act? Mill, unfortunately, failed to provide us with an adequate account of the basis of our duties and rights.

Bentham provided us with one solution. Rule utilitarianism provided us with another. Unfortunately, both brands of utilitarianism suffered from at least two important conceptual weaknesses which rendered utilitarianism inconsistent with the absolute inviolability of the inner sphere of life. Faced with these obstacles we examined, in chapter V, John Rawls' theory of fundamental freedom. We found that Rawls' theory rested upon a prior ontological hypothesis concerning the principle of self-respect. Rawls' principle might very well provide us with a basis by which we can overcome the conceptual limitations of utilitarianism. It might also provide a principled criterion with which to anchor the existence of fundamental rights. Let us see whether that is so by examining whether Rawls' principle of self-respect provides us with an argument as to why the "inner sphere of life" ought to be protected.

Chapter IV argued, in addition, that Mill's *On Liberty* was written from the perspective of utilitarianism.[1] Interspersed throughout Mill's writings, on the other hand, there appeared an idea which resembles Rawls' ontological assumption. It is in our interest to grasp and elaborate the idea if we are to try to develop an alternative perspective with which to view the issue of the "inner sphere of life" in particular and fundamental rights in general. The idea to which I refer is that the ultimate norm in a democratic society is the development of individuality rather than the "greatest happiness of the greatest number". At the outset of his *On Liberty*, for example, Mill expressed concern for the tyranny of the majority because it invariably fettered "the development and, if possible, prevent[ed] the formation, of any individuality not in harmony with its ways..."[2] And, when he began his discussion as to why individuality was "one of the elements of well-being",[3] he explained that he found it necessary to justify liberty on utilitarian grounds simply because people were indifferent to individuality as an independent ground of argument. In Mill's words, "the common modes of thinking" hardly recognized individual spontaneity "as having any intrinsic worth."[4]

Section 1. The Development of Individuality

Mill provided us with two interpretations of what he meant by the term "the development of individuality".

On several occasions he conceived the "self" as an empirically identifiable person with real feelings, impulses, desires, hopes and thoughts. A person whose desires and impulses were his own possessed a strong character, according to Mill.[5] Indeed, Mill insisted that the individual with strong desires and impulses of his own constituted the "perfect human being". Without impulses of one's own, a person possessed no character: he had "no more [character] than a steam-engine has a character." Society needed "strong natures". Spontaneity and individuality, therefore, were to be encouraged. Society was obligated to cultivate personal impulses, to stimulate the unfolding of the individuality of desires and impulses.

In Mill's *On Liberty* there lies hidden an alternative and, as we shall see, a conflicting conception of the "self". According to his alternative version, the "self" was not an empirically ascertainable given. Rather, the nature of the "self" was unknown. The person was always in the process of becoming. That is, rather than existing in a physiological sense, the individual existed as an ideal potentiality, the *daimon* within us. In one well-known passage, for example, Mill asserted that "human nature is not a machine to be built after a model, and set to do exactly the work prescribed for it, but a tree, which requires to grow and develop itself on all sides, according to the tendency of the inward forces which make it a living thing."[6] For Mill, the ultimate end of man was, quoting from Wilhelm von Humbolt,

> the highest and most harmonious development of his powers to a complete and consistent whole; that, therefore, the object towards which every human being must ceaselessly direct his efforts..., and on which especially those who design to influence their fellow-men must ever keep their eyes, is the individuality of power and development.[7]

Elsewhere in *On Liberty* Mill asked "What more or better can be said of any condition of human affairs than that it bring human beings themselves nearer to the best they can be?"[8]

It was from this latter perspective that Mill examined the constitution of the ideal government in his *Representative Government*. The most important element of good government, he wrote, was that it "promote the virtue and intelligence of the people themselves."[9] The ideal government should "foster in the members of the community the various desirable qualities, moral and intellectual; or rather (following Bentham's more complete classification) moral, intellectual, and active."[10] We should judge a government, he continued two pages later, by "the degree in which they [that is, its political institutions] promote the general mental advancement in intellect, in virtue, and in practical activity and efficiency."[11] Secondly, he emphasized, we should examine "the degree of perfection with which they organize the moral, intellectual, and active worth already existing, so as to operate with the greatest effect on public affairs."

Mill seems to have given us very little further direction in his writings as to what he meant by the term, "the development of individuality". Unfortunately, the notion has sometimes been held out as the basis of democratic theory without an adequate examination of what it means to "develop" the "self". One philosopher who has attempted such an inquiry is T. H. Green, who delivered his *Lectures on Political Obligation* at Oxford between 1879 and 1882.[12]

T. H. Green's conception of the "development of the self" seems to have had two themes. First, he argued that one should resolve all political questions by reference to the essence of man or, using a more common term, human nature. Man's essence was, in Green's view, to strive toward an ideal unattained condition of man himself.[13] The true function of government was to maintain the conditions essential for a person to fulfill his moral nature.[14] The justifiability of laws and the existence of "natural" rights depended upon whether the laws or rights were directly related to "the moral vocation of man."[15] An individual's rights and a society's counterclaim to exercise certain authority over the individual rested upon the fact that such rights and powers were "necessary to the fulfilment of man's vocation as a moral being, to an effectual self-devotion to the work of developing the perfect character in himself and others."[16]

As a second theme, Green argued that man could develop only as a social being. Rights could exist only in a society where society's members recognised a common good as the ideal good for each member.[17] Why was society so important? On the one hand, rights were necessary to allow the moral personality to develop. On the other hand, the personality could develop only when the society's members recognised that an individual contributed to a common good.[18] In this light, Green insisted that:

> there can be no right without a consciousness of common interest on the part of members of a society. Without this there might be certain powers on the part of individuals, but no recognition of these powers by others as powers of which they allow the exercise, nor any claim to such recognition; and without this recognition or claim to recognition there can be no right.[19]

Accordingly, the individual had to be conscious of society's good as well as his own. What rights he had, he had by virtue of his membership in society.

Freedom, for Green, had a positive as well as negative element. The "mere removal of compulsion", or what some have called negative freedom, served as a necessary though insufficient condition of "true freedom".[20] "When we speak of freedom as something to be so highly prized," Green insisted, "we mean a positive power or capacity of doing or enjoying something worth doing or enjoying... in common with others."[21] One could measure the progress of any society only "by the greater power on the part of the citizens as a body to make the most and best of themselves."

More to the point, freedom had more than merely a legal connotation. For freedom to be meaningful, one had to be in a position to exercise the freedom effectively. We must, that is, consider the economic and social as well as the legal elements of freedom. Thus, a contract into slavery was void because it violated positive freedom:

> No contract is valid in which human persons, willingly or unwillingly, are dealt with as commodities, because such contracts of necessity defeat the end for which alone society enforces contracts at all.[22]

Similarly, positive freedom could justifiably restrict freedom of contract when a man bargained to work in conditions fatal to his health,[23] or when the contract itself constituted "an instrument of oppression."[24]

Section 2. The "Self" for Whom We Should Have Respect

John Stuart Mill's brief excursion into self-development theory and T. H. Green's more extensive elaboration of it raise important questions with respect to the nature of the "self" which is to be

192

developed and respected. One can find at least three different conceptions of the "self" in Mill's and Green's writings. Each conception, if adopted, would lead to very different implications for the protection of "self-regarding" conduct in particular and fundamental rights in general.

One conception which played a role in Mill's analysis defined the "self" as an actuality, as someone who actually feels, eats, drinks and breathes. He is a "real" person in the "real" world. The development of his "self" entails the development of his *subjective desires* and *impulses*. He realises himself if he is permitted to do what he *desires* to do. Thus, the standards which we should use to judge his conduct are solely his desires. The variety of standards is as diverse as there are desires within each individual and amongst all individuals in society.

This first conception of the "self" has at least two important consequences for the problem of "self-regarding" conduct. In the first place, a person with no impulses or desires would be freer than someone whose desires remained unfulfilled.[25] A "contented" slave would be freer than his frustrated master. The "contented" prisoner would be freer than the professor who always wanted to be the dean of a law school or the president of a university.

Secondly, whether an individual could legitimately infringe the "self-regarding" conduct of another would depend upon the outcome of the power relationship between the two persons. Each individual would try to persuade or, ultimately, physically to force the other to recognise the superiority of his desires over the wishes of others. Society would be characterised by a permanent conflict between and amongst citizens with their unlimited desires. The "self" in this first conception is a "possessive individualist", someone who is "essentially the proprietor of his own person or capacities, owing nothing to society for them."[26] He is neither "a moral whole" nor a part of a larger social whole, but simply an owner of himself. As a consequence, important socio-economic and political issues in society will be resolved only through an open or, possibly, disguised power struggle. The politically stronger will eventually win out, no matter how meritorious the position of minorities. Though the politically stronger could prevail through persuasion or appeals to the self-interest of the weak, tyranny would not be precluded. And tyranny was the very state of affairs which Mill loathed.

The second conception of the "self" is defined in "objective" terms of higher goodness, independent of one's actual desires and impulses. T. H. Green's first theme with respect to the development of the "self" elaborated above would seem to fall under this conception. Whether one owes a duty toward others depends upon whether the fulfilment of a duty would bring him closer to his "true", "higher" self. This "self" is not an empirical self of subjective desires, impulses and the like.

But how would one determine the nature of the "true" self? It would seem from the writings of Green and others that the "true" self is determined through reason. Indeed, it would seem that this "objective" conception of the self presumes that we should adopt a "rationalist" perspective toward moral problems.[27] That is, it assumes that the truth can be ascertained through reason and that misjudgments as to what factors most contribute toward the development of the self can be and should be rationally resolved in favour of what is right. Because the "true", ideal self is the same for all persons, according to our second conception, society may legitimately interfere with "self-regarding" conduct when the reason of society's leaders dictates that such intervention is necessary for the fulfilment of the "true" self. The existence, nature and scope of fundamental rights are thereby readily ascertainable, unless society's leaders misjudge what constituted self-development in any particular case. In the latter event, reason would eventually resolve all differences.

Isaiah Berlin has raised an important objection to this notion of a "higher" "true" self.[28] Historically, according to Berlin, the "true" self has become identified with the social "whole" of which the individual is merely an element: he has become identified with a race, class, state or religion. Also, authoritarian leaders have professed to have insight into the "ends" toward which individuals ought to be developing. Society's members would pursue the "ends" were they more enlightened but, according to those leaders, society's members do not do so because they are blind, ignorant or corrupt.[29] This "monstrous impersonation", according to Berlin, has confronted the application of all political theories of self-realisation.

This second, "objective" conception of the self could be used to justify even subtler infringements of "self-regarding" conduct than Berlin contemplated. Mill himself pointed to some examples. Paternalism was justifiable for children, adolescents, persons "in a state to require being taken care of by others" and "those backward states of society in which the race itself may be considered to be as in its nonage."[30] Presumably these persons were incapable of comprehending the nature of their "true" "higher" selves. Society had to teach, persuade or coerce them into maturity. Society or society's representatives — elected or otherwise —

194

alone monopolised insight into the "true" nature of members of the human species.

There is, however, a third conception of the "self". As Mill suggested in his analogy of a tree,[31] the self is a potentiality, always in the process of becoming. The self is one's *daimon*, "the ideal possibility which each individual bears within him and which it is his destiny progressively to actualise."[32] Unlike the first conception, the self is not conceived by reference to one's impulses or desires: he is continually growing. Unlike the second conception, the self cannot be imposed nor be discovered by some great leader because the self is *always* in the process of becoming. The "monstrous impersonation" about which Berlin was concerned is conceptually impossible with this third notion of the self because our fallibility prevents us from ever knowing its nature. The meaning of the self is, of necessity, open-ended. Any one person's conception is of equal weight and equal respect relative to another's. Consequently, the basis of freedom in this third conception cannot logically lead to tyranny.

If I am correct in my assessment of the nature of this third conception of the self, who would qualify as a "person" under it? Could we justifiably exclude children and adolescents as Mill did? Could we exclude "barbarians" "incapable of being improved by free and equal discussion"?[33] This exemption from the category of "persons" would presumably extend to those whom our society deemed insane and senile and, possibly, even to the "uneducated", apathetic and conformist-minded members of society. Nevertheless, although such an exemption from the class of "persons" would be consistent with our second conception of the "self" as a rationally conceived, "true" individual, the exemption would clearly be inconsistent with the third. Because the third conception is by its very nature open-ended, a state or society has no claim to define who qualifies. A person is merely a potentiality and, therefore, the class of "persons" contemplated would presumably include children, adolescents, the alleged insane, the senile and persons of all races.

Not surprisingly, this third conception of the "self" ushers forth at least two problems. First, how could the conception of the "self" as an open-ended potentiality ever serve as a viable basis for legislators to design social policy or, alternatively, for judges to adjudicate legal disputes? Before I can face this question it is important to appreciate what it means *to respect* the person as a potentiality. After fleshing out the meaning of respect, I shall attempt to show how respect for persons as a concept can be used to resolve theoretical and practical issues regarding the three categories of "self-regarding" conduct examined in chapter IV. In chapter VII I shall attempt to elaborate how respect for persons can provide a viable basis to resolve the critical civil liberties issues which have plagued jurists in the common law tradition: that is, which rights are fundamental rights; what standard of judicial scrutiny should be expected; at what point and for what reason(s) may the state circumscribe fundamental rights; and, what method of justifying judicial decisions is most consistent with the existence of fundamental rights?

A second problem with the third conception of the "self" is as follows: how can I criticise jurists and lawyers in chapters I to III for not adequately defending fundamental rights when they may well have adopted one of the other two conceptions of human nature? My point is that jurists and lawyers cannot consistently adopt one of the latter two conceptions of the "self" and, at the same time, claim they are defending fundamental rights.

The Introduction to this book began with the claim by constitution framers, legislators, judges and legal scholars that fundamental rights in fact exist in and are the foundation of their respective legal systems. Chapters I to III documented variations of the same theme. My conclusion to chapters II and III was that lawyers could ultimately justify legal rights only by raising moral considerations concerning the individual and the state. I have now suggested that the two conceptions of the "self" adopted in liberal political theory are conceptually consistent with tyranny. If jurists, lawyers and legislators want to live by their claim that their opinions, decisions, and conduct consistently support fundamental rights, then the character of their arguments must be rooted in the conception of the person as a potentiality, always in the process of becoming. The very fact that they may have adopted either of the two traditional conceptions of the "self" serves as an added reason why the juristic arguments for the existence of fundamental rights have proved unsatisfactory in the common law tradition.

Section 3.   What Does It Mean to Respect a Person?

What does it mean to say that we ought to respect persons as persons rather than as things? If our argument adopting the third conception of the "self" is valid, what would it mean to say that we ought to respect the person as a potentiality? In addition, how could we connect that respect to the issue of "self-regarding" conduct?

Stephen Darwell has recently pointed out that there are at least two different senses of respect which are commonly confused.[34]

196

We ought to distinguish between the two, he suggests. And so we should. For, the one meaning, which he labels "appraisal respect", appears inconsistent with our third conception of the self as an open-ended potentiality. Whereas the second sense, referred to as "recognition respect", is more consistent with the self as a potentiality, "appraisal respect" is appropriate for a conception of the self as an empirically ascertainable entity. "Recognition respect" provides, therefore, a more coherent connection with our theory of fundamental rights.

Darwell defines "appraisal respect" as "a positive appraisal of an individual made with regard to those features which are excellences of persons."[35] So, for example, we might have great respect for a tennis player because of his demonstrated ability at tennis. Similarly, we might have great respect for a scientist, doctor or lawyer because of the development of their talents and capacities amidst obstacles. Appraisal respect contemplates that we grade persons with reference to what we consider to be valuable human traits acquired by an individual throughout his lifetime. The traits are empirically ascertainable capacities. Because human traits and capacities vary from one individual to the next, appraisal respect admits of degree: we may respect the cancer research scientist more than the tennis player. Or, we may have more esteem for one tennis player over another. The pivotal issue in our evaluation of someone is merit. We have appraisal respect for him/her, in other words, when he/she has *merited* or *deserved* our respect. What we are concerned with here is the esteem we hold of one's abilities and achievements.

There are several implications of appraisal respect which run counter to the existence of fundamental rights.

In the first place, not every one in a society will be worthy of "appraisal respect". Some persons will not possess natural ability because of aptitude, physical handicap, or emotional make-up. Furthermore, our success in life's enterprises, it seems, depends to a great extent upon the family and other environmental factors surrounding our early childhood upbringing. We are neither naturally endowed nor nurtured on equal terms. As a consequence, appraisal respect will be owed to some persons and not to others. When we consider men and women in terms of their professional or social titles we acknowledge the conspicuous existence of inequality amongst persons.

Secondly, in addition to being shared unequally, one's right to appraisal respect may be waived, taken away or even unrecognised. The reason why this is so is that, as in the case of Benthamite utilitarianism, the existence, nature and scope of one's rights to appraisal respect will vary according to society's preferences toward a particular enterprise at any one time. What constitutes achievement is culturally and socially conditioned. So, for example, if a society gives more weight to economic rather than to artistic achievement, the rights derived from appraisal respect will be more extensive in number and wider in scope for a successful businessman than for an accomplished actor. The former might justifiably be afforded the right to counsel upon being charged with impaired driving whereas the latter might not. Similarly, one would have more difficulty in justifying an interference with a corporate president's "self-regarding" conduct than, say, that of the manager of a shoe store.

In addition, assuming that a society did set out a scale of priorities of occupations, the criteria employed to assess each profession would vary in time and place. If, for example, society places high esteem upon economic ability, should merit be judged by a company's profit margin or should it be evaluated by the company's success at expanding the number of its outlets? Similarly, if architecture is to be a socially preferred profession, should merit be evaluated upon the basis of the architect's ability to design a functional building or should one look to his ability to design a building of aesthetic beauty? Whichever criterion we choose will alter the outsome. As a consequence, if the existence and very nature of fundamental rights hinge upon appraisal respect for persons, our rights will be *ad hoc* in that they may exist one day in one circumstance but not the next in a similar circumstance. As in the case of the "shock the conscience" form of fundamental rights examined in chapter II,[36] appraisal respect leaves us with no principled criteria upon which to determine the nature and scope of a fundamental right.

The critical problem with the character of an argument for fundamental rights based on appraisal respect is that if we value someone for his meritorious qualities he is, as a person, dispensable. For, it is his merit that we value, not his individuality. Appraisal respect, by its very nature, contemplates inequality of rights.

Darwall offers us a second sense in which we can use the term "respect". This second sense avoids the above limitations. The second sense, referred to as "recognition respect", is defined as "to give appropriate weight to the fact that he or she is a person by willing to constrain one's behaviour in ways required by that fact [of being a person.]."[37] Recognition respect does not necessarily infer that we must give someone esteem for his accomplishments or abilities. Rather, it requires that from respect for the person flows moral constraints upon our conduct. These moral constraints involve rights and responsibilities. When we fail to show recognition respect towards someone, we also fail to respond to him in a manner which takes his person seriously.

But what are the rights and responsibilities which flow from the recognition of a person? What does it mean to say that we ought to take the potentiality of a person seriously?

The first point to note is that, if my earlier argument concerning the nature of the "self" is valid, recognition respect requires that we recognise the human potentiality in others. We must recognise the *daimon*, the "ideal possibility" within him. We recognise him not because he *deserves* or *merits* our recognition, nor because he has successfully won esteem for his professional, athletic or artistic accomplishments. The latter consideration, which focuses upon one's empirical abilities, accepts the person's impulses and desires as givens which fundamental rights should supposedly protect. Recognition respect, in contrast, considers the person in a normative rather than an empirical sense. Each person is always an open-ended potentiality in the process of becoming. When we respect the person in this sense we recognise him, to use Mill's words, "as a tree which requires to grow and develop on all sides according to the tendency of the inward forces which make it a living thing."[38] The basis of recognition respect, therefore, is independent of one's actual abilities and deserts.

This point leads us to a further implication for our analysis of fundamental rights. Because of the independence of recognition respect from merit, there is a sense in which all persons are equal. Though differing in intelligence, psyche and environmental endowments, we are all equal in the sense that recognition respect is owed to all persons rather than just to some. It is owed equally because we are members of the same species. Though citizens of different secular states, though members of diverse cultural, religious or political groups, and though born into different families, we are also members of the *gens humana*. As Bernard Williams reminds us, all members of the species *homo sapiens* possess the capacity to feel pain, both physical and emotional.[39] We also have the capacity to feel affection toward others.

Recognition respect requires that we shed the conspicuous labels of social, political and professional status. It insists that, underlying the unequal human abilities and underlying our grading of those capacities, there is a common humanness enveloping each person. That common humanness is found in one's potentiality, in the unchartered individuality which is always in the process of becoming. This, it is submitted, is what is meant by the term "the human point of view". And this is what is meant by the assertion that we ought to respect a person as a person, rather than as a thing.

Henry Higgins certainly failed to show recognition respect toward Eliza Doolittle in George Bernard Shaw's *Pygmalion*. Eliza resented being treated "for dirt". She was not a thing which Henry Higgins could manipulate at will. She was an "end", not a means. She had her own feelings, her own hopes, her own beliefs. She wanted to be able to make her own judgments rather than to have them made for her. Stanley Benn has perceptively put the philosophic idea underlying Eliza's feelings in the following more positive way:

> To *conceive* someone as a person is to see him as actually or potentially a chooser, as one attempting to steer his own course through the world, adjusting his behaviour as his apperception of the world changes, and correcting course as he perceives his errors. It is to understand that his life is for him a kind of enterprise like one's own, not merely a succession of more or less fortunate happenings, but a record of achievements and failures; and just as one cannot describe one's own life in these terms without claiming that what happens is important, so as to see another's in the same light is to see that for him at least this must be important.[40]

Thus, according to Benn, we should show respect towards others as persons when we see how their aims and conduct could be important for them. The recognition that others are engaged in "self-creative enterprises" makes a claim upon us. That is, when we proceed in a manner which is "other-regarding" we have a duty to take account of the way in which our conduct may affect another person's "self-creative enterprise".

Recognition respect has a final important implication for fundamental rights. This relates to the primacy of the individual — a problem, one should recall, which prevented utilitarianism from consistently justifying the protection of "self-regarding" conduct. We saw in chapter IV that the reason why Benthamite and rule utilitarianism could not support the inviolability of the "inner sphere of life" lay in the fact that the ultimate norm in utilitarianism was "the greatest happiness of the greatest number". Society's welfare provided the vantage point from which both act and rule utilitarianism assessed all human behaviour. In contrast, the alternative perspective elaborated here argues that the individual is the reference point for our analysis of fundamental rights. However man grows in a social environment, the source of our fundamental rights is found in the recognition respect which we have for the *individual*.

200

Section 4. Respect for Persons and the "Inner Sphere of Life"

We have elaborated the sense in which we should use the terms "person" and "respect" if we are consistently to consider rights and freedoms as fundamental. But we are still left with the problem of connecting the notion of "respect for persons" with the rights and duties which the principle imposes. I shall commence the examination of this connection by returning to the question as to whether an argument can be made for the protection of the "inner sphere of life".

We have examined three possible conceptions of the "self" for whom we should have respect. The first conception defined the self as an actuality — as a real, empirically ascertainable person whose capacities could be graded. The second conception defined the "self" "from the outside", as it were, in terms of a "higher", "true" self. We rejected both conceptions as incompatible with the sustained existence of fundamental rights. The third conception, which considered the "self" as a potentiality, proved a more satisfactory basis. What the third conception of respect for persons tells us is that the inviolability of the "inner sphere of life" is intrinsic to the very nature of the "self" and, in particular, that the protection of the inner sphere of life is an important example of how we should show recognition respect towards persons. This is so for at least four reasons.

In the first place, that society should be able to interfere with one's "self-regarding" conduct simply because of society's "preferences" is entirely alien to the notion of respect for the "self" as a potentiality. There is no "true self" or, if there is, our fallibility prevents us from ever knowing its nature. By imposing its own religious, political or moral preferences upon an individual, society is admitting that there is one "true" or "higher" self — and this is something which the third conception of the "self" does not admit. We are obliged, therefore, to discard Lord Devlin's instruction that "if the reasonable man believes that a practice is immoral and believes also — no matter whether the belief is right or wrong, so be it that is honest and dispassionate — that no right-minded member of his society could think otherwise, then for the purpose of the law it is immoral."[41] The issue of whether society may justifiably intervene with "self-regarding" conduct cannot be resolved by ascertaining society's offended sensibilities, its paternalistic beliefs, or its feelings of "intolerance, indignation and disgust."[42] The notion of the person as a potentiality precludes the outcome of such an examination as a legitimate grounds for interfering with one's "self-regarding" conduct as that term was understood in chapter IV.

The notion of the "person" as a potentiality is related to the protection of the inner sphere of life, secondly, in that the potentiality of the individual "develops" if he is able to make his own choices in life rather than having them imposed upon him. Mill seemed conscious of this point when he asserted,

> He who lets the world, or his own portion of it, choose his plan of life for him, has no need of any other faculty than the ape-like one of imitation. He who chooses his plan for himself, employs all his faculties. He must use observation to see, reasoning and judgment to foresee, activity to gather materials for decision, discrimination to decide, firmess and self-control to hold to his deliberate decision...[43]

It may be that the individual does not know best what his "interests" dictate, contrary to what Mill suggested at one point. Despite his ignorance, however, his nature is such that no one else can claim to "know" it. When the self is conceived as a potentiality he is seen as being, in Stanley Benn's words, "engaged on a kind of self-creative enterprise, which could be disrupted, distorted or frustrated even by so limited an intrusion as watching."[44] Man, as a potentiality, is a *chooser* whose only criterion of "achievement" is not in terms of his worth to society but in terms of whether he himself has come to a judgment on the basis of the exercise of his own choice. By exercising choice the individual "grows" and "develops" his latent potentiality.

The notion of the person as a potentiality provides more forcefulness to Mill's theme of the need to protect "self-regarding" conduct. Mill's point was that only when a person is left to his own, to think and choose on his own, will he develop. Even though a customary rule could appropriately guide an individual in his decisions in any case,

> yet to conform to custom, merely *as* custom, does not educate or develop in him any of the qualities which are the distinctive endowment of a human being. The human faculties of perception, judgment, discriminative feeling, mental activity, and even moral preference, are exercised only in making a choice. He who does anything because it is the custom makes no choice.[45]

This idea also underlies Mill's explanation of why society is unwarranted "in saying to another human creature of ripe years that he shall not do with his life for his own benefit what he *chooses* to do with it... but in each person's own concerns his individual spontaneity is entitled to free exercise."[46] The individual must be allowed to exercise his own judgment because the exercise of choice is the very condition of the making of a person.

The thrust of an argument for the protection of self-regarding conduct is that "self-regarding" conduct is intrinsic to the very nature of the self as a potentiality. The "essential conditions" for the fulfillment of human nature are, in Mill's words, "freedom and variety of situations."[47] The protection of self-regarding conduct is central to the latter. One inherently values self-regarding conduct because it is the epitome of all that man is.

In this light one may more fully appreciate Mill's approval of the sale of drugs without prescriptions on the one hand and, on the other, his abhorrence of a contract of slavery. The purchase of a drug without a prescription provides an important opportunity for the exercise of choice. But, with a contract of slavery, the contractee "defeats, in his own case, the very purpose which is the justification of allowing him to dispose of himself... The principle of freedom cannot require that he should be free. It is not freedom to be allowed to alienate his freedom."[48] In other words, such a contract forever destroys the contractee's opportunity to exercise fundamental choices and the contract, therefore, contradicts the very nature of a human being.

Recognition respect requires the protection of the inner sphere of life for a third reason. We have already seen that we do not show recognition respect merely because someone deserves or merits it. If we were to do so, our protection of "self-regarding" conduct would vary in scope according to the same circumstances as examined in our discussion of utilitarianism in chapter IV.[49] Rather, recognition respect requires us to constrain our behaviour in ways required by the fact that an individual is a member of the species *homo sapiens* and that he possesses an "ideal possibility" within himself. This requires a disposition to perceive another person's "self-regarding" conduct from his/her point of view. Adopting Bernard Williams' meaning of respect, John Rawls emphasized that mutual respect is shown "in our willingness to see the situation of others from their point of view, from the perspective of their conception of the good; and in our being prepared to give reasons for our actions whenever the interests of others are materially affected."[50]

Appraisal respect, in contrast, does not require this disposition. One may respect another's athletic or business prowess, but not be disposed to perceive political or religious beliefs from his point of view. Even if one were so disposed, his disposition might well be dictated out of self-interest or fear rather than out of recognition respect. On the other hand, we are obligated to see things from the other's point of view once we start to recognise the potentiality in persons. As one commentator has suggested, "trying to see the world from another's point of view is a means of acknowledging that she/he has a conception of the good and that one attaches some value to this."[51] One might add that, even if he/she does not in fact have a conception of the good (for, after all, probably only a very small minority in a society have any conscious, articulate conception of the good), perceiving the world from his/her point of view is a means of acknowledging that he/she is equally worthy of having such a conception.

This leads to a fourth reason why respect for persons consistently supports the inviolability of the inner sphere of life. In contrast to utilitarianism, respect for persons assures that one's duties toward others will emanate from within the individual rather than from society. If the individual's nature is that of an open-ended potentiality and if one is to think and behave consistently with man's nature in his dealings with others, one is required to recognise that society is composed of persons whose potentiality is *equally* worthy of respect. In this way, one's obligations are not posited by society. Rather, they emanate from within the individual. Respect for persons necessitates an imminent rather than an imposed freedom.

One might wonder whether the latter two points do not require us to give active approval and social esteem to another's point of view. If so, does not our distinction between appraisal and recognition respect thereby collapse? This quaere clarifies the thrust of the above points. Recognition respect merely requires an attitude of non-interference. Such an attitude does not mean that we must hold others in admiration or awe. Rather, in one commentator's words, it means "mainly the willingness to leave the respected alone as deserving such independence:"[52] It implies a toleration of religious, political and moral conduct. The required attitude of non-interference explains why our philosophic basis of fundamental rights leaves no room for a paternalistic society. It goes some distance to explain why Lord Devlin's instructions were so alien to our own intuitive notions of democratic theory. Respect for persons demands that society give a minimal degree of consideration to the inner sphere of life to every human being.

It is important to note, in this context, that seeing things from another person's point of view does not mean that we are estopped from pursuing our own affairs if others are morally repulsed by our conduct. We would have been so prevented if we had adopted the first conception of the "person" — that is, the actual, empirical self of desires and impulses. But, as we have just

204

seen, another person's, deep-felt moral convictions of the Devlinite variety are an illegitimate ground for obstructing our conduct once we adopt the third conception of the "person". We have, instead, only a duty to take into account the manner in which our conduct may directly affect the *capacity* of other persons to exercise their *choices* in their "self-creative enterprises". The fact that my homosexual conduct or my selling of pornographic material, for example, instills deep feelings of "intolerance, indignation or disgust" in others does not affect their capacity to exercise choice in their own "self-creative enterprises". Such considerations are irrelevant, therefore, in our assessment of our duties towards others. Indeed, in order to be consistent with the third conception of the "person", society is obliged to have an attitude of non-interference towards my conduct unless, of course, my conduct truly affects the capacity of society's other members to exercise their choices.

The key criterion to decide whether society may intervene with an individual's conduct, therefore, is not that the conduct sets off deep-felt feelings of "intolerance, indignation or disgust", as Lord Devlin would have it. Nor is the issue that one's conduct interferes with the interests of others, as John Rees suggests.[53] Nor is it that the conduct causes harm upon others, as John Stuart Mill sometimes would have it. Rather, the test is whether the exercise of the person's choice in pursuing the conduct is necessary for a "self-creative enterprise" and, if so, whether that conduct interferes with the capacity of other members of society to exercise choice. And this, as we have seen,[54] is because choice is the very condition of the making of persons.

Section 5.   The Application of a "Respect for Persons" Argument to "Self-Regarding" Conduct

We have just seen that under a respect for persons argument feelings of "intolerance, indignation and disgust" by society towards homosexual behaviour or obscene materials is an illegitimate reason for restraining the homosexual's or publisher's "self-regarding" conduct. Let us examine another example in the same class of cases.

Let us assume that an employer A in Winnipeg believes that it is "within his rights" not to admit Indians into his employment. He believes that it is not in the community's interest nor in the interest of the Indian's family that he seek employment off the Reserve. Indians, he believes, are uncivilised and disgusting. In addition, the employer believes that his decision is solely a matter of his own "self-regarding" conduct which, in itself, needs no justification. We have seen that a Benthamite utilitarian could accept the employer's explanation after having measured the complex pains and pleasures of the Indian on the one hand and the intensity of the employer's and community's feelings on the other. A rule utilitarian would be obliged to assess the long-term consequences of a rule prohibiting employment of Indians. A rule utilitarian might be able to justify the rule if, for example, the rule did not lead to political or social dissatisfaction within the Indian community towards law enforcement officers. He might also be able to justify the rule if the non-existence of such a rule would gravely loosen the moral fabric of society.

A respect for persons argument, in contrast, would not limit itself to an inquiry into the Indian's family, the employer's feelings or the community's short or long-term welfare. It would be unsatisfactory to say that society possesses jurisdiction simply because the employer causes harm to the interests of the Indian or because the Indian, by moving away from his family to work in Winnipeg, causes harm to his family's interests. Rather, under a respect for persons argument, the employer is obligated to respect the Indian as a potentiality.

This duty of respect, we have seen, would entail two elements. First, the employer must be willing to let the Indian himself decide whether he should leave the Reserve. That is, respect for the Indian involves an "attitude of non-interference" by the employer in his dealings with the Indian. The Indian's exercise of choice is an inherent element of his own nature and it is not for any one else to exercise that choice for him. For the same reason, it is unjustifiable for the employer to forbid employment to an otherwise qualified person on the grounds that the person's lifestyle or the colour of his hair repulses the employer.

Secondly, the employer's respect towards the Indian must be a personal, not an impersonal, respect.[55] The employer must perceive the potential conflict between his own conduct and the Indian's from the Indian's point of view and the employer must communicate that attitude to the Indian. He would project that attitude by permitting the Indian to work in his enterprise. It would not be enough for the employer to forbid employment however politely and to pray for the Indian on Sunday: such a respect would be an impersonal one. To deny employment to the Indian because of the colour of his skin would be to treat him as an object.

How would a respect for persons argument deal with the second category of cases we discussed in the context of act and rule utilitarianism in chapter IV (that is, where society interferes with an individual's conduct in order to protect him from self-inflicted

206

harm)? We have seen that society may not intervene simply because the suicide or slavery infringes upon society's moral code. Nor may society interfere out of a paternalistic concern that the individual's behaviour is contrary to his interests: choice is an intrinsic element in the conception of the self as a potentiality. On the other hand, the two imperatives of the respect for persons argument both operate in favour of letting the suicidal person be. As a result of the second requisite (that is, personal respect towards the individual as a person), society has an obligation to warn him of the consequences of taking an inappropriate quantity or combination of drugs. Society also has a duty to warn him of the "poisonous" features of all drugs, whether the drugs be taken alone or in combination with alcohol. But the "attitude of non-interference" would appear to leave it to the individual to choose whether to end his life after he had been adequately informed of his choices and the consequences of those choices.

What makes the suicide case different from a contract into slavery is that in the former case there is only one party directly involved while in the latter case there are two. That is, using Mill's terminology, in the suicide case there is no party to whom the duty to prevent the suicide can be assigned unless, of course, the suicidal individual expressly informs a friend, druggist or physician of his intention to use the drugs to kill himself. In the slavery case, on the other hand, the distinct duty is assignable to the slave-owner who is a contractee. Although the prospective slave-owner is obligated to let the prospective slave choose on his own whether to become a slave, the prospective slave-owner is also obligated to communicate a personal respect towards the prospective slave — that is, to see things from the other's point of view. If the prospective slave-owner signs a contract of slavery he is communicating disrespect for the other party. By signing the contract, the slave-owner denies the very nature of the contractee as a potentiality worthy of consideration. The only exit from the prospective slave-owner's dilemma would seem to be for him to attempt to alleviate the social, economic and political circumstances which induced the individual to seek a contract of slavery.

The prospective slave-owner's general duty to project personal respect towards the prospective slave by seeing things from the latter's point of view is both distinct and assignable. In the same vein, if an individual with suicidal propensities requested drugs from a physician with the express purpose of attempting suicide, the doctor would be obligated to try to alleviate the psycho-social factors which induced the individual to seek the drugs. The general duty of personal respect explains why Mill believed that a father owed a duty to his family, and why a drunkard owed a duty to his wife. It also explains why Mill felt compelled to emphasize that

> it would be a great misunderstanding of this doctrine [of the protection of self-regarding conduct] to suppose that it is one of selfish indifference which pretends that human beings have no business with each other's conduct in life, and that they should not concern themselves about the well-doing or well-being of one another, unless their own interest is involved. Instead of any diminution, there is need of a great increase of *disinterested* exertion to promote the good of others...[56]

And how would a respect for persons argument deal with the third category of cases where the society is concerned that the individual may harm himself at some future time? Let us consider, for example, a regulation which authorizes a policeman to confiscate a motorcycle whenever the driver fails to wear a motorcycle helmet. We have seen that the exercise of choice is the very condition for the making of persons. Thus, it would seem that even though one's choice may eventually cause harm to himself, even though the collective welfare stands to lose economically from one's choice, the motorcyclist must be left alone.

But can we say that a motorcyclist is pursuing a "self-creative enterprise" when he decides not to wear a helmet? Whether or not he is pursuing such an enterprise, it is not for society to judge: the motorcyclist alone is the valuator of his own ideas and behaviour. But does a motorcyclist consciously exercise the "human faculties of perception, judgment, discriminative feeling, mental activity and even moral preference" — to use Mill's terms — when he regularly mounts his motorcycle and, out of habit, fails to put on his helmet? Does he really *exercise* choice? In response to this problem I can only suggest that, in the first place, the motorcyclist may be exercising choice unconsciously or subconsciously and that society is not in a position to determine whether that is actually so. Secondly, as in the case of the suicidal individual, I can only repeat that the "attutude of non-interference" would seem to necessitate that it be left to the motorcyclist to decide the issue. Society's role only arises out of our second imperative: that is, that society owes a duty of personal respect towards the motorcyclist. This would entail a societal duty to make the motorcyclist fully aware of the alternatives and consequences. Society has a duty, for example, to make him aware of the statistical probability of his death if the motorcyclist falls from the motorcycle without a helmet. But that is all society may do.

The problem is more complicated in the case of seat-belts in automobiles. Usually more than the driver's life is at stake. The driver's decision not to have seat-belts installed in his car reflects his own personal disrespect towards his future passengers. Thus, society is obligated to require that seat-belts be installed in the passengers' seats of every automobile[57] but society has no claim to compel passengers to use them. Society is obligated to inform all potential passengers with respect to their choices and the consequences of those choices.

Section 6. An Argument in Support of Fundamental Rights

The conception of the "self" as an open-ended potentiality goes a long way towards resolving the conceptual problems incurred with utilitarianism in chapter IV. The primacy of the "greatest happiness of the greatest number" and the external societal source of one's obligations towards others in utilitarian theory had militated against the inviolability of the inner sphere of life. Recognition respect for the individual as a potentiality, in contrast, places the individual rather than the community happiness as the ultimate reference point for analysis. Recognition respect for persons also necessitates an immanent rather than a posited freedom. Finally, the conception of the person as an open-ended potentiality avoids the tyrannical implications which flow from the other two conceptions of the self traditionally adopted in liberal political theory.

In chapter IV I set out to construct an argument as to why neither the state nor society ought to penetrate, burden, abrogate or infringe the inner sphere of life. I have now shown how such an argument can be rooted in the notion of recognition respect for the person. For one thing, the very open-endedness of the content of the self, aside from its initial definition, precluded the conceptual possibility that society could ever justifiably interfere with one's "self-regarding" conduct for reasons only of society's religious, political, moral or emotional preferences.

Furthermore, I suggested that the exercise of choice in "self-regarding" conduct is the very condition for the making of a person. The individual becomes truer to his nature if he can make his own choices in life rather than have the choices imposed upon him.

Thirdly, recognition respect necessitates that we perceive another person's thoughts, feelings, beliefs and conduct from his/her point of view. If the nature of an individual is that he is an open-ended potentiality always in the process of becoming, and if the individual is to behave consistently with his own nature in his dealings with others, then he will come to recognise the potentiality in others. Once we begin to recognise that potentiality in others, we will be required to attempt to perceive things from the others' point of view.

An argument as to why neither the state nor society ought to penetrate the inner sphere of life can be rooted in the notion of respect for persons in one final manner. If we adopt a recognition respect for persons' perspective, our obligations towards others emanate internally from within ourselves. Neither society nor the state may transgress the inner sphere of life under the pretention of positing social or legal obligations upon individuals. Rather, in contrast to utilitarianism, the existence of one's social or legal obligations initiate internally within the individual.

Having constructed an argument which justified why neither the state nor society ought to penetrate the inner sphere of life, we can now legitimately describe the rights which entrench the boundaries of that sphere as fundamental rights. The rights are fundamental in the sense that they are "essential", "basic", "underlying", "primary", "formative" elements in the inviolability of the inner sphere of life. It may be that these rights are few in number and limited in scope. However that may be, we have constructed an argument which justifies why neither the state nor society ought to penetrate a certain minimum sphere of life. Consequently, the rights which prop up the boundaries of that sphere exist independently of the state and society.

The rights rooted in respect for persons, however, extend beyond the mere protection of the inner sphere of life. They can do so and yet remain fundamental for several reasons.

First, the rights are tied to the recognition respect rather than to the appraisal respect of a person. The connection between recognition respect and one's rights is crucial because, by being so connected, the rights are permanent. The criteria which society chooses to appraise meritorious conduct may vary over time and place. Any rights which might be tied to appraisal respect could be waived, abrogated or even remain unrecognised. The rights would be *ad hoc* rights.

In contrast, the rights grounded in recognition respect are permanent. The respect is owed to an individual for reasons independent of one's ability, worth or desert. The respect is owed to an individual simply because he is a member of the human species. This membership, in turn, possesses an element of permanence which does not exist for the criteria for merit respect. The legal consequences of any attempt to abrogate or abridge the rights will be examined in chapter VII.

The rights which are rooted in respect for persons are fundamental in a second sense. The rights are "basic", "the root of the

210

matter", or "essential" to the recognition of the person in that the rights themselves demonstrate our manner of taking that person seriously as a member of the human species. The rights are also basic in that the rights constitute the essential conditions for the fulfilment of human nature as we have conceived of it. The rights thereby acknowledge that the individual is a potentiality who always has the possibility to grow. Finally, the rights ensure that the individual's point of view is of sufficient worth to be heard and considered.

The rights embedded in respect for persons are fundamental in a final sense. The rights are shared *equally* by all members of the human species. The fact that the rights are owed because we are *all* members of the same species prevents the rights from being owed to some persons, but not to others.

Curiously enough, my argument in support of fundamental rights does provide a viable basis for social policy. I have attempted to show how this is so in this chapter by resolving theoretical and practical issues related to "self-regarding" conduct. In chapter VII I shall demonstrate how my argument can be translated back to constitutional principles and constitutional analysis.

The person is not alone in the world. He is, as T. H. Green emphasized, a social being. Indeed, my argument contemplates that that one owes obligations towards others in society.

The individual's obligations are of two kinds: an attitude of non-interference in the activities and thoughts of others, and a duty of personal respect towards others. That respect need not take account of society's deep-felt convictions of "intolerance, indignation and disgust" because of the open-endedness of the nature of the person. The two obligations explain why one's own good, "whether physical or moral", is not a sufficient warrant for society to punish a motorcyclist who does not wear a helmet or to create a crime for anyone who attempts suicide. The two obligations explain why slavery is inconsistent with the protection of "self-regarding conduct". At long last we have elaborated a philosophic perspective which can consistently support the existence of fundamental rights in general and the absolute inviolability of the inner sphere of life in particular.

1. Text supra, chap. 4 between notes 71 and 83.
2. John Stuart Mill, *On Liberty* (Mary Warnock ed., Glasgow: William Collins Sons & Co., 1962), p. 130.

Some scholars have suggested that this theme is not hidden in the least. See, for example, David Spitz, "Freedom and Individuality: Mill's Liberty in Retrospect," in *Liberty: Nomos IV*, J. Roland Pennock and John W. Chapman, eds., (New York: Atherton Press, 1962); Richard B. Friedman, "A New Exploration of Mill's Essay *On Liberty*," 14 *Political Studies*, pp. 281-304 (1966); Albert W. Levi, "The Value of Freedom: Mill's Liberty," 70 *Ethics*, pp. 37-46 (1959); Gertrude Himmelfarb, *On Liberty and Liberalism: The Case of John Stuart Mill* (N.Y.: Knopf, 1974).

3. This is the title to chapter 3 of his *On Liberty*.
4. John Stuart Mill, *On Liberty*, supra note 2, p. 185.
5. Ibid., p. 188.
6. Ibid.
7. Ibid., p. 186.
8. Ibid., p. 193.
9. John Stuart Mill, *Considerations on Representative Government*, Currin V. Shields, ed., (New York: Bobbs-Merrill Co., 1958), p. 25.
10. Ibid.
11. Ibid., p. 28.
12. T. H. Green, *The Principles of Political Obligation*. J. R. Rodman, ed., (New York: Crofts, 1964).
13. Ibid., p. 110, para. 25.
14. Ibid., p. 105, para. 18.
15. Ibid., p. 106, para. 20(2).
16. Ibid., p. 107, para. 21.
17. Ibid., p. 111, para. 25.
18. Ibid., p. 112, para. 26.
19. Ibid., p. 116, para. 31. Green made the same point at p. 118, para. 113:

> But in truth it is only as members of a society, as recognising common interest and objects, that individuals come to have these attributes and rights; and the power, which in a political society they have to obey, is derived from the development and systematisation of those institutions for the regulation of a common life without which they would have no rights at all.

20. T. H. Green, *Liberal Legislation and Freedom of Contract*, supra, note 12, p. 52.
21. Ibid., pp. 51-52.
22. Ibid., p. 54.
23. Ibid., p. 55.
24. Ibid., p. 62.

25. This problem is developed in Robert F. Sassen's "Freedom as an end of Politics," 2 *Interpretation* 105, p. 117 (1971).

26. C. B. Macpherson, *The Political Theory of Possessive Individualism* (Oxford: Clarendon Press 1962), p. 3. Mr. Justice Holmes' conception of human nature coincides closely with this view. His conception is documented and connected to his judgements in William E. Conklin, *The Political Theory of Mr. Justice Holmes*, 26 Chitty's L. J. 200, p. 201-203 (1978).

27. I use the term as described in Micheal Oakeshott's, "Rationalism in Politics" and "Political Education" in *Rationalism in Politics and Other Essays* (London: Methuen, 1962).

28. Isaiah Berlin, "Introduction" and "Two Concepts of Liberty" in *Four Essays on Liberty* (London: Oxford U. Press, 1969).

29. Ibid., pp. 133 ff.

30. John Stuart Mill, *On Liberty*, supra, note 2, pp. 135-136.

31. See text, supra, between notes 5 and 12.

32. This notion of the *daimon* is borrowed from Norton & Norton, "From Law to Love: Social Order as Self-Realization," 6 *J. Value Inquiry* 91, p. 92 (1972).

33. Mill, *On Liberty*, supra, note 2, p. 136.

34. Stephen L. Darwall, "Two Kinds of Respect," 86 *Ethics* 36 (1977).

35. Ibid., p. 45.

36. See text, supra, chap II at note 30.

37. Stephen Darwall, supra, note 34, p. 45.

38. John Stuart Mill, *On Liberty*, supra, note 2, p. 188.

39. Bernard Williams, "The Idea of Equality," in Peter Laslett and W. G. Runciman, eds., *Philosophy, Politics and Society (Second Series)* (Oxford, 1972), p. 112.

40. Stanley I. Benn, "Privacy, Freedom and Respect for Persons", in *Privacy: Nomos 13*, J. Roland Pennock and John W. Chapman, eds., (New York: Atherton Press, 1971), p. 9.

41. Lord Devlin, "Morals and the Criminal Law", in *The Enforcement of Morals* (London: Oxford, 1965), pp. 22-23.

42. Ibid., p. 17.

43. John Stuart Mill, *On Liberty*, supra, note 2, p. 187.

44. Stanley Benn, supra, note 40, p. 187.

45. John Stuart Mill, *On Liberty*, supra, note 2, p. 187.

46. Ibid., p. 206. Emphasis added.

47. Ibid., pp. 203, 194.

48. Ibid., p. 236.

49. See text, supra, between notes 33 and 41, and between notes 52 and 64.

50. John Rawls, *A Theory of Justice* (Cambridge: Harvard U. Press, 1971), p. 337.

51. C. Cranor, "Toward a Theory of Respect for Persons," 12 *American Philosophical Quarterly* 309, pp. 305-316 (1975).

52. Herbert Spiegelberg, "Human Dignity: A Challenge to Contemporary Philosophy," in *Human Dignity: This Century and the Next*, R. Gotesky & E. Laszlo, eds., (N.Y.: Gordon and Breach, 1970).

53. John Rees, "A Re-Reading of Mill on Liberty," in *Limits of Liberty: Studies on Mill's On Liberty*, P. Radcliffe ed., (Belmont Calif.: Wadsworth, 1966). See generally, text, supra, chap. IV between notes 17 and 21.

54. See text, supra, between notes 42 and 49.

55. This point is stressed by Spiegelberg, supra, note 52.

56. John Stuart Mill, *On Liberty*, supra, note 2, p. 206. Emphasis added.

Mill's use of the word "disinterested" would seem to run counter to the thrust of our second imperative. Mill continued his discussion, however, in this way:

> Human beings owe to each other help to distinguish the better from the worse, and encouragement to choose the former and avoid the latter. They should be forever stimulating each other to increased exercise of their higher faculties, and increased direction of their feelings and aims towards wise instead of foolish, elevating instead of degrading, objects and contemplations.

57. And the driver's seat if more than the owner would drive the automobile.

214

Part Three

Implications for
Constitutional Analysis

Chapter VII

Some Implications for Constitutional Analysis

In the last chapter I developed an argument in support of fundamental rights. The argument was rooted in one of John Rawls'
ontological hypotheses: the notion of "respect for persons". I put
some content into that notion both in terms of a consistent conception of human nature and in terms of what it means to say that
we ought to *respect* a person. I connected "respect for persons" to
the principle of the inner sphere of life generally and tried to show
how "respect for persons" could be a viable basis for social policy
concerning such issues as homosexual conduct, obscenity, racial
discrimination, contracts into slavery, suicide, the wearing of
motorcycle helmets, the fastening of seat belts, and the involuntary detention of mental patients. Each of the latter involves the
larger question of whether the state or society ought to interfere
with "self-regarding" conduct. Because the traditional legal resources can take the common law lawyer only so far before he
must begin to ask normative questions, the line of argument in
chapter VI can legitimately be incorporated into the lawyer's defence of fundamental rights.

I wish now to suggest further implications which my argument
for fundamental rights provides for constitutional analysis. And I
shall do so by confronting the four critical issues which have faced
constitution framers, legislators, judges, bureaucrats and lawyers in
common law countries. First, is there a principled criterion in
ascertaining why fundamental rights are fundamental? Secondly,
what level of judicial scrutiny is expected of legislation which
burdens a fundamental right? Thirdly, may the state circumscribe
a fundamental right in the interest of the state or, to use the
wording of one draft of the Canadian Government's proposed
entrenched Bill of Rights, "in the interests of public safety, order,health or morals, [or] of national security..."?[1] Finally, what
method of justifying judicial decisions would appear to be most
consistent with the existence of fundamental rights?

Section 1. Which Rights are Fundamental?

We saw in the first three chapters of my study that one of the elementary but significant obstacles to a theory of fundamental rights was that traditional juristic arguments did not provide a satisfactory criterion with which to determine which rights were fundamental and which were not. Even an entrenched Bill of Rights, such as an American, could not definitively provide such a criterion because traditional Bills of Rights used such terms as "due process of law" and "equality before the law" without indicating the criterion to determine the demands of such principles. We examined how some American Justices had attempted to incorporate other entrenched rights into such principles "totally" and "selectively". We also studied how Justices Frankfurter and Harlan tried to justify why some rights were fundamental and others were not by relying upon the "ordered liberty" of Anglo-American jurisprudence. With each approach the courts could justify neither their starting point nor their conclusions. We found, in addition, that even if the incorporationist perspective could explain why some rights were more fundamental than others, the court still had to define the meaning and scope of the incorporated provisions. A court could not adequately elaborate a definition or determine the scope of entrenched provisions without some initial "fundamentality" notion.

Rawl's ontological hypothesis of "respect for persons" provides a starting point for such analysis. In the last chapter I distinguished three conceptions of a "person".[2] I found that the only conception of the "person" consistent with the existence of fundamental rights was the person as a potentiality, always in the process of becoming. This conception was open-ended and, because it was, our fallibility prevented us from ever knowing its nature in concrete terms. Each individual's person, as a consequence, was on an *equal* footing with another's. Those fundamental rights which were bound up with the recognition of a person were, therefore, shared equally amongst all members of the human species rather than just to some.

Chapter VI also distinguished two different senses of what it means to say that we *respect* someone: appraisal and recognition respect.[3] The former concerns the esteem which we hold of someone's abilities and achievements. The latter reflects the weight we give to the fact that someone is an open-ended potentiality. Out of this respect and out of the nature of the person there flow minimum moral constraints upon one's conduct. These moral constraints are the "intermediate premises" for which Justice Harlan

218

searched in vain. They are our fundamental rights and duties. The ontological hypothesis of "respect for persons", then, provides us with a perspective with which to determine whether any particular right is a fundamental right.

How do the fundamental rights flow from the nature of a person as a potentiality? Neither politician, nor judge, nor public servant knows the true nature of a human being. They are, therefore, in no position to impose their will upon an individual under the alibi that they know the true nature of human beings. Human fallibility prevents them from ever knowing the true nature of human beings in concrete terms. Fundamental rights acknowledge that fact. Fundamental rights encircle an individual so as to ensure that the individual's process of becoming will not be altered or burdened by paternalistic or self-righteous political officials or institutions.

By what method, then, are we to determine whether a right is fundamental? The state, its instrumentalities or its officials do not give us fundamental rights. The state's officials (which include judges) merely metaphorically acknowledge their existence because we already possess them as members of the human species. Similarly, the state's officials may not take fundamental rights away under the pretext that such rights must be earned. They are rights "of man", "of the person" — not "of the citizen". They are held independently of statute, judicial decision, custom or even written constitution. They are held independently of one's utility to society.

Thus, we cannot determine whether a right is fundamental by looking backward to the principles embedded in legal tradition as Chief Justice Coke would have us do. Nor is it satisfactory for us to investigate the contemporary values of society. Nor, indeed, does a written constitution resolve our problem. Rather, in order to determine whether a right is fundamental, a judge, legislator, bureaucrat or citizen must be prepared to examine normative political philosophy. My own study indicates that such an inquiry should ask whether any particular right is bound up with "the recognition" of a "person". Those fundamental rights which are indispensably entangled with "the recognition" of a "person" are "minimum floors" which *must* be fulfilled if we are to claim in all honesty and consistency that our society is founded upon the existence of fundamental rights.

"Recognition respect for persons" would appear to require at least three avenues of constitutional inquiry. First, recognition respect for persons proscribes discrimination on grounds of race, sex, national origin and colour. Secondly, it precludes interference with a person's life, his inner sphere of life, his thoughts and feelings, the modes of his own expression and due process. Thirdly, it requires that we ensure the equal worth of these fundamental rights. This demands, in turn, that one examine the socio-economic considerations surrounding the effective exercise or non-exercise of the rights.

The first inquiry is exemplified in chapter VI by the case of the employer who discriminated against Indians as a group because of his own racial and paternalistic preferences.[4] A "respect for persons" inquiry, we found in chapter VI, would not restrict itself to a consideration of the Indian's family, the employer's own opinions or the community's overall short- or long-term welfare. We found from our analysis in chapter IV that one could not consistently defend fundamental rights and, at the same time, suggest that society possessed jurisdiction simply because the employer had caused harm to the interests of the Indian. Rather, under a "respect for persons" perspective, the employer owed a duty to respect the Indian as a potentiality. This involved a willingness on the employer's part to let the Indian decide on his own whether he should leave the Reserve: that was what we meant by the term "an attitude of non-interference". "Respect for persons" also required that the employer perceive the potential conflict between his own conduct and the Indian's from the latter's point of view. The employer had a duty to project that attitude by employing the Indian notwithstanding the employer's racial opinions.

This line of argument, it is submitted, underlies proscriptions against burdening racial, sexual, national origin or colour classifications in legislation or human endeavour. By not projecting a personal respect toward a racial group, a legislator, employer or landlord is not treating *all* persons as "persons", as "humans". The latter notion exists independently of the laws posited by the legislature or the moral values of any employer or landlord. The notion of the person as a potentiality is also shared *equally* amongst all members of the human species. Furthermore, by imposing their own racial, religious, moral or political preferences upon others, the legislative majority, the employer and the landlord are admitting that there is one "true" or "higher" self. But this admission has led to tyranny, as Isaiah Berlin so rightly pointed out. The offended sensibilities, the paternalistic beliefs and the feelings of "intolerance, indignation and disgust" were found in chapter VI to be illegitimate grounds upon which to justify legislative or social categories of race.

This first type of constitutional inquiry does not preclude the possibility of an oppressive, tyrannical government. A government would still be able to take away rights to life, thought, expression, due process and the like without discrimination according to race, sex, national origin and colour. A constitution based upon fundamental rights, therefore, would have to take account of this possibility and constitutional analysis should attempt to connect such rights with the "recognition respect for persons".

It would seem, for example, that the paramount fundamental right is life. For, with death so dies all possibility for growth in the human world. Furthermore, life itself would appear to be a common condition precedent to the exercise of all other fundamental rights. Finally, the conscious taking of life violates in the most compelling sense the recognition that an individual is a member of the human species. That is, the execution of life, commonly known as capital punishment, denies what it is the very nature of fundamental rights to affirm.

Closely related to respect for life is respect for one's thoughts, beliefs and feelings. Aside from life itself, the most significant core to the "inner sphere of life" is one's thoughts, beliefs and feelings. If my arguments for the protection of the "inner sphere of life" in chapters IV and VI are valid, then a fundamental freedom of thought has also been established. This would include, for example, a fundamental right not to be involuntarily detained in a mental hospital by reason only of the "patient's" thoughts or feelings.[5] Since the state possesses no jurisdiction to pry into one's thoughts or feelings, the courts have a serious obligation to develop a constitutionally protected zone of impenetrability encircling the individual's life and his thoughts.

The second avenue of constitutional inquiry incorporates the fundamental freedoms of political participation, speech, religion, due process and assembly into a constitution founded upon the existence of fundamental rights. These freedoms would appear to be fundamental largely because they provide critical means of recognising the *daimon* or "ideal possibility" within the individual. With respect to the recognition element, a zone which constitutionally protects one's political participation, expression and due process demonstrates respect toward the ideal possibility within an individual. By participating, for example, the individual becomes someone "who counts for something in the community's decision making processes."[6] That is, his humanness which he shares equally with others is being *recognised*. With respect to the second element, participation in a common enterprise, expression through speech, assembly or religion, or being assured of due process in matters that might burden one's person: these elements delineate the boundary lines within which the individual will fulfil his own potentiality, his own *person*. Donald Keim has expressed the latter point quite aptly in this way:

> Part of what it means to be a complete human being is to participate with one's fellow men in the creation of a "political space" where men may display their humanity as doers of deeds and speakers of words. Deprived of this experience men lose that quality which separates them from other living organisms. When men choose to create a public realm in which they are inexorably linked by common bonds of joint enterprise, they actualize their natures as political beings. This concept requires that political activity be viewed not as an instrument for achieving private satisfactions but as an activity whose reward is (political) being itself.[7]

Political participation, free expression, and due process, in other words, enlarge the scope of one's experience and fulfilment.

Because of the nexus between political participation and the "recognition" of a "person", my defence of fundamental rights does not necessarily contradict democratic norms as might be initially supposed. When one begins with the ontological value of "respect for persons" rather than the "greatest happiness of the greatest number", the "right to vote" is not an end in itself but rather only one facet of a wider freedom to *participate* actively in decisions which affect (rather than merely touch)[8] the individual. Other facets include freedom of political dissent, freedom of the press and the freedom of assembly. As William Bishin has shown, a system of government "where the vote has meaning" and "citizens feel free to come to their own conclusions and to criticize" discourages abuses and the concentration of power.[9] A wide scope of these other freedoms places effective political participation upon firmer ground. The right of political participation is, as a consequence, interdependent with other fundamental rights.

The right of political participation, in turn, is entangled with the principle of "respect for persons" much as are the fundamental rights of non-discrimination, life and thought. When the "right to vote" and majority rule are placed in this perspective, one can better appreciate the serious responsibilities of our courts and our lawyers to elaborate a deeper meaning and wider scope to the fundamental rights of non-discrimination, life, thought and expression. The latter are interdependent with the effective exercise of a right of political participation. The political demise of the legislature in Canada and England over the past century with the consequential decline in the scope of political participation described in chapter II suggests that the principle of legislative supremacy justifies intense judicial activism rather than passivity in the protection of other fundamental rights and freedoms.

222

This judicial responsibility to take account of the complete picture of fundamental rights in terms of their source in the ontological principle of "respect for persons" reflects a cohesiveness and interrelatedness amongst rights uncharacteristic of utilitarian theory. What constitutional lawyers must concern themselves with is the *effective exercise* of the rights rather than merely an abstract declaration of their existence. Indeed, we saw in the American voting cases that the United States Supreme Court had precisely this distinction in mind.[10] The court in *Reynolds*,[11] *Harper*[12] and *Kramer*[13] expressed concern over "the debasement or dilution of the weight of a citizen's vote" and "the danger of denying some citizens any effective voice in the governmental affairs which substantially affect their lives." It is in this vein that constitutional lawyers must seriously incorporate the socio-economic considerations into their arguments.

In chapter V I emphasized amongst other things that John Rawls erred by insisting, on the one hand, that the basic liberties be held equally and, on the other, that the liberties could be of unequal worth.[14] The worth of basic liberties varied with one's economic, intellectual, social and political capacity to exercise those liberties effectively. We noted Norman Daniels' successful argument that the unequal worth of one basic liberty could have a multiplying effect upon the effective exercise of other basic liberties.[15] In this manner, liberty and equality were not so contradictory as liberal political and legal theorists have generally assumed. Even if one starts with liberty rather than equality as the primary social good in a just society, the effective exercise of liberty will require at least a minimum floor of equality.

The point has been most recently made by John D. Hodson[16] in his critique of Robert Nozick's *Anarchy, State and Utopia*.[17] Nozick had tried to justify "a minimal state limited to the narrow functions of protection against force, theft, fraud, enforcement of contracts, and so on."[18] These minimal functions arose out of conduct where one individual intentionally caused harm against another. The legitimate state, according to Nozick, could not force one to aid another. Redistribution of wealth, except to redress historic injustices, was unjustified.[19] Hodson's reply is that harm against Nozick's rights may be caused unintentionally as well as intentionally. If we take the right to life or health as fundamental, for example, the unfettered exercise of capitalism might cause such harm as to prevent the ability of some persons from maintaining their health and lives. The more "successful" members of society may not have actually intended such a consequence in the least. Thus, re-distribution of wealth by the state may be necessary to ensure the effective exercise of a fundamental right to life or health.

The *Rodriquez*[20] case examined in chapter III exemplifies how counsel could make a constitutional argument for the worth of liberty.[21] In *Rodriquez* the Texas system of financing public education through local property taxes was at issue. As a consequence of the system, substantial interdistrict disparities in per-pupil expenditures were incurred. Mr. Justice Marshall directed his attention to the repercussions which the financing system had for the effective exercise of a child's constitutional rights when that child happened to have resided in a low-income district. Education directly affected the capacity of a child to exercise his First Amendment rights and to participate in the political process when he/she grew older. Because personal wealth was directly correlated to education, the Texas system of financing public education directly involved one's constitutional rights.

A similar argument would apply, it is submitted, to the problem of language rights in a country such as Canada. If one looks to the written Constitution (the British North America Acts) as a source of Francophone language rights, one finds only relatively minor language guarantees. Section 133 of the British North America Acts, 1867, protects the French language in the debates of the Houses of Parliament, in the debates of the Quebec Legislature, in the journals of those Houses, and in pleadings before federal and Quebec courts.[22] The written constitution fails to protect the use of French in many other facets of court procedure, subordinate legislation, and in the actual conduct of government.[23] If, on the other hand, one were to follow the approach advocated by Chief Justice Coke, one would also be hard pressed to find Francophone language rights. The Articles of Capitulation of Quebec and Montreal[24] in 1760, the Treaty of Paris, 1763,[25] and the Quebec Act, 1774,[26] did expressly safeguard the Roman Catholic religion in Quebec. Legislative enactments did expand the use of French before the courts and legislatures during the latter eighteenth century[27] and the 1840s.[28] One judicial decision did acknowledge in 1813 that

> the French language has been used by His Majesty in his communications to His subjects in this province, as well as in His executive as in His legislative capacity, and been recognized as the legal means of communication of His Canadian subjects.[29]

As in the case of freedom of religious conscience as examined in chapter I, however, it is difficult to find *express* judicial support for a fundamental right of the individual to speak, assemble or communicate with government officials in the French language in the sense of the right being immune from legislative, administrative or judicial denial. What is more, Chief Justice Coke's approach would require that we take account of the legislative, judicial and administrative treatment of French language rights in the federal as well as the Manitoban, Ontario and New Brunswick Governments during the past one hundred years. It would seem that, if Chief Justice Coke's line of argument is followed, constitutional history since Confederation works against the existence of fundamental language rights for Francophone citizens.[30] This has been the case notwithstanding the constitutional obligation to protect the Francophone Quebecois as a cultural entity in the Canadas prior to Confederation in 1867. Consequently, neither a "written constitution" form of argument nor Chief Justice Coke's "backward-looking" theory of fundamental rights can consistently sustain the existence of French linguistic rights over time.

It is submitted that when counsel incorporate the equal worth of fundamental rights into their frame of analysis, a firmer constitutional foundation for French language rights exists in Canada. For one thing, if a Francophone does possess fundamental rights of political participation, thought, expression and due process and if those rights are to be shared equally amongst all Canadians, then one must seriously question how the rights can be exercised effectively and equally if Francophones cannot participate and express or defend themselves in the language most natural to them. This point extends to communications between French-speaking residents on the one hand, and the courts, legislatures and bureaucracies on the other. In the same manner that education was directly connected with the capacity of one to exercise First Amendment rights and political participation rights in *Rodriquez*, so language ia directly related to the effective exercise of fundamental rights by French-speaking residents in Canada. Language rights are constitutionally required in order that fundamental rights be shared *equally* in fact as well as in theory.

Language rights do not flow from the principle of "respect for persons" with the same facility as do the rights to life, thought, political participation, speech, assembly, religion and due process. Language rights are not owed to each person as a member of the human species. But their importance to the principle of "respect for persons" arises from the fact that, in the Canadian circumstances, language rights are essential conditions for the effective exercise of those fundamental rights which are integrally entangled with "respect for persons". In some societies, constitutional recognition of a minority language is not essential for the effective exercise of fundamental rights. But in the Canadian context, a constitutional obligation to respect the Francophone language in a variety of institutional settings better ensures that the exercise of fundamental rights are *equally* shared. As a consequence, such an obligation shows recognition *respect* for the *persons* who express themselves in the French language.

Section 2. The Level of Judicial Scrutiny of Legislation

The interdependency of one fundamental right with another and of liberty with equality leads to an important implication for the judiciary in a country such as Canada. The Canadian Government has submitted various drafts of an entrenched Bill of Rights as a part of its "solution" to the threat of Quebec independence. And yet, we found in chapter III that an entrenched Bill of Rights does not provide definitive answers to civil liberties problems.

The American experience has demonstrated that the level of judicial scrutiny to a great extent determines the outcome of any civil liberties issue. According to the "reasonable relationship" test, the Supreme Court examined whether there was a reasonable connection between the statutory classification and the statute's overall purpose. For the reasons expressed in chapter III,[31] the United States Supreme Court had sustained the constitutionality of all but one state statute challenged upon equal protection grounds between 1937 and 1970 using the "reasonable relationship" test.[32] According to the "compelling state interest" test, the court scrutinized the legitimacy of the state's purpose, questioned whether that purpose could be more adequately served by some "less onerous alternative" and, thirdly, weighed the importance of the purpose as against the undesirability of the classification. With respect to the latter requisite, only *compelling* state purposes could sustain the constitutionality of a statute. A judicial decision to proceed under the one test or the other virtually determined the result without any analysis of the nature of the fundamental rights allegedly burdened or the extent to which they were burdened or the relative importance of possible conflicting fundamental rights. The American approach has been both *ad hoc* and "all or nothing".

In the above section I pointed to a cluster of questions which one must ask in order to ascertain whether a right is fundamental. Having suggested that the central issue is the connection between a right and the "recognition respect of persons", we now have a principled criterion to guide the courts in their choice of a level of scrutiny. The interdependency of fundamental rights with each

226

other and the critical significance of socio-economic considerations point to a "spectrum of standards" for reviewing legislation similar to that advocated by Mr. Justice Marshall.[33] Justice Marshall has emphasized three considerations in the ascertainment of the level of scrutiny: the character of the classification, the relative importance to the class of the governmental benefits which the class did not receive, and the "constitutional and societal importance of the interest [fundamental right] adversely affected." I have argued in section 1 above that recognition respect translates itself into at least three avenues of constitutional analysis in determining which rights are fundamental. These three areas correspond surprisingly with Mr. Justice Marshall's three-pronged criteria.

First, our norm of "respect for persons" proscribed certain legislative classifications which violated respect for the person vis-à-vis all other members of the human species. That is, the law did not treat all persons "as persons", "as humans". Discriminatory classifications such as race, sex, national origin and colour seemed pressing examples. These categories reflect Justice Marshall's first concern.

Secondly, for the reasons explained, the principle of "respect for persons" precluded interference with another category of rights and freedoms. In apparent order of priority they were the right to life, the freedom of thought and feeling, and the freedom of political participation, speech, press, assembly, due process and religion. These rights and freedoms were bound up with my analysis of the "inner sphere of life" and the nature of a person as a potentiality. This category of rights corresponds to Justice Marshall's third criterion, although it would be more consistent to refer to the importance of the right to "respect for persons" rather than to the "constitutional and societal importance" of any particular right.

Now, each of these two categories of rights could operate independently of the other. The first category might be satisfied under an oppressive, tyrannical government. That is, the state could erode the freedoms of life, thought, political participation, expression and due process without discrimination on the basis of race, sex, national origin and colour. Similarly, the rights to life, thought, political participation, expression and due process do not logically preclude the possibility of a slave society based upon race, sex, national origin or colour. But both tyranny and slavery are alien to any society which wishes to grounds its rights in the norm of "respect for persons".

As a consequence, legislative, administrative or common law

infringement of either group of rights should trigger off strict judicial scrutiny. In other words, a legislative, administrative or common law rule must show on its face that the rule was enacted so as to protect other conflicting more important fundamental rights. This is what is meant by an inquiry into "the legitimacy of the state's purpose". Furthermore, the state must establish that its purpose could not have been more adequately served by some alternative, less restrictive of fundamental rights. Finally, the court must be able to weigh the relative importance to the principle of "respect for persons" of the fundamental right it wishes to protect on the one hand, as against the fundamental right(s) which will be burdened on the other.

The third avenue of constitutional inquiry elaborated in section 1 above flows from the fact that fundamental rights are inter-dependent with each othera and with socio-economic considerations. The courts must choose a level of scrutiny which accurately reflects this inter-relatedness. In the *Rodriquez* case, for example, Justice Marshall held that education directly affected the capacity of a child to exercise his/her First Amendment rights and his/her right to participate in the political process as an adult. This relationship between education and constitutional rights was more marked with disadvantaged or powerless groups in contrast to wealthy or powerful groups. Justice Marshall was justified, therefore, in exercising a stricter level of scrutiny with respect to the former group than with respect to the latter. Group wealth represented a particularly serious obstacle to education because disadvantaged persons possessed little significant control over group wealth.

Another recent example of how this line of constitutional analysis can arise is the United States Supreme Court decision of *Buckley* v. *Valeo*.[34] This case involved the Federal Election Campaign Act of 1971, as amended in 1974. The Act had laid down guidelines governing financial contributions and expenditures to election campaigns, reporting and public disclosure of contributions and the public financing of presidential election campaigns. Although the eight Justices differed with respect to each issue, the majority upheld the restrictions for financial contributions, the reporting and disclosure provisions and the financing of presidential campaigns. The court held the expenditure restrictions to be unconstitutional as a violation of the spender's First Amendment rights to communicate his opinions and to associate.

The *per curiam* judgment, which was joined only by Justices Brennan, Stewart and Powell in all portions, adopted a "close scrutiny" standard with respect to the contribution and expendi-

228

ture restrictions because they operated "in an area of the most fundamental First Amendment activities." The court acknowledged that one could sustain significant interference with the First Amendment if the state could establish a sufficiently important "interest" and if the state could not have protected that interest by less onerous means. The court weighed the conflicting fundamental rights. Whereas it sided with the rights protected by the state in the contribution limitations (the right of political participation which was undermined by corruption and the appearance of corruption through political contributions), the majority gave more weight to the freedoms of speech and assembly in the context of expenditure restrictions. The latter, the court held, could not adequately curtail the appearance of corruption. In addition, the expenditure limitations heavily burdened core First Amendment rights. In the court's words,

> a restriction on the amount of money a person or group can spend on political communication during a campaign necessarily reduces the quantity of expression by restricting the number of issues discussed, the depth of their exploration, and the size of the audience reached. This is because virtually every means of communicating ideas in today's mass society requires the expenditure of money... The expenditure limitations contained in the Act represent substantial rather than merely theoretical restraints on the quantity and diversity of political speech.
>
> By contrast with a limitation upon expenditures for political expression, a limitation upon the amount that any one person or group may contribute to a candidate or political committee entail only a marginal restriction upon the contributor's ability to engage in free communication.[35]

The court in *Buckley* v. *Valeo*, it is submitted, gave inadequate attention to the interdependence of the rights to speak and to assemble on the one hand with the socio-economic context in which the rights are exercised on the other. Whereas the court could give less weight to the latter in an economically egalitarian society, the court cannot do so in a society such as the American or Canadian where money plays such an important part in political and social life. The statutory purpose of equalizing the relative financial resources of candidates is more than merely "an ancillary interest" — to use the court's description. As Justice Marshall explained in his dissent on the issue of expenditure restrictions:

> In my view the interest is more precisely the interest in promoting the reality and appearance of equal access to the political arena... The wealthy candidate's immediate access to a substantial personal fortune may give him an initial advantage that his less wealthy opponent can never overcome. And even if the advantage can be overcome, the per-

ception that personal wealth wins elections may not only discourage potential candidates without significant personal wealth from entering the political arena, but also undermine public confidence in the integrity of the electoral process.[36]

What is at issue is not the fundamental freedoms of speech and assembly as abstract notions but rather the *equal* fundamental right to exercise the freedoms of speech and assembly *effectively*.

Section 3. The Scope of Fundamental Rights

The sorts of constitutional issues which I have raised with respect to the level of judicial scrutiny of legislation burdening fundamental rights leads to a third implication which recognition respect for persons poses for constitutional analysis. Namely, the Benthamite notion of "the greatest happiness of the greatest number" or, its contemporary term, the "interest of the state", the "national interest" or the "national security" will not suffice as a justification for the restriction of a fundamental right. Rather, a fundamental right may be restricted only when compelling reasons have explained why the exercise of one fundamental right interferes with the effective exercise of another fundamental right and why the latter serves as a more important element of "respect for persons" in the circumstances. In other words, the only legitimate limit to the scope of a fundamental right is the existence and exercise of another fundamental right.

This implication flows from chapter II where it was argued and demonstrated, with reference to the constitutional experiences of Canada and the United States, that the general welfare as reflected in the contemporary values of society provides an inadequate basis for fundamental rights. The "shock the conscience" form of the societal interest was highly subjective and discretionary. Furthermore, it was conceptually consistent with a system of *ad hoc* rights, rights which existed one day in a given circumstance but denied the next in the same circumstance because of changes in popular opinions. In addition, shocking society's conscience seemed inapplicable in a society such as Canada's with centuries-old conflicting legal traditions. Finally, it provided no principled basis for deciding which rights were fundamental and which were not. Similar obstacles were incurred with respect to the two other forms of determining the general welfare. Neither the "will of the majority" nor the "supremacy of the legislature" left any theoretical limit to the repression of fundamental rights. A society could hardly be said to be based upon fundamental rights if politician, judge or bureaucrat could, in the name of the general welfare or

230

national interest, create all rights, determine their meaning and scope, and possess the authority to destroy them.

The implication also flows from my examination of the principle of the protection of "self-regarding" conduct in chapter IV. We found there that the reason why Benthamite and rule utilitarianism could not support the absolute inviolability of the inner sphere of life lay in the fact that the ultimate norm in utilitarian theory was "the greatest happiness of the greatest number" and that the source of one's obligations in that theory was directed from without rather than from within the person. Utilitarian theory contemplated the infringement of "self-regarding" conduct whenever *society* calculated that such an infringement was necessary to the general welfare. Despite Mill's desire to support the inviolability of the "inner sphere of life", his adoption of utilitarianism led him to value "self-regarding" conduct for its instrumental relationship to the societal welfare rather than out of respect for the instrinsic worth of the individual himself. Furthermore, Mill conceded that, although society was not founded upon a social contract, each citizen owed "distinct and assignable obligations" toward society. But he explicitly and implicitly left it to society to impose those obligations. This, in turn, invited the very tyranny of the majority which Mill so dreaded. The obligations would vary with the cultural values, if not whims, of any particular society. And the scope of what was considered "self-regarding" conduct could be enlarged only by a corresponding shift in public norms.

Finally, the constitutional implication that the interest of the state or "of the public" cannot justifiably restrict fundamental rights flows from my examination of John Rawls' notion of the "common interest" in chapter V. Rawls had contemplated that the state could restrict the basic liberties in the "common interest". But he failed to guide us as to when the common interest necessitated such restrictions. His generalities were so vague as to chill the exercise of basic liberties even in normal circumstances. Further, he did not clarify *who* was to determine whether a threat to the public order could reasonably be expected from the continued exercise of a basic liberty. In addition, his introduction of the new norm of the "common interest" placed serious qualifications upon his own espoused departure from utilitarianism, at least as far as fundamental rights were concerned. Finally, Rawls wrongly assumed that there existed a substantial and direct relationship between the existence and exercise of basic liberties on the one hand, and political instability on the other. Although the onus was on Rawls to substantitate that claim, I tried to show that there was little evidence to suggest that the exercise of basic liberties had any direct causal connection with political instability.

a. *The Place of Ronald Dworkin's Analysis of Rights*

The implication which my defence of fundamental rights bears upon the scope of fundamental rights can be better appreciated in the light of a distinction made by Ronald Dworkin in his recently published *Taking Rights Seriously*.[37] In his chapter entitled the same, Dworkin distinguishes a weak from a strong sense of rights. In words very similar to Bentham's,[38] Dworkin describes the weak sense as something "that it is the 'right' thing for him to do."[39] According to the strong sense, some special grounds are needed to justify interference with one's conduct.[40] In his chapter "Constitutional Cases," Dworkin defines a right in the strong sense as a "special claim", as something which protects an individual group or citizen against the majority.[41] And, in "Justice and Rights," Dworkin asserts that an individual possesses a right to something

> if the failure to provide that act, when he calls for it, would be unjustified within that (political) theory even if the *goals* of the theory would, on the balance, be disserviced by that act. The strength of a particular right, within a particular theory, is a function of the degree of disservice on the whole, that is necessary to justify refusing an act called for under the right.[42]

Dworkin argues that if American citizens are supposed to have certain fundamental rights against their government, "if this idea is significant, and worth bragging about",[43] then one should adopt the second stronger sense of rights. If someone claims that American citizens possess a right against the government, according to Dworkin,

> what he cannot do is to say that the Government is justified in overriding a right on the minimal grounds that would be sufficient if no such right existed. He cannot say that the Government is entitled to act on no more than a judgment that its act is likely to produce, overall, a benefit to the community. That admission would make his claim of a right pointless, and would show him to be using some sense of "right" other than the strong sense necessary to give his claim the political importance it is normally taken to have.[44]

That is what Dworkin means by "taking rights seriously".

I said that Dworkin's weak sense of rights was very similar to Bentham's. In order to understand the importance of Dworkin's distinction between a weak and strong sense of rights let us return

232

to Bentham's conception of a right as initially summarized in chapters II and IV above.

For Bentham, all laws were directed towards the common end of happiness.[45] The utility of any proposed law was measured by its tendency to create or diverge from happiness.[46] A "right" was something which ought to be done: it was a right or correct action as opposed to a wrong one.[47] And a right action was one which increased the community's happiness. In this manner the "rights" of an individual were conflated into the *felicitic calculus* of the "greatest happiness of the greatest number". A right, for Bentham, was a "social concession" which the state granted to the individual because the right improved the community's overall happiness. The utilitarian right was, for the individual, a very weak right indeed.

What needs emphasizing is that utilitarian theory contemplated restrictions on liberty whenever such restrictions were reasonably necessary to the community's welfare. As Bentham's follower, John Austin, explained, "since the power of the government is incapable of legal limitation, the government is legally free to abridge their political liberty, at its own pleasure or discretion."[48] Or, as Mill argued in chapter 4 of his essay on *Utilitarianism*, "all persons are deemed to have a right to equality of treatment, except when some recognized social expediency requires the reverse."[49]

Why could liberty be restricted in a wide range of circumstances? This was in part because one examined the reasonableness of a restriction by reference to the majority's welfare rather than the intrinsic worth of the individual. One could challenge restrictions only by establishing that more appropriate means could achieve the social welfare. Secondly, utilitarians defined the community's welfare in very vague and wide terms. Bentham defined "the community", for example, as "a fictitious body, composed of the individual persons who are considered as constituting as it were its members."[50] The interests of this "fictitious body" were "what the legislative majority of the legislature said they were."[51] Mill, who himself loathed the "tyranny of the majority", acknowledged the open-endedness of the concept by suggesting that it was capable of accomodating such diverse interests as money, fame, power, music, health, virtue and the like. One of the Canadian Government's earlier proposals for the constitutional entrenchment of the utilitarian perspective did not even appear to express the community's welfare in concrete terms: the "fundamental rights" which the government wishes to entrench may be limited by restrictions "as are reasonably justifiable in a democratic society in the interests of public safety, order, health or morals, of national security, or of the rights and freedoms of others..."[52]

One should note that Professor Dworkin conpromises his stronger sense of rights in at least two ways. First, he admits that not all special claims will win out since one claim may conflict with another. This potential conflict underlies Dworkin's distinction between an abstract and concrete right. An abstract right "does not indicate how that aim (i.e., political aim) is to be weighed or compromised in particular circumstances against other political aims."[53] A concrete right, on the other hand, reflects a particular resolution of the conflict of rights "in particular complex social situations." Thus, once a court renders a decision in a hard case, the decision asserts concrete rather than abstract rights.[54] In this manner a concrete right reflects the outcome of society's weighing of various rights which conflict with one another.

Dworkin compromises his stronger sense of rights in a second, more critical fashion, however. He suggests on several occasions that, although a right cannot be outweighed by all collective goals, a right may well be legitimately outweighed by collective goals of "special urgency" or "to prevent a catastrophe or even to obtain a clear and major public benefit."[55] Dworkin acknowledges in his chapter entitled "Taking Rights Seriously" that this latter restriction of a right treats "the right in question as not among the most important or fundamental."[56] He admits on another occasion that his is "a low-keyed theory of moral rights against the state."[57]

Because he does permit restrictions upon "stronger" rights in some circumstances, the question arises as to how Dworkin's theory of rights really differs from the weaker Benthamite sense initially elaborated. It would seem that Dworkin is arguing that his "stronger" rights are "special" or *prima facie* claims which cannot legitimately be outweighed by any of the invalid reasons for a moral judgment which Dworkin himself rejects in his chapter entitled "Liberty and Moralism".[58]

In that chapter Dworkin disqualifies four categories of factors as valid reasons for a moral judgment: prejudice, personal emotional reaction, "patently false" propositions of fact and the "parroting" of other persons' beliefs. These "invalid" reasons are of some consequence in a Benthamite perspective. For, as I just noted, Bentham conflated the "rights" of an individual into the *felicitic calculus* of the greatest happiness of the greatest number. One calculated the greatest happiness by measuring the pains and pleasures which flowed from a proposed measure to each and every person in the community. But those pleasures and pains include the very considerations which Dworkin disqualifies as valid reasons for a moral judgment. An over-all benefit to the community is an inadequate justification to override a *prima facie* claim because any over-all collective benefit is often found by measuring the invalid reasons or "preferences" of society's members. Dworkin has this point in mind when he asserts in his chapter on "Reverse Discrimination" that a right could not be outweighed

> when the gains that outweigh the losses include the satisfaction of *prejudices* and *other sorts of preferences* that it is *improper* for officials or institutions to take into account at all.[59]

For Dworkin, a moral judgment is a very different phenomenon from a "preference" which, quoting from Lord Devlin,[60] is "largely a matter of feeling" for which reasons need not to be given. I shall call this weak sense of rights R_1.

Professor Dworkin's theory of rights leaves at least one important ambiguity. On the one hand, he advocates a "low-keyed" theory of rights which does conceive their compromising by collective goals "to obtain a clear and major public benefit." Ordinarily, under this conception, an over-all benefit to the community is an inadequate justification to override a prima facie claim. This is because the over-all benefit to the community is usually found by measuring the "preferences" of society's members. And the "special urgency" or "clear and major public benefit" would appear to be ascertained by non-preference reasons. On the other hand, essays such as "Hard Cases"[61] and "Taking Rights Seriously"[62] seem to suggest that even collective goals based upon non-Devlinite preferences ought not to outweigh rights. In the latter category, only other rights may outweigh a constitutional right.

As a consequence of the dilemma, there appears to be two "strong" senses of rights embedded within Dworkin's writings. There are rights (R_2), in the first place, which cannot be outweighed by any collective goal which has been determined simply by measuring the emotional preferences of society's members. Rights are special claims in a second stronger sense (R_3) in that they cannot be outweighed even by collective goals which have been ascertained by a consideration of "valid" or non-Devlinite factors. The only circumstances when the second strong sense of rights may be comprised are when they conflict with other more important rights. This is the sense of a fundamental right which consistently flows from my own examination of the principle of "respect for persons". It is a "high-keyed" theory of fundamental rights.

b. *An Analysis of the "Sense of Rights" in the "Subversive Advocacy" Cases in the United States*

If one finds my defence of fundamental rights convincing, then serious practical implications lie for the scope of fundamental rights in concrete cases. I wish to demonstrate this by returning to a series of "subversive advocacy" cases in the United States from the *Schenck*[63] to *Dennis*[64] decisions. Most of the Supreme Court Justices in these cases, I shall argue, shared the Benthamite weak sense of rights (that is, R_1).

Mr. Justice Holmes' judgments in *Schenck* v. *United States*,[65] *Frohwerk* v. *United States*,[66] and *Debs* v. *United States*,[67] for example, contemplated that collective goals could outweigh freedom of speech if Congress deemed the speech a "clear and present danger" to the state. Section 3 of the Espionage Act made it a criminal offence wilfully to make false reports or statements with the intent of interfering with military success, wilfully to cause insubordination in the armed foces and wilfully to obstruct recruitment. Schenck was charged with a conspiracy to violate Section 3. Schenck's pamphlet intimated in impassioned language that conscription constituted the worst form of despotism. Mr. Justice Holmes held that, although such language was permissible "in many places and in ordinary times," circumstances alter the character of any conduct. The issue "in every case," according to Justice Holmes, was whether words are expressed in such circumstances as to create "a clear and present danger" to the state.

Justice Holmes reaffirmed this pronouncement in the same year in *Frohwerk* and *Debs* by asking whether, in the particular circumstances, the court could detect a "presumed intent" and whether the words caused a "bad tendency". In *Debs*, for example, the accused had spoken on the subject of socialism, prophesying the eventual success of that philosophy. Justice Holmes held that the natural and intended effect of Debs' speech was to oppose the war. Justice Holmes' adoption of a weak sense of rights is not surprising in that his personal correspondence during the period indicates that he was entirely insensitive to any claim for special judicial protection of free speech.[68]

Justice Holmes' dissent in *Abrams* v. *United States*[69] is noted by constitutional commentators[70] as a departure from the "clear and present danger" test in favour of a more protected place for free speech. And yet, this judgment too presumed a weak sense of rights. In *Abrams*, the defendants had published two leaflets condemning the American complicity in the anti-Bolshevik struggle. The Supreme Court upheld the conviction of the defendants for

236

curtailing production of war materials necessary to the prosecution of the war with Germany, with the intent to hinder the prosecution of that war.

Justice Holmes, who dissented, began his analysis by examining whether Abram's acts came under any legislative rule.[71] The only relevant rule prohibited conduct where "the proximate motive of the specific act" was to cripple or hinder the American prosecution of the war. Justice Holmes construed a specific intent requirement into the pertinent legislative rule. Holmes J. concluded that the defendants' conduct did not come within this rule because the defendants did not possess the required specific intent: the immediate target of their conduct was American military intervention against the Russian revolution.

Holmes J. then went to a constitutional analysis which elaborated the clear and present danger as a constitutional test for protecting freedom of speech. The principle, which he believed to be consistent with *Schenck*, *Frohwerk* and *Debs*, was stated as follows:

> But when men have realized that time has upset many fighting faiths, they may come to believe even more than they believe the very foundations of their own conduct that *the ultimate good* desired is better reached by free trade in ideas — that the best test of truth is the power of the thought to get itself accepted in the competition of the market, and that truth is the only ground upon which their wishes safely can be carried out. That at any rate is the theory of our Constitution.[72]

Although Justice Holmes' theory protected free speech in the *Abrams* case, he justified "the free trade of ideas" in terms of the "ultimate good" for the collective welfare. In that light he could easily appreciate why a government would wish to restrict free speech whenever necessary for the state's interest. As he explained in *Abrams*,

> persecution of the expression of opinions seems to me perfectly logical. If you have no doubt of your premises or your power and want a certain result with all your heart you naturally express your wishes in law and sweep away all opposition. To allow opposition by speech seems to indicate that you think the speech impotent, as when a man says that he has squared the circle, or you do not care whole-heartedly for the result, or that you doubt either your power or your premises.[73]

Holmes J. adopted the primacy of the collective welfare as the focal point of his "clear and present danger" test.

The majority of the Supreme Court as well as Justice Holmes accepted a weak sense of a right to free speech in *Gitlow* v. *New York*.[74] Gitlow's newspaper "The Revolutionary Age" had published sixteen thousand copies of a "Manifesto" advocating a "Communist Revolution". It had urged mass industrial revolts and "revolutionary mass action". Gitlow was charged pursuant to Section 161 of the New York Penal law which had made it an offence for anyone who by word of mouth, writing, publishing, or selling "advocates, advises or teaches the duty, necessity or propriety of overthrowing or overturning organized government by force or violence... or by any unlawful means." The issue was whether Section 161 required the United States Government to produce evidence of "some definite or immediate act" of violence or unlawful activity which flowed from the Manifesto's publication. No such evidence had been proferred and the Supreme Court (per Sanford J.) held that none was necessary.

The initial portion of Justice Sanford's judgment assessed whether Gitlow's conduct came within the scope of Section 161. After holding affirmatively, he examined the social consequences of ruling Section 161 unconstitutional. The Manifesto's utterances were, Justice Sanford stressed, "inimical to the general welfare" and entailed "such danger of substantive evil." They involved "danger to the public peace and to the security of the State." Even the immediate consequences were "real and substantial."

As with Justice Sanford, Justice Holmes too believed that he could resolve the issue of the scope of freedom of speech by reference to the social consequences involved. The state's interests were paramount, according to Justice Holmes. The only question was whether Gitlow's utterances obstructed the interests of the state. Holmes J. still adhered to the *Schenck* "clear and present danger" test. It was "manifest," he concluded, "that there was no present danger of an attempt to overthrow the government by force on the part of the admittedly small minority who shared the defendant's views." Furthermore, it was not in the interest of society to repress freedom of speech.

Another great liberal judge, Mr. Justice Brandeis, shared the weak sense of rights (R_1) in *Whitney* v. *California*.[75] Whitney had been charged as a member of a syndicalist organization pursuant to the *Criminal Syndicalism Act*[76] of California. She had attended the 1919 national convention of the socialist party. This party eventually split and she became a member of the more "radical" faction. At a later convention of the new party she supported a resolution endorsing "the value of political action" for workers. The Supreme Court held that the California Syndicalism Act could constitutionally be applied to her case.

Justice Brandeis, who gave a concurring judgment, began by setting out two competing legal principles. According to the first, the rights of free speech could be restricted only when "the speech would produce, or is intended to produce, a clear and immanent danger of some substantive evil." According to the second principle, the legislature usually decided which circumstances constituted "a clear and present danger of substantive evil." In difficult cases, however, the court assessed the remoteness and degree of evil. Because no legal standard existed to guide the courts in the immediate case, Justice Brandeis found it necessary to ask the basic philosophic question as to "why a State is, ordinarily, denied the power to prohibit dissemination of social, economic and political doctrine which a vast majority of its citizens believes to be false and fraught with evil consequence.[77] Brandeis J.'s own "theory of the Constitution" rings clear:

> Those who won our independence believed that the final end of the State was to make men free to develop their faculties; and that in its government the deliberative forces should prevail over the arbitrary. They valued liberty both as an end and as a means. They believed liberty to be the secret of happiness and courage to be the secret of liberty. They believed that freedom to think as you will and to speak as you think are means indispensable to the discovery and spread of political truth; that without free speech and assembly discussion would be futile; that with them, discussion affords ordinarily adequate protection against the dissemination of noxious doctrine; that the greatest menace to freedom is an inert people; that public discussion is a political duty; and that this should be a fundamental principle of the American government.[78]

A close look at this "theory of the Constitution" discloses Justice Brandeis' acceptance of a weak sense of rights. Free speech secured "order". Discouragement of thought "menaces stable government." The government may suppress free speech if there are "reasonable grounds to fear that *serious evil* will result." The "danger must be imminent." Brandeis J. was clearly speaking of a "serious evil" to the collectivity as a whole, not to the rights of others. It was "harm to society" or "injury to the state" — to use his words — that was at issue. The important question for Justice Brandeis was merely whether the *means* used to satisfy the collective welfare were reasonable. Clearly, the "clear and present danger" test initiated by Mr. Justice Holmes in *Schenck*, applied by Justice Holmes in *Frohwerk* and *Debs*, and elaborated by Justice Brandeis in *Whitney* protected the "right" to free speech only when other important *collective* goals did not conflict with the "right".

Furthermore, even if Brandeis J. can be said to have given paramount "fundamentalness" to the individual's right of free speech (he did acknowledge it to be an end as well as a means), he translated that parmountcy into a legal principle which justified restrictions on free speech when those restrictions were reasonably justified from the state's viewpoint. Clearly, if Brandeis J. were to accept rights as "fundamental", he should have questioned whether the state could restrict free speech whenever the state so desired or, alternatively, whether the state could do so only when it was essential to protect more important rights. Furthermore, Justice Brandeis should have asked whether the state and the society were one and the same thing and, if not, whether there were occasions when the state's restriction of free speech contradicted the interests of society. A further question which Brandeis J. might have faced was whether he could consider free speech as fundamental in any true sense when the "right's" existence was contingent upon the state or, alternatively, whether there was a constitutionally protected area of free speech which the state could not legitimately penetrate. This is not to suggest that the notion of a fundamental right requires a particular answer to any of these questions. Consistency between Justice Brandeis's political theory of the Constitution and his "intermediate" constitutional principles does require in this context, on the other hand, that the questions be asked and that Justice Brandeis' own legal responses be internally consistent with his conclusion that free speech is valuable as an "end in itself". Brandeis J. failed to ask the questions and he failed to give any explanation for his conclusion which, on its face, is inconsistent with his political theory that free speech be an end in itself.

One final Supreme Court decision which we might examine is the 1951 decision of *Dennis* v. *United States*.[79] At issue was whether Sections 2 or 3 of the Smith Act violated the First Amendment. Section 2 created an offence for anyone "knowingly or wilfully advising or teaching the overthrow or destruction of the Government." Justices Vinson, Frankfurter and Jackson expressly held that one could determine the scope of fundamental rights only by reference to the dictates of the collective welfare. Speech, Justice Vinson held, was a "societal value" which "must be subordinated to other values and considerations." The state's interest was "the ultimate value of any society." The state could restrict speech if the speech posed a "substantial threat to the safety of the community." According to Vinson J., the court's role was to examine whether any speech posed such a threat. Quoting from Learned Hand's Court of Appeal judgment in *Dennis*, the judicial function in every case was simply to ask whether the gravity of the "evil", discounted by its improbability, justifies such invasion of free speech as is necessary to avoid the danger.[80]

Nothing could be closer to Bentham's "weak sense" of a right.

Justice Vinson's colleagues in *Dennis* shared his weak sense of a freedom of speech. Justice Frankfurter, for example, emphasized that "the historic antecedents of the First Amendment" gave to the courts the role of balancing the "competing interests" which compose the collective welfare. The central interests were the public's interest in protecting speech, the state's interest in protecting its security and the court's interest in assuring public acceptability of its future decisons. Justice Jackson concurred that a right to free speech should be protected when "it was the right thing to do" from the collectivity's viewpoint. Speech had been protected in those circumstances, according to Justice Frankfurter, when the right was "vital to our society." Even Justice Douglas, who dissented, fell back upon his own assessment of collective goals as determinative of the issue. Speech may lose its "constitutional immunity", he asserted, when this was "in the interests of the safety of the Republic." The crucial issue was simply whether the danger to society was real and imminent.[81]

c. *The Adoption of a Weak Sense of Rights by the Canadian Supreme Court*

The American Supreme Court has not been alone in its adoption of a weak sense of rights. Indeed, a good argument can be made that the weak sense of rights has pervaded the Canadian judicial and legislative approaches toward civil liberties problems until the present. This is reflected in recent decisions involving equality before the law,[82] the right to counsel,[83] cruel and unusual punishment,[84] contempt,[85] obscenity[86] and censorship.[87] The utilitarian perspective underlies several Reports of the Canadian Law Reform Commission[88] as well as the federal government's proposed entrenched Bill of Rights.[89] Finally, it is embedded in the reasoning process of the Supreme Court decision of *Boucher* v. *R.*,[90] a case which at least one learned Canadian scholar[91] has described as having a "tacit assumption" that freedom of expression is "a basic value which was protected by legal principles built into the structure of our legal system." I shall try to show how the political presuppositions of the Supreme Court Justices in the *Boucher* case were very alien to the existence of a fundamental right to freedom of expression as that right has been defended in this book.

The jury in *Boucher* had convicted the accused of publishing a seditious libel, contrary to the Criminal Code.[92] The Quebec Court of Appeal, with two dissents, affirmed the conviction. Boucher, who belonged to the Jehovah's Witness, had published a pamphlet entitled "Quebec's Burning Hatred for God and Christ and Freedom is the shame of all Canada." Over 1,500,000 copies had been printed in English, French and Ukrainian. The pamphlet began with a plea for a calm and sober consideration of the evidence presented in the pamphlet. It referred to instances of destruction of the sect's Bibles, of "mob violence" and of public violence against private property owned by Witnesses who were engaged in the distribution of Bibles and religious pamphlets. Hundreds of Witnesses were allegedly subjected to heavy fines, prison sentences, delay in the disposition of charges and exorbitant bail arising out of the violence. Upon alleging that the "force behind Quebec's suicidal hate is priest domination," the pamphlet attacked the Quebec courts for being "so under priestly thumbs that they affirmed the infamous sentence" in *Roncarelli* v. *Duplessis*.[93]

In the first hearing three Justices (Rinfret, Kerwin and Taschereau JJ.) set aside the conviction and ordered a new trial on the grounds that the trial judge had misinstructed the jury. Two Justices (Rand and Estey JJ.) quashed the conviction and ordered an acquittal. The issue involved the nature of *mens rea* required for seditious libel. Because the court's decision lacked a clear *ratio* which could guide future trial judges in their instructions, the full court reñheard the case and, by a vote of four to five, ordered an acquittal.

A close look at each of the judgments in both hearings finds the Supreme Court explicitly adopting a weak sense of rights. Rinfret J. asserted, quoting from another source, that "there must be a point where restriction upon an individual's freedom of expression is justified and required on the grounds of reason, or on the ground of the democratic process and the necessities of the present situation."[94] Canadian residents could not insist on an unrestricted freedom of speech "utterly irrespective of the evil results which are often inevitable." Justice Taschereau, ushering forth a series of precedents, stressed that the purpose of the seditious offences was to punish those who had *slandered the state* or who had caused disaffection and stirred up "ill-will and hostility" between different classes of subjects.[95] Although Justice Rand rejected the latter category of conduct as coming within the purview of the crime in favour of "the clash of critical discussion on political, social and religious subjects,"[96] he maintained that seditious libel encompassed words intended "or... so likely to do so as to be deemed to be intended" to cause disorder "directly or indirectly *to Government in its broadest sense.*"[97]

Kerwin J., in the re-hearing, elaborated upon his judgment that the seditious intent had to incite people "against *constituted authority*" or to create a public disturbance or disorder *"against such authority."*[98] Kellock J. similarly expressed the importance of the interest of the state by approving dicta from Fitzgerald J. in *R. v. Sullivan*:[99]

> Sedition is a crime *against society*, nearly allied to that of treason... Sedition in itself is a comprehensive term, and it embraces all those practices, whether by word, deed, or writing, which are calculated to disturb *the tranquillity of the state*, and lead ignorant persons to endeavour to subvert *the Government* and the laws of the empire. The objects of sedition generally are to induce discontent and insurrection, and stir up *opposition to the Government*, and bring the administration of justice into contempt...[100]

Justice Estey, notwithstanding his order for an acquittal in the second hearing, emphasized that "I am of the opinion that in all cases the intention to incite violence or public disorder or unlawful conduct *against His Majesty* or *an institution of the State* is essential."[101] Cartwright J. also understood the scope of the crime in terms of the "disturbance of or resistence of *the authority of* lawfully constituted Government."[102] Whether the Justices used the term "public disorder", "society", "the laws of the Empire", the "government", "an institution of the state" or the "state", the message reigned clear: rights were to be protected only to the extent that they did not collide with the collective welfare or *raison d'état.*

d. *An Alternative Analysis of the Scope of Free Speech in the "Subversive Advocacy" Cases*

If the American Supreme Court in the *Schenck* to *Dennis* line of cases as well as Candian legislators and judges have adopted a weak sense of rights, how should one conceive the scope of free speech if one wishes to adhere to a stronger sense of a right? It would seem that one line of constitutional analysis which approaches R_3 is that advocated by Professor Emerson[103] and applied by Mr. Justice Black in *Yates v. United States*.[104]

Professor Emerson has argued that the framers of the American Constitution had already balanced out fundamental policy conflicts when they had drafted the First Amendment. As a consequence, the judiciary's function was "not to re-open this prior balancing but to construct the specific legal doctrines which... will

243

govern the concrete issues." These "doctrines" appear to be Justice Harlan's "intermediate principles" or Ronald Dworkin's "conceptions".[105] According to Dworkin, the First Amendment is a series of concepts. When one appeals to the *concept* of freedom of speech, one appeals to what free speech means objectively speaking. In contrast, when one lays down a conception of free speech, one elaborates what *he* means by the guarantee. With a concept one poses a moral issue but with a conception one tries to answer it. Professor Emerson's "doctrines" recognise the special claim surrounding the individual's right to free expression as against the collective welfare. As Emerson puts it, his theory "rests upon the general proposition that expression must be free and unrestrained, that *the state may not seek to achieve other social objectives through control of expression...*"[106] Emerson's point is that there is a clearly marked constitutional zone encircling an individual which the state may not penetrate in pursuance of collective goals.

In *Yates* the Supreme Court (per Harlan J.) reversed convictions of lower echelon members of the communist party made pursuant to the Smith Act. Justice Harlan held that the advocacy of the overthrow of a government differed from the mere doctrinal justification of forcible overthrow. The former urged action whereas the latter represented mere belief. Harlan J. emphasized that freedom of expression marked off a constitutional zone protecting beliefs. Justice Black, who dissented, reaffirmed the *principle* of the inviolability of the inner sphere of life:

> The choice expressed in the First Amendment in favour of free expression was made against a turbulent background by men such as Jefferson, Madison, and Mason — men who believed that loyalty to the provisions of this Amendment was the best way to assure a long life for this new nation and its Government. Unless there is complete freedom for expression of all ideas, whether we like them or not, concerning the way government should be run and who shall run it, I doubt if any views in the long run can be secured against the censor. The First Amendment provides the only kind of security system that can preserve a free government — *one that leaves* the way wide open for people to favour, discuss, advocate, or incite causes and doctrines however obnoxious and antagonistic such views may be to the rest *of us*.[107]

Several points should be made with respect to the connection between the Emerson-Black approach towards the First Amendment on the one hand and a strong sense of rights on the other. First, the connection between the two lies in the ultimate test adopted rather than Professor Emerson's justification of it. Emerson did, as a whole, justify his test by use of utilitarian arguments and utilitarian theorists (such as John Stuart Mill). But the similar-

244

ity between Emerson's approach and a strong sense of rights (R_3) lies in Emerson's idea that collective goals ought not to outweigh freedom of speech.

The second point to note is that Professor Emerson's test adopts the stronger (that is, R_3) of Dworkin's two strong sense of rights in that, under R_2 collective goals may justify the restriction of free speech in circumstances of "special urgency", "a catastrophe" or to obtain "a clear and major public benefit." Although Emerson's justification of the existence of a freedom of speech represents a "low-keyed" theory of rights against the state (R_2), his ultimate test seems to be more of a higher-keyed theory (R_3) in that it does not account for the compromising of free speech when that speech conflicts with collective goals of "serious urgency".

Section 4. Judicial Decision-Making in Constitutional Cases

The final area of constitutional analysis which I wish to connect with my argument for fundamental rights is the manner in which judges ought to justify constitutional decisions. A useful starting point is Professor Ronald Dworkin's theory of judicial decision-making. Dworkin, briefly, elaborates a theory of judicial decision-making which gives a high place to the role of principles in the law. He also emphasizes that a judge must find institutional support for those principles. Unlike legal rules, principles do not necessarily originate in a particular legislative or judicial decision; rather, their origin lies "in a sense of appropriateness developed in the profession and the public over time." In order to determine whether a principle has continued weight, a judge must set his own convictions aside. He must construct a constitutional theory demanded by the institutions in any given society.

a. *Dworkin's Model of Constitutional Decision-Making*

As mentioned, Professor Dworkin gives a high place for the role of principles in the law. We first encounter his emphasis of the role of principles in "The Model of Rules II". In "The Model of Rules II" Dworkin asks whether we can say that we have a legal obligation simply by applying "the law" to the particular facts of a case. He agrees with the accepted view that "the law" includes legal rules. But he insists that "the law" also includes legal principles. Principles play a particularly important part in "hard cases" where the result is not clearly dictated by statute or precedent. Principles are important, for example, when one legal rule conflicts with another. A judge may resolve such a conflict only by determining which of the two rules is valid. But a judge does not decide the validity of a rule by reference to some master rule of recognition. Rather, he assesses its validity by an examination of the rules and principles which "support", "underlie" and are "embedded" in the legal system.[108] As Dworkin explains,

> but we cannot say that one rule is more important than another within the system of rules, so that when two rules conflict one supercedes the other by virtue of its greater weight. If two rules conflict, one of them cannot be a valid rule. The decision as to which is valid, and which must be abandoned or recast, must be *made by appealing to considerations beyond the rules themselves.* A legal system might regulate such conflicts by other rules, which prefer the rule enacted by the higher authority, or the rule enacted later, or the more specific rule, or something of that sort. A legal system may also prefer the rule supported by the more important principles. (Our own legal system uses both of these techniques).[109]

Once a judge has identified those "other considerations", he will be in a position to assess which alternative legal rule is more consistent with those considerations. Indeed, principles are so important that before a judge may justifiably alter an existing legal rule, he must advance some principle or policy served by the change.[110] Unless a judge does elaborate some principle, he fails in his judicial duty.[111]

But what are these "other considerations"? More particularly, what is a principle? How, for example, does it differ from a legal rule? A rule has a "compelling" character in the sense that if a case falls within the fact condition contemplated by the rule then the rule automatically applies "in an all-or-nothing fashion": "the answer it [that is, the rule] supplies must be accepted."[112] If a particular case does not come within the fact category contemplated in the "if" clause of the rule, then the rule does not apply. A principle contrasts with a rule in at least two ways. First, a principle does not indicate the legal consequences which automatically flow from its application.[113] A principle points to a particular decision in particular circumstance but a principle does not dictate, necessitate or compel a particular decision in an automatic sense. Unlike a rule, a principle has the dimension of weight and it may be outweighed by a principle arguing in another direction. Secondly, some principles do not even set out an "if" clause or fact condition which makes its application necessary.[114] An example would be the principle that "the courts will not permit themselves to be used as instruments of inequity and injustice."[115]

What, then, is a principle? Again, we are told what it is not. It is not a policy. Dworkin elaborates his notions of a principle and a policy in his essay "Hard Cases". An argument of principle is intended to establish an individual or group right or an *"individuated* political aim".[116] His example is that a minority has a right to equal respect and concern. On the other hand, an argument of policy demonstrates that a decision advances or protects some collective goal of the community.[117] His example is an argument that a subsidy for aircraft manufacturers will protect national defence.

A judge's role in hard cases is to assess the relative weight and importance of principles and policies. Whereas two conflicting rules cannot both be valid,[118] principles and policies may conflict with one another. Because this is so, a legal right in a hard case is usually less than absolute. A right's weight is heavy if the argument for the principle establishing the right can withstand competition from other arguments of principle or policy. The potentiality of conflict amongst principles and policies underlies Dworkin's distinction between an abstract and a concrete right. An abstract right "does not indicate how that aim [that is, political aim] is to be weighed or compromised in particular circumstances against other political aims."[119] A concrete right reflects a particular resolution of the conflict of rights "in particular complex social situation".[120] Thus, once a decision is given in a hard case, the decision asserts concrete rather than abstract rights.[121]

Dworkin goes to even greater lengths to emphasize that an adequate theory of judicial decision-making must rely upon institutional, not background rights. The latter provide a justification for a political decision in the abstract.[122] The former provide a justification for a decision in the "insulated" context of some specific situation. A judge must fall back upon institutional rather than background rights because the citizen consents to "the autonomous enterprise of making rules."[123]

Dworkin's emphasis on the necessity for institutional support underlying a right provides greater understanding of his distinction between a forward-looking and a backward-looking model of judicial decision-making. He raises the distinction in an early book review entitled "Does Law Have a Function?"[124] A forward-looking model is one which looks to the future. There, the judge's function is to ask the *normative*, teleological question "what desirable state-of-affairs should be pursued in the future." In a backward-looking model the judge's function is to *find* a principle which existing or past institutional materials *require*.

This process of finding a principle by looking backward is an entirely different process from construing and applying the principle once it is found.[125] A judge *construes* a principle when he attempts to determine its meaning by reading it in the light of other principles and policies. He construes the initial principle so as to limit or enlarge its scope in much the same way that a judge ought to construe the scope of a statutory provision in the entire context of the statute. The judge applies a principle when, after construing its scope, he applies the principle to the facts of the case before him. These two judicial functions in statutory construction cases take place *after* the judge has found the appropriate statutory provision. In "hard cases", however, this initial pursuit is not so easy because the case is not clearly dictated by statute or precedent. The judge must, in a hard case, still *find* the potentially appropriate principles and, according to Dworkin, he does so by looking backward into the institutional materials.

Dworkin clearly contemplates in "Hard Cases" that once the judge has found the principles by looking backward into the institutional materials, he may then go on to consider the consequences which will flow towards other conflicting principles and policies when the initial principle is construed narrowly or widely. To use Dworkin's example,[126] a judge would *find* a right to equal respect and concern by examining institutional materials such as anti-discrimination statutes. But a judge would have to *construe* and *apply* that right so as to limit its scope in the light of its logical or foreseeable consequences for other principles and policies. Policies could outweigh the right of equal respect, for example, if the application of fair employment practices proved "especially disruptive or dangerous." This process of decision-making is certainly "more inclusive" — to use Dworkin's own term[127] — than a model which only provides for forward-looking considerations.[128]

Dworkin's distinctions between principles and rules, principles and policies, concrete and abstract rights, and institutional and background rights do not affirmatively tell us what is a principle. The underlying point in Dworkin's notion of a principle, it seems, is Dworkin's own understanding of what constitutes a valid moral judgment. Unlike a legal rule, a principle "states *a reason* that argues in one direction."[129] Unlike a policy, a principle is "*a requirement* of justice or fairness or some other *dimension of morality*."[130] We shall see that Dworkin's use of the words "reason" and "dimension of morality" have extreme importance once one

248

understands his notion of a valid moral judgment. The latter notion also helps to explain why Dworkin emphasizes that a judge must seek his reasons from institutional rather than background support.

Dworkin's understanding of a valid moral judgment is found primarily in two of his essays. In the first article he appears to have ever written, later published in *Taking Rights Seriously* as a chapter entitled "Liberty and Moralism",[131] Dworkin argues that for one to take a moral position one must be able to give a reason for it. But not every reason will do. We have seen in the previous section that reasons which do not count are those of prejudice, personal emotional reaction, patently false propositions of fact (that is, they challenge "the minimal standards of evidence and argument I generally accept and impose upon others"), and the "parroting" or simple citation of other persons' beliefs.[132] Certain propositions, however, are so "axiomatic and self-evident" that one does not have to give reasons for them (presumably an example might be "murder is immoral"). Every valid reason will presuppose "some general moral principle or theory" even though one may not be able to state that principle or theory. Dworkin emphasizes that despite the preclusion of the irrational elements cited above, a person's general moral theory must be sincere and consistent with the positions he takes on any given issue. Following the terminology also used by John Stuart Mill,[133] any moral belief which does not meet with Dworkin's criteria are mere prejudices or "preferences".

The second source of Dworkin's meaning of a valid moral judgment arises in his description in "Hard Cases" of Hercules, the ideal judge. Hercules, "a lawyer of superhuman skill, learning, patience, and acumen," will always decide his cases by elaborating reasons. Hercules' reasons are principles initially derived from the construction of "a full political theory which justifies the particular rules of the constitution." If Hercules finds two or more plausible theories, he must turn to the institutional rules and practices in order to ascertain which theory provides "a smoother fit with the constitutional scheme as a whole." That is, he must choose "the soundest theory of law" which is "consistent", "coherent" and "appealing" in terms of the constitutional scheme and existing institutional rules.[134] The origin of a legal principle, therefore, lies not in a judicial decision itself, "but in a sense of appropriateness developed in the profession and the public over time."[135] If the settled institutional practices are insufficiently detailed, the ideal judge must elaborate a general political theory which is consistent with those institutions. He must then translate that theory into legal principles. Although the judge exercises judgment in the latter context, it is a weak sense of discretion.

There is an important connection between Dworkin's account of the role of principles in hard cases and his own understanding of what constitutes a valid moral position as enunciated in "Liberty and Moralism". One finds the connection in at least three different contexts in his writings.

First, in "Justice and Rights",[136] Dworkin expressly connects his distinction between principles and policies on the one hand, and his notion of a valid moral position on the other hand. We have seen that he came to hold in "Hard Cases" that an argument of policy is intended to establish a collective goal. He believed that hard cases were decided on the basis of principles which, in turn, establish individual rights. In "Justice and Rights", Dworkin explicitly cites his first article "Lord Devlin and the Enforcement of Morals" (now entitled "Liberty and Moralism") for further explanation as to why a goal-based theory of the law could legitimately take into account "Devlinite" considerations.[137] More precisely, Lord Devlin had believed that the secondary effects of punishing immorality could be beneficial. But in "Lord Devlin and the Enforcement of Morals", Dworkin had argued that Lord Devlin's arguments for the enforcement of morals included the sorts of reasons which Dworkin disqualified as appropriate considerations in a valid moral position. A rights-based theory of the law, in contrast, would not give weight to Devlinite considerations, Dworkin argued.

Secondly, Dworkin emphasizes in "Hard Cases" that Hercules' reasons for judgment are principles initially derived from constructing "a full political theory which justifies the particular rules of the constitution" and which have institutional support.[138] Decision-making by intuition is to be condemned.[139]

In "Justice and Rights" Dworkin writes in similar terms but he does so *in a quest to elaborate a philosophic technique of a valid moral argument*. He develops what he calls a "constructive model" of moral argument which he asserts "is not unfamiliar to lawyers."[140] It is "analogous to one model of common law adjudication." The "constructive model" is not based on a judge's intuitions. Rather, it assumes that "men and women have a responsibility to fit the particular judgments on which they act into a coherent program of action..."[141] That is,

> it demands that decisions taken in the name of justice must never outstrip an official's ability to account for these decisions in a theory of justice, even when such a theory must compromise some of his intuitions. It demands that we act on principle rather than on faith. Its

engine is a doctrine of responsibility that requires men to integrate their intuitions and subordinate some of these, when necessary, to that responsibility. It presupposes that articulated consistency, decisions in accordance with a program that can be made public and followed until changed, is essential to any conception of justice. An official in the position I describe, guided by this model, must give up his apparently inconsistent position; he must do so even if he hopes one day, by further reflection, to devise better principles that will allow all his initial convictions to stand as principles.[142]

The constructive model will "not allow appeals to unique intuitions that might mask prejudice or self-interest in particular cases."[143] Precisely because prejudice and self-interest are precluded, the coherent program provides "independent reasons of political morality."[144] The constructive model of moral argument requires the same traits required of Hercules: coherence, consistency, rationality and impartiality.

Thirdly, we find a connection between the role of principles in judicial decision-making on the one hand and Dworkin's own understanding of a valid moral position on the other in his three major articles on judicial decision-making. In "The Model of Rules" Dworkin argues that when we say we have a legal obligation we must include principles as well as rules as part of "the law". When he defines a principle he does so expressly in terms of morality: "it is a requirement of justice or fairness or some other dimension of morality."[145] This definition as well as his conclusion that principles are part of "the law" certainly leave no doubt where Dworkin stands with respect to the rhetorical question with which he introduces his essay entitled "The Model of Rules":

> Why do we call what "the law" says a matter of legal "obligation"? Is "obligation" here just a term of art, meaning only "what the law says"? Or does legal obligation have something to do with moral obligation? Can we say that we have, in principle at least, the *same reasons for meeting our legal obligations that we have for meeting our moral obligations?* "[146]

In "The Model of Rules 1" Dworkin expressly places the issue of a judge's legal duty in moral terms.[147] If we want to claim that judges have a *duty* to follow the legislature or the constitution, Dworkin writes, then we must give *grounds* for asserting that duty: "this requires that we face the issue of moral philosophy." That issue is not resolved by reference to the community's moral standards in the sense of a consensus of belief about a particular issue.[148] Rather, it refers "to *moral principles* that underlie the community's institutions and laws, in the sense that these principles would figure in a sound theory of law..."[149]

251

Finally, in "Hard Cases" Dworkin continually emphasizes that Hercules' theory of the Constitution is a moral theory. In hard cases "judges must sometimes make judgments of political morality in order to decide what the legal rights of litigants are."[150]

The connection between Dworkin's account of principles and his own understanding of a valid moral position is important for a better grasp of the role of principles in hard cases. In hard cases the judge *must* make a moral judgment. But as Dworkin argues in "Liberty and Moralism", a person making a valid moral judgment must give reasons for his decision. Although legal rules are sufficient in easy cases, in hard cases a judge must find grounds for his judgment by taking account of considerations outside of legal rules. In this process the judge must construct a moral theory consistent with institutional materials. The "moral case" which he makes for a particular decision will depend upon the coherence, impartiality and rationality of his constructive theory. His "moral case" will be weak if it includes his own personal convictions, his own intuitions. That is, if the judge's own personal convictions are inconsistent with an impartial assessment of the settled institutional practices, his personal convictions must fall because they represent personal emotional reactions. For, as Dworkin set out in "Liberty and Moralism", not all reasons will count if one is to take a moral position. A personal preference is such a disqualified reason.

Having grapsed the underlying theory in Dworkin's model of judicial decision-making, how would this theory lead a judge in a first amendment case? The First Amendment provides that

> Congress shall make no law respecting an establishment of religion, or prohibiting the free exercise thereof: or abridging the freedom of speech, or of the press; or the right of the people to peaceably assemble, and to petition the Government for a redress of grievances.

According to Dworkin, the First Amendment provides a series of concepts. I have already noted Dworkin's distinction between a concept and a conception in section c. of this chapter. When one appeals to the *concept* of freedom of speech, one appeals to what free speech means objectively speaking. In contrast, when one lays down a conception of free speech, one lays down what *he* means by the term. With a concept one poses a moral issue but with a conception one tries to answer it.

Accordingly, the first stage of a Dworkinian analysis would be to enunciate what one means by free speech — that is, to set a conception which answers the central moral-political issues in the First Amendment. The judge should then determine whether that conception accords with "settled practices and rules" as reflected in previous judicial decisions in which the conception was cited or figured in the argument, statutes, preambles of statutes, legislative committee reports, other legislative documents, administrative decision, custom and general moral standards of the community or "some identifiable segments thereof."[151] The constitutional text is not *necessarily* the overriding source of institutional history.[152]

In the second stage the judge must "try to put himself, so far as he can, within the more general scheme of beliefs and attitudes of those who value the concept, to look at these clear cases through their eyes."[153] If his conception has insufficient institutional support, the judge must set out some alternative political conception which might be more coincident with existing practices. If he finds a political conception when he does so, he must accept that conception even though his personal convictions depart from it. But if the institutional materials are vague or if past judicial assessment of them cannot be reconciled,[154] the judge must translate his general political philosophy into legal principle.[155]

b. *An Application of Dworkin's Model to Two Cases*

I suggested in section c. above that Mr. Justice Brandeis did not adopt a strong sense of rights in the *Whitney* decision.[156] His reasons for judgment lead us to conclude that even if a judge were to justify his decision in a hard case in the manner Dworkin advocates, it would not necessarily follow that the judge would come out supporting a strong sense of rights. Because no legal standard existed to guide him, Justice Brandeis found it necessary to elaborate a "theory of the Constitution" which he believed flowed from the moral-political values of "those who won our independence." This is just what Dworkin expects of a judge. And yet, Justice Brandeis' theory of the Constitution embodied a weak sense of rights as did the legal principles which he derived from that theory.

Learned Hand's district court judgment in *Masses Publishing Co.* v. *Patten*[157] represents a second judgment which was justified according to the Dworkinian model but which supported a weak sense of rights. *The Masses* was an alleged revolutionary journal published by the plaintiff company. The defendant, acting under the Postmaster General's direction, advised the plaintiff that the mails would be denied to the August issue of *The Masses* since the issue was contrary to the Espionage Act. Section 3 of the said Act made it an offence to wilfully make or convey false reports or false statements with intent to interfere with the operation or success of the military or naval forces of the United States or to promote the success of its enemies...

The issue was whether the court should construe Section 3 in a way which extended to cover *The Masses*.

Judge Learned Hand began his judgment by stressing that it was "beside the question" whether the August issue, by inculcating dissension, had the *consequence* of interfering with the success of the United States military forces. Judge Hand went to the word "wilfully". By a literal construction he held the word to mean "only a statement of fact which the utterer knows to be false." The statements made in the August issue of *The Masses*, however, were believed by the utterer to be true. But Judge Hand went on to suggest that an important political principle underlay this narrow "conception" of the word "wilfully": namely,

> the right to criticise by temperate reasoning, or by immoderate and indecent invective, which is normally the privilege of the individual in countries dependent upon the free expression of opinion as the ultimate source of authority.[158]

Section 3 of the Espionage Act made it an offence to "willfully *cause* or attempt to cause insubordination, disloyalty, mutiny, or refusal of duty, in the military or naval forces of the United States." Judge Hand held that to construe the word "cause" broadly

> would contradict the *normal assumption of democratic government* that the suppression of hostile criticism does not turn upon the justice of its substance or the decency and propriety of its temper.[159]

By so holding, Judge Hand was in effect appealing to a political theory of the Constitution which justified a narrow construction of the word "cause". And, as Dworkin would advocate, Judge Hand supported his theory by reference to "the use and want of our people."

Judge Hand followed this initial Dworkinian analysis by elaborating how his general theory of the Constitution would be translated in other circumstances. According to Judge Hand, his theory did not recognise an absolute freedom of expression:

> Words are not only the keys of persuasion, but the triggers of action, and those which have no purport but to counsel the violation of law cannot by latitude of interpretation be a part of that public opinion *which is the final source of government in a democratic state.*[160]

But, Judge Hand continued, counselling or advising violation of the law did not include political agitation which might eventually

254

stimulate men to violate the law. The reason Judge Hand gave was that such a wide legal principle would, again, be contrary to his general political theory of the Constitution:

> Yet to assimilate agitation, legitimate as such, with direct incitement to violent resistance, is to disregard the tolerance of all methods of political agitation which in normal times is *a safeguard of free government.*

Judge Hand concluded his judgment by, once more, appealing to the institutional history which supported his political theory. More specifically, his theory was supported by "a hard-bought acquisition in the fight for freedom."[161] This institutional framework underlay Congress' enactment of Section 3 of the Espionage Act, Judge Hand assured us.

Judge Hand justified the *The Masses* decision in a manner which was consistent with Dworkin's model of how judges actually decide constitutional cases. First, when faced with two alternative constructions or, to use Dworkin's term, conceptions of the words "wilfully" and "cause", Judge Hand found that his own general theory of the Constitution precluded consideration of one of them. Secondly, Judge Hand found a constitutional principle by looking backward into institutional materials, "referring alternately to political philosophy and institutional detail" — although the detail of his history was somewhat weak. Having so *found* a governing principle he construed and applied the principle in a way that would not have a harmful effect upon the principle. Indeed, the logical consequence of construing the words "wilfully" narrowly and "cause" broadly would be that "every political agitation which can be shown to be apt to create a seditious temper is illegal." Finally, Judge Hand accepted that construction of the words "wilfully" and "cause" which was consonant with Dworkin's own conception of the judicial function. Rather the positing a test which had the courts "balance" the potential political consequences of an utterance for the state, Judge Hand formulated a test which looked to the utterance itself. As Professor Gerald Gunther has remarked,

> To second-guess enforcement officials about provable consequences of subversive speech was to him a questionable judicial function: judges had no special competence to foresee the future. ...
>
> Hand's solution to the problem of an appropriate and effective judicial role was to focus on the speaker's words, not on their probable consequences. . . he sought a more "absolute and objective test" focusing on "language" — "qualitative formula, hard, conventional, difficult to evade", as he said in his letters.[162]

Although Judge Hand's method of judicial decision-making in this constitutional case ressembled the Dworkinian model, Judge Hand did not conclude with a strong sense of rights (R_3). Judge Hand, like Justice Holmes, justified his interpretation of the Espionage Act in terms which contemplated that collective goals could outweigh the right of free speech. For one thing, he emphasized in his theory of the Constitution that "there has always been a recognised limit to such expressions, incident indeed to the existence of any compulsive power of the state itself."

Secondly, Judge Hand went on to assert that

> words are not only the keys of persuasion, but the triggers of action, and those which have no purport but to counsel the violation of the law cannot by any latitude of interpretation be a part of that *public opinion* which is the *final source of government* in a democratic state.

This passage shows how Judge Hand hinged the limits of free speech upon collective goals. The state enacts "the law" presumably in the name of the collective goals. Since Judge Hand placed no limit to the jurisdiction of the state to legislate, the state could conceivably repress freedom of speech *in toto* under Judge Hand's analysis. That is, "the law" could declare that there is no freedom of speech. All speech, as a consequence, could be deemed a violation of "the law".

b. *Implication of Chief Justice Coke's Theory of Fundamental Rights*

But why did Justices Brandeis and Hand not adopt a strong sense of rights? The argument in chapter I of this study suggests at least a partial answer to the question. We saw that under Chief Justice Coke's "backward-looking" approach of searching out weighty common law precedents in order to sustain his propositions of constitutional principle, there could conceivably be very few fundamental rights. And their scope would be very limited. For, *if* there were a fundamental right, it had to have already existed in the law. In addition, it must have been consistently embedded as a principle over several decades — if not centuries. We saw that, as a consequence, Chief Justice Coke's approach could be used to justify both tyranny and slavery if the legal tradition lacked principles proscribing such practices.

Or, as may have been the circumstance at the time of Justices Brandeis and Hand, the legal tradition may have been a utilitarian one which accepted a weak sense of rights. The "institutional background" of the subversive advocacy cases in the United States

256

during the *Schenck* to *Dennis* period provides little precedential support for either of the two stronger senses of rights (R_2 and R_3). Clearly, although it is not the case in the United States, Dworkin's model of judicial decision-making could be used to legitimize grave inhumanities in the same manner in which positivism was alleged to have supported Nazi atrocities. What if the community's moral-political traditions demonstrated no respect toward individual rights? What if the "institutional background" consisted of consistent a-morality which denied the authority of any right, human or otherwise? [163]

Professor Dworkin offers neither argument nor evidence why his moral theory of rights would be chosen over an amoral theory. Indeed, his model of judicial decion-making could solidify an amoral regime, contrary to his own desire that rights be taken seriously. We have already seen that Hercules may oppose popular morality only when "the community's morality is inconsistent on the issue."[164] In "Justice and Rights", Dworkin clearly sets out that his theory of the sources of decision-making is a "theory of the community rather than of particular individuals, and this is an enterprise that is important, for example, in adjudication."[165] Rather than following "troublesome intuitions", Dworkin's judge must subordinate his intuitions to a constructive program demanded by the enterprise of an institution.[166] An official is like a sculptor who must "carve the animal that best fits a pile of bones he happened to find."[167] Institutional constraints are "pervasive and endure to the decision itself."[168]

Precisely because judicial decisions about rights "reflect, rather than oppose, political decisions of the past," the injustices in the law and the inadequacies of the political presuppositions embedded in institutional history will be carried over into the present. Consequently, Professor Dworkin's model of judicial decision-making is not only inaccurate as a description of the judicial process in one series of American cases. The logic of Professor Dworkin's own prescriptions as well as the judgments of Mr. Justice Brandeis in *Whitney* and Judge Learned Hand in *Masses* demonstrate that even if a judge follows a Dworkinian method of decision-making, his method is undesirable if one whishes to take rights seriously.

c. *Implications of "Contemporary Values" and "Entrenched Bill of Rights" Arguments for Fundamental Rights*

A further set of problems arises from Dworkin's model of judicial decision-making. The "institutional background" may well direct that the existence, nature and scope of our fundamental rights be determined by the contemporary values of society or the express or implied guarantees of a written Constitution. Chapters II and III of my study argued, however, that these two arguments do not necessarily ensure a solid foundation for fundamental rights. Under the former, the determination and scope of fundamental rights was highly subjective, discretionary and *ad hoc*. I suggested that it was difficult to quantify the social welfare in practice, as Bentham had urged. The conceptual possibility remained that contemporary values could create, limit or even destroy rights. Although an entrenched Bill of Rights provided a more steadfast institutional foundation for fundamental rights, it too was found to possess serious shortcomings. An entrenched Bill did not resolve the meaning and scope of the provisions of a Bill of Rights. In addition, an entrenched Bill did not guide the courts as to the degree of judicial scrutiny required of legislation which burdens a fundamental right.

One issue pervades both arguments: from whence comes the rule that the "contemporary values" or a written constitution have the force of law? A Dworkinian analysis would presumably suggest that the "institutional background" of society demands the one or the other constitutional theory. But the issue persists: why must the force of law be given to principles embedded in institutional history? Professor Dworkin would probably reply that such a method of justifying judicial decisons will result in the protection of fundamental rights. But this response has been scrutinised and been found wanting. Legal rules can take the lawyer only so far. At some point he must ask normative political questions such as "ought the state or society protect the inner sphere of life?" Chapter II concluded that the source of constitutional rules lies in political norms, in political morality.

Dworkin's model of judicial decision-making does help us a great deal in this regard. Dworkin has emphasized much more openly than, if not in direct contradiction of, Anglo-American legal scholars before him that in hard cases the judge *must* make a moral-political judgment. A valid more judgment should give reasons and certain types of reasons, such as prejudices, are precluded. In this process of reasoning the judge must construct a coherent and impartial moral theory.

Contrary to what Professor Dworkin has suggested, however, the moral theory is not "found" embedded within institutional history. Nor is it confined merely to "hard" cases. Rather, the theory must be "found" in the world of moral-political philosophy. Moral-political philosophy provides the background against which judges must elaborate intermediate principles of constitutional law. And the moral theory must be constructed to more than merely "hard" cases. It must be the foundation of justifying every decision where fundamental rights have been burdened.

This conclusion begs that judges justify their decisions by asking deep questions of moral and political philosophy. It directs that judges be prepared to examine the connection between fundamental rights and the principle of "recognition respect for persons".

This, in turn, requires that our judges be forward-looking as well as backward-looking. Looking forward in an effort to ascertain whether the application of constitutional principle in any particular case will lead to logical or empirical consequences which contradict a philosophic perspective of "respect for persons". Backward-looking with the intent of analyzing the coherency between the political presuppositions of principles embedded in the law on the one hand and "respect for persons" on the other. Unlike the Anglo-Canadian judicial tradition, however, the judge who wishes to justify his decisions in a manner which allows for the existence of fundamental rights must be prepared to examine the socio-economic conditions surrounding the effective exercise of fundamental rights. For, it is the equal worth of fundamental rights which should be his concern if he wants to live up to his claim that his decisions support the existence of fundamental rights.

Notes

1. Until June 1978 the major proposal for an entrenched Bill of Rights in Canada, known as the Victoria Charter, expressly permitted in Article 3 "limitations on the exercise of the fundamental freedoms as are reasonably justifiable in a democratic society in the interests of public safety, order, health or morals, of national security, or of the rights and freedoms of others..." This limitation immediately followed express guarantees of the traditionally considered "fundamental" freedoms and a provision (Article 2) which supposedly guaranteed that "no law of the Parliament of Canada or the Legislatures of the Provinces shall abrogate or abridge any of the fundamental freedoms herein recognized and declared."

Similarly, the Recommendations of the *Final Report* of the Molgat-MacGuigan Special Joint Committee of the Senate and of the House of Commons on the Constitution of Canada, 1972 provided in Recommendation 21 that "the rights and freedoms recognized by the Bill of Rights should not be interpreted as absolute and unlimited, but should rather be exercisable to the extent that they are reasonably justifiable in a democratic society." The Report explained that the Victoria Charter's use of terms such as "public safety, order, health or morals, of national security, or of the rights and freedoms of others" too narrowly qualified the exercise of the enumerated "fundamental" rights. The Committee's reasoning for omitting the vague terms "public safety, order, health or morals, of national security..." is even more frightening than the content of Article 3 in the original proposal itself.

In June 1978, the Canadian Government introduced Bill C-60 into Parliament. This Bill, known as *The Constitutional Amendment Bill*, 3rd. sess., 30th Parl. (Canada), 26-27 Eliz. II, 1977-78 (1st reading: June 20, 1978), set out a proposed Bill of Rights which provided in Article 25 that

> nothing in this Charter shall be held to prevent such limitations on the exercise or enjoyment of any of the individual rights and freedoms declared by this Charter as are justifiable in a free and democratic society in the interests of public safety or health, the interests of the peace and security of the public, or the interests of the rights and freedoms of others...

For the weaknesses of Article 25 see generally, Appendix A at the end of this study.

2. Text, supra, chap. VI, sect. b.

3. Text, supra, chap. VI, sect. c.

4. Text, supra, chap. VI between notes 54 and 56.

5. The former *Mental Health Act* in Ontario was sufficiently general in its terms as to legitimize detainment in a mental hospital for such reason. Section 8(1) provided for involuntary detention if "any person"

> a suffers from mental disorder of a nature or degree so as to require hospitalization *in the interests of his own safety* or the safety of others; and
>
> b is not suitable for admission as an informal patient.

260

Section 9(1) provided that a Justice of the Peace may require a psychiatric examination if a person

    a is believed to be suffering from *mental disorder*; and
    b should be examined *in the interest of his own safety* or the safety of others.

Section 10 provided that a peace officer may detain a person for medical examination if the person is

    a *apparently* suffering from *mental disorder*; and
    b acting in a manner that in a *normal* person would be disorderly.

The Mental Health Act, R.S.O. 1970, c. 269. Emphasis added.

The latest amendments to the Ontario Mental Health Act (Bill 124, 1st sess., 31st Leg., Ont., 26 Eliz. II, 1977) do try to foreclose detainment for reason only of the patient's thoughts or feelings in that "bodily harm" is the criterion. However, the Bill does, in a paternalistic fashion, legalize detainment when the patient is likely to cause "serious bodily harm" or "imminent and serious physical impairment" to himself (Sections 2, 3 and 4). In addition, the police officer would appear to be able to consider the person's feelings and thoughts in that Section 4 gives the officer authority to detain if he "observes a person who acts in a manner that in a *normal* person would be disorderly and..." Emphasis added. For the objectionable features of such provisions see generally, text, supra, chap. VI, sect. e.

    6.   Kenneth L. Karst, *Foreward: Equal Citizenship under the Fourteenth Amendment*, 91 Harv. L. Rev. 1, p. 8 (1977).

    7.   Donald Keim, "Participation in Contemporary Democratic Theories," in *Participation in Politics: Nomos XVI*, J. Roland Pennock and John W. Chapman, ed., (N.Y.: Lieber-Atherton, 1975), p. 29.

    8.   Donald Keim, ibid., p. 12. Keim questions "the facile identification of participation in decisions that significantly *affect* one's destiny with participation in decisions that immediately *touch* one's life." Keim continues, "objective control and the subjective sense of political efficacy may be related, but the latter is not an adequate substitute for the former."

    9.   W. R. Bishin, *Judicial Review in Democratic Theory*, 50 Southern Calif. L. Rev. 1099, p. 1126 (1977).

    10. Text, supra, chap. III between notes 58 and 71.

    11. *Reynolds* v. *Sims*, 377 U.S. 533, 84 S. Ct. 1362, 12 L. Ed. 2d 506 (1964).

    12. *Harper* v. *Virginia Board of Elections*, 383 U.S. 663, 86 S. Ct. 1079, 16 L. Ed. 2d 169 (1966).

    13. *Kramer* v. *Union Free School District No. 15*, 395 U.S. 621, 89 S. Ct. 1886, 23 L. Ed. 2d 583 (1969).

    14. Text, supra, between notes 51 and 67.

    15. Text, supra, between notes 62 and 67.

    16. John D. Hodson, *Nozick, Libertarianism and Rights*, 19 Arizona L. Rev. 212 (1977).

    17. Robert Nozick, *Anarchy, State and Utopia* (N.Y.: Basic Books, 1974).

18. Nozick, ibid., pp. ix, 26.

19. Ibid., chap. 7.

20. *San Antonio Independent School Dist* v. *Rodriquez*, 411 U.S. 1, 98 S. Ct. 1278 (1973).

21. Text, supra, chap. III at note 82.

22. Section 133 of the British North America Act, 1867 provides that

> either the English or the French language may be used by any person in the debates of the Houses of the Parliament of Canada and of the Houses of the Legislature of Quebec; and both those languages shall be used in the respective records and journals of those houses; and either of those languages may be used by any person or in any pleading or process in or issuing from any Court of Canada established under this Act, and in or from all or any of the Courts of Quebec.

23. See generally, for example, Claude-Armand Sheppard's *The Law of Languages in Canada* (Information Canada, 1971), pp. 67-69.

24. *Articles of the Capitulation of Quebec, 1759 and of Montreal, 1760* as reprinted in William Houston, *Documents Illustrative of the Canadian Constitution* (New York: Books for Libraries Press, 1891, 1970 reprint), pp. 27 ff., 33 ff.

25. *Treaty of Paris, 1763* extracts of which are reprinted in William Houston, ibid., p. 61.

26. *Quebec Act, 1774* as reprinted in William Houston, ibid., p. 90.

27. The Legislative Assembly confirmed the primacy of the French language in Quebec by resolving 21 to 15 on December 27th, 1792 that the Journals of the Assembly be printed in both languages. After 1791 statutes were enacted in both languages. On January 23rd, 1793, the Assembly made both languages equal as a source of law. See generally, Sheppard, ibid., pp. 3-53.

28. The Legislature in the United Canadas reaffirmed and expanded the use of French in pleadings, judicial proceedings and jury selection in enactments dated 1843, 1846, 1847, 1849, 1855 and 1864. For documented support for these and other judicial and legislative acknowledgments of the French language see generally William E. Conklin, "Constitutional Ideology, Language Rights and Political Disunity in Canada," to be published in *Language, Law and Development*, L. Marasinghe and William E. Conklin, eds., (Colombo: Lake House Publishers, 1980) and 1979 U.N.B.L.J. 39.

29. *R.* v. *Talon* K.B., 1813 as reported in Nantel, Marechal, "La langue française au palais," 5 *R. du B.* pp. 201-216 (1945) and cited in Sheppard, supra, note 23, p. 31.

30. For example, notwithstanding the fact that the constitutional document which established the province of Manitoba (The Manitoba Act, 1870, Sect. 23) required the use of French or English in the Legislature, the legislative records, journals and statutes, and in the Courts, the Manitoba Legislature abolished these guarantees in 1890 (Stat. Man. 1890, 53 Vict., c. 14). The latter has only recently been challenged in the higher courts. Also see *Ottawa Separate School Trustees* v. *Mackell* [1917] A.C. 62 where the Privy Council (per Lord Buckmaster L.C.) held constitutional certain Ontario regulations

which had provided that the use of French was not to be continued beyond the first grade in either public or separate schools without the approval of the government's chief inspector (cl. 3). The inspectors were required to report if any school was not properly enforcing this regulation. All teachers in schools where French was the language of instruction, were required to possess a sufficient knowledge of English to teach the prescribed courses of study (d.13).

For the lack of support for fundamental linguistic rights for the French speaking community in our constitutional history over the past 100 years see generally Claude-Armand Sheppard, *The Law of Languages in Canada* (Ottawa: Info. Can., 1971); Ontario Advisory Committee on Confederation, "French-language Public secondary schools in Ontario," in *The Confederation Challenge (Background Papers and Reports)*, (Toronto: Govt. of Ont., 1970), vol. 2, p. 256 ff.; and Royal Commission on Education in Ontario, *Report* (Toronto: Queen's Printer, 1950), chap. 16.

31.   Text, supra, chap. III between notes 26 and 39.

32.   Richard Fielding cited the single anomalous case as *Morey v. Doud*, 354 U.S. 457, 77 S. Ct. 1344 (1957); Fielding, *Fundamental Personal Rights: Another Approach to Equal Protection*, 40 U. Chi. L. Rev. 807, p. 811 (1973).

33.   Text, supra, chap. III between notes 76 and 82.

34.   *Buckley* v. *Valeo*, 424 U.S. 1, 96 S. Ct. 612, 46 L. Ed. 2d 659 (1976).

35.   *Buckley* v. *Valeo, per curiam* ibid., at U.S. 19, S. Ct. 634-5.

36.   *Buckley* v. *Valeo*, per Marshall J. ibid., at U.S. 287, S. Ct. 759.

37.   Ronald Dworkin, *Taking Rights Seriously* (Cambridge, Mass.: Harv. U. Press, 1977).

38.   See generally, text, infra, between notes 44 and 52.

39.   Ronald Dworkin, "Taking Rights Seriously," in *Taking Rights Seriously*, supra, note 37, p. 188.

40.   Ibid., p. 188.

> The claim that citizens have a right to free speech must imply that it would be wrong for the government to stop them from speaking, even when the government believes what they will say will cause more harm than good. The claim cannot mean... only that citizens do no wrong in speaking their minds, though the government reserves the right to prevent them from doing so.

41.   Ibid., pp. 133, 139 ("Constitutional Cases").

42.   Ibid., p. 169 ("Justice and Rights").

43.   Ibid., p. 190 ("Taking Rights Seriously").

44.   Ibid., pp. 191-192.

45.   Jeremy Bentham, *An Introduction to the Principles of Morals and Legislation*, (L. J. Lafleur ed., New York: Hafner, 1948), chap. 3, para. 1 [hereinafter cited as *An Introduction*]:

> The happiness of the individuals, of whom a community is composed, that is their pleasures and their security, is the end and the sole end

which the legislator ought to have in view: the sole standard, in conformity to which each individual ought, as far as depends upon the legislator, to be MADE to fashion his behaviour.

See also Jeremy Bentham, *A Fragment on Government* (F. Montague ed., Oxford: Clarendon Press, 1891), [hereinafter cited as *A Fragment*]; John Stuart Mill, *Utilitarianism* in *Essential Works of John Stuart Mill* (Max Lerner ed., New York, Toronto, London: Bantam Books, 1961), p. 194: "pleasures and freedom from pain are the only things desirable as ends"; and John Austin, *Lectures on Jurisprudence*, 2nd ed., (1861, New York: Lennox Hill reprint, 1970), vol. 1, p. 264.

46. Jeremy Bentham, *An Introduction*, ibid., chap. 1, para. 2; *A Fragment*, ibid., chap. 1, para. 45.

47. See text, supra, chap. II, notes 53 and 54.

48. John Austin, *Lectures*, supra, note 45, p. 241.

49. John Stuart Mill, *Utilitarianism*, supra, note 45, p. 247. Mill suggested that an individual would succumb to the dictates of social expediency because "a human being is capable of apprehending a community of interest between himself and the human society of which he forms a part", ibid., p. 236. When he asked himself a few pages later as to why society ought to protect an individual's rights he could only respond, "I can give him no other reason than general utility". Ibid., p. 238.

50. Jeremy Bentham, *An Introduction*, supra note 45, chap. 1, para. 4.

51. David J. Manning, *The Mind of Jeremy Bentham* (London: Longmans, 1968), p. 78.

52. See generally, supra, note 1 as well as the Appendix infra.

53. Ronald Dworkin, "Hard Cases", supra, note 37, p. 93. His examples are the rights to free speech, dignity and equality.

54. Ibid., p. 82. See his treatment of Learned Hand's theory of negligence at pp. 98-100.

55. Ibid., p. 92 ("Hard Cases"). He cites "the ordinary, routine goals of political administration" as an example of the situation where a collective goal cannot outweigh a right.

Also see Dworkin's essays "Taking Rights Seriously" and "Constitutional Cases" in supra, note 37, at pp. 188 and 138 respectively.

56. Ibid., p. 188 ("Taking Rights Seriously").

57. Ibid., p. 138 ("Constitutional Cases").

58. This essay, initially entitled "Lord Devlin and the Enforcement of Morals", seems to have been Dworkin's first major published effort. His later essays appear to build upon it. See generally, text, infra between notes 130 and 134.

59. Ronald Dworkin, "Reverse Discrimination," supra, note 37, p. 228, note 1. Emphasis added. See especially Dworkin's critique of Bentham's "preference utilitarianism" at pp. 231-234.

60. Ibid. pp. 253-254 ("Liberty and Moralism"), quoting from Lord Devlin, *The Enforcement of Morals* (New York, Toronto: Oxford Univ. Press, 1965), pp. 15 and 22-23.

61. Ronald Dworkin, supra, note 37, chap. 4.

62. See text, supra, corresponding to note 44. Also see text, supra, corresponding to note 42. In addition, Dworkin defines "individual rights" in his "Introduction" as "political trumps held by individuals. Individuals have rights when, for some reason, a collective goal is not a sufficient justification for denying them what they wish, as individuals, to have or to do, or not a sufficient justification for imposing some loss or injury upon them" at p. xi. And in "Constitutional Cases" at pp. 138-9 of *Taking Rights Seriously*, Dworkin asserts that his essay "Taking Rights Seriously" had defined a moral right against the state in this way: "if for some reason the state would do wrong to treat him in a certain way, even though it would be in the general interest to do so."

63. *Schenck* v. *United States*, 249 U.S. 47, 39. S. Ct. 247, 63 L. Ed. 470 (1919).

64. *Dennis* v. *United States*, 341 U.S. 494, 71 S. Ct. 857, 95 L. Ed. 1137 (1951).

65. *Schenck* v. *United States*, 249 U.S. 47, 39 S. Ct. 247, 63 L. Ed. 470 (1919).

66. *Frohwerk* v. *United States*, 249 U.S. 204, 39 S. Ct. 249, 63 L. Ed. 561 (1919).

67. *Debs* v. *United States*, 249 U.S. 211, 39 S. Ct. 252, 63 L. Ed. 566 (1919).

68. See Justice Holmes' letters uncovered by Gerald Gunther in *Learned Hand and the Origins of Modern First Amendment Doctrine: Some Fragments of History*, 27 Stanford L. Rev. 719 (1975).
Holmes' letters to Laski and Pollock during the same period, however, do indicate that Holmes found it quite difficult to write the court's judgments in *Schenck, Frohwerk* and *Debs*. He regretted that the government had pressed the cases and hoped that the President would pardon the convicted parties. He seemed to believe that he had no choice but no apply the law and that the law gave little protection to free speech. See *Holmes-Laski Letters: 1916-1935*, M. D. Howe ed., (Cambridge: Harvard U. Press, 1953), pp. 190 and 203.

69. *Abrams* v. *United States*, 250 U.S. 616, 40 S. Ct. 17 (1919).

70. See, for example, Gerald Gunther's *Cases and Materials on Constitutional Law* (9th ed., Mineola Foundation Press, 1975) at pp. 1061-1068 and *Learned Hand and the Origins of Modern First Amendment Doctrine: Some Fragments of History*, supra, note 68.

71. The only possible rule was Section 3 of Title I of the 1917 Espionage Act which was also at issue in the *Schenck Frohwerk* and *Debs* cases. See text, supra, following note 67.

72. *Abrams* v. *United States*, 250 U.S. 616, 630; 40 S. Ct. 17, 22 (1919). Emphasis added.

73. Ibid.

74. *Gitlow* v. *New York*, 268 U.S. 652, 45 S. Ct. 625, 69 L. Ed. 1138 (1925).

75. *Whitney* v. *California*, 274 U.S. 357, 47 S. Ct. 641, 71 L. Ed. 1095 (1927).

76. The Criminal Syndicalism Act provided that anyone "who is or

knowingly becomes a member of any organization... organized or assembled to advocate, teach or aid and abet criminal syndicalism" was guilty of a felony. Criminal syndicalism was defined as "any doctrine or precept advocating, teaching or aiding and abetting the commission of crime, sabotage... or unlawful acts of force and violence or unlawful methods of terrorism as a means of accomplishing a change in industrial ownership or control, or affecting any political change."

77. As Justice Brandeis explained in *Whitney* v. *California*, 274 U.S. 357, 376, 47 S. Ct. 641, 648:

> This Court has not yet fixed the standard by which to determine when a danger shall be deemed clear; how remote the danger may be and yet be deemed present; and what degree of evil shall be deemed sufficiently substantial to justify resort to abridgment of free speech and assembly as the means of protection. To reach sound conclusions on these matters, we must bear in mind why a state is, ordinarily,...

78. Ibid.

79. *Dennis* v. *United States*, 341 U.S. 494, 71 S. Ct. 857, 95 L. Ed. 1137 (1951).

80. Ibid., per Vinson J. at U.S. 510, S. Ct. 868 quoting from Justice Hand, who wrote the majority judgment in *Dennis* in the Court of Appeals, Second Circuit, 183 F. 2d 201, 212.

81. Ibid., per Douglas J. at U.S. 585, S. Ct. 905:

> There comes a time when even speech loses its constitutional immunity. Speech innocuous one year may at another time fan such destructive flames that it must be halted in the interests of the safety of the Republic. That is the meaning of the clear and present danger test...

Douglas J. went on to state that although the First Amendment provides no exception to free speech, this did not mean "that the nation need hold its hand until it is in such weakened condition that there is no time to protect itself from incitement to revolution. Seditious conduct can always be punished. Ibid., at U.S. 590, S. Ct. 907.

82. See generally, William E. Conklin, *The Utilitarian Theory of Equality Before the Law*, 8 Ottawa Law Rev. 485 (1976).

83. The Supreme Court of Canada has adopted such a weak sense of rights in the "right to counsel" cases that one is hard pressed to suggest that there is a right, let alone fundamental right, to counsel in Canada. See the cases summarized in text, supra, chap. II, notes 82 and 86.

84. *R.* v. *Miller & Cockriell* (1977) 70 D.L.R. (3d) 324, [1976] 5 W.W.R. 711 (S.C.C.); *R.* v. *Shand* (1977) 70 D.L.R. (3d) 395, (1977) 13 O.R. (2d) 65 (Ont. C.A.); *McCann et al* v. *The Queen* (1976) 68 D.L.R. (3d) 661 (Fed. Ct., T.D.). See generally, William Conklin, "Capital Punishment and a Democratic Society," to be published in Julio Menezes, ed., *Decade of Adjustment: Legal Perspectives on contemporary Canadian Issues*, (Toronto: Macmillan & Co., 1979).

85. The utilitarian presuppositions of contempt are most clearly articulated in *A-G* v. *Times Newspapers*, [1974] A.C. 292 (H.L.). For some Cana-

dian examples see *R.* v. *McKeown,* [1971] S.C.R. 446; *R.* v. *Carocchia* (1974), 43 D.L.R. (3d) 427, 15 C.C.C. (2d) 175 (Que, C.A.); *Re Ouellet (Nos. 1 & 2)* (1977), 72 D.L.R. (3d) 95 (Que, C.A.); *Vallieres* v. *The Queen; Gagnon* v. *The Queen* (1974), 47 D.L.R. (3d) 378, 25 C.R. (N.S.) 217 (Que. C.A.).

86. See, for example, *R.* v. *Brodie,* [1962] S.C.R. 681, 132 C.C.C. 161, 37 C.R. 120; *Dominion News & Gifts Ltd.* v. *The Queen,* [1964] S.C.R. 251, (1964) 3 C.C.C. 1, 42 C.R. 209; *R.* v. *Coles Co. Ltd.,* [1965] 1 O.R. 557, [1965] 2 C.C.C. 304, 44 C.R. 219, 49 D.L.R. (2d) 34 (Ont. C.A.). Note, in particular, the Canada Law Reform Commission's justification of "public obscenity" laws, infra, note 88; Graham Hughes, *Morals and the Criminal Law,* 71 Yale L.J. 662, pp. 665-666 and 678-683 (1962), and Robert Paul Wolff, *The Poverty of Liberalism* (Boston; Beacon Press, 1968).

87. *The Nova Scotia Board of Censors for A-G for N.S.* v. *McNeil,* [1978] 2 S.C.R. 662.

88. See, for example, *Limits of Criminal Law* (Working Paper # 10, 1975). At p. 16 the paper argues that immorality alone is an insufficient reason to apply the criminal law sanction. Only the most harmful conduct justifies its use. But at pp. 21, 35 and 44 the paper identifies harmful conduct with conduct which threatens or infringes upon "essential" societal values. The paper can thereby justify the validity of a crime of public obscenity (see pp. 23-25) in that public obscenity causes harm to "important" values. There is a sense in which the paper justifies public obscenity in Devlinite terms, notwithstanding its initial disclaimer that immorality alone is an insufficient reason to apply the criminal law sanction. See, e.g., pp. 29-31, 37-38, 42. The paper does not explain why it chooses the "essential values" that it does (i.e., "dignity", "liberty" and "peace"). Nor does it put much, if any, content into those values. Note the paper's utilitarian concern with the most appropriate *means* to control obscenity such as by administrative control rather than criminal sanction at p. 47 (for utilitarianism's focus upon the means rather than the ends see text, supra, between notes 49 and 50). Clearly, the paper is subject to the same criticisms which I made of the "shock the conscience" form of determining society's contemporary values in chapter two. In the light of my arguments raised in chapter II, IV and VI, it is difficult to support the reasoning of the paper if we want a society founded upon fundamental rights.

For other examples of the weak sense of rights adopted by the Canada Law Reform Commission see, e.g., *Report: Our Criminal Law* (Ottawa: Info. Can., 1976), pp. 5-7, 27-30; *Contempt of Court* (Working Paper 20), (Ottawa: Info. Can., 1977), pp. 22-24, 34, 41; *Report: Mental Disorder in the Criminal Process* (Ottawa: Info. Can., 1976), p. 2; *The Meaning of Guilt: strict liability* (Working Paper 2), (Ottawa: Info. Can., 1974), pp. 4-8; *Sexual Offences* (Working Paper 22), (Ottawa: Info. Can., 1978), pp. 4-5.

89. See supra, note 1.

90. *Boucher* v. *R.,* [1951] S.C.R. 265; (1951), 2 D.L.R. 369; (1950), 99 C.C.C. 1; (1951), 11 C.R. 85, (S.C.C. 2nd hearing); revg (1950), 1 D.L.R. 657; (1949), 96 C.C.C. 48; 9 C.R. 127 (S.C.C., 1st hearing).

91. Paul Weiler, *In the Last Resort* (Toronto: Carswell/Methuen, 1974), p. 192.

92. Boucher was convicted under Sect. 133 of the Canadian Criminal Code:

> 1) Seditious words are words expressive of a seditious intention.
> 2) A seditious libel is a libel expressive of a seditious intention.
> 3) A seditious conspiracy is an agreement between two or more persons to carry into execution a seditious intention.
> 4) Without limiting the generality of the meaning of the expression "seditious intention" everyone shall be presumed to have a seditious intention who publishes, or circulates any writing, printing or document in which it is advocated, or who teaches or advocates, the use, without the authority of law, of force, as a means of accomplishing any governmental change within Canada.

This must be read with Sect. 133A which provides

> No one shall be deemed to have a seditious intention only because he intends in good faith, —
> a) to show that His Majesty has been misled or mistaken in his measures; or
> b) to point out errors or defects in the government or constitution of the United Kingdom, or of any part of it, or of Canada or any province thereof, or in either House of Parliament of the United Kingdom or of Canada, or in any Legislature, or in the administration of justice; or to excite His Majesty's subjects to attempt to procure, by lawful means the alteration of any matter in the state; or
> c) to point out, in order to their removal, matters which are producing or have a tendency to produce feelings of hatred and ill-will between different classes of His Majesty's subjects.

For a study of the political context surrounding the origins of the chief elements of this offence see William E. Conklin, *The Origins of the Law of Sedition*, 15 Crim. L.Q. 277, pp. 290-300 (1973).

93. *Roncarelli* v. *Duplessis*, [1959] S.C.R. 121; 16 D.L.R. (2d) 689 (S.C.C.).

94. *Boucher* v. *R.*, [1951] S.C.R. 265, 277; (1950) 1 D.L.R. 657, 666 (S.C.C., 1st hearing).

95. (1950) 1 D.L.R. 657, 676-677 (1st hearing).

96. [1951] S.C.R. 265, 288; (1950) 1 D.L.R. 657, 682.

97. Ibid., S.C.R. 289; D.L.R. 683. Emphasis added.

98. *Boucher* v. *R.*, [1951] S.C.R. 265, 283; (1951) 2 D.L.R. 369, 379 (S.C.C., 2nd hearing). Emphasis added.

99. *R.* v. *Sullivan* (1868), 11 Cox C.C. 44, 45.

100. *Boucher* v. *R.*, [1951] S.C.R. 265, 296-297, (1951) 2 D.L.R. 369, 384 (S.C.C., 2nd hearing). Emphasis added.

101. Ibid., S.C.R. 315, D.L.R. 393. Emphasis added.

102. Ibid., S.C.R. 333, D.L.R. 409. Emphasis added.

103. Thomas I. Emerson, *Towards A General Theory of the First Amendment*, 72 Yale L.J. 877 (1963). Also see Charles L. Black, *The People and The Court* (New York: Macmillan, 1960), pp. 217-221.

268

104. *Yates* v. *U.S.*, 354 U.S. 298, 77 S. Ct. 1064 (1957).

105. See text, infra, between notes 150 and 151.

106. Thomas Emerson, supra, note 103, p. 955. Emphasis added.

107. *Yates* v. *U.S.*, 354 U.S. 298, 344, 77 S. Ct. 1064, 1090 (1957).

108. Ronald Dworkin, supra, note 37, pp. 14-15 ("The Model of Rules I"), p. 62 ("The Model of Rules II") and pp. 101-105 ("Hard Cases").

109. Ibid., p. 27 ("The Model of Rules I").

110. Ibid., p. 37 ("The Model of Rules I"):

> First, it is necessary, though not sufficient, that the judge find that the change would advance *some policy* or serve some principle, which policy or principle thus justifies the change. [Emphasis added].

111. Ibid., p. 67 ("The Model of Rules II").

112. Ibid., p. 24.

113. Ibid., p. 25.

114. Ibid., p. 26:

> A principle like "No man may profit from his own wrong" does not even purport to set out conditions that make its application necessary.

115. Ibid., p. 24.

116. Ibid., pp. 82, 90 ("Hard Cases").

117. Ibid., p. 90.

118. Ibid., p. 27 ("The Model of Rules I").

119. Ibid., p. 93 ("Hard Cases"). His examples are the rights to free speech, dignity and equality.

120. Ibid., p. 93.

121. Ibid., p. 82. See his treatment of Learned Hand's theory of negligence at pp. 98-100.

122. Ibid., p. 93.

123. Ibid., pp. 104-105.

124. Ronald Dworkin, *Does Law have a Function? A Comment on the Two-Level Theory of Decision*, 74 Yale L.J. 640 (1965). The example which Dworkin provides is a constitutional restraint forbidding slavery even though an economist might demonstrate to everyone's satisfaction that slavery of persons whose I.Q. falls below a given level would advance the forward-looking goal of "the greatest happiness of the greatest number".

In "The Model of Rules 1" in *Taking Rights Seriously*, supra, note 37, p. 22 he defines a "policy" as "that kind of standard that sets out *a goal* to be reached, generally an improvement in some economic, political, or social feature of the community... I call a principle a standard that is to be observed, not because it will advance or secure an economic, political, or social situation *deemed desirable*, but because it is a *requirement of justice or fairness in some other dimension of morality*." Emphasis added.

125. I use these terms in the sense elaborated by E. A. Driedger in *The Construction of Statutes* (Toronto: Butterworths, 1974).

126. Ronald Dworkin, *Taking Rights Seriously*, supra, note 37, pp. 82-83 ("Hard Cases").

127. Ronald Dworkin, *Does Law have a Function?: A Comment on the Two-Level Theory of Decision*, 74 Yale L.J. 640, 647 (1965):

> Indeed, it might be that the legal process should itself be viewed as operating on two levels, like the two levels on which Wasserstrom urges that courts should operate. Perhaps an assumed, overriding goal like utility is best advanced if courts make rules on the basis of PRESENT community standards, principles, and policies... without reference to their utility, and legislatures or other institutions test the utility of such principles and policies, substituting others if they find the incumbents wanting. I indicated earlier that I regard the assumption of a fundamental social goal as chimerical, even as a legislative standard. But it is odd that Wasserstrom, who apparently does not, never considers a more inclusive two-level procedure as a possible technique for insuring the long-distance progress of the entire legal system toward that goal.

128. This is not to suggest, however, that Wasserstrom's model is entirely forward-looking. Wasserstrom's model is backward-looking at the "first level" of analysis when a judge must initially examine whether a particular court relates to some general moral or legal rule. His model is alleged to be "forward-looking" in that the judge must then question whether the rule is justifiable in the great majority of cases in terms of its consequences upon the general welfare. See Richard A. Wasserstrom, *The Judicial Decision* (Stanford: Stanford U. Press, 1961), pp. 119-120 and chap. 7.

129. Ronald Dworkin, supra, note 37, p. 26 ("The Model of Rules I"). Emphasis added.

130. Ibid., p. 22. Emphasis added.

131. Ibid., chap. 10 ("Liberty and Moralism").

132. Ibid., pp. 249-250.

133. John Stuart Mill, *On Liberty*, (Mary Warnock ed., Glasgow: William Collins & Sons, 1962), p. 131:

> but an opinion on a point of conduct, not *supported by reasons*, can only count as one person's *preference*; and if the reasons, when given, are a mere appeal to a similar preference felt by other people, it is still only many people's liking instead of one. [Emphasis added].

134. Ronald Dworkin, supra, note 37, p. 119 ("Hard Cases").

135. Ibid., p. 40 ("The Model of Rules I").

136. Ibid., pp. 172-173 ("Justice and Rights").

137. Ibid., chap. 10 ("Liberty and Moralism").

138. See text, supra, corresponding to notes 133 and 135.

139. Ronald Dworkin, supra, note 37, p. 87 ("Hard Cases"). Note that Dworkin expressly refers the reader to his chapter on "Justice and Rights" in his note 1 at p. 87.

140. Ibid., p. 161 ("Justice and Rights").

141. Ibid., p. 162.

142. Ibid.

143. Ibid., pp. 162-3.

144. Ibid.

145. Ibid., p. 22 ("The Model of Rules I").

146. Ibid., p. 14. Emphasis added.

147. Ibid., p. 49 ("The Model of Rules II").

148. Ibid., p. 79.

149. Ibid., Emphasis added.

150. Ibid., p. 89 ("Hard Cases").

151. Ibid., p. 40 ("The Model of Rules I"). Also see Raz, *Legal Principles and the Limits of Law*, 81 Yale L.J. 823, p. 848 (1972).

152. Ronald Dworkin, "Constitutional Cases", supra, note 37, p. 136.

The customary principles which Dworkin considers as a source of law are no more entrenched than the principles of customary constitutional law of the Canadian and British Constitutions. See, e.g., the writings of Sir Ivor Jennings who once defined the English Constitution as "the rules governing the composition, powers and methods of operation of the main institutions of government and the *general principles* applicable to their relations to the citizen" as cited in J. D. Whyte and W. R. Lederman, *Canadian Constitutional Law* (Toronto: Butterworths, 1975), p. vi. Also see Dicey, *The Law of the Constitution*, (Wade ed., 1962, London: Macmillan, 1885), especially his chapter on "The Nature of Conventions of the Constitution", chap. 14; J. N. Lyon and R. G. Atkey, *Canadian Constitutional Law in a Modern Perspective* (Toronto: Univ. of Toronto Press, 1970), pp. 70 ff.; and M. Dawson, *The Government of Canada* (5th ed., Toronto: Univ. of Toronto Press, 1970), chap. 4.

153. Ronald Dworkin, "Hard Cases", supra, note 37, p. 127.

154. Ibid., pp. 129, 121. A mistaken assessment would be one which is inconsistent with the principles embedded in the materials or which is inadequate in its assessment.

155. Ibid., pp. 89, 105-106.

156. See text, supra, between notes 74 and 79.

157. *Masses Publishing Co.* v. *Patten*, 244 Fed. 535 (1917), Dist. Ct., S.D. New York.

158. Ibid., 539.

159. Ibid., 539-540. Emphasis added.

160. Ibid., Emphasis added.

161. Ibid., 540, 542-543.

162. Gerald Gunther, *Learned Hand the Origins of Modern First Amendment Doctrine: Some Fragments of History*, 27 Stanford L. Rev. 719, 725 (1975).

163. The reader might consider my criticism unrealistic since a lawyer's "soundest theory of law" under the Dworkinian model would include "virtually every principle of social or political morality that has currency in his community and that he personally accepts, except those excluded by constitutional considerations..." There would be variant conclusions about difficult legal issues presumably even in a society with amoral traditions.

In response to this possible objection, history has not witnessed my point to be unrealistic. Furthermore, Dworkin clearly intended his model to cover all societies — not just the American society with its abundance of "institutional support" for individual rights. Even if the problem as described were an "unrealistic" one, Dworkin's requirements of coherence and articulate consistency would demand that we examine the conceptual implications of his own model. Finally, my criticism arises because Dworkin contemplated that a judge may realize that some of his own moral beliefs do not have currency in the community.

164. Ronald Dworkin, "Hard Cases," supra, note 37, p. 126 and "Constitutional Cases," ibid., p. 139. Also see text, supra, between notes 132 and 136.

165. Ibid., pp. 162-163 ("Justice and Rights").

166. Ibid., pp. 161-163.

167. Ibid., p. 169.

168. Ibid., p. 87 ("Hard Cases").

Conclusion

This study has asked whether an argument could be made which could consistently support the existence of fundamental rights. Why is any fundamental right fundamental? What distinguishes a right from a fundamental right? If a society wishes or believes itself to be founded upon fundamental rights, how does one proceed to translate that belief into legislative, judicial and constitutional principles? These issues have been placed before us.

The inquiry began by examining the responses which have been offered by jurists in Canada, the United States and Great Britain. One argument for fundamental rights, initially developed by Chief Justice Coke in the early seventeenth century, looked backward into underlying common law principles. The Chief Justice had responded to the Tudor monarchs who, in turn, had shifted ultimate constitutional authority from the common law courts to the King's Council and the prerogative courts. Various factors had undermined the judiciary's independence and the judicial function itself. Chief Justice Coke wanted to restore the authority of common law judges by a technique of argument which uncovered legal precedents of centuries past. Coke C.J. demonstrated this technique of analysis in such cases as *Prohibitions del Roy*, the *Case of Lords President of Wales and York*, the *Case of Prohibitions*, and *Dr. Bonham's Case*. His approach was reflected in his *Institutes* and in his commentary on judgments as he reported them in his *Reports*.

Two American and one Canadian constitutional judgments were then used to show how Chief Justice Coke's backward-looking argument is unsatisfactory. First, the Chief Justice's method of argument was designed to secure a static, confining society. Secondly, conceptually speaking, his argument could sustain very few fundamental rights for if there were a fundamental right, it had to have already existed in the law and consistently persisted as a principle over past centuries. This problem, in turn, had several consequences. There could be no fundamental right if a legal tradition were silent upon an issue. There could be few rights in any society which evolved fairly rapidly. Those rights which did exist would unlikely grow in scope or number. The uncovering of long standing principles could be a highly subjective pursuit. In addition, Chief Justice Coke's argument could consistently sustain both tyranny and slavery if the legal tradition lacked principles proscribing such practices. I ushered forth historical evidence of Coke C.J.'s own day to demonstrate the serious possibility of these problems.

The Chief Justice's method of argument was then used to see whether one could uncover fundamental rights of political participation and religious conscience in the Canadian legal tradition. The conclusion is warranted that the equal right of political participation was established only relatively recently, and by statute rather than by common law principles. Although the Roman Catholic religion in Ontario and Quebec occupied a protected constitutional position in our legal tradition, constitutional documents as well as judicial pronouncements in *Saumur, Henry Birks* and *Robertson and Rosetanni* suggested that freedom of religious conscience is not a fundamental freedom in Canada in the sense of being "at the root of the matter", "essential", "basic", "underlying", "primary", "formative", or "irreducible".

A second method of argument which Canadian, British and American jurists have employed has been to ascertain the contemporary values of society. Lord Devlin on the British side and Justices Marshall, Cardozo and Frankfurter on the American attempted to ascertain those values by questioning whether any particular conduct shocked the conscience of society. Jeremy Bentham advocated an intricate method of determining the "majority will". Mr. Justice Pigeon and other Canadian jurists have fallen back upon the supremacy of the legislature as the means for depicting society's contemporary values.

The constitutional experiences in the United States and Canada have demonstrated that each of these forms of argument had major shortcomings. The determination and scope of fundamental rights under the "shock the conscience" form was highly subjective, discretionary, productive of *ad hoc* rights, inapplicable in a country such as Canada which possesses a variety of cultures with centuries-old conflicting legal traditions, and unsatisfactory as a means for providing a principled criterion for deciding which rights are fundamental and which are not.

Bentham's "majority will" form of argument proved impossible to apply to moral values. Bentham's argument provided for no theoretical limit upon which the majority could restrict rights. As a consequence, rights under his scheme could not be considered fundamental.

The final form, legislative supremacy, ironically could not foreclose the necessity for judges to make significant moral-political judgments. As the experience with the Canadian Bill of Rights demonstrates, the Canadian judiciary have been compelled to construe the meaning and scope of freedoms which Parliament clearly and imperatively declared to be fundamental. The Canadian experience also shows that, where the roots of fundamental rights are considered to be society's contemporary values as reflected in legislative enactments, those roots can be very shallow in practice. In addition, a right can hardly be considered fundamental if the legislature creates all rights, determines their meaning and scope, and may destroy them. Finally, political science studies have showed how legislative supremacy is no longer a realistic viable foundation for fundamental rights in Canada or England in that the legislature is no longer the supreme political institution in the body politic.

It is often believed that the ultimate protection of fundamental rights is the entrenchment of a Bill of Rights in a written Constitution. The conclusion is warranted from chapter III that this is not so because judges, legislators and bureaucrats must still make normative political judgments. An entrenched Bill of Rights, for example, does not resolve the meaning and scope of the guarantees. Nor does it resolve the problem of the level of judicial scrutiny of legislation, administrative conduct and common law principles. The American constitutional experience demonstrates that counsel cannot possibly approach these issues without journeying beyond the traditional common law resources into the world of normative political philosophy.

Because the initial problem of trying to elaborate an argument in support of fundamental rights compels one to go beyond the traditional resources available to a common law lawyer, Part Two examined the two most important contributions to the concept of liberty in Anglo-American political philosophy during the past century: John Stuart Mill's *On Liberty* and John Rawls' *A Theory of Justice*. Chapter IV elaborated what Mill meant by the term "the inner sphere of life" and it showed how his notion was related to liberty generally. Two forms of utilitarianism, Benthamite and rule utilitarianism, were then examined in order to see whether either form could justify the protection of "self-regarding" conduct in a variety of concrete cases. Neither form of utilitarianism could do so. Indeed, a Benthamite utilitarian could not even accept a *prima facie* presumption that "self-regarding" conduct ought to be protected. Generally, the outcome of a Benthamite calculation hinged upon the circumstances of any particular case. Factual circumstances were conceived whereby society could interfere with "self-regarding" conduct in the three classes of cases considered. A rule utilitarian could not accept the proposition that the individual ought to reign uncontrolled in the "inner sphere" of his life in all cases. The rule utilitarian had to take account of exceptions as, for example, a case where it could be established that the public display of homosexual conduct would gravely loosen society's moral fabric. As in the case of attempted suicide, one's own good, both physical and moral, could justify intervention into "self-regarding" conduct in some cases, by some means but not by others. Society's "preferences" were relevant if those feelings of disgust were "essential to [society's] existence."

Because of utilitarianism's unsatisfactory conclusions, one is led to re-examine Mill's own arguments for the protection of "self-regarding" conduct. Chapter IV found that Mill's own arguments did not succeed and that this stemmed in large part because he valued "self-regarding" conduct for its instrumental importance to society's welfare rather than for the intrinsic worth of the individual. In addition, Mill left it to society as a whole to impose initial obligations upon the individual. These two problems characterised the utilitarian perspective as a whole as well as Mill's *On Liberty*.

John Rawls seriously attempted to break away from the utilitarian trap. Chapter V outlined the central elements of his theory of fundamental rights: namely, that one basic liberty should be weighed against another so as to produce "the best total system of equal liberty"; that the basic liberties "roughly speaking" compose the traditional liberal civil rights; and, thirdly, that liberty could be restricted only for a greater system of liberty for all. Each of these elements, however, left critical issues unresolved. Rawls did not guide us as to the relative values of the several liberties. He found it unnecessary to elaborate priority rules in the weighing of conflicting rights. Further, Rawls treated the basic liberties as something which one can measure mathematically. Secondly, with respect to Rawls' priority of basic liberties over socio-economic equality, Rawls treated the two packages as an "all-or-nothing" affair: either socio-economic conditions allowed for the effective establishment of rights or they did not do so. He seemed unclear as to the cut-off point between the general and special conceptions of justice. Rawls underestimated the complexity of resolving a conflict between the two principles of justice in concrete cases.

Finally, he appeared to share the liberal assumption that liberty and equality contradicted each other.

With respect to his "common interest" principle, chapter IV found that Rawls did not specify whether there were any conceptual limits to the restrictions of basic liberties. Nor did he provide any criterion to decide when the common interest necessitated restrictions upon the basic liberties. The terms he did employ were so vague as to chill the exercise of freedoms and to encourage abuse in practice. The Canadian Government's handling of the FLQ crisis in Quebec, 1970-71 exemplified the problems incurred in the application of Rawls' "common interest" principle. Not least of these, Rawls was not entirely clear as to who was to determine when a threat to the public order could be reasonably expected. Since it seems that he left the determination to persons holding political power, his "common interest" doctrine provided the conceptual framework for authoritarian government. Indeed, one is led to conclude that the primacy of public order and political stability rather than basic liberties served in effects as the real First Principle in Rawls' just society.

Finally, chapter V showed how Rawls' system of basic liberties was not as self-contained as he suggested. His system was premised upon two ontological hypotheses. The one, "liberty of conscience", proved an inadequate basis for justifying the primacy of basic liberties. The other, "self-respect", provided a far sounder foundation for understanding why liberty is truly fundamental.

Chapter VI completed the long journey with which we began our study by rooting an argument in support of fundamental rights in John Rawls' notion of respect for persons. Some content was incorporated into his concept by an examination of three different conceptions of "the person" embedded in the writings of Mill and T. H. Green. Two of the conceptions were found to be consistent with tyranny and slavery. Only the third, the idea that the self is a potentiality always in the process of becoming, could lead to a coherent theory of fundamental rights. Chapter VI then raised two conceptions of what it means to say that we ought to *respect* someone. The one, appraisal respect, is not shared equally. It may be waived, taken away or even remain unrecognised. In addition, it may vary in time and place with the consequence that the rights derived from it will be *ad hoc*. The second conception, recognition respect, avoids these problems. Not only is it consistent with the idea that a person is a potentiality, but it contemplates a sense in which all persons are equal. It recognises the primacy of the individual rather than the individual's instrumental relationship with the social welfare.

Having elaborated the meaning of the norm "respect for persons", chapter VI then showed how it formed the basis of a consistent argument for the protection of the "inner sphere of life". The argument was applied to the same categories of cases examined in chapter IV under the utilitarian perspective but, unlike the latter, it was now possible to justify the necessity for the absolute inviolability of the inner sphere of life.

Students of the law might invariably respond with a characteristic "so what!" Why should one be bothered by the fact that an argument can consistently be made that neither society nor the state ought to penetrate the "inner sphere of life"? Why should one be concerned that a philosophic perspective has finally been found within which one can now defend the existence of fundamental rights? Conceiving the law as a self-contained system of non-contradictory legal rules Canadian jurists, in particular, have comfortably declined from asking philosophic questions of a moral-political nature. When pressed, common law lawyers have tautologically relied upon such notions as society's conscience, the majority's will, the supremacy of the legislature or the intent of the constitution.

There are many reasons why the "so what?" response proves inadequate. Not least is the fact that legislators, judges, bureaucrats and lawyers boast the claim that fundamental rights exist in their respective societies. So long as one persists in that claim, then one cannot consistently legislate, adjudicate, apply or argue concrete problems using the traditional analytic skills, forms of argument and legal resources with which common lawyers are familiar. Neither the rhetoric of legal rules nor the unconditional reflexes of inherited political principles will satisfy the claim.

For too long the political assumptions underlying legal rules have gone unchallenged when liberty and equality were at issue. Trained within an intellectual tradition which prides itself for its barren insularity from the insights of other disciplines and initiated into a profession which accepts as an act of faith that learning legal rules constitutes the most "practical" method of understanding the law, the common law lawyer has for too long analyzed judicial decisions, statutes and constitutional documents without questioning the validity of the moral-political assumptions of his resource material. From chapters I to III one can conclude that the lawyer's traditional arguments in defence of fundamental rights have proceeded on false political assumptions — false, that is, if the lawyer is to live by his own claim that he is defending the existence of fundamental rights. From chapter IV one can conclude that the orthodox liberal tradition, which hovers over the lawyer's arguments, also contradicts that very claim. Chapter VII and the following Appendix demonstrate that one can reach very different conclusions to concrete problems if one adopts a moral-political perspective rooted in respect for persons rather than in utilitarianism.

In particular, a philosophy rooted in respect for persons can be linked to hitherto unresolved constitutional issues. For one thing, respect for persons tells us why some rights are fundamental and others are not. It provides an argument for non-discrimination rights as well as for the fundamental rights of life, thought, political participation, speech, press, due process, assembly and religion. More importantly, it explains why counsel and judge alike are compelled to incorporate socio-economic considerations into their analyses of concrete cases.

Secondly, respect for persons finally provides lawyers with a principled basis to ascertain what level of scrutiny should be expected of legislative, administrative or judicial conduct which allegedly burdens the exercise of fundamental rights.

Thirdly, respect for persons signifies a principled criterion to decide whether and, if so, when the state may interfere with the exercise of fundamental rights. Professor Dworkin's writings suggest three different senses for the term "a right against the state". The *Schenck* to *Dennis* "subversive advocacy" decisions of the American Supreme Court and the *Boucher* decision of the Canadian Supreme Court presupposed a very weak sense of rights. Indeed, the sense of a right to free speech and free assembly which the courts adopted foreclosed the very possibility that the rights were fundamental rights. Justice Black in *Yates* and Professor Emerson's sense of a right to free speech point to a direction in which a fundamental freedom of speech can be defended before a legislature or court.

Finally, respect for persons is integrally linked to the manner in which judges ought to justify their decisions in cases where fundamental rights are at issue. Contrary to the advice of America's most eminent scholar on the subject of judicial decision-making, jurists must look forward and to the present as well as backward. They must look forward to the consequences which their decisions might pose for the effective exercise of fundamental rights, both as an empirical and logical issue. They must look to the present in order to ensure that all residents in a society can, given the socio-economic conditions, exercise the fundamental rights effectively and equally. Finally, jurists must look backward into legal tradition.

Again contrary to the advice of Professor Dworkin, however,

jurists must not be confined to a political theory of the Constitution from the principles and policies embedded in institutional history. Rather, if Justices are to justify their decisions in a manner consistent with the existence of fundamental rights, they must look backward into institutional history in order to determine whether the political presuppositions underlying any principle or policy are consistent with respect for persons. Jurists, legislators and constitution framers must ask normative political questions and they must be prepared to carry on a dialogue in the world of moral-political philosophy. Consciousness that a defence of fundamental rights demands such an inquiry raises to the fore new questions and, possibly, new answers.

Appendix

Some Problems Concerning the Bill of Rights Provisions of Bill C-60[1]

(Brief submitted to Special Joint Parliamentary Committee on the Constitution of Canada, Sept. 15th, 1978)

Referring to a Public Notice inviting written briefs concerning the Government of Canada's constitutional proposals as set out in Bill C-60, I wish to raise some problems with respect to the proposed provisions setting out a Bill of Rights in the Constitution. The government's decision to constitutionalise a Bill of Rights is commendable as is its elaborate provision for of "Official Languages and Language Rights" in sections 13 to 22. On the other hand, there appear to be several issues arising out of sections 5 to 12 and sections 23 to 29 which the draftsman, no doubt under the pressure of time, overlooked. The issues arise primarily from the judicial treatment of the Canadian Bill of Rights during the past four years, the Warren and Burger Courts' examination of the American Bill of Rights since the late 1960s, and the experience of several Commonwealth countries with respect to similar provisions in their Constitutions.

The issues, which I hope the Committee will scrutinize, are divided into two parts. In Part A I shall deal with sections 5 to 12 and sections 23 to 29 generally. In Part B I shall raise what seem to me to be serious problems arising out of section 25 from the point of view of draftsmanship as well as political theory.

A. Concerning Sections 5 to 12 and 23 to 29 Generally

1. First, is it the intent of Bill C-60 that the meaning and scope of the entrenched rights should be "frozen" as of the date of the commencement of operation of Bill C-60 or, alternatively, is it the intent of Bill C-60 that the meaning and scope of the rights should expand in the future?

Whereas section 20 of Bill C-60 expressly provides for the expansion of language rights in the future, Bill C-60 does not so provide with respect to the "political and legal rights". Section 26 enacts only that the Charter shall not be held "to abrogate, abridge or derogate" from any right or freedom which may have existed at the time of the commencement of Bill C-60 or thereafter. Indeed, the draftsman of Bill C-60 does not appear to have given sufficient consideration to the kinds of indicia which Canadian courts have used to freeze the meaning of the words and phrases in the Canadian Bill of Rights as of the date of the commencement of that statute (that is, 1960).

One indicium which the Canadian Supreme Court has used to justify its "frozen meaning" doctrine, for example, is the term *"have existed and shall continue to exist"* in section 1 of the Canadian Bill of Rights.[2] Martland, J. has explained the relevance of this term in this manner:

> Section 1 of the Bill declared that six defined human rights and freedoms "have existed" and that they should "continue to exist". All of them have existed and were protected under the common law. The Bill did not purport to declare new rights and freedoms...[3]

Section 6 of Bill C-60 similarly provides that "every individual *shall enjoy and continue to enjoy* the following fundamental rights and freedoms..." Although the draftsman of Bill C-60 has erased the past tense "have existed", the retention of the future tense "shall *continue* to enjoy" imports an inference that the rights already existed and were protected under the statutory and common law prior to the commencement of Bill C-60. One can draw this inference notwithstanding the fact that the draftsman of Bill C-60 may have merely intended to emphasize that the rights should be enjoyed in the future. This is so because the future imperative verb "shall enjoy" in section 6 already accomplishes that purpose. As a consequence of the statutory interpretation principle that seemingly repetitious words are presumed to add something which should not otherwise be there if the words had been omitted,[4] a court would be justified in adopting the "frozen meaning" inference to the words "shall continue to enjoy".

A second indicium which the Canadian Supreme Court has used as a ground for its "frozen meaning" doctrine is section 5(1) of the Canadian Bill of Rights.[5] Section 5(1) provides that

> nothing in Part 1 shall be construed to abrogate or abridge any human right or fundamental freedom, not enumerated therein that may have existed in Canada at the commencement of this Act.

The court has inferred from this section that the fundamental rights declared in the Canadian Bill of Rights had already existed in 1960 and, therefore, Parliament could not have intended that the rights be given a different or enlarged meaning from that which they had in 1960. Although a good argument can be made that the court has misconstrued section 5(1),[6] the fact remains that the court has not overruled its use of section 5(1) as a basis for the "frozen meaning" doctrine. As a result, future courts might well fall back upon a similar indicium in Bill C-60. For, section 26 of Bill C-60 adopts very similar wording to section 5(1) of the Canadian Bill of Rights; namely, that

> nothing in this Charter shall be held to abrogate, abridge or derogate from any right or freedom not declared by it that may have existed in Canada at the commencement of this Act...

It is submitted that it is preferable that a Bill of Rights be drafted to take account of the above issue and to allow for the expansion of the meaning and scope of fundamental rights in the future. This submission rests upon at least two reasons:

a) For one thing, a great strength of the judiciary in the United Kingdom has been its ability to re-interpret words and phrases over the centuries without which the law would never have evolved as we know it today. The courts, as well as philosophers, have recognised that a word derives its meaning from the context in which it is used. As the context changes, so does its meaning. An entrenched Bill of Rights should be drafted so as to take account of this phenomenon rather than to pose an obstacle to it with negative consequences for the protection of the individual's fundamental rights.

b) Secondly, and closely related, political and technological circumstances change so rapidly over a period of a few years that the frozen meaning of a right will prevent the courts from protecting the individual from new intrusions into his/her life or liberty.

The technological "advances" in the detection of crime and in the pursuit of political goals (such as electronic surveillance) would no doubt have been unforeseen by any framer of a Bill of Rights in the nineteenth century.

Similarly, political changes in the institutions of society (such as the shift in political power from the Members of Parliament and legislative assemblies to large bureaucracies, senior public servants and a Prime Minister) were unforeseen when initial constitutional obligations and rights were set down following the Articles of Capitulation in Montreal. Whereas the law of the Constitution did import serious obligations toward French-speaking citizens who expressed themselves before the courts and legislative assemblies for about a century and a quarter following the capitulation in 1759, no such obligations were extended to communications between French-speaking citizens and governmental bureaucracies.[7] One can account for the contrast in that a bureaucracy as such did not exist until the late nineteenth century. The major political institutions during the late eighteenth and the nineteenth centuries were legislative councils, legislative assemblies and courts. The failure of our courts and legislatures to extend the constitutional obligation to the new political circumstance (the growth of a public service whose decisions and conduct affected the lives and liberties of one of the founding races) led to the relative diminution of the effective exercise of fundamental rights by French-speaking citizens during the twentieth century.

2. Secondly, *further attention should be given to section 11(2) of Bill C-60.* Section 11(2) expressly provides that Parliament or a legislative assembly of a province may be prolonged beyond five years from the date of the return of the writs "in time of real or apprehended war, invasion or insurrection" "if such continuation is not opposed by the votes of more than one-third of the members of the House of Commons or the legislative assembly, as the case may be." Section 11(2) raises at least three issues which must be faced:

a) Does section 11(2) take account of the long-standing principle of the "conclusiveness of statutes"?

This principle finds its most recent expression in the House of Lords decision of *British Railways Board* v. *Pickin*[7] and the Ontario High Court decision of *Drewery et al* v. *Century City Developments Ltd. et al (No. 1).*[8] Briefly, this principle lays down that the courts have no jurisdiction to examine the legislative process lying behind the enactment of a statute. This exclusion encompasses the facts as well as the policy ushered forth in support of a bill. The principle is a weighty one in that it has been followed in England and Canada since 1835. As a consequence, it is highly unlikely that a Canadian court would look behind a government's declaration that "a real or apprehended war, invasion or insurrection" existed. A government's misrepresentation of the facts to Parliament or a Legislative Assembly would not serve as a pretext for judicial scrutiny of the declaration. It would be sufficient for an enacting section of a bill to set out the declaration. Indeed, it would even appear to be adequate for the government to make mere reference to a "real or apprehended... insurrection" in the preamble of a bill. Because of the principle of the "conclusiveness of statutes" a complainant would not succeed in requesting a court to scrutinize whether "a real or apprehended war, invasion or insurrection" *in fact* existed.[9]

284

b) Is the government of the day constitutionally obligated to record the vote of a bill which prolongs the life of Parliament or a legislature?

My research respecting this issue leads me to the opinion that the recording of votes in the *Journals* and the publication of the latter is merely a practice for which there is no written constitutional requirement in the present Constitution nor in Bill C-60. If the government of the day did not wish to record the vote for a bill prolonging Parliament's life, the courts would not be able to go beyond a declaration in, say, the preamble that the continuation was "not opposed by the votes of more than one-third of the members of the House of Commons or the Legislative Assembly, as the case may be." Several Commonwealth cases indicate that this seemingly technical point is crucial to the effectiveness of an entrenched Bill of Rights.[10]

c) Is the condition precedent for the prolongation of the life of a parliament or legislative assembly adequate in that it is drafted in the negative terms "not opposed by the votes of more than one-third of the members..."?

The past years have witnessed a growth in party discipline with attendant consequences for non-conforming Members of the Legislature or Parliament. In addition, one could characterize both the national and provincial political systems, during the past fifty years, as one party systems in that one political party has served as the governing party with one minority party infrequently gaining power for short time periods.[11] As a result of these and other factors, section 11(2) of Bill C-60 should be reexamined. Consideration should be given to omitting it entirely from the Bill or, alternatively, drafting a positive condition precedent such as "is passed by the votes of more than two-thirds of the members..."

3. Thirdly, what is the meaning and effect of section 8[12] of Bill C-60?

a) Does section 8 constitutionalize a distinction between two classes of individuals in Canada: citizens and non-citizens? Whereas all other enumerated rights in Bill C-60 apply to *every individual* in Canada, section 8 expressly applies only to citizens. It is most ironic to find a "Charter of Rights and Freedoms" explicitly making any such distinction.

b) Furthermore, why has the draftsman guaranteed "the equal protection of the law" to citizens only in section 8 whereas section 6 already provides for the "equal protection of the law" to every individual in Canada? It is not inconceivable that a future court would construe the two together and hold that the right to "equal protection of the law" in section 6 applies only to citizens.

c) Does the phrase "equal protection of the law" in section 8 have a different meaning from the same term as it is used in section 6?

The draftsman has, in section 8, related the right of "equal protection of the law" to "the right to move to and take up residence in any province or territory of Canada." This would seem to indicate that "equal protection of the law" in section 8 is intended to mean "the equal application and administration of the law" as elaborated by Dicey.[13] This Diceyan construction is confirmed in that section 8 expressly contemplates inequalities in the content of "any laws of general application" so long as those laws are apparently applied and administered equally. But this is the thrust of the phrase "equality before the law" as defined by the Supreme Court of Canada in *A.-G. Canada* v. *Lavell, Isaac* v. *Bedard*[14] and *The Queen* v. *Burnshine*.[15] Because our courts presume that every word or phrase in a statute is intended to have some meaning by Parliament and because the meaning of "equal protection of the law" as inferred from its context in section 8 is the very meaning attributed by our courts to "equality before the law" in section 6, the phrase "equal protection of the law" may well mean different things in sections 6 and 8. This is confirmed by the fact that the American courts have, since the 1880s, understood "the equal protection of the laws" to mean more than merely "the equal application and administration of the law" in the Diceyan sense.[16] Some weight must be given to the American cases in construing section 6 in that the phrase "equal protection of the law", in contrast to "equality before the law", is lifted from the American Bill of Rights.

It is submitted that a basic constitutional document such as Bill C-60 should be as free as possible from such ambiguity in order to lessen litigation costs and in order to assure residents in Canada as to their constitutional rights.

d) The above ambiguity and uncertainty is magnified in that section 8 expressly exempts the right of the citizen to inter-provincial travel, "equal protection of the laws" and the acquisition of property if a restriction to any such right is "reasonably justifiable..."

Aside from rendering the stated rights in section 8 entirely ineffective,[17] the express exclusion is in direct conflict with the right to "equal protection" "given" to *all* individuals in section 6 in that section 6 does not contemplate any restrictions to the right except for those in section 25 (see my discussion of section 25 in Part B below). Why does Bill C-60 give an unqualified right to equal protection (subject to section 25) to both citizens and non-citizens in section 6 but the same right in expressly qualified terms to citizens in section 8?

e) Does the interpretation principle *expressio unius est exclusio alterius* apply to the prohibited classifications in section 8 so that the additional proscribed classifications in section 9 do not apply to section 8?

According to this interpretation principle, "the mention of one thing is the exclusion of another..."[19] As a result of the operation of this principle, one could conceive a future court holding that the proscribed grounds for restricting the stated rights in section 8 are *only* "the place of his or her residence or domicile, or birth" notwithstanding the apparent intent of section 9 to add "race, national or ethnic origin, language, colour, religion, age or sex" as proscribed grounds for restricting the rights in section 8.

In the light of this possible construction and in the light of the strong arguments that can be made with respect to the above four subissues, the government's proposed entrenched Bill of Rights could not successfully have been used to invalidate the orders for the deportation of the Japanese-Canadians in 1943 — one of the more anti-libertarian incidents in Canadian history. My arguments below concerning section 25 consolidate this opinion.

4.   Fourthly, will section 24 have the practical effect of rendering the entrenched rights in Bill C-60 of little practical utility?

By section 24 an individual may request a court "to define or enforce any of the individual rights and freedoms declared by this Charter" but only "where no other remedy is available or provided for by law." It would seem that this section will have the effect of delaying an individual's recourse to the courts if he/she pursues his/her constitutional rights. Any challenge to legislative, administrative or judicial conduct will be immediately met by an argument from Crown counsel or the defendant's counsel that some other remedy is available from the precedents of centuries past. That issue alone might take up several days of court time during which period one's rights may be irrevocably harmed.

Section 24 makes the entrenched rights *merely rights of a last resort*. Bill C-60 places them in a tertiary rather than a preferred position in practice. And this is accomplished notwithstanding the declared intent of Bill C-60, as reflected in sections 3 to 5, its preamble and the government of Canada's self-congratulatory pamphlets, of raising our fundamental rights to a paramount position in our moral-political system.

5. Fifthly, what is the effect of section 27 of Bill C-60? Is section 27 incongruous in the light of the context of the Charter as a whole? Even if it is not incongruous, can it be justified as being consistent with democratic theory?

Section 27 provides that "for greater certainty" the individual rights and freedoms declared by Bill C-60 are those "assured by or by virtue of sections 6 to 10, 14, 16, 19 and 21." Thus, several other rights and freedoms which the Charter expressly enumerates are explicitly precluded from consideration as constitutionally protected rights. More particularly:

a) the five year maximum rule for the life of a Parliament or Legislative Assembly (sect. 11);

b) the requirement of a legislative session at least once per year (sect. 12);

c) the principle that French and English be official languages (sect. 13);

d) the principle that the statutes, records and journals of Parliament and the Legislatures of Ontario, Quebec and New Brunswick be printed and published in both French and English (sects. 15(1) and (2));

e) the requirement that both language versions be "equally authoritative" (sect. 15(3));

f) the requirement that all rights, privileges and obligations regarding French and/or English that exist at the date of the commencement of Bill C-60 or that continue to exist thereafter shall not be abrogated, abridged or derogated therefrom by Bill C-60 (sect. 18). This includes rights provided for in statutory, common law and customary constitutional law.

g) the privilege of extending the preferential treatment to the French and English languages beyond that guaranteed in sections 13 to 19 (sect. 20).

Because section 27 of Bill C-60 has excluded the above rights and privileges as "individual rights", the Charter has expressly distinguished between two classes of fundamental rights. The Charter has placed the rights listed from a) to g) above in a secondary position in that an individual will not be able to request a court to define or enforce them pursuant to section 24 of Bill C-60. One is given to wonder why the draftsman has placed them in an entrenched Bill of Rights at all. What sections 11, 12, 13, 15(1), (2) and (3), 18 and 20 give, section 27 takes away by denying the individual the sole remedy expressly contemplated by Bill C-60 for a violation of constitutional rights!

A deeper problem is that the Charter, by section 27, expressly precludes the fundamental right of political participation from its list of individual rights which should be constitutionalized.[19] Although an argument can be made that many of the rights in section 6 are conditions precedent for a general individual right of political participation,[20] sections 10, 11 and 12 are the only sections directly bearing on the issue and section 27 specifically excludes sections 11 and 12 as individual rights. A government could, as a consequence of section 27, constitutionally take away the right to vote or participate in elections from *all* individuals without regard to race, national or ethnic origin, language, colour, religion or sex. Section 10 would not be violated. And we have already seen how easy it would be for a government to prolong the life of a House or legislative assembly in the context of the overlooked issues raised above concerning section 11(2).

A very strong argument can be made that the right to political participation is an "individual" right owed to the individual as an individual.[21] This right stems from the underlying themes of democratic theory. Indeed, it is as important as any of the enumerated rights and freedoms in sections 6 and 7 with the possible exception of the right to life. The individual has as good a claim to insist that his/her constitution protect that right and that the courts enforce that right than he/she has with respect to the rights elaborated in sections 6 to 9. And any constitution which advertises a "Charter of Rights and Freedoms" as Bill C-60 does falls far short of its pretention unless it elevates the ideas underlying sections 11(1) and 12 to a higher plane.

A similar argument can be made with respect to the individual's right to the freedom of information.

B. Concerning section 25

The problems raised above with respect to Bill C-60 are magnified when one examines section 25 closely. Section 25 provides that

> nothing in this Charter shall be held to prevent such limitations on the exercise or enjoyment of any of the individual rights and freedoms declared by this Charter as are justifiable in a free and democratic society in the interests of public safety or health, the interests of the peace and security of the public, or the interests of the rights and freedoms of others, whether such limitations are imposed by law or by virtue of the construction or application of any law.

This section expressly authorizes any government, court, parliament, legislature, administrative agency, administrator or police officer to restrict the so-called "individual rights" which are supposedly entrenched. Section 25 expressly permits and validates the alienation "by the ordinary exercise of such legislative or other authority as may be conferred by law," notwithstanding section 5's acknowledgment that the declared rights in Bill C-60 "if they are to endure, [must] be incapable of being alienated by the ordinary exercise of such legislative or other authority as may be conferred by law..." So long as this provision or any similar provision is in an entrenched Bill of Rights in this country, there is no basis for one to claim that the purpose and effect of the Bill is "to guarantee the rights and freedoms, and ensure that these rights and freedoms are inalienable" as has the Government of Canada.

1. Does section 25 take account of the weighty and long-standing principle of the conclusiveness of statutes?

By this principle the courts have no jurisdiction to examine the legislative process lying behind the enactment of a statute. Any claimant who believes his rights have been infringed will, as a result of this principle, be unsuccessful in requesting a court to scrutinize the evidence or possible reasons why a government, legislature, administrator or other official believes the restriction to be in "the interests of public safety or health, the interests of the peace and security of the public..." A governmental or other declaration that the restriction is in such interests is conclusive of the matter. Although possible constitutional arguments have been raised which a lawyer might attempt to make before a Canadian court in an effort to break the rigidity of this weighty principle,[22] the reverence of the Canadian judiciary to legislative supremacy in general[23] and the conclusiveness of statutes in particular suggest that the issue is too important to be left to the whims of future Canadian courts whose judges will be even more hesitant to strike down legislation than they are at present. To strike down a statute or the construction or application of any statute because it conflicts with an entrenched Bill of Rights is a "once-for-all" decision whereas at present any statute or administrative conduct which is held in conflict with the Canadian Bill of Rights can always be immediately validated by a new statute which has a "notwithstanding the Canadian Bill of Rights" clause.

2. Secondly, and closely related, what level of judicial scrutiny of the "justifications" for legislative or administrative conduct does section 25 contemplate?

It appears that the draftsman has adopted the same test for judicial scrutiny that the Canadian courts have read into the Canadian Bill of Rights, namely, the "reasonable classification" or "reasonable relationship" test.[24] This test, which was initially developed by the American courts in the early twentieth century, contemplates that the judiciary need only try to find some "reason" or rationale for the legislation or administrative conduct which allegedly infringes a fundamental right. During the late 1960s the American Supreme Court began to realise that this level of judicial scrutiny had proved inadequate if the American courts were to fulfil their constitutional position required by an entrenched Bill of Rights. Indeed, between 1937 and 1970, the American Supreme Court used this test to sustain the constitutionality of all but one state statute challenged under the "equal protection" clause of the Fourteenth Amendment (The anomolous case was *Morey* v. *Doud* 354 U.S. 457, 77 S. Ct. 1344 (1957)). The Court was able to strike down state statutes only when it used a higher level of judicial scrutiny than that contemplated by the "reasonable relationship" test. Interestingly, the majority and minority judgments in the Canadian Supreme Court's treatment of Canadian Bill of Rights cases have followed much the same pattern.

The reasons why the section 25 test of mere "justifiability" has proved inadequate have been examined above.[25] What is important to note is that a draftsman who wishes to design an entrenched Bill of Rights which will fulfil the objectives of inalienability as set out in sections 3 and 5 as well as the government's "information" pamphlets should take into account at least the following factors:

a) Not any reason or "justification" should be able to sustain the constitutionality of legislation or government conduct which allegedly infringes fundamental rights. Only *compelling* reasons should be permitted;

b) Furthermore, those compelling reasons must be related to the infringement of other fundamental rights or, alternatively, the exercise of the same fundamental right by another person. To permit the restriction of constitutional rights in the name of "a free and democratic society" "in the interests of public safety or health" or the "interests of the peace and security of the public" is merely to beg the question "what constitutes the fundamental elements of a 'free and democratic society' " rather than to provide standards. In addition, such latter terms as "the public interest" bring in a calculation which is quite alien to the existence of fundamental rights as is argued in point 6 below.

c) In addition, the onus of proof should be placed upon the state to establish the evidence and to articulate the compelling reasons demonstrating why the challenged legislation, administrative or police conduct, or judicial principle is necessary to protect the exercise of more important constitutional rights.

291

Section 25, in contrast, places the onus on the individual complainant.[26]

3. Thirdly, does section 25 of Bill C-60 take account of the issue whether the justification can be made *ex post facto* by the government or, alternatively, whether the justification must be given at the time of the enactment of the legislation or the commencement of the administrative conduct which allegedly infringes the constitutional right?

The former possibility gives grave latitude to the state and its agents to rationalise its conduct and legislation upon the basis of events which occurred after the conduct or enactment or, even to hypothecate incidents which it would try to use as grounds for the initial enactment of the legislation. It is far too easy for a government to rationalise repressive measures *ex post facto* on the basis of such terms as "the public interest" or the "national security". It also appears very easy for a government not to give any evidence or reasons for its burdening of fundamental rights even *ex post facto* as has been the experience of the present government concerning its legislation and conduct during and after the "Quebec crisis" of October, 1970.[27]

4. Fourthly, does the wording of section 25 take account of the experiences in several Commonwealth countries with constitutions with similarly worded provision(s)?

Provisions similar to section 25 of Bill C-60 serve as the constitutional basis for some of the more authoritarian and anti-human rights conduct which the world has witnessed since the Second World War. Provisions similar to section 25 have provided the constitutional authority for Idi Amin to pursue the activities he has, for Indira Ghandi to impose authoritarian government in 1976, and for the Government of Bangladesh to impose martial law on August 20th, 1975. Examples can be found in other Commonwealth constitutions and in the experiences of other Commonwealth countries such as Sri Lanke, Cyprus, Nigeria and Malaysia.[28] Also note that the Soviet Constitution has a similarly worded provision (along with an "entrenched" Bill of Rights).[29] Surely the experiences of these countries renders section 25 of Bill C-60 suspect if one is to take the objectives of Bill C-60 at face value.

5. Fifthly, what is the meaning, scope and effect upon fundamental rights of such terms as "the interest of public safety", "the interest of health", "the interest of the peace... of the public" and the interest of "the security of the public"?

292

In addition to the problems incurred by the use of such terms as discussed in point B2 above, the vagueness and open-endedness of the terms have the following consequences:

a) When society constitutionally permits the restriction of fundamental rights with such vague words without expressly providing guidelines in the constitution, *society leaves the political decisions of whether to restrict the fundamental rights to the supposed experts* — the bureaucrats, the lawyers, the judges and a few cabinet members — with no political scrutiny by the public and with no certainty that only compelling reasons related to the infringement of other fundamental rights will be the basis of a decision. That is, by accepting section 25 in an entrenched Bill of Rights, Canadian society is shirking its political responsibility.

b) The open-endedness of such terms *chills* the exercise of the supposedly entrenched rights. That is, the individual will be *deterred* from exercising his/her constitutional rights supposedly guaranteed in sections 6 to 22 of the Charter out of the fear, apprehension or expectation that section 25 will render the exercise of the rights illegal even though the ultimate constitutional decison in the case would be resolved in favour of the individual's rights. Section 25 serves as an "invisible hand" lying behind the exercise of the declared rights.

c) Even though one's constitutional rights are protected on the face of a statute or regulation, the vagueness of the terms in section 25 serve as a pretext for abuse in the application or construction of the statute or regulation by government officials.

6. Sixthly, does section 25 of Bill C-60 incorporate and entrench a particular political philosophy which, on close examination, has little room for the existence of fundamental rights?

Section 25 does in fact adopt a particular political philosophy known as utilitarianism.[30] The phrase "the interest of the peace and security of the public" is the legalistic synonym for Jeremy Bentham's notion of the "greatest happiness of the greatest number". One's fundamental rights do not form the ultimate value in a society contemplated by this Constitution. Rather, one's rights are secondary to and hinge upon the higher value of the "national security" and the "public interest" — whatever those terms mean at any particular point in time.

The consequences of adopting this political perspective are serious for fundamental rights:

a) First, the state, as represented by the Government of Canada or a province, may proscribe any conduct so long as it can claim that such proscription is in the interest of the "public peace" or "national security".

b) Secondly, because section 25 contemplates that the courts, government officials and administrators may legitimately restrict the constitutional rights (note the phrase "whether such limitations are imposed by law or by virtue of the *construction or application* of law"), such persons may also exercise their functions by reference to the vague terms "public peace" and "public or national security".

c) Thirdly, implicit in the terms of section 25 is a political theory of majoritarianism. Notwithstanding the very weak protection given to the individual right of political participation in Bill C-60 as noted above in A6, the terms "public peace" and "national security" open up the opportunity for any government or official to rationalise the restrictions of fundamental rights in terms of the "greatest happiness of the greatest number". I have tried to explain elsewhere the problems arising out of such a perspective.[31] In particular, the utilitarian outlook is conceptually consistent with both slavery and tyranny.[32] As a consequence of these problems and as a result of the drafting problems raised in this memo, it would seem to be very difficult to assert that Bill C-60 accomplishes what the Liberal Government of Canada claims that the Bill has accomplished.[33]

All of which is respectfully submitted,

William E. Conklin

Notes

1. Bill C-60, "The Constitutional Amendment Bill", June, 1978.
2. 8-9 Eliz. II (1960). Sect. 1 provides that

> it is hereby recognized and declared that in Canada there have existed and shall exist without discrimination by reason of race, national origin, colour, religion or sex, the following human rights and fundamental freedoms, namely, ...

For a discussion of the "frozen meaning" doctrine in the context of the arguments raised in this study see text, supra, chap. II between notes 73 and 83.

3. *R.* v. *Burnshine and Attorney-General for Ontario (Intervenants)*, [1975] 1 S.C.R. 693, 44 D.L.R. (3d) 584, (1974), 25 C.R.N.S. 270, 277.

4. See generally, Elmer A. Driedger, *The Construction of Statutes* (Toronto: Butterworths & Co., 1974), pp. 72-74.

5. *Robertson and Rosetanni* v. *The Queen*, [1963] S.C.R. 651, 654 per Ritchie J.

6. The argument is elaborated in William E. Conklin and Gerald A. Ferguson, *The Burnshine Affair: Whatever Happened to Drybones and Equality before the Law?*, 22 Chitty's L.J. 303, pp. 306 ff. (1974).

7. This proposition is documented in William E. Conklin, "Constitutional Ideology, Language Rights and Political Disunity in Canada," to be published in Laksman Marasinghe and William E. Conklin, ed., *Law, Language and Development* (Colombo: Lake House Publishers, 80) and reprinted in (1978) U.N.B.L.J. 39. Also see text, supra, chap. VII, between notes 20 and 31.

8. [1974] 2 W.L.R. 208 (H.L.).

9. For a discussion of the political basis of this principle see generally text, supra, chap. II following note 108.

10. See, for example, *Akar* v. *A-G Sierra Leone*, [1970] A.C. 853 (P.C.), *Bribery Commissioner* v. *Ranasinghe*, [1965] A.C. 172, [1964] 2 All. E.R. 785, [1964] 2 W.L.R. 1301 (P.C.).

11. See generally, text, supra, chap. II corresponding to notes 102 to 108.

12. Section 8 provides as follows:

> (c) Rights Within Canada of Canadian Citizens
> 8. Every citizen of Canada, wherever the place of his or her residence or domicile, previous residence or domicile or birth has
> — the right to move to and take up residence in any province or territory of Canada, and in consequence thereof to enjoy the equal protection of the law within that province or territory in the matter of his or her residence therein; and
> — the right to acquire and hold property in, and to pursue the gaining of a livelihood in, any province or territory of Canda;
> subject to any laws of general application in force in that province or territory but in all other respects subject only to such limitations on his

or her exercise or enjoyment of those rights as are reasonably justifiable otherwise than on the basis of the place of his or her residence or domicile, previous residence or domicile, or birth.

13. See text, supra, chap. II between notes 90 and 94.

14. [1974] S.C.R. 1349, (1973) 38 D.L.R. (3d) 481, 23 C.R.N.S. 197, 11 R.F.L. 333 (S.C.C.).

15. [1975] 1 S.C.R. 693, 44 D.L.R. (3d) 584, [1974] 4 W.W.R. 49, 25 C.R.N.S. 270 (S.C.C.).

16. See text, supra, chap. III corresponding to notes 33 to 44.

17. See discussion in text, infra, part B of Appendix.

18. See generally, R. Cross, *Statutory Interpretation* (London: Butterworths, 1976) pp. 120-121.

19. For the importance of this fundamental right see text, supra, chap. VII between notes 5 and 10.

20. See text, supra, chap. VII between notes 7 and 10.

21. See esp. text, supra, chap. VII between notes 7 and 10.

22. See generally, William E. Conklin, *Pickin and its Applicability to Canada*, 25 Univ. Tor. L.J. 193 (1975). Also see text, supra, chap. II, sect. 3.

23. See esp. text, supra, chap. II between notes 60 and 87.

24. See text, supra, chap. III, sect. 2 esp. corresponding to notes 33 to 44.

25. See text, supra, chap. III corresponding to notes 35 to 44.

26. For the reasoning lying behind the above submission see esp. text, supra, chap. III, sect. 2 and chap. VII, sect. 2.

27. The above criticisms are explained in connection with John Rawls' principle of the "common interest" in text, supra, chap. V, corresponding to notes 66 and 101.

28. See text, supra, chap. III at note 29.

29. See, supra, Introduction, note 1.

30. See generally text, supra, chap. IV.

31. For the objections to this from the point of view of the existence of fundamental rights see esp. text, supra, chap. II.

32. For this and other objections see ibid.

33. See, for example, "The Constitutional Amendment Bill, 1978: Explanatory Document," pp. 8-12, "A Time for Action: Toward the Renewal of the Canadian Federation," p. 8, and "A Time for Action: Highlights of the Federal Government's Proposals for the Renewal of the Canadian Federation," pp. 2, 9, each of which is published by the Government of Canada. Also note section 5 of Bill C-60 which provides that Bill C-60 affirms "the conviction and belief" that "there are certain rights and freedoms which must be assured to all of the people of that [a free and democratic] society as well as to people within that society individually and as members of particular groups, and which must, if they are to endure, be incapable of being alienated by the ordinary exercise of such legislative or other authority as may be conferred by law on its respective institutions of government."

Index

act utilitarianism
   definition 5, 140
ad hoc rights
   appraisal respect 197-198, 210
   majority will 68
   society's consience 62
appraisal respect 197-198

backward-looking
   amoral regime 257
   Coke 14-21
   consequences 24-25
   Dworkin 256-257
   examples 21-23
   generally 4, 273-274
   seditious advocacy 256-257
   seditious libel created 25-27
   sense of rights 256-257
   static 23-24
   utilitarian tradition 256
   Wasserstrom 270 n.128
Bentham
   assumptions 133-134
   extent 156 n.34
   fecundity 156 n.32
   generally 4, 55
   greatest happiness 87 n.37, 88
     n.42, 230
   majority will theory 64-66
   pains 134
   pleasures 134
   psychological harm 134-135
   purity 156 n.33
   state intervention 68, 230
   rights 69-70, 233
Berlin
   authoritarianism 194

generally 3
monstrous impersonation 194,
   195
paternalism 194
social whole 194
true self 194
Bill of Rights, 1689
   political participation 28
Black
   total incorporation 99
Blackstone
   natural law 93 n.109
Bracton
   precedent 13
   rule of law 62
   seditious libel 26
Brandeis
   principles 254
   reasonable justification 240
   substantial evil 239
   theory of Constitution 239, 253
   weak rights 239, 240
British North America Acts
   constitutional obligation 80-83
   exhaustiveness 36
   division of powers analysis 39-40,
     72-73, 81
   language 224-226, 262 n.22, n.27,
     n.28, n.30
   legislative supremacy 81-82
   political basis 83
   preamble 81
   religion 32-45, 42-44
   section 93 36, 42, 43-44
   section 133 224, 262 n.22

About the Author

Mr. Conklin received his undergraduate education in political science and economics and in law at the University of Toronto. He did his graduate work in political science at the London School of Economics and in law at the Columbia Law School. During recent years he has written articles which attempt to bridge the gap between law and political theory with respect to such topics as legislative supremacy, equality before the law, language rights in Canada, capital punishment and the decisions of Mr. Justice Holmes. Mr. Conklin is presently an Associate Professor of Law at the University of Windsor.

Colophon

letter: baskerville 11/12, 9/11
setter: Pecasse-Eurozet b.v.
printer: Samsom Sijthoff Grafische Bedrijven
binder: Callenbach
cover-design: W. Bottenheft